It's Bet

"Besides providing new ammunition for optimists, Mr. Easterbrook's aim in this important book is to identify what we've been doing right and to consider what we can do about the still pressing problems we face... Mr. Easterbrook wants to make optimism intellectually respectable again, and he has done so with cogent arguments and bountiful evidence."

—**Wall Street Journal**

"*It's Better Than It Looks* makes many good arguments about inequality...Easterbrook is good on democracy and dictatorship (democracy is better at money and better at war). He is also good on climate change (the technical solutions are there, and all will be fine 'if society chooses reform,' though that choice is surely the crux of the problem)."

—**New York Times Book Review**

"Easterbrook sets out to disabuse readers of any casual pessimism and equip them with enough facts and arguments to silence dinner parties from now till kingdom come... rich in detail and observation."

—**Weekly Standard**

"Countering the usual pessimism disseminated by the 'experts' and rebroadcast by the 'if it bleeds, it leads' media, *It's Better Than It Looks* ably defends the view that the grand sweep of history has gone from generally bad to generally good for the vast majority of the world's populace. Whether the book surveys global food supply, infectious diseases, the natural system, the economy, violence, technology or governance, the overall outlook consistently comes up positive, according to Mr. Easterbrook. His impressive, rather objective, amply-referenced, perspicacious analysis supports his optimism."

—**Washington Times**

IT'S BETTER THAN IT LOOKS

Also by Gregg Easterbrook

This Magic Moment
A Moment on the Earth
Beside Still Waters
Tuesday Morning Quarterback
The Here and Now
The Progress Paradox
Sonic Boom
The Leading Indicators
The King of Sports
The Game's Not Over

IT'S BETTER THAN IT LOOKS

REASONS FOR OPTIMISM IN AN AGE OF FEAR

GREGG EASTERBROOK

PUBLICAFFAIRS
New York

PublicAffairs
Hachette Book Group
1290 Avenue of the Americas, New York, NY 10104
www.publicaffairsbooks.com
@Public_Affairs

Printed in the United States of America

First Edition: February 2018
First Trade Paperback Edition: March 2019

Published by PublicAffairs, an imprint of Perseus Books, LLC, a subsidiary of Hachette Book Group, Inc. The PublicAffairs name and logo is a trademark of the Hachette Book Group.

The Hachette Speakers Bureau provides a wide range of authors for speaking events. To find out more, go to www.hachettespeakersbureau.com or call (866) 376–6591.

The publisher is not responsible for websites (or their content) that are not owned by the publisher.

Library of Congress Cataloging-in-Publication Data

Names: Easterbrook, Gregg, author.
Title: It's better than it looks : the case for optimism in an age of fear / Gregg Easterbrook.
Description: First edition. | New York : PublicAffairs, [2018] | Includes bibliographical references and index.Identifiers: LCCN 2017048518| ISBN 9781610397414 (hardcover) | ISBN 9781610397421 (ebook)
Subjects: LCSH: Progress. | Quality of life. | Civilization, Modern—21st century. | Economic history. | Social history.
Classification: LCC HM891 .E268 2018 | DDC 306.09—dc23
LC record available at https://lccn.loc.gov/2017048518

ISBNs: 978-1-61039-741-4 (hardcover), 978-1-61039-742-1 (ebook); 978-1-54177-403-2 (paperback)

LSC-C

10 9 8 7 6 5 4 3 2 1

For William Whitworth
from the Arkansas Gazette *to* The New Yorker
to editor-in-chief of The Atlantic:
the consummate editor

The great fact to remember is that the trend of civilization is forever upward.

—Franklin Delano Roosevelt,
shortly before his 1945 death

Contents

Preface:
Optimism Goes Out of Style

ON THE NOVEMBER 2016 DAY Donald Trump was elected president of the United States, unemployment was 4.6 percent, a number that would have caused economists of the 1970s to fall to their knees and kiss the ground. In real-dollar terms, gasoline prices were the same as when teenagers rushed to record stores to buy the latest 45-rpm monaural singles. Natural resources and foodstuffs were plentiful. Middle-class wages and household income were rising. The economy had expanded for eighty-nine consecutive months. Private-sector jobs had grown for eighty consecutive months, nearly doubling the previous record of forty-eight months; a net of eight million jobs had been added in less than a decade. US industrial output was at an all-time record. Inflation had been low for a decade, while mortgage rates and other borrowing costs were at historic lows. Crime, especially homicide, was in long-term decline. All forms of pollution except greenhouse gases were in long-term decline; all forms of discrimination were in long-term decline; most disease rates were in long-term decline. Education levels and longevity were the highest ever. Two-thirds of the globe's reserve currency was held in the USD, which meant the rest of the world judged America's prospects to be excellent. The United States military not only was the strongest—it was stronger than all other militaries of the world combined. Objectively, America was in the best condition it had ever been in.

Yet Trump convinced voters that "our country is going to hell." Despite the industrial output record, Trump convinced voters that "we don't make things anymore." Despite the glittering numbers, Trump convinced voters that the economy "is always bad, down, down, down." Despite the urban comebacks of Boston, Chicago, Cleveland, Denver, Philadelphia, Pittsburgh, and Washington, DC, Trump convinced voters that "American cities have no education, they have no jobs." Despite the United States being viewed by other nations as the eight-hundred-pound gorilla, Trump convinced voters that in America's interactions with the world, "we're losing all the time, we lose with everything." Addressing a rally in Colorado a few days before the election, Trump told voters they were living through "the lowest point in the history of our country."

In the aftermath of the 2016 presidential election, there was a scramble to attach culpability to the pollsters, the pundits, the Russians, the FBI, WikiLeaks, sexism, and Hillary Clinton's egregious campaign. What mattered is that when Trump told voters things were awful, they believed him.

Trump hardly was alone in being all negative all the time. In the same year, Bernie Sanders came out of left field and nearly upset heavily favored insider Hillary Clinton for the nomination of the Democratic Party via a campaign that relentlessly described contemporary America as foundering on the rocks. The United States, Sanders contended, has been "destroyed" except for the wealthiest few. Sanders's backers shouted approval at his flamboyantly downbeat assertions, some every bit as kooky as any by Trump. Sanders proclaimed that Americans are being "poisoned" by pollutants caused by corporate greed. If our bodies are being poisoned, living longer is a funny way of showing it.

Believing things much worse than they are hardly was confined to the United States. Objectively, in 2016, the United Kingdom was in the best condition it has ever been in—judged by strong economic growth, by the lowest unemployment rate of any European Union member, by high levels of personal freedom and public health, by inflation-adjusted per capita income, by almost any other leading indicator. During current generations, no Britons have died in great-power European wars, versus the two million dead and five million severely wounded in European wars among recent prior generations. Yet, in 2016, British voters angrily demanded separation from the European Union, seeming to believe their tranquil, prosperous polity was "down, down, down."

The feelings of irate voters are not just some lapse. Voters in the United States and Europe have been barraged with rapid-fire reports of bad news, causing a deep sense that today's society has broken yesterday's promises. It is easy to feel this way, but feeling this way also is a choice. Too often we try to force the world to match our feelings, when we'd be on a more even keel—and experience life more fully—if instead our feelings matched the world.

There are four basic types of knowing. One is certainty: we can be certain the sun is ninety-three million miles from Earth. Another is faith or doubt: we can neither prove nor disprove beliefs about God. A third is opinion: there's no right or wrong on questions such as which beer tastes best or whether baseball should have the designated hitter rule.

Then there is what we want to believe. What we *want* to believe can upend any degree of evidence, provability, or subjectivity. Trump, Sanders, and the Brexit movement struck a chord because people *wanted* to believe the worst about society. They wanted to believe the worst though the United States at the time was in the best condition it had ever been in, the same could be said of the United Kingdom, and the world overall had never been better.

Of course there are many individuals and families experiencing personal, physical, or financial hardship: there never will be a moment when no one is sick, distressed, or brokenhearted. On the whole, though, at no juncture in American history were people better off than they were in 2016: living standards, per-capita income, buying power, health, safety, liberty, and longevity were at their highest, while women, minorities, and gays were free in ways they'd never been before. There had been no juncture in history at which the typical member of the global population was better off either.

Consider a metric. During the same period when Trump and Sanders were cheered for saying carnage was everywhere, the Misery Index—unemployment plus inflation—was at its lowest in half a century (and the lower the better with this metric). Average people get hammered when unemployment and inflation are high at the same time; in 2016, both were unusually low at the same time. Union leaders speak of the 1960s as a golden age for the working man, but the Misery Index was higher then. Republicans speak of the Reagan presidency as a golden age for families, but the Misery Index was higher then. Democrats speak of the Bill

Clinton presidency as a golden age for prosperity, but the Misery Index was higher then. If the Misery Index is the best indicator of conditions for average Americans—and arguably it is—then 2016 was a golden year. Yet voters did not respond to indices, however favorable: they responded to the negativity with which they were assaulted by the forces of the moment.

My 2003 book *The Progress Paradox* proposed that people in the United States and other developed nations suffer "collapse anxiety"—a concern that their way of life soon will be no more. Many fear that the formula of free-market economies, resource consumption, personal freedom, and democratic government by laws not men will not last. This book will show a range of reasons why the Western way of life is more robust than meets the eye—and why a better world is closer than it looks.

But the primary causes of a mostly-improving life—progress, both social and technical—entail a lot of change, at a pace that in recent generations has quickened. Change may benefit some more than others; even universally desirable change may be greeted with trepidation. As changes occur more frequently, these negative feelings rise, regardless of whether, on balance, changes serve the common good.

Consequent is the conundrum I've studied since the publication of *The Progress Paradox*: as life gets better, people feel worse. By "life gets better" I surely do not mean all aspects of life are better, nor that life is better for every individual. By "life gets better" I mean that in the contemporary world most people are better off in most ways when compared to any prior generation.

This seems close to an inarguable proposition—yet runs against conventional wisdom, because optimism has gone out of style. Reflecting on this, I decided to research and write the book you now hold, which has three goals.

The first goal is to show that for all the apprehension, digitized clamor, and grating superficiality of the present day, conditions in the United States and European Union, as well as in most though of course not all of the larger world, are more auspicious than generally understood.

The second goal is to ask why this is so. What influences—especially, what types of reform—have prevented decline? Why do so many think the world is getting worse when by almost every objective measure the reverse is true? Why are we in this predicament of general gloom—a sense that preceded Trump—even as most indicators point toward the better world we all want?

Third, this book seeks to take the lessons learned from successful reforms of the past and apply them to the dilemmas of the twenty-first century, such as inequality and climate change.

Through these three contentions, I hope to show that the arrow of history points up. I do not suppose that history is deterministic, wrought by forces external to our choices. Nor do I suppose that history is teleological, guided toward some end. I do not suggest history is cyclical, or bound to do that which can be predicted from previous events. (Cycles-of-history contentions hinge on pretending there are "secrets" that "control" history; for this reason, it is disturbing that some top advisers to Donald Trump endorse cycles-of-history mumbo jumbo.) I do assert that as time passes, in the main the human condition improves and this can be expected to continue.

THE MID-NINETEENTH-CENTURY FRENCH PHILOSOPHER FRÉDÉRIC Bastiat maintained that when assessing any situation, it is vital to consider what might have occurred instead. His essay on this topic, *That Which Is Seen and That Which Is Not Seen,* became the foundation of what economists now call "opportunity-cost analysis." Don't think solely about what happened; think as well about what did not happen, and thereby is unseen. In our great spinning world, what do we not see? As a prelude to the book's three goals, ponder for a moment the tribulations our world does not have.

Granaries are not empty. It has been two centuries since Thomas Malthus said rising population would lead to mass starvation—unavoidably, as an iron law. During the 1960s, it was predicted that hundreds of millions, perhaps billions, soon would die of hunger. Instead, by 2015, the United Nations reported global malnutrition had declined to the lowest level in history. Nearly all malnutrition that persists is caused by distribution failures or by government corruption, not by lack of supply. Hunger could be eliminated in our lifetimes.

Resources are not exhausted. In the 1970s, it was commonly forecast that petroleum and natural gas would be gone by around the year 2000, leaving society desperate for fuel. Instead, oil and gas are in worldwide oversupply, so readily obtained and so inexpensive that the greenhouse gases they release are causing climate change. Minerals and ores, also expected to run out, instead are abundant. Resources have not been depleted despite the incredible proliferation of people, vehicles, aircraft, and construction.

There are no runaway plagues. Unstoppable outbreaks of super-viruses and mutations were said to menace a growing world; instead, nearly all disease rates are in decline, including the rates of most cancers. In 2000, the US Centers for Disease Control and Prevention (CDC) reported that infectious diseases have declined so much that obesity is killing far more Americans than germs. Death rates from infectious disease have fallen in nearly all nations, including the poorest.

With each passing year, global longevity improves, and not just in the United States and European Union. In almost all nations, the human family is living longer, while suffering fewer heart attacks and strokes. And even in the poorest nations, there is no sign that longevity increases have peaked.

The Western nations are not choking on pollution. A generation ago, Denver, Houston, Los Angeles, and San Diego were becoming uninhabitable owing to smog, while air pollution in many areas of the United States and Europe did widespread respiratory damage. Today Los Angeles air quality has improved so much that the LA basin goes years between serious air quality alerts, while in 2014 San Diego had its lowest smog levels since record-keeping began. Nationally, since 1990, winter smog is down 77 percent and summer smog down 22 percent—improvements achieved as the US population grew rapidly. As recently as the 1980s, acid rain was expected to destroy forests in the eastern United States and central Europe. Since 1990, sulfur dioxide, the main cause of acid rain, has decreased by 81 percent in the United States and is down sharply in Europe. Appalachian forests in the United States and the Black Forest in Germany are in the best condition they have been in since the eighteenth century.

Cities in Africa, Asia, and India remain afflicted by smog and also by smoke, the latter long since eliminated from Western air except around wildfires. But in most developing nations the trend lines are toward less air and water pollution, even as ever more people are alive, engaging in ever more economic activity. There is one global exception to these trend lines: greenhouse gases. And don't believe talk radio—artificial climate change is scientifically proven.

The economy drives everyone crazy but keeps functioning. Many have gotten airsick from economic turbulence, but there hasn't been a global crash since the Great Depression eight decades ago. Living standards keep rising for almost everyone, especially for those to whom that trend is most important—the poor. Goods and services are in ample supply; in almost every year, global per capita GDP sets a record. Middle-class income growth is soft throughout the Western nations, but middle-class buying power, which matters more than pretax income, keeps rising. That "shrinking middle class" you've heard so much about? In the United States, the main reason the middle is shrinking is large numbers of people moving up, not down.

The global economy is hitting on all cylinders in one respect that cannot be observed within the United States or European Union— developing-world indigence rapidly being reduced. In 1990, 37 percent of humanity lived in what the World Bank defines as extreme poverty; today that number is 10 percent. It may be small consolation to anyone in the American upper Midwest or the northern part of England who lost a manufacturing job because of global trade, but the same forces that caused a relatively small share in the United States and United Kingdom to experience economic distress also caused a gigantic reduction of suffering in Africa, Asia, and Latin America. The decline of developing-world poverty should be viewed as the focal story of the last quarter-century. Since that story cannot be observed from the United States and Europe, Westerners largely are unaware.

Crime and war are not getting worse. A generation ago, as murder rates rose and the superpowers stocked their arsenals, a horrific future of violence-ravaged cities and constant warfare seemed in store. Instead, since 1990 crime rates have declined sharply in the United States and many other nations—Central Park after dark now is as safe as Yellowstone Park at noon. The crime decline led to an urban revival that benefits almost everyone, including African Americans, who today are much less likely to be homicide victims than a generation ago and also less likely, despite horrific exceptions to this rule, to be harmed by police than in decades past.

Although there are poignant exceptions, including the Syrian civil war, since about 1990 the frequency and intensity of combat have gone down worldwide, while global per-capita arms spending has entered a cycle of decline. Rather than add nuclear bombs, the United States and the Russian Federation have disassembled tens of thousands of these nightmare devices, then destroyed the parts in the presence of witnesses.

Since about 1990, a person's chance of dying because of violence has dropped to the lowest it has ever been, stretching back to the mists of prehistory. That statement holds even considering the 2016 wave of Islamist terror attacks in Europe and the mass shootings in America. Other than in Afghanistan, Iraq, Sudan, and Syria, in 2016 the chance of anyone in any nation dying by violence was at a historic low. Even under population pressure, the world grows steadily safer.

The dictators aren't winning. During World War II, when darkness spread across both hemispheres, only a handful of free societies held the line against tyranny. After the war, communism brought police-state poverty to China and the Soviet Union, seemingly to finish the job fascism started. Far-sighted thinkers, such as George Orwell, predicted the coming of global absolute dictatorship that would crush freedom out of existence.

Instead, it's been victory after victory for the ballot box, human rights, and public opinion. Some nations are relapsing (Russia, Turkey), and others are in disarray owing to what the democracy theorist Larry Diamond calls "predatory government" (Nigeria, Venezuela). But during the current generation, no nation has gone from freedom to dictatorship, while the largest nation (China) is dipping its toes into liberty and the second-largest (India) holds on, however tenuously, to free expression and free elections. The technological developments that Orwell feared would allow dictators to oversee every minute of life instead have given average people broad access to information their governments cannot control.

*   *   *

THERE ARE MANY OTHER ARENAS in which it's easy to overlook the problems we do not have. Despite video games and a short-attention-span culture, ignorance has not flourished: education levels keep rising, while in the developing world, schooling for girls has stopped being rare. Not only is there justice in having well-educated girls and women take positions of responsibility in business, government, and science, this doubles the world's supply of ideas. Technology has not run amok: cars, aircraft, medicine, and even many weapons have grown less dangerous. Tremendous attention has been paid to the decline of factory jobs, which began long before trade with China and which, driven by automation, was always inevitable, globalization or no. Scant attention has been paid to the fact that more than 60 percent of Americans now hold some form of white-collar employment. White-collar work involves stress and boredom, but no backbreaking manual labor or inhalation of factory fumes.

Detailed support for all the above points will be provided in coming chapters.

That the US, European, and global situations are better than commonly perceived should not lead to complacency. On the contrary, awareness of progress should inspire greater reform. The challenges of the present day are daunting: inequality, racial tension, climate change, illegal immigration, refugees forced to flee war zones or failed states, never-ending conflagration in the Middle East, tyrants and warlords in parts of Africa, low-achieving public schools, a shallow and corporate-driven culture that makes the task of public schools Sisyphean, public discourse contaminated by rage—and these are just for starters.

Plus surely there's a huge problem barreling down the tracks directly toward us. Pick any year of the past: some major problem arrived unexpectedly. A law of nature seems to dictate that for each problem solved, another is created. So this book will not say, don't worry, be happy. There is a great deal to worry about. But while worrying, be optimistic. Optimism does not make us blind to the many faults of the world. Rather, optimism is the conviction that problems can be solved if we roll up our sleeves and get to work.

Optimism was once the frame of the forward-thinking. The Progressives of a century ago were optimists through and through: they sought for all men and women freedom of speech, freedom of religion, freedom from fear, and freedom from want, believing these were not slogans but advances that could be achieved on a practical basis. They saw a future when, in the wonderful final verse of "America the Beautiful," "alabaster cities gleam undimmed by human tears."

Then pessimism became fashionable, starting in academia and expanding to the public square, brought there by politicians, social media, and our apprehension regarding change. Today the conventional wisdom is that any informed person should feel the world is falling apart. If you don't think everything is awful, you must not understand the situation!

Campaigning for the White House, Trump mixed pounding pessimism about the present with woolly longing for the past, saying, "I love the old days." When exactly *were* those "Good Ole Days"? And where did they happen? At every stage in the past, life spans were shorter, disease was more common, living standards were lower, discrimination and pollution were worse, and liberty was more imperiled.

The conservative intellectual Yuval Levin has written that Americans are engaged in "a politics of competitive nostalgia" that demands return to an idealized past that can never be reached because it never existed in the first place. A better future, on the other hand, can be reached. Optimism needs to become intellectually respectable again. Optimism is the best argument for reform—and the bow that propels the arrow of history.

Bethesda, Maryland
July 2017

A Few Notes to the Reader

- All money references in this book are converted to constant dollars or other constant currency; thus, past money values are stated in current terms.
- Modern names of nations are employed.
- Where the text reads that a person "said" or "has said," the quotation comes from the public record. Where the text reads that a person "says," the quotation comes from an interview with me.

Part I

∞

Why the World Refuses to End

Chapter 1

Why Don't We Starve?

ON A CHILLY WINTER MORNING in 1914, on a farm in tiny Cresco, Iowa, the most important person of the twentieth century was born. He learned his three Rs in a one-room schoolhouse, hurrying home each day to tend animals. Winning a scholarship to college, he studied agronomy and pondered an idea about how to make crops produce more food using less soil. Then he went out into the world and saved a billion people.

At a time of creepy politicians and cringe-worthy cultural figures, it is said the young lack heroes. A shame, then, that hardly any young people recognize the name Norman Borlaug, despite his entirely admirable life, including the 1970 Nobel Peace Prize. Borlaug lived most of his years far from the land of his birth, assisting African, Asian, and Mexican researchers and extension officials in what would come to be called the Green Revolution.

The movement Borlaug started is the reason most of the seven billion people on our planet have plenty to eat—and all would have plenty if food distribution were improved. In 2015, the United Nations' Food and Agriculture Organization (FAO) reported that malnutrition had declined to the lowest level in history, with just 13 percent of the human family going to bed hungry. Because the human family has become so large, "just 13 percent" means about 900 million souls. In a world of excess, this is a tragically large number, but a half-century ago, 50 percent of humanity was malnourished.

Even as the global population has soared, the proportion who want for food has declined sharply, and malnutrition is on track to decline further as the global population continues to rise. "Because of the Green Revolution, the world can produce enough calories and protein for 10 billion or even 20 billion people," says Rajiv Shah, who ran the US Agency for International Development (USAID) from 2010 to 2015. "There are questions about protecting the environment and agricultural equity. But the Malthusian fears are disproven. If there's a collapse coming, food supply will not be the reason."

No MATTER WHERE YOU ARE in the world, the meals you will consume today trace in part to that Iowa farm boy and his gift for making plants grow. Actions taken by him and others in the Green Revolution bear on both the centrality of farming to our existence and the ways in which reform is the essential ingredient in human progress.

Because so many citizens of contemporary nations take food supply for granted, it is easy to forget that every successful society in history has been grounded, as it were, in agriculture. Farming has no sex appeal compared to miniature electronics or launching rockets, but if plants don't grow, little else matters. A fundamental reason Argentina, Australia, Canada, the United States, and most of Europe are prosperous is that they mastered farming, producing a bounty of grain, fruits, vegetables, dairy, meat, fowl, wine, and fiber. Extending mastery of farming to the rest of the world will make other nations prosperous too.

The production of food is the first window to understanding why many expected calamities give way to mostly positive trends. The kinds of steps that prevented expected starvation can work against other challenges to come.

Historically, expectations of starvation have been keen. Two centuries ago, Thomas Malthus declared that population would increase faster than food production, leading to general ruin. This would happen inexorably, Malthus said, because nature uses scarcity to control species, and it would be physically impossible to cultivate enough land to feed all those being born.

Famines that struck China, India, Ireland, and Japan about a generation after Malthus seemed to confirm his contention. The idea of looming general starvation was taken up by others. Publishing the *Communist*

Manifesto in 1848, Marx and Engels made the "establishment of armies for agriculture" one of their ten planks. They believed that the sole hope for feeding humanity was diversion of the world's soldiers from military duties to working the fields.

Terrible food shortages would come to China, Germany, Greece, India, Russia, and Vietnam in the first half of the twentieth century—manmade, to a certain extent, by war and by dictatorship—while the Dust Bowl of the 1930s caused Americans and Canadians to fear that their farm productivity was ending. By the 1960s, the notion of inexorable starvation had become cant. A best-selling book of 1967, *Famine 1975!*, predicted global food riots no later than 1975, with the United States having to make the horrifying Sophie's choice of deciding which nations to save and in which nations everyone must be allowed to die to alleviate pressure on the food supply and "reduce the surplus population," as Dickens had Ebenezer Scrooge say. In 1970, the Stanford University theorist Paul Ehrlich, a beloved figure to the declinist worldview because he called the United States "doomed," appeared on *The Tonight Show*—then having an audience larger, per capita, than any show today—to tell Johnny Carson that mass starvation killing hundreds of millions soon would occur not just in Africa or Asia but in North America. "Sometime within the next 15 years the end will come," Ehrlich declared to the national audience—"the end" in this sense meaning of humanity. Famine contentions would even cross over into popular entertainment. A recent box-office smash movie franchise, *The Hunger Games,* is based on the premise that future US society will possess force fields and antigravity devices—but have no idea how to grow tomatoes.

Yet we don't starve. When Malthus's *Essay on the Principle of Population* appeared, there were one billion people. Now the human family has seven times as many members, and there is sufficient food that obesity is a public health problem not just in rich nations but in parts of the developing world. Today there are twice as many people who are overweight as the *total* number who were alive when Malthus said there were far too many mouths to feed. Farmers around the world complain that despite having seven billion customers, overproduction of food causes supply to exceed demand. ("Crop Glut Expected to Worsen"—*Wall Street*

Journal, April 2017. Read that twice.) And while war- or government-created food distribution failures continue in North Korea, South Sudan, and Venezuela—if North Korea simply opened its borders, ample supplies would be available—the term "crop failure" has not been heard since the Soviet grain debacle two generations ago.

BORLAUG LIVED IN MEXICO IN the 1940s and 1950s, then in India and Pakistan in the 1960s and 1970s, working with farmers and communes to replace backbreaking subsistence agriculture with high-yield techniques that featured rapid development of new crops. Men and women have altered crops and animals since antiquity: there may not be anyone alive today who has consumed any plant, beef, or fowl that was entirely naturally evolved. Ancient Mesoamericans crossed *teosinte,* a wild grass, with the ancestor of maize. Changing *teosinte* into corn took hundreds, if not thousands, of years because traditional crop breeding is agonizingly slow. Borlaug and other agronomists stationed in Mexico at the International Maize and Wheat Improvement Center—known by its Spanish initials CIMMYT—discovered several ways to accelerate how plants become hybrids. The CIMMYT techniques allowed Borlaug to hasten the perfection of dwarf spring wheat, now a staple across the world. Malthus and Marx did not know that new ideas could speed hybridization, raising crop yields; they assumed a static, invariant agricultural system. Instead, farming became dynamic.

Though it is conventionally assumed farmers want a tall, impressive-looking harvest, shrinking wheat and other cereals has proven beneficial. Cross-bred for short stalks, plants expend less energy on inedible columns and more on growing fruit. Stout, short-stalked wheat neatly supports the edible kernels, whereas tall-stalked wheat bends over at maturity, complicating reaping. Nature favored genes for wheat tallness because in nature plants compete for access to sunlight. In high-yield agriculture, competition is eliminated because rows of uniform crops receive equal sunlight. Using insights into accelerated selective breeding, Borlaug and his colleagues also developed wheat strains resistant to rust fungus, long the bane of grain farmers. Wheat was Borlaug's cereal of choice because it is naturally resilient against insects. He and his assistants cross-bred for wheat that grew fast, did not rust, tolerated drought and shade, and, most of all, increased yield.

As Borlaug labored at CIMMYT to perfect new versions of wheat, researchers at the International Rice Research Institute in the Philippines and the Hunan Rice Research Institute in China were using accelerated cross-breeding to seek high-yield rice strains; later they would be joined by agronomists at the Africa Rice Center in Côte d'Ivoire. These research institutions, whose existence is unknown even to most well-educated people, would provide the means for feeding a growing world. In 1997, *The Atlantic* magazine estimated Borlaug's high-yield cereal innovations had saved a billion lives. Two decades along, the count may now be two billion.

Barely resembling the ancestor plant, selectively bred dwarf wheat needed little pesticide but could not prosper without fertilizer and irrigation. Like most agronomists, Borlaug advocated organic fertilizers—a fancy name for manure—to restore soil nutrients. But the way to attain large quantities of manure is to have large herds of livestock consume grain that would otherwise feed people. Fertilizers based on fossil fuels and minerals can renew soil on a global scale, trading inedible substances for grain, fruits, and vegetables. Converting the world to commercial-scale inorganic fertilizer entails making peace with industrial production. To Borlaug, that choice was noncontroversial, since the interest of humanity, especially the poor, would be served.

Borlaug and many Mexican agronomists would travel to India and Pakistan, working during the Indo-Pakistani War of 1965 to bring high-yield techniques to that food-short region. (Mexico's national contribution to the reduction of global malnutrition has never received adequate recognition.) Some developing-nation governments were suspicious because having highly educated American and Mexican technical experts in contact with illiterate peasant farmers might shake up feudal cultures, to the discomfort of landed aristocratic families. At the same time, some Western commentators were suggesting it would be wrong to increase the food supply in the developing world; better to let nature do the dirty work of restraining the human population.

Everywhere Borlaug and his acolytes went, agricultural yields rose and hunger declined. The numbers are in every case striking. When Borlaug was a boy, US farms produced 10.8 bushels of wheat per acre. By 1950, 13 bushels of wheat an acre were grown; by 2015, yield was up to 36 bushels per acre. Higher yields meant steadily more calories and protein per person, not just in the West but in most of the developing world. The Worldwatch Institute, a sustainable growth organization, would declare in 2009, "The global grain harvest has nearly tripled since 1961, during a time when world population doubled."

In 1961, the world produced 760 million tons of grain; by 2015 the figure was 2.4 billion tons, holding, roughly, to the pattern of trebled output for doubled population. Yield numbers for dairy and meat increased in sync. In 1950, the world produced 37 pounds of beef per capita. By 2015, beef production had risen to 99 pounds per capita. Those numbers equate to production of calories and protein rising faster than population growth not just once in a while, rather, throughout the postwar era.

NEARLY AS IMPORTANT, HIGH-YIELD AGRICULTURAL techniques allow more food from less land. The 1.1 billion bushels of wheat the United States harvested in 1950 required 84 million acres for cultivation. The 2 billion acres harvested in 2015 required 55 million acres—nearly twice as much yield from one-third fewer acres. Other forms of yield increase reduce stress on nature. For one, cows produce steadily more milk: in the United States, a cow produced about 80 percent more milk in 2015 than in 1980. The result is the same level of milk production as in 1980 from a million fewer cows, with less land devoted to cow grazing.

High-yield agriculture has many results that the well-informed rationalist of a half-century ago would have viewed as impossible—among them, India not only feeding itself but also becoming a net exporter of foodstuffs. Terrible street poverty continues in Kolkata and other Indian cities, but the expected waves of mass starvation have given way instead to impressive farm production. In 2013, India shipped $13 billion worth of cereals to the international market.

Following Borlaug's example, contemporary research teams led by Yuan Longping in China and Monty Jones in Sierra Leone developed a rice cultivar, *nerica,* that combines the high yield and dwarf stalks of the most productive kind of Asian rice with the qualities needed for Africa's climate, and with the taste of traditional African rice. (Green Revolution advocates learned early on that a crop must appeal to the local palate.) Nerica rice is beginning to grow across Africa, replacing imports with domestic production.

A generation ago, some Western environmentalists asserted, for ideological reasons, that only subsistence agriculture—plows drawn by animals, traditional seeds—was appropriate for Africa. One can romanticize backbreaking, low-yield, old-style agriculture when there's an air-conditioned Panera across the street. Trendy opposition to high-yield agriculture for Africa made it hard to farmers there to obtain World Bank and other kinds of financing for threshers, cross-bred seeds, and similar supplies—access to credit being as essential as rain to the success of farming in the United States and European Union. Borlaug told me in 1995 that many Western lobbyists "have never experienced the physical sensation of hunger. If they lived just one month amid the misery of the developing world, as I have for fifty years, they'd be crying out for tractors and fertilizer and irrigation canals and be outraged that fashionable elitists back home were trying to deny these things."

Part of what was at work was the common confusion of Green Revolution farming techniques with assumptions about mad scientists inventing living chimeras. Many Green Revolution approaches to the soil don't involve chemicals: for instance, drip irrigation, a Green Revolution idea that employs lots of ground-level hoses releasing small amounts of water to eliminate the evaporation associated with big rotating sprayers. Farmers likewise have adopted conservation tillage—which leaves the last season's crop residue in place to preserve soil—and no-till agriculture.

Hostility to the Green Revolution changed in 2006, when the Bill and Melinda Gates Foundation came down on the side of high-yield farming for Africa. Gates's imprimatur prompted funding institutions to begin advancing credit to African farmers, enabling them to adopt modern techniques. Yields—for instance, of Kenyan maize—headed upward in the same way they did on the Great Plains during Borlaug's youth. Gates Foundation research brought breakthroughs such as a means to increase the number of hours in the day that plants metabolize sunlight. This 2016 finding appears to promise another 10 to 20 percent yield boost for many types of crops.

BECAUSE MOST AFRICAN FARMING DOES not yet use modern techniques, there is ample room for improvement, both to generate more food for the continent and then to produce the value-added exports that enhance economic growth. Olusegun Obasanjo, a former president of Nigeria, noted in 2016 that "agribusiness is Africa's biggest opportunity to not only end hunger and malnutrition, but also for generating income and employment." If agriculture exports are to help boost the GDPs of African nations, Western trade barriers must be dropped. For instance, the European Union allows green coffee beans from Africa to be imported without tariff, but imposes heavy taxes on the importation of roasted coffee. In so doing, the European Union accepts the sweat of African field labor but reserves the skilled value-added component for itself. In 2014, African coffee plantations sold $2.4 billion worth of green beans to Germany, where the crop was roasted and resold to European baristas and supermarkets for $3.8 billion.

While trade barriers should fall, the development of high-yield seeds optimized for Africa is needed even more. When Shah became USAID director, he pushed the agency toward supporting agricultural research specific to the soil and climate of Africa. This was the sort of reform that has no constituency inside the United States because—and keep this thought in mind—the results are invisible to Americans.

Some agronomists have viewed Africa as a lost cause because the continent was never glaciated—glacial scouring was the ice age's gift to topsoil. There is a hypothesis that bounces around historical sociology that the reason Europe developed faster than Africa is that Europe's glaciated soil was productive and Africa's depleted soil was not. "This does not take into account continental drift," Shah says. "If you map where the continents were in the far past, you find African soil is really similar to the Brazilian soil once considered unsuitable for tilling." Brazil's *cerrado*, a vast savanna, was made to flower through the application of crushed limestone. Brazil has countless problems, but its soybean and cattle sectors run like clockwork. A dose of lime may help African farms do so as well.

Should the kind of agricultural success achieved in Brazil come to Africa, not only will lives on that continent improve, but the long-term food security picture for the world will brighten. In turn, population growth will moderate: probably along a curve on which the human family peaks at around 11 billion, according to the United Nations Population Division, whose projections have a track record of accuracy. Everywhere that subsistence farming has given way to high-yield, population growth has slowed while education levels have risen, especially for girls.

In subsistence farming, children are valuable only for their muscles or ability to birth more children. Technology-based farming shifts the focus onto understanding agronomy as a science and learning about economic markets for the crops produced. This muscles-to-books transition in the economics of farming is an essential reason that global fertility has been declining for decades. The global population growth rate peaked in 1960, at about 2.1 percent per annum, and has been declining since, now down to 1.2 percent. Lower death rates and the "demographic momentum" of huge numbers of young people who have yet to start families guarantee that the human family will continue to expand; demographic momentum ensures that even if the population growth rate keeps diminishing, the global census will go up until around 2100. But the long-term social transition—from high fertility with little education to moderate fertility with moderate education to low fertility with high education—already is close to complete.

For food production to continue to outpace population growth, not only must high-yield practices spread to practically all tilled earth, nations in Africa and elsewhere must adopt market-based agriculture. It is not a coincidence that the big increase in cereal production in China began when central planning was replaced by market forces. Free-market systems have many defects—only ideologues consider market economics to be flawless—but have shown themselves better than central planning at allocating agricultural resources, getting food where it's needed, and rewarding those farmers who increase yields.

*   *   *

MANY PARTS OF THE WORLD need the Hamilton solution—not *Hamilton* the musical but Alexander Hamilton's eighteenth-century policy for the United States. His prescription was three-part: a national bank to underwrite commercial investments, temporary tariffs to protect young industries, and federal funding of roads and canals so markets for agricultural goods could develop, encouraging farmers to produce more than their own community could buy. The British horticulturalist Noel Kingsbury has noted that until the development of long-distance transportation, farming was a local business: once they could ship to distant markets, farmers had a reason to increase crop yields. Many parts of the world would benefit from improved infrastructure for delivering food where supplies are short, and while fresh.

Hamiltonian policy has stood the test of time. All prosperous nations have a national lending institution; tariffs help new industries develop, though must be removed once new industries mature; one reason the United States became affluent is that federal infrastructure investments allowed the breadbasket potential of the country to develop. Much of the developing world needs roads, bridges, and railroads because farmers in rural areas (especially in Africa and some parts of South America) can't get their goods to urban markets and so do not benefit from raising production. The malnutrition that continues links more to distribution problems, lack of infrastructure, and local corruption than to farm output. Perhaps as *Hamilton* is performed around the globe the program notes could include an endorsement of its hero's beliefs on infrastructure for agriculture.

Because high-yield farming involves use of chemicals and, increasingly, genetically modified plants, some feel uneasy about modern agriculture— the sense of unease being in many ways the modern condition. Perhaps too much planting of genetically identical crops could set the stage for natural selection to create a fast-moving plant disease. This hasn't happened in nearly a century of use of high-yield techniques, but the possibility cannot be ruled out. It's a reason that agricultural research—one of the most cost-effective forms of research—should seek ever-varied seeds, in the same way that medical research seeks ever-varied antibiotics. In the main, high-yield agriculture is good for nature. Why has there been no second Dust Bowl? Because high-yield crops don't fail.

The UN's Food and Agriculture Organization projected in 2014 that calorie production per acre could rise 70 percent by 2050, well ahead of expected population growth, while irrigation water and agricultural chemicals used per acre could decline, as could the total number of cultivated acres relative to production. The virtue of less chemical application is obvious, though not necessarily appreciated—much of the early focus in the genetic modification of crops was on enabling plants to resist insects without pesticide application. According to studies by the US Department of Agriculture, pesticide application in the United States rose steadily from the end of World War II to a peak in 1981 and has been declining since, as insect-resistant crops came into general use. Pesticides still are perilous. A class called chlorpyrifos may cause developmental problems in infants; in the United States, chlorpyrifos have been banned for home use but remain legal on farms, protecting consumers but not pregnant women working in fields.

But the trend is toward lower levels of pesticides. Many consumers don't like foodstuffs with the spooky-sounding stamp GENETICALLY MODIFIED ORGANISM, yet such plants are less likely than other kinds to be dusted with chemicals. In 2013, the American Association for the Advancement of Science concluded that eating GMO crops is safe; by 2017, research had shifted to "editing" crops, not by adding anything, but by switching some naturally occurring genes (mainly the ones that cause spoilage). Biotechnological farming may improve long-term health by increasing the supply of fresh fruits and fresh vegetables relative to processed foods: one goal of current research is to develop vegetables that stay fresh for long periods at room temperature.

The virtue of reducing water use in agriculture means more than meets the eye. Freshwater supplies are strained in much of the Middle East, while China is pumping aquifers at an alarming rate. The most populous and thus most food-needy nation, China has only about 25 percent of the world average of freshwater per person. As Li Jiao has written, the North China Plain water table, on which the nation's rice crop depends, may become depleted in just one generation.

The temperature impacts of global warming may be manageable; its impact on freshwater could be another matter. As the UCLA geographer Laurence Smith has noted, 98 percent of the world's water is salty: the 2 percent that is fresh is not held in lakes and rivers but mainly in glaciers and snowpack, which global warming is melting. When meltwater from ice and snow flows downhill to the sea, the water cycle eventually moves it back to high-altitude cold storage. But this happens much too slowly to replenish humanity's freshwater needs.

Desalinization creates freshwater, but is expensive. That makes reducing agriculture's freshwater consumption a global priority, given that farms use two gallons of freshwater for every one gallon needed by people for drinking and bathing. Genetically modified crops generally require less moisture than the plants they replace; the Green Revolution has been a friend of water protection.

In the last twenty years, California has taken steps to rationalize use of freshwater in agriculture. Market pricing has been the key to California's reduction of water waste, which is more closely tied to agriculture than watering lawns. Other Western nations need to take similar steps—for example, Belgium heavily subsidizes production of potatoes, a water-intensive crop, though it's been fifty years since potatoes were in short supply anywhere.

Both for nature and for society, the pivotal aspect of technological agriculture is its ability to produce more food from less land. Today the United States has 21 percent less land under cultivation than in 1880, yet that smaller acreage produces six times as much food and fiber. Since the Soviet Union collapsed in 1991, with heavy-handed centrally planned farming supplanted by market forces, Russia has removed from cultivation a land area the size of Poland—and Russian agricultural production has gone up. This kind of result—more food produced on fewer acres—is needed everywhere.

WHEN THE GLOBAL POPULATION BEGAN its steep rise—there were a billion people in 1800, 1.6 billion in 1900, and 6 billion in 2000—the hopeful view was that everyone could be fed, but only by leveling every forest and tilling every last scrap of land. Instead, food production rose while acres under tillage went down; in most cases land withdrawn from farming was returned to its natural condition, not paved over. Currently only about 0.45 percent of the globe is covered in concrete, a figure that excludes Antarctica: add the austral continent, and one-third of 1 percent of the globe is paved.

Jesse Ausubel, director of the Human Environment Program at Rockefeller University in New York City, says, "Farmers have so effectively learned to extract more crop from a given area that land needed for agriculture is shrinking at the same time people become more numerous and eat a higher-quality diet." Today the Appalachian forest covers the most acreage since Europeans first saw North America, despite the huge boom in population on the America East Coast, because so much land has been withdrawn from farming and returned to nature. Ausubel continues: "This reversal in land use—orders of magnitude larger in scale than all urban expansion combined—could foretell a great landscape restoration by 2050, expanding the global forest by 10 percent. That's about 750 million acres, the area of India, returned to a natural condition during the same period as the biggest population boom the world has ever known."

Politicians, lobbyists, activists, mainstream news organizations, and now social media prefer negative spins. Something that ought to be seen as great news—the world has plenty of food, including in most of the developing world—instead is spun as sinister agribusiness experimenting on crops. Something else that ought to be seen as great news—each year in Western nations there are fewer farms, more agricultural land is retired from cultivation and returned to nature, and farms still operating cover less acreage—instead is spun by newscasters and by lobbyists as a shocking crisis of "vanishing farms."

Zhifeng Liu, a researcher at Beijing Normal University, found in 2014 that cities, suburbs, and roads cover about 3 percent of Earth's surface; by contrast, 11 percent of Earth's landmass is tilled, meaning agriculture is by far the largest anthropogenic use of land. This makes declining need for farm acres good both for nature and for the expansion of cities. The year 2013 was the first in which more men and women around the world lived in cities than outside of them. In 2015, the world reached thirty-five cities of at least 10 million persons. Many are unfamiliar in the West: Shenzhen, a thriving Chinese metropolis that did not exist a generation ago, today is larger than Chicago or London.

Progress in agriculture is the main reason the ongoing global expansion of cities does not imperil land supply; the secondary reason is that evolving technology causes women and men to need less land in all respects. The Dutch scientist Louise Fresco has noted that in Paleolithic times each human being required about 125 acres for hunting food and gathering supplies. Today each person on Earth requires about one acre for food production, resource extraction, and living space—though today's lifestyle involves a far higher level of materialism than lifestyles of the Stone Age. She further notes it was just a century ago that a burger—red meat on white bread—was "available exclusively to the rich and powerful." Today a billion people eat steer-based food on a steady basis, another two billion eat such fare occasionally, and for good or ill, most of the rest of the world aspires to join the cheeseburger party.

Obviously the West would have better health if its dietary habits improved. Signs of improvement are guardedly positive, from little changes (McDonald's switched in 2016 to cage-free eggs and meat raised without antibiotics) to major indicators (schools and cities are discouraging the consumption of sugared sodas, the number-one source of empty calories). Dietitians would rather Americans simply ate less. Agronomists would rather they favored chicken sandwiches over cheeseburgers, since cattle require about five times the resources, per pound of meat, as birds do. Tilapia sandwiches would be better still, as fish require fewer resources per pound of protein produced than do poultry. Plant burgers would be ideal.

One reason India was able to defy expectations and feed itself is that the nation's largely vegetarian diet requires less grain production than meat-based nourishment. It would be nice if, for ethical reasons, the whole world followed India's example and went vegetarian. This won't happen anytime soon. Perhaps a middle ground could be found between plants-only fare and the Western—and increasingly Asian—cuisine of beef, pork, and fowl. A possible practical compromise is meat produced absent an animal.

Today's veggie burgers taste like compressed sawdust. In the research lab are plant-based meat substitutes that are scrumptious, triggering the satisfaction sensors in the tongue. Several start-up companies are working on plant-based recipes that activate our biological pathways for the taste of meat, leading to a veggie burger that is healthful, satisfying to chow down on, and doesn't require any cattle, nor the considerable agricultural inputs involved in raising cattle.

Another possible alternative is cultured meat grown directly as tissue, no animal required. Sounds weird? To most in the Western world, going out in the yard, catching a chicken, and wringing its neck sounds weird—yet that's what great-grandma considered normal for preparation of a nice dinner. Culturing tissue for meat does work, though so far it results in steak that would sell for $1,000 a pound. But numerous staples of contemporary life—television, cell phones, home printers, jetliners—began as very expensive and then became affordable. Ausubel says, "Posterity may view the twentieth century as this odd period when huge numbers of people consumed meat from cattle, which the future will consider both unethical and an unwise use of resources, as diners continue to order double cheeseburgers—just double cheeseburgers made without animals." Should this happen, feeding an ever-larger global population will be ever more practical.

LET'S SHIFT GEARS FOR A moment to introduce two ideas that will recur throughout this book. The first is that there has been a historically unprecedented transition in how most societies relate to land. This transition, which has drawn little notice, is one of the driving forces behind positive change in our world. The second idea is that most positive change is happening in the developing world, not in the United States or the European Union. Both these ideas link to the question of why we don't starve, and both expand into larger issues.

First consider land. The steady reduction of the acreage required for farming has an impact on geopolitics that is unrelated to food. For centuries, nations have gone to war over land in part because acquiring acres was the sole means to grow more to eat, and thus a key to wealth for the aristocratic class—the "landed gentry." When European settlers reached the United States west of the Mississippi, they were thrilled to claim large tracts of land—to have what the rich of Old Europe most treasured. John

Steinbeck's *East of Eden*, published in 1952, says of nineteenth-century California that the reason new arrivals were so excited by the open, fertile expanses was not so much the chance to pan for gold as the chance to own land.

Control of tillable land for farming was one aspect of the many centuries of European and Asian battles that preceded the twentieth century's world wars, which were also in some respects about control of land. The American Civil War was in part a fight about the desire of the Confederacy to retain a slavery-based agricultural lifestyle—farming of the time had not changed meaningfully in a millennium, with the lord sitting on his veranda as serfs hewed the soil the same way it had been hewed for centuries—while preventing encroachment of the fast-changing industrial, education-based lifestyle of New England. Land was the essence of the old plantation lifestyle, while land was a secondary or tertiary concern to the rising industrial, education-based lifestyle.

The arrival of high-yield farming made it possible to grow ample food and also to acquire wealth without dominating large swaths of land—or exploiting slaves, serfs, or peasants. In turn, one reason for the striking decline of war during the last quarter-century has been that nations no longer need to seize land to obtain sufficient food. African, American, Chinese, Mexican, and Filipino agronomists crossing cereal strains to develop hybrid vigor were trying to feed the hungry, not reduce combat, but their efforts had that highly positive, if unanticipated, consequence. A coming chapter will detail both the decline of war—no matter how things seem on cable news, the frequency and intensity of wars, as well as military and civilian casualties, are in a quarter-century cycle of decline—and the role of changes in land use in this trend.

Now consider progress in the developing world. Not only is most of the decline of malnutrition happening there, but so are most of the declines of poverty, pollution, violence, and lack of education.

Just a century ago, 80 percent of humanity could neither read nor write. Today global illiteracy is down to 15 percent—of a far larger population base. Agricultural improvements help reduce illiteracy. Subsistence farming requires constant manual labor, but no book learning; families want lots of children to work the land, but each child has little value, so why waste time with school? Today life on the farm, even in the developing world, requires less exertion than in the past, but knowledge has become essential; families have fewer offspring, then invest in their schooling because each child is worth more.

The word "incredible" is overused, but still, the decline of global poverty in the current generation is an incredible story. Because the gains occur outside the United States and European Union, the good news is happening largely unacknowledged in the West. One might say to today's America: wonderful things are happening, just not here.

Ninety percent of the world lived in extreme poverty 150 years ago, while 10 percent lived well. The extreme-poverty share began a mild decline around the turn of the twentieth century; by the onset of World War II, only three-quarters of the global population lived in destitution, while one-quarter enjoyed good material circumstances. The crossover moment—when more people had achieved a decent living standard than were living in destitution—came sometime in the 1970s. By 2015, the most recent year for which statistics are available, complete reversal had occurred—only 10 percent of the global population lived in extreme poverty, rather than 90 percent, as once was the case. Max Roser, an economist at the University of Oxford, notes that this trend works out to about 130,000 people escaping from poverty *each day* for the last twenty-five years.

The World Bank reports that the number living in extreme poverty—defined as an income of no more than $1.90 per day—dropped from 1.9 billion in 1990 to 710 million in 2015. Seven-hundred-ten million is a huge total, more than the population of North America. But since the world census rose from 5.3 billion to 7.4 billion in the period measured, that means the share of humanity that does not live in extreme poverty nearly doubled, from 3.4 billion to 6.6 billion, between 1990 and 2015. The 3 billion additional men and women who are not impoverished—most in the developing world—represent more than the total number alive in the entire world on the day Donald Trump was born.

The mainstream American press confers attention on civil unrest and air pollution in China and India, daunting issues to be sure, while saying little regarding reduction of poverty in those nations. The former are negative stories, the latter a positive one—that's all you need to know about editors' choices. A 2013 survey by Novus, a social change organization in Sweden, found that two-thirds of Americans and Britons believed extreme poverty in the developing world has doubled. Correct is that such poverty has halved. But how would Americans and Britons know this when reporters, editors, presenters, and political leaders look askance at developing-world progress? In 2015, Georgetown University professor Steven Radelet published an exceptional book, *The Great Surge,* about improving conditions in most developing nations. Heard of this volume? I didn't think so. Had the title been *Doomsday 2020!,* television bookers surely would have sought out the author.

China and India, where most of the decline in extreme poverty is occurring, are the globe's most populous nations, and have something essential in common: about a generation ago, both switched from state-controlled economies to market forces. In 2016, Pope Francis denounced the free market, saying that only socialism serves average people. Actual use in China and India has shown that replacing socialism with market forces causes the lot of average people to improve dramatically, while actual use in Cuba, North Korea, and Venezuela has shown state economic control imposes destitution, except of course for insider elites.

The switch from socialism to market forces in the largest nation, China, has drawbacks: even as poverty and hunger decline and education expands, inequality has risen and corruption has increased exponentially. The result is average people being better off combined with a richer, more arrogant One Percent.

MANY OF THE EXAMPLES IN this chapter—altering crops to increase yield and prevent soil loss, cross-breeding plants from different regions of the world, researching ways to produce a meatless steak dinner—represent dynamism, the ability of knowledge to adapt to changing conditions.

One of the fundamental conflicts in human attitudes about life is between catastrophism and dynamism. The catastrophism view, embraced by a strange coalition of far left and far right types, is that the world not only is going downhill but can only go downhill. The contrasting view, dynamism, is that we'll muddle through and, in the main, circumstances will improve. People and technology will adjust to evolving conditions—which is what's happened so far, since the human story began. Dynamism hardly promises that we'll approve of the future—only that we'll be able to live in it, and that a better world is coming.

THE SUMMATION OF WHY WE don't starve might be this: agricultural output gets higher because farms get smaller. This is an example both of dynamism and of the virtue of reform.

More reforms in agriculture will be needed if climate change diminishes the current breadbasket regions while creating new ones—say, a dry Kansas but a warmer Siberia. In a world of climate change, keeping farm output high may be a daunting challenge, but fundamentally is an engineering problem, and dynamic systems are good at engineering.

So we won't starve. Will we instead die of some runaway disease?

Chapter 2

Why, Despite All Our Bad Habits,
Do We Keep Living Longer?

THE WORLD HEALTH ORGANIZATION (WHO) warns of a pandemic that could cause rapid mass deaths, rendering whole regions of the planet uninhabitable. A top official at the US National Institutes of Health (NIH) declares the disease outbreak "almost certain." The secretary of the Department of Health and Human Services (HHS) advises Americans to stockpile canned food and medicine, in case the economy collapses because of unstoppable contagion. ABC News declares the death toll could reach 150 million. White House officials advise the president to prepare to send the Army into cities to put down riots caused by the pandemic.

Ebola? Zika? Forecast for a bioweapon attack? Treatment for a big-budget science-fiction movie starring Gal Gadot and Chris Pine?

The opening paragraph describes actual events from 2005 and 2006, when the avian flu known as H5N1 was expected to devastate humanity. Instead, at this writing, avian flu has killed about 450 people worldwide—which is 450 tragedies, but a negligible total compared to expectations, or to routine causes of mortality.

Other twenty-first-century disease outbreaks followed a similar pattern. In 2009, swine flu was widely believed to be proliferating relentlessly, predicted to cause millions of deaths. Instead, the 2009 swine flu killed around 18,000 people worldwide, which was terrible, but far less than the death toll from pneumonia that year.

In 2012, a coronavirus was detected moving from camels to people in Saudi Arabia. The disease, Middle East respiratory syndrome (MERS), was declared an extraordinary threat. An official of the Council on Foreign Relations, citadel of the American establishment, said MERS could be the "new Black Death," predicting that one-quarter of the population of Europe and Africa would die from the condition. Instead, virologists determined the disease is not especially contagious. MERS is known to have taken about 500 lives, far fewer than died during the outbreak year by drowning in bathtubs.

In 2014, Ebola was detected in Guinea. Normally transmitted solely by close contact, Ebola appeared to have mutated and become airborne, which would make it much more dangerous. Experts predicted the contagion would spread unstoppably, killing huge numbers of people and leading to sealed borders around the globe. The US Centers for Disease Control and Prevention (CDC) estimated 1.4 million Ebola infections by spring 2015, warning of "the next AIDS."

Instead, by spring 2015, new cases had nearly stopped. Researchers at the National Institutes of Health determined there were no unusual mutations in Ebola: the outbreak was caused not by an airborne variation but by a long-existing strain that, like other forms of Ebola, communicates only during intimate contact. By summer 2015, an Ebola vaccine—a joint project of the World Health Organization and the pharmaceutical firm Merck—was in trials. Some 11,300 people worldwide died from Ebola in 2014 and 2015, an awful result, but a tiny fraction of what had been expected, and negligible compared to deaths during the same period from routine conditions such as hypertension. In the United States, Ebola killed five people versus, during the same period, the 20,000 who died from seasonal flu.

INFECTIOUS ILLNESS WAS THE BANE of our ancestors. Even in a world of vaccines and positron scanners, there is fear of the runaway pathogen whose spread cannot be stopped, a fear every one of our ancestors felt. This fear has become keener as the global population continues to expand. It took thousands of years for the human family to reach one billion, then two hundred years to add the next two billion, then just fifty years to add the two billion after that. Today another 100 million—the population of the Philippines—is added biennially. Historically, more people meant more disease. Historically, crowding into cities also triggered disease, and with each passing year, the human family lives closer together. There seems every reason to think a novel virus or bacterium will cut people down like wheat.

Diseases are further expected to run wild because politicians and the media favor scare stories, while television shows seek experts who will make dramatic predictions rather than those who offer measured or optimistic observations. "Always predict the worst and you'll be hailed as a prophet," the troubadour Tom Lehrer once sang.

Yet plaguelike outbreaks don't happen, though of course there is no guarantee they never will. Adjusting for age—ever-elongating life spans cause people to be around for sufficient years to develop chronic conditions—nearly all disease rates, including rates of heart disease and cancer, are diminishing in the United States, the European Union, and most other parts of the world.

For the United States, the five leading causes of death—heart disease, cancer, chronic respiratory disorders, accidents, and stroke—are in long-term slopes of decline, according to data from the CDC. Coronary mortality shot upward in the early postwar era when packs-a-day cigarette smoking became common: smoking causes lung cancer and also damages the heart. As Jane Brody has noted, had heart disease fatality continued to rise in the United States at the rate of the 1950s and 1960s, 1.7 million Americans would die each year of heart attacks: instead, in 2016, about 425,000 did, about 75 percent fewer than would have been expected. The cancer death rate is down 25 percent since 1991, according to the American Cancer Society, "translating to approximately 2.1 million fewer cancer deaths than would have been expected if death rates had remained at their peak," Rebecca Siegel, a research officer for the society, said in a 2017 study.

But you'd never know this from midmorning talk shows, which continue to promote the notion of an ongoing cancer pandemic, or to focus on single instances of rare cancers while glossing over the macro numbers.

It's not just declining disease rates in the West from which the media avert their eyes. One generation ago—not the dim past but the 1980s—in India only the children of the upper class, about 2 percent of youth overall, received measles vaccination. Today 85 percent of Indian children are vaccinated against measles, with even the poorest children of the Delhi area receiving the advanced MMR inoculation. You've seen sexual violence and smog in India—serious matters to be sure—covered in detail in the Western press, but have you seen improving public health mentioned? In August 2015, a milestone was reached: the continent of Africa went a full year without a polio case. Being positive, this health story drew little notice. And it's not just social media and cable talkfests that slant negative on human well-being. From late 2013 to early 2015, the *New York Times,* the world's leading newspaper, ran twenty-two page-one stories suggesting a pending Ebola catastrophe. When in mid-2015 the NIH concluded there was no mutated Ebola strain, the *Times* put this development at the bottom of page 4. A dispatch headlined "Ebola Cases Fall Sharply, World Health Organization Says" was positioned on page 5. The success of the Ebola vaccine was reported on page A9.

Intercontinental air travel has gone in just a few generations from non-existent to rare to amazingly common. Jetliners create a means that does not exist in nature to transfer pathogens quickly over long distances. Fast food, junk snacks, microwaved fare, sweeteners, and sodium would seem another pervasive health harm: "Do you want fries with that?" might replace "In God We Trust" on US currency. During the Barack Obama presidency, First Lady Michelle Obama crusaded against processed sugar—even as the US government was underwriting sugar production at the wholesale level and providing, according to a 2016 US Agriculture Department study, about $15 billion annually in candy and sweetened soda to food stamp recipients. Western super-sized eating is spreading to Asia and South America, in no small part because the dynamics described in the previous chapter make calories plentiful and inexpensive. Air travel and poor dietary habits are people-caused health threats that nature could not have mounted.

The American car-centric, walking-averse lifestyle is rightly implicated in expanded waistlines and metabolic syndrome, the cluster of chronic disorders associated with too many calories and not enough activity. Weight gain and metabolic syndrome are proliferating in places where cars are not king. When in 2016 the summer Olympics were held in Rio de Janeiro, home of beach-body culture and "The Girl from Ipanema"— "tall and tan and lean and lovely"—the world learned that obesity is Brazil's leading health problem, despite car ownership levels far lower than those found in the United States. Half a century ago, the pressing social problem in Mexico was malnutrition. Now Mexico has the most obesity in the world, with one-third of its population severely overweight; Mexicans are more likely to die from weight-caused conditions than from violence. Across the globe today there are more people who overeat than who go to bed hungry, a statement that would have seemed fantastical to our great-grandparents, if not to our parents.

As the human population has grown spectacularly in the postwar period, diminished harm from contagions is deceptively important because, in all prior centuries, crowded conditions communicated disease. Once, people wanted to get out of polluted, filthy cities for health reasons. Today, in the United States and European Union, urban pollution is in long-term decline, while cities offer health care facilities close at hand. American city-dwellers walk more than rural Americans, who go everywhere in cars or trucks, and walking is associated with longer life. In the twenty-first century, the city has replaced the countryside as the healthful place to be.

The arrival of genetic engineering creates another apprehension, engaging the threat that some laboratory will produce an organism that functions as a weapon. Determined attempts by the old Soviet Union to invent bioweapons got nowhere, compared to packing bullets. Once "weaponized" smallpox accidentally was released from a Soviet military facility. Three people died. Accidentally firing a machine gun at the same place would have killed more. In 1979, an explosion at another Soviet site released a large quantity of weapons-grade anthrax; sixty-eight people died, but there was no runaway effect. In that time and place, weapons-grade anthrax caused less mortality than vodka. In 1989, workers at an American government laboratory near Washington, DC, accidentally were exposed to Ebola; no one died. A coordinated anthrax attack on Washington in 2001 was expected to trigger unstoppable plague; five people died. Actual use has shown chemical and biological weapons to be pound for pound less dangerous than bullets or explosives: the 1995 sarin gas attacks in the Tokyo subway killed twelve people, while conventional bombs of about the same size and weight killed fifty-two people in the 2005 London Underground terror attacks. None of this ensures that a potent bioweapon will not someday emerge from a laboratory. But the engineered germ must overcome the same obstacle faced by the naturally occurring germ—that mammals have spent hundreds of millions of years evolving defenses against biological assault.

DISEASES CAUSE SUFFERING BUT DO not run wild mainly because the biosphere is elaborately conditioned to defeat germs and viruses. So far as is known, there has never been an unstoppable contagion—"never" in this sense not meaning "recently" but *never:* not during the 3.8 billion years life has existed. Mammal bodies contain an amazing range of proteins and biological pathways that arose to counteract contagion. Animals, plants, and pathogens developed jointly: the living ecosystem has been resisting disease for eons. Had any disease ever "won," the result would have been lights-out for the disease, which would have lost its hosts. That plants, mammals, and people are here is proof the diseases don't win.

Beyond the natural evolution of immune systems are the social evolutions of medical science and public health practices. "People seem to believe society is becoming more vulnerable to plagues, but public health gets better all the time," says Margaret Liu, a researcher at the Karolinska Institute, a medical school in Stockholm, who is among the world's leading vaccine specialists. The body of a person in basic good health—that is, not already sickened by something else—can fight off most pathogens. This is why hospital patients contract staph or strep while doctors and nurses do not contract these diseases: the patients are weakened by sickness or surgery; the nurses and physicians are in basic good health. And year by year, more of the human family is in basic good health.

The influenza pandemic of 1918–1919 killed at least 20 million people, from a far smaller population than today's. At the time, health care institutions were rudimentary and food shortages—agriculture was reeling from the Great War—resulted in entire regions of men and women who were malnourished. Hungry people are more prone to infection than the overfed, who form the contemporary global majority. Broad access, first to sulfa drugs, then to antibiotics, has made people less likely to be sick. Steadily improving sanitation standards in most of the world have reduced public exposure to diseases, causing the majority to be in better health when they strike. There were three flu pandemics during the twentieth century, and each was less virulent than the previous one. First the horrific post–World War I pandemic; next a 1957 pandemic, caused by the H2N2 virus, which killed one million to four million worldwide, though the global population was significantly higher than in 1918–1919; then the 1968 Hong Kong flu, caused by the H3N2 strain, which also killed one million to four million, again from a larger population base. As public health steadily improved, including in most developing nations, viruses took fewer lives, setting the stage for the 2014 Ebola outbreak, which would prove far less harmful than anticipated.

Yet people expect runaway contagions. At the Cineplex and on primetime television, Hollywood stars wander post-apocalyptic landscapes where, viewers are told, all but a remnant of humanity was wiped out in weeks by an unstoppable ailment: *The Walking Dead, I Am Legend, Twelve Monkeys,* many others. Why audiences find the end of the world entertaining is anyone's guess. What matters is viewers may think there is scientific plausibility to television shows and movies that present the RNA and DNA of pathogens as super-ultra-unstoppable. Movies and primetime TV are the same mediums that depict time travel and lovelorn teen vampires: entertainment on the screen is not exactly fact-checked. Audiences laugh off most of what Hollywood produces, but cinematic warnings of plagues are harder to dismiss. You know you will never climb into a time machine; you don't know you will never inhale a plague bacillus.

Microbes and viruses cannot be seen. There is a certain logic in fearing the invisible more than obvious risks, such as car crashes. Globally, traffic accidents kill substantially more people than exotic diseases. We have commonsense mechanisms to assess what kinds of behavior while driving are reasonable and what kinds are perilous. We have no commonsense means of knowing whether a stranger sauntering down the street is a carrier of a deadly pathogen.

*   *   *

WHY HAS PUBLIC HEALTH STEADILY improved? High-quality hospitals and health clinics, once mainly for the privileged, increasingly are open to everyone: in most of the European Union and in Japan, sick people are admitted to hospitals regardless of ability to pay, while in the United States, emergency rooms accept patients regardless of ability to pay. During the US debate about the Affordable Care Act, popularly known as ObamaCare, commentators on both sides referred to the legislation as providing health care. What it provides is insurance coverage; health care is already provided, at least to anyone in medical distress. That anyone can get high-quality health care, rather than the rich being in teaching hospitals while the poor are in dingy charity institutions, has been a boon to public health.

As more workers in nearly all nations, including China and India, shift from manual labor to white-collar or service industry employment, public health improves. Deindustrialization is spoken of by politicians and pundits as if referring to something dreadful—in health terms, deindustrialization is a major plus. Commentators like to glamorize factory labor and underground mining: both lead to chronic degenerative health problems that arrive during the prime of life. The more people there are who sit at desks rather than work in factories, the more public health improves. In 1900, some 80 percent of Americans were employed at manual or semiskilled labor, 20 percent in professional roles. Today only 4 percent of American employment is manual labor; 35 percent is semiskilled and 61 percent is white-collar, treble the share of a century ago. Health and longevity have improved in sync.

PUBLIC INVESTMENT IN SANITATION INFRASTRUCTURE has further improved overall health, making runaway pandemics less likely. As recently as the 1970s, many large Western cities discharged untreated sewage into rivers, lakes, or oceans; now none do. Chicago has invested about $4 billion in a deep-tunnel system that keeps storm runoff out of waterways; the Chicago River, once disgusting, has become popular for dinner cruises. (The Chicago River is dyed green for Saint Patrick's Day—generations ago, there was so much muck that dying the river was out of the question.)

Boston spent several billion dollars to clean the Charles River and nearby parts of the Atlantic Ocean; Los Angeles, Milwaukee, and San Diego are among cities that have made significant investments in sewer discharge abatement. Water sanitation has a long way to go in the developing world: in Pakistan, where I once lived, open sewage trenches run through densely populated parts of cities. But the trend is toward cleaner water in the developing world, which means less disease transmission.

Pollution reduction improves public health. As recently as the 1970s, millions of pounds of toxic chemicals were released annually by US industry or disposed of untreated. Today toxic emissions are down—though US manufacturing output is up—and most industrial waste either is treated or recycled. As the next chapter will detail, all forms of air pollution except greenhouse gases are in long-term decline in the United States and European Union; better air quality is good for public health. Air in China, India, and parts of the developing world is dangerously polluted; across the contemporary globe it is the poor nations that are the polluted ones, not the advanced industrial regions. In poor nations, indoor air pollution—caused by burning wood, coal, or agricultural wastes for heating and cooking—may be worse than outdoor air pollution. The World Health Organization estimates that indoor air pollution causes 4.3 million deaths annually in the developing world; by contrast, outdoor air pollution causes little if any mortality in the United States and European Union. Indoor cooking smoke in the developing world is far more harmful to the human family than conjectured super-plagues.

Public investments to reduce pollution are joined to a better public health response model, the latter tending to nip problems in the bud. Neither Ebola nor Zika ran wild in part because public health teams in Africa and elsewhere acted immediately. For generations, governments have devoted more resources to denying problems exist than to addressing them. Increasingly, governments admit the truth about pollution and disease, while health organizations act promptly to prevent pathogens from spreading.

Improved medical care, better sanitation, ample food, less pollution, the shift toward white-collar work—these and other trends add up to rising longevity. In 2016, the government agency Public Health England reported that a sixty-five-year-old British man was likely to live to age eighty-four, and a sixty-five-year-old British woman to eighty-six, both representing record longevity. Numbers are similar throughout the West. Despite observing the increase in their older fellow citizens, Americans and Europeans, polls show, think they will die sooner than actuarial tables suggest. This not only is a factor in too-low retirement savings—assuming you won't live as long as you probably will can become an excuse not to put money away—but has broader applications to society's misunderstanding of ever-better public health.

For millennia if not for eons—anthropology continuously pushes backward the era of human origin—life expectancy was short. A few became gray and stooped, assumed, because of their years, to have won the favor of the gods. The typical person was fortunate to reach middle age. Beginning in the nineteenth century, this changed.

Birth and death data show that since about 1840, each year new babies live three months longer than those born the prior year; each decade, new babies live two and a half years longer. When the nineteenth century began in America, life expectancy at birth was forty-seven years. Now it's seventy-nine years, just about an added three months of life for every passing year. Should this trend continue, by midcentury, American life expectancy at birth will be eighty-eight years. By the end of the twenty-first century, longevity will reach one hundred years. Centenarians may become the norm, no longer meriting a phone call from the president.

Those who live longer live taller. As recently as the middle nineteenth century, the upper class in Britain and other European nations was notably taller, on average, than the working class, owing to better nourishment and protection from debilitating labor. By the middle of the twentieth century, all persons averaged about the same height. Tallness for men and women across social classes has been increasing nearly everywhere in the world. For example, in 1900 the typical man in the Netherlands was five feet, seven inches tall. Today the typical man in the Netherlands is five-foot-eleven. A gradual, global increase in tallness tracks the gradual, global increase in longevity, and both began around the same time. Perhaps in 1840 the Earth transited a comet tail and life span dust fell around the world. More likely, as time passes, the human condition improves.

The longevity rise seems not to link to specific events. It didn't accelerate much as antibiotics and vaccines became common, nor decline much during wars or health alarms such as the AIDS spread. Global trends in life expectancy are smooth and almost uninterrupted: graphs look like an escalator rising at a 45-degree angle. The improvement obtains nearly everywhere. A century ago, African life expectancy at birth was just twenty-five years; today life expectancy is sixty years—lower than most other regions but a leap compared to the African past. Until recent decades in the United States, African Americans on average died much sooner than whites, both a sorrow and a reason blacks had so much trouble building family net worth. The gap steadily has narrowed and now is nearly gone; in 2017, the CDC reported that older black males live about the same length of time as older white males. China, which was deeply impoverished, with wretched public health, two generations ago, today has seventy-six-year life expectancy at birth, only slightly below that of Scotland. The whole world is riding the escalator.

As recently as the 1990s, no medical institution focused on science-based attempts to increase life expectancy. That changed in 1999 with the opening of the Buck Institute in Marin County, California—home to fading hipsters and towering redwoods, the place to which the Golden Gate Bridge leads. Already Buck Institute researchers have been able to double the life spans of common laboratory animals. Whether their techniques will work in people is unknown, but the research is nascent.

If artificial intervention can add longevity, very long-lived men and women may be in the cards. Natural selection favors adaptations that allow animals, including humans, to reach the age of reproduction. Adaptations that add post-reproductive years are lost to evolution, since the animal that lives longer than its peers has no mechanism to pass longevity fitness to offspring. Brian Kennedy, former director of the Buck Institute, says, "Because natural selection did not improve us for aging, there's a chance for rapid gains. The latest BMWs are close to perfect, how can an engineer improve them? But the Model T was easy to improve. When young, genetically we are BMWs. In aging, we become Model Ts. The improvements haven't started yet."

Impressed by the Buck Institute, in 2014 Google founded a longevity research project called Calico. Already Calico researcher Cynthia Kenyon has shown that in some worms, altering just two genes causes the invertebrate to live twice as long, and in good vigor by the standards of worms. The genetic tweaks activate what seems to be a naturally occurring life-span pathway that evolution turned off, perhaps to favor a pathway that raises the odds of reaching reproductive age—which once was unlikely in nature and today in human society is highly likely. Many natural selection outcomes are poorly grasped. Whales don't get cancer; polar bears consume an extremely high-fat diet yet don't develop arterial plaque. If the biology of such outcomes was understood, a drug might be designed to mimic the no-cancer no-plaque pathways in people. Should it be found that people already have life-span extenders in their DNA makeup—turned off by some past evolutionary event—turning on genes that already exist seems a lot more promising than designing new DNA in a lab.

Projections for still-longer life spans do not, however, assume medical discoveries will be made—simply that the escalator ride will continue.

THE STEADY IMPROVEMENT OF HUMAN life spans with each passing year was noticed by James Vaupel, founder of Germany's Max Planck Institute for Demographic Research. In 2002, Vaupel published an influential article in the technical journal *Science,* documenting the eerily linear rise in life expectancy since 1840. Controversially, he concluded that "reductions in mortality should not be seen as a disconnected sequence of unrepeatable revolutions but rather as a regular stream of continuing progress." No specific discovery or innovation was causing people to live longer, Vaupel thought; improvements in nutrition, sanitation, and medical knowledge obviously help, but the operative impetus was, he wrote, the "stream of continuing progress." In 2017, Vaupel told me data collected since 2002 support his conclusion: "Life expectancy continues to rise at a pace of a bit less than two and a half years per decade, or about six hours per day." A baby born at the end of the week will live a full day longer than one born at the beginning of the week.

Vaupel's 2002 paper described a "reasonable scenario" in which longevity increases continue at least until life expectancy at birth in the United States and European Union surpasses one hundred years, with life expectancy in the developing world rising at least until it surpasses the standard for the West today.

There are counterarguments to this view. From 2014 to 2015, life expectancy at birth in the United States declined slightly, the first downturn in a generation, while life expectancy for men in China has been in slight decline for a decade. More broadly, the standout factor in twentieth-century longevity gains was reduction of infant mortality, since saving an infant saves the entire span of that person's life. Infant mortality is now so low—1 in 175 in the United States, 1 in 230 in the European Union—that little room for improvement remains. By contrast, health interventions for senior citizens do not add notably to longevity, as senior citizens have little remaining life to save. S. Jay Olshansky, a professor of public health at the University of Illinois at Chicago, calculates that if cancer among the aging were eliminated altogether, US life expectancy would rise only three years.

The increased mortality the United States experienced from 2014 to 2015 seems to link to deaths caused by drugs—not so much street highs like heroin but legally obtained prescription pharmaceuticals, especially opioid painkillers. The 33,000 opioid intoxication deaths in the United States in 2015 exceeded the number of murders: in that year, police were more likely to be summoned to the scene of an overdose than of a homicide. Painkiller intemperance by adults is doubly disturbing because, as Claire McCarthy, a pediatrician at Boston Children's Hospital, has written, alcohol and street-drug consumption by teens has been declining for a quarter-century. Kids are getting smart about not getting blasted, grown-ups are getting dumb. (Binge drinking at college fraternities and sororities is bad, but same-age Americans not enrolled in school are more likely to abuse alcohol than college students.) The CDC reports, "Deaths from prescription drugs like oxycodone, hydrocodone and methadone have more than quadrupled since 1999." Yet government spares no expense, and imposes long prison sentences, to oppose marijuana, which can replace narcotic painkillers at a fraction of the addiction and overdose risk, even as government looks the other way on prescription opioids and their marketing.

The mortality uptick brought on by self-inflicted death—prescription drug overdose, suicide, alcohol poisoning—is pronounced among whites. Princeton University researchers Angus Deaton and Anne Case have shown that in 2000 one out of every 4,400 white Americans died from alcohol or drug overdose or at his or her own hand; by 2014, it was one in 1,800. Of all American citizens, in 2000, one in 9,500 took his or her own life by suicide, while in 2014 one in 7,700 did so. Both figures represent less self-inflicted death than a century ago, when one American in 6,200 committed suicide annually. But since contemporary Americans live much better than their forebears, a dramatic decline in suicide might be expected. Instead, the decline is modest and has now been joined by a rise in overdose deaths.

Less smoking contributes to lower mortality, though cigarettes going out of fashion coincides with the expansion of pants sizes: smoking suppresses the appetite. Europeans scratch their heads about the United States, where cigarettes and cigars are zealously restricted to protect health yet junk food is omnipresent and guns are sold to those with mental health issues or who have never taken a firearm safety class. Smoking is down in the West but all the rage in China, which has become the world's leading producer of smartphones, high-speed elevators, Disney toys, and cigarettes. Christopher Buckley's 1994 humor novel *Thank You for Smoking* had a subplot about the Chinese government wanting citizens hooked on cigarettes so they would stay alert and productive during adulthood, then die before filing for pensions. As men's mortality in China rises, what once was wacky satire draws closer to documentary.

Childhood obesity rose alarmingly from about 1970 to about 2000, then began a shallow decline as parents and schools became aware of links between obesity and fried or sugared cuisine. The Robert Wood Johnson Foundation reports that since 2007, in the United States there has been a 78-a-day per-capita drop in consumption of calories—trivial over the short term, important if sustained for a generation.

The medical writer Margot Sanger-Katz notes that most measures of childhood health are improving, while researchers increasingly think a good metabolic reading in youth portends "health span," the late-life years of vigor: "Today's children and young adults may grow up to enjoy longer lives and fewer health problems than their parents." For example, researchers led by Matthew Pase of Boston University found in 2017 that drinking lots of sugary soda early in life is associated with memory loss and Alzheimer's late in life. The postwar period saw a huge increase in consumption of sugary soda, peaking in the year 1998, as well as an increase in dementia diagnoses. Should young people continue to favor water and sports drinks over sugary soda—2016 was the first year in which bottled water outsold carbonated soft drinks in the United States—they may suffer less memory loss when they age. Stepping further back, research suggests that if pregnant women eat seafood, their babies' IQ will be higher. Insights such as these could improve long-term health for large numbers.

WHILE LONGEVITY IS RISING AND disease rates are declining, in the United States disability is increasing, at least as defined by those who qualify for two similarly named federal programs run by the Social Security Administration (SSA): Social Security Disability Insurance (SSDI) and Supplemental Security Income (SSI), which pay $10,000 to $14,000 per year to working-age adults classified as disabled and also make payments to disabled minors and senior citizens. Two decades ago, SSDI, the program that is mainly for working-age adults, had 4.5 million recipients; by 2017, there were 8.8 million Americans on SSDI. If the number of recipients had risen in sync with population growth, today there would be about 5.2 million Americans on SSDI, so the actual number, 8.8 million, represents a 70 percent increase compared to expectations. A parallel program for veterans has seen the number of disability recipients nearly double, compared to population increase, in the past two decades. Combining numbers for the two SSA-run programs and the veterans' programs, then subtracting the aged, results in about 7 percent of Americans under age sixty-five now receiving disability subsidies—a proportion that's not just big in comparison with past populations but big period.

America's forever-wars in Afghanistan and Iraq may explain the rise in disabled veterans: not only have many members of the armed services been exposed to harm in recent decades; improved field hospitals make them more likely to survive with injuries. Wounded warriors are always preferable to buried warriors, but bring with them costs—financial to the public, personal to families—that politicians and cable-news talking heads don't like to address while expounding grand theories.

For the civilian population, the total of disability recipients might be diminishing as ever-improving therapies, coupled to teleworking, allow men and women with serious physical problems to fulfill many tasks. Yet even discounting for aging and population increase, disability rolls are up. Does this tell us something about health—or something about society?

Chana Joffe-Walt, a reporter for the public radio show *This American Life,* proposes a disturbing answer: in the contemporary economy, being poorly educated and overweight are, of themselves, disabilities. In 2013, she interviewed an Alabama physician who said he approves federal disability payments to anyone who did not graduate from high school and is severely overweight because on today's job landscape no employer would want such a person.

Joffe-Walt found that federal disability subsidies are more common in rural areas than in cities; rural residents are more likely to be poorly educated and to be too heavy to stand. Census Bureau statistics reinforce this view: in Alabama's largely rural Fourth Congressional District, 17 percent of working-age adults are classified as disabled, more than double the nationwide rate. She noted that a diabolical calculation can be involved. Getting $14,000 a year for life from government, plus health care through Medicaid, while sleeping late then watching TV all day, may be attractive compared to earning $13,500 per year—that's the federal minimum wage at forty hours per week, minus payroll taxes—while worrying about being laid off, running the risk of losing health insurance, and rising at dawn to obey an irritable boss.

Being "on the draw," as is said in rural areas, is a fast lane to nowhere: no dignity, no chance of advancement, no ability to help your family. So you might as well drink bargain vodka and take painkillers! Here is where disability subsidies, substance abuse, cigarette smoking, and the mortality increase found by the Princeton researchers Case and Deaton intersect. Health outcomes and longevity are improving nicely for the educated. For those with no college, it's another matter.

Today in the United States the best-educated males live fourteen years longer than the least-educated men. Olshansky's research suggests American women who lack a high school diploma have experienced no life-span increase since the 1950s, while the life expectancy of highly educated women has soared in the same period. "Nothing pops out of the data like the link between education and life expectancy," Olshansky says. "The good news is that share of the population that is low-educated is in gradual decline. The bad news is that lack of education seems even more lethal than it was in the past."

Education does not sync with life expectancy because reading Hemingway lowers blood pressure: college is a proxy for other aspects of a person's life. The Centers for Disease Control have found that those who never attended college are three times more likely to smoke than those holding bachelor's degrees. The educated generally have higher incomes, are less sedentary—chronic health failings are associated with couch-potato behavior—and follow doctors' instructions. Physicians lament that poorly educated patients may ignore directives on matters as rudimentary as how often to take medicine. John Rowe, a professor of public health at Columbia University and former CEO of the insurer Aetna, says, "If someone walked into my office and asked me to predict how long he would live, I would ask two things—what is your age and how many years of education did you receive?"

Many developments that improve longevity—better sanitation, less pollution, technologically upgraded emergency rooms—are provided to everyone on an egalitarian basis. Education is not. Public schools are dreadful in many places, including much of California, Michigan, and the former Confederate states; legislatures are cutting support for public universities; private colleges are prohibitively expensive to many families. Educational issues often are discussed in terms of social justice—perhaps health should be added as a concern. If education is the ace card of longevity, the top quintile may pull away from the rest.

TODAY MANY REVERE NATURE AS a benign goddess, but to our ancestors nature was an enemy, bringer of suffering through disease, predation, and natural disaster. That humanity first evolved from nature, then engaged in a millennia-long duel to the death with nature, then finally established peaceful coexistence with the found world, will form a pleasing narrative, assuming our descendants can look back and analyze events in this manner. But peaceful coexistence is not yet won. In parts of the world, the battle against nature continues. Anti-vaccine sentiment, founded in left-wing science illiteracy and right-wing propaganda, has allowed polio to make a resurgence. Bill Gates noted in 2014 that the tsetse fly, assassin bug, and freshwater snail—nearly unknown in the West—kill about 30,000 men and women a year in Africa, Central America, and South America. Mosquitoes are far worse. In 2014, some 475,000 people worldwide were slain by their fellow human beings via crime, war, and domestic violence. That same year mosquitoes killed 725,000 people.

Progress against malaria does continue. Samir Bhatt of the University of Oxford has shown that, since 2000, the incidence of malaria in Africa has declined 40 percent, despite population growth. So far the most effective counter to the *Anopheles* mosquito is insecticide-treated sleeping nets. These are not enough: the hot parts of the world, which may be expanding, need vaccines against mosquito-borne disease. Perhaps some other plan of attack will work: one promising line of research involves releasing altered mosquitoes that do not carry dengue fever. The altered insects proliferate and still bite but don't transmit disease, leading to a less-dangerous mosquito population. If this technique can work against malaria, or a vaccine can be found, global health may take a giant step.

Imagine if the United States or European Union had the same malaria incidence as sub-Saharan Africa, where large numbers die of the disease and millions of others become sickly and unproductive, requiring care rather than pulling their own weight. If malaria were common in the West, voters and leaders of the United States and European Union would consider the quest for a vaccine the number-one issue facing the world.

EVEN IF RUNAWAY DISEASE OUTBREAKS have been contained in the current generation, how can we be sure this will continue to be the case? Today, making new vaccines is a slow process, since attenuating an existing pathogen is required: the varicella vaccine, for instance, took three decades to perfect. In development are "vaccine platforms" of recombinant proteins—the goal is a sort of blank that can be turned into a potent vaccine quickly in response to disease mutations. Vaccines also are hard to produce in quantity, as one-by-one injection into chicken eggs, or other cumbersome processes, may be required. In principle, transgenic plants could grow vaccines more simply than pharmaceutical facilities can manufacture them.

In the near future, mutation of a new pathogen might lead to this public health response: first inoculation perfected quickly from a vaccine platform, then a transgene plant that grows the necessary proteins in the same manner crops are grown. At some juncture in this century, the communicable vaccine may be developed. People can give each other diseases; what if they could give each other immunity?

THE SUMMATION OF WHY DISEASES don't wipe us out might be this: they don't because they can't. Natural selection prepared genus *Homo* to defend itself against pathogens, while public health improvements make the world's people less likely to succumb. Still, as the global population continues to rise, society will need reforms to make health care better, less expensive, and more equitably distributed.

So we won't starve and won't be wiped out by plagues. What if nature collapses?

Chapter 3

Will Nature Collapse?

THERE'S NO NOSTALGIA FOR THE 1970s. The global economy was stagnant, the Cold War tangible. China, the Subcontinent, most of Africa, and much of South America were impoverished. Extensive areas of the world were police-states or officially racist or both.

And nature was thought to be on the verge of collapse. Petroleum was said to be in such desperate supply that grandees in Washington and London spoke of waging war to seize the oil of the Arabian Peninsula. Natural gas was viewed as so close to exhaustion that Congress enacted a law nearly banning its use. Many minerals and ores, even the river-bed sand essential for concrete, were said to be reaching depletion. Miasmic air pollution was common; Los Angeles averaged 125 "stage 1" smog alerts annually. Industry dumped toxic wastes as it pleased, while cities discharged untreated sewage into lakes and oceans. Dangerous chemicals such as daminozide (Alar) and dioxin were showing up in groundwater, even on apples. High-altitude ozone depletion threatened to allow passage of radiation the stratosphere once blocked. From the White House, Richard Nixon declared that by the year 2000, "our cities are going to be choked with pollution." Forests were sickened by acid rain, burning in the Amazon, or slicked off by logging. "Charismatic megafauna"—big, cute animals—were imperiled, including the sea otter, rarely seen off the California coast. Huge numbers of species were supposedly close to extinction, among them the North American bald eagle, symbol of the United States.

Two factors threatened to make the situation worse still. One was the incredible acceleration of population growth in response to the food supply and health improvements discussed in the first two chapters. The other was early indicators of artificially triggered changes to the climate.

In 1970, anchorman Walter Cronkite, America's best-known television presence, intoned that "population growth is totally out of control." The global census has since doubled. If a time traveler told Walter Cronkite in 1970 that the world soon would host twice as many people, and that warming caused by artificial greenhouse gases would become scientifically incontrovertible, surely the anchorman would have employed his famed avuncular baritone to predict the biosphere would collapse.

INSTEAD, IN 2017, I WATCHED a bald eagle glide peacefully above my home near Washington, DC. North American eagles have proliferated so much that the International Union for the Conservation of Nature (IUCN), which keeps the books on species gains and losses, now classifies the bird under "least concern."

The eagle flew through air that was free of smog, as air almost always is in American cities. Newspapers in my driveway reported that oversupply of petroleum and natural gas was pushing energy prices toward record lows. "Oil Glut Worries"—page 1, *Wall Street Journal*, March 10, 2017; "Natural Gas Glut Deepens," same paper, same page, a week later. Society was expected by now to be in full panic mode regarding oil and gas exhaustion, and instead the apprehension is too much fuel. Another newspaper in the driveway reported so many otters frolicking off California that tourists were crowding seaside enclaves to watch. Acid rain was nearly stopped, the stratospheric ozone hole was closing. Water quality alarms were ongoing in Flint, Michigan, and along Long Island Sound, but in general cleanliness was rising, with Boston Harbor, Chesapeake Bay, Puget Sound, and other major water bodies, filthy a generation ago, mostly safe for swimming and fishing, meeting the 1972 Clean Water Act's definition of success. Nearly every environmental barometer in the United States was positive and had been so for years if not decades.

Watching the bald eagle soar did not make me feel complacent regarding the natural world, rather, made me feel that greenhouse gases can be brought to heel, just as other environmental problems have been. Climate change reforms will be the subject of a coming chapter. Here, let's contemplate why nature did not collapse, despite ever more people consuming ever more resources.

Man-made damage to nature can be atrocious. Think of the *Exxon Valdez* oil spill, which destroyed forever the wildlife in Prince William Sound, Alaska. At least that's what was said in 1989 when the tanker struck Bligh Reef. Today most sea and intertidal life in Prince William Sound has returned to pre-spill numbers, while the sound's combination of beauty and biology makes it a popular destination for whale-watching tours. Exxon, now ExxonMobil, deserved the billions in fines and settlements the company paid. But the whole thing was over in a snap of the fingers in geologic terms.

Humanity is hardly the only force that damages nature. In 1980, pressurized magma inside Mount Saint Helens in Washington State exploded with the power of about 1,500 Hiroshima bombs. "Some 19 million old-growth Douglas firs, trees with deep roots, were ripped from the ground and tossed about like cocktail swizzles," one analyst wrote. Hundreds of square miles burned to cinders, animals and fifty-seven people near the eruption turned to char. Commentators of the time called the Mount Saint Helens area destroyed forever. When I hiked the blast zone in 1992, I was amazed to behold areas that had been lifeless moonscapes in 1980; just a dozen years later, they were bright with biology: wildflower, elk, sapling firs. Today Mount Saint Helens National Volcanic Monument is a recommended destination for backpackers.

Through the eons, nature has healed after insults far worse than the worst ever done by people—ice ages, asteroid strikes, thousand-year periods of volcanism so extreme that global ash clouds blocked the sun for years at a time. The mega-volcanism that long ago created Siberia is estimated to have unleashed three billion times the force of the Hiroshima blast, plus far more smoke than humanity's wars and factories combined. Nature has evolved defenses against such harm in the same way that the body has evolved defenses against pathogens. This does not make harm to nature insignificant, any more than having an immune system makes germs insignificant. But before asking whether nature will collapse, it's good to remind ourselves that our ongoing existence is evidence that the biosphere is a green fortress.

Similarly, it is important to cast aside the common misconception that the guiding imperative of human interaction with the found world should be to preserve nature's correct form. Nature has no correct form but, rather, continuous transformation. The Harvard University evolutionary biologist Richard Lewontin has written, "Human existence cannot proceed rationally under the banner 'save the environment,' as 'the environment' does not exist to be saved. The world inhabited by living organisms is constantly changed and reconstructed by the activity of all these organisms, not just by human activity." If men and women vanished from the Earth tomorrow, the environment would continue to change.

AN IMPORTANT INDICATOR OF THE health of nature is trees. During the nineteenth century, when wood was a primary heating fuel and cleared land was needed for farming, forested acreage declined fast. Careless logging often had the unintended consequence of leading to erosion and mudslides. By the 1980s, emissions from power plants of sulfur dioxide, which changes to acid in the air, threatened forests of the Appalachian Mountains and the eastern regions of Europe. A "new silent spring" was forecast: if forests died and ceased to provide habitat, no songbirds would greet spring. By 1999, the climate activist Bill McKibben would write that forest health was a solved issue, noting "the forest cover of the eastern United States is today as extensive as it was prior to the American Revolution."

When Al Gore was vice president, widespread obliteration of the Amazon rain forest was forecast. Gore liked to shock audiences by saying one football field per second of jungle was being burned or leveled in the Amazon Basin. That figure works out to 14 million football fields' worth—or 21 million acres—of forest gone from Brazil by today. Gore's prediction turned out to be correct—and this may be the only time anyone has ever written those words! But while 21 million acres may sound, to a resident of a tightly packed place such as San Francisco or Tokyo, like the expanse of the Andromeda galaxy, the number represents roughly 1 percent of the Amazon rain forest.

Beginning around 2015, Amazon deforestation accelerated to an annualized rate of two million acres, according to satellite data compiled by

Brazilian researchers. That is a concern, but Amazon deforestation could continue at such a rate for several generations and the rain forest would remain dauntingly vast. Regardless, there are reasons the word "deforestation" should give pause. One is that clearing rain forest releases carbon from soil: the global warming implications of rain-forest clearing may be greater than the wild-lands implications. The second is that, because trees take so much longer to replace than other kinds of plants, deforestation has in the past been coincident with the failure of societies. The UCLA geographer Jared Diamond has argued that the Anasazi and Maya civilizations ended because rapid deforestation caused topsoil loss (via erosion and wind) that prevented farming. Modern forms of agriculture would seem to insulate today's world from this result, but it's not playing the percentages to repeat a practice that, in the past, brought woe.

Tree indicators beyond the Amazon have been positive at least for a generation. Researchers led by Thomas Crowther of the Yale School of Forestry have used satellite images to estimate that most tree loss caused by human civilization occurred before the twentieth century, not in the contemporary era. The planet now has about three trillion trees, or 425 trees per person, Yale determined. In 2015, researchers led by Simon Lewis of University College London compiled satellite data on South America and found that nearly all of the continent's forests, including most rain forests, fell into the category of "least disturbed."

AS SOME HAZARDS TO FORESTS were diminishing, acid rain was increasing, particularly from about 1950 to the 1980s. The acid rain threat to forests of the eastern United States stopped because 1990 legislation created a cap-and-trade program that placed limits on power plant releases of sulfur dioxide and similar gases. Since passage of the bill, sulfur dioxide emissions have declined 81 percent in the United States, the Environmental Protection Agency reported in 2016. The cap-and-trade system, developed by a nonpartisan think tank called Resources for the Future and backed by early-1990s EPA administrator Bill Reilly, turned out to work faster and to cost far less than anticipated. Reilly further is admired for having pressured oil companies in the early 1990s not to "flare" natural gas that impedes petroleum drilling—those scenes of towers of flame near oil derricks are scenes of flaring. Not only should natural gas be employed as a source of clean power, Reilly correctly surmised that flaring releases methane into the atmosphere, and methane is a more potent greenhouse gas than carbon dioxide.

Controlling acid rain was inexpensive because the system relied on market forces rather than top-down regulation: power plant engineers were free to reduce pollution in whatever manner they saw fit, and if they "overcontrolled"—cut pollution more than the law required—they could sell permits to power plants having trouble meeting the mandate. Editorialists who frothed over the program for entailing the sale of a right to pollute always skipped that the total degree of pollution steadily went down.

Since the acid-rain cap-and-trade program in the United States, the European Union and China have adopted similar policies and also seen sulfur dioxide emissions drop. This raises a little implication and a big implication. The little implication is that protecting forests turns out to be less expensive and more practical than once assumed. The big implication is that acid rain has been bested without international mandates or United Nations oversight—indeed, without acid rain even mentioned in treaties. Nations have dealt with acid rain without being compelled to do so, because addressing the problem is both affordable and in the national self-interest. This example is an underlying reason to be sanguine that greenhouse gases can be controlled.

BACK IN THE DAYS WHEN commentators assumed a forest collapse was looming, a man named Roger Sedjo was the sylvan issues analyst at Resources for the Future. He wrote academic treatises forecasting that trees and the habitats they foster—much forest biology occurs below the canopy, for that matter, below ground—would be just fine. "The old view was that farming would require clearing of every scrap of land, but even when I was young, you could see from leading indicators that farming would need less land," Sedjo says. He estimates that global forest cover has increased by about 15 percent since 1980, and that forest cover in the United States today is the same as it was in 1950, while the wood stock— the volume of timber, not the concert—has risen nearly 50 percent since

1980. These forest-and-tree improvements have happened as the number of people alive has risen dramatically.

Sedjo believes less land for farming, coupled to improved management of logging, is why trees are rebounding. In this context, improved management of logging is plantation forestry: rows of fast-growing trees that a business plans to harvest for wood. Such logging may be perceived as an offense to nature. "People seem to object to plantation forestry on some mystical level, because they have spiritual reactions to wild stands of trees," Sedjo says. "No one has a spiritual reaction to rows of tomatoes. Vegetables in a row seems normal, trees in a row seems wrong. In both cases, it's just people growing plants."

Conceptually, trees are really big stalks of wheat—they can be planted, harvested, and replanted in an endless cycle. A field clear-cut of wheat is a visual image of prosperity and autumnal harvest, while a field clear-cut of mature trees is thought bad. To the extent one may impute awareness to the natural world, nature would be perplexed that people admire the regimented growing and harvesting of fruits and vegetables while thinking trees should rise only in haphazard manner.

EVEN IF THE TREES ARE okay, what about the animals? The conclusion of Rachel Carson's haunting 1962 book *Silent Spring* was that most Northern American bird species soon would fall extinct. Instead, by three decades after the book was published, of the forty bird species Carson named as about to cease existing, thirty-three had stable or increasing populations in the United States; seven were in decline but far from lost. The National Audubon Society's annual Christmas Bird Count, the most extensive tracking of specific numbers, finds "alarming" decline in a few bird species, but rising numbers for most. Audubon's 2016 count tallied 646 avian species in the United States, including 182 bird species in Los Angeles, once so polluted wildlife seemed on the verge of annihilation there.

About a week after watching the bald eagle above my home, I went for a hike in a forest preserve situated just sixteen miles from the White House. I got a clear glimpse of three wild turkeys—though I did not approach them, as these are ornery animals. Populations of wild turkey and some other birds have bounced back because supermarket-fed Americans no longer shoot wild fowl for dinner. Populations of eagles and other birds have bounced back because society heeded Carson's warnings and restricted the rash use of insecticides, including DDT.

These winged examples point to the larger perspective on species: there are problems, but not to the scale that was anticipated when experts predicted rapid human-caused mass extinctions akin in scale to the after-effects of the asteroid that killed the dinosaurs. The International Union for the Conservation of Nature assesses the majority of known species—probably there are many living things in no one's taxonomy—as in good shape. The IUCN finds 1.3 percent of species in clear danger of falling extinct and about 20 percent under some form of pressure, whether man-made or natural. Research shows negative trend lines for corals, which, being temperature-sensitive but immobile, are imperiled by ocean warming. Katherine MacKinnon, an anthropologist at St. Louis University, found in 2017 that primates—apes, chimpanzees, bonobos, the animals most similar to people—are the most-threatened class, because their isolated habitats increasingly come into contact with people.

That past predictions of widespread human-caused species loss did not come true does not mean the peril to other living things has concluded. Nor that the peril to us is over: the medical researcher Frank Fenner, who was a motivating force behind the eradication of smallpox, in 2010 predicted humanity would fall extinct by the end of the twenty-first century. But so far, observed human-caused extinctions have been less than forecast.

OZONE IS MORE THAN THE name of a street in Venice, California. Ozone is an oxygen molecule with three atoms, rather than the more common two-atom gas (diatomic oxygen). This distinction sounds arcane, but because mammal lungs evolved to process two-atom oxygen, the three-atom version, new to lungs as an ingredient in urban smog, causes respiratory harm. The human family does not want to breathe ozone: especially, children and seniors should not. Miles up in the stratosphere, ozone is beneficial. There the bad-for-lungs chemistry is irrelevant, while ozone's absorption of ultraviolet radiation is beneficial: three-atom oxygen helps screen the dangerous part of the sun's rays.

That ozone's impact depends on location is one of the zany equilibria of the natural world. Ozone harms the lungs but also keeps radiation off your skin: there was a point in the recent past when it was safer, for your skin, to sunbathe on a beach in smoggy California than in some dangerously clean place like Hawaii. Sulfur dioxide exists in another zany equilibrium: low in the atmosphere this compound becomes acid rain; high in the air it forms particles that cause solar heat to bounce back into space, retarding global warming. Given the rise in atmospheric greenhouse gases, the world might have warmed more than has happened. There are many possible reasons observed warming is slower than seemed likely: one is that sulfur dioxide is a reverse greenhouse gas, cooling the planet. Those initiatives to reduce sulfur dioxide—reforms this chapter just praised? The less acid rain, the more warming.

In the early postwar period, chemicals called chlorofluorocarbons (CFCs) and halons came into widespread use as refrigerants and fire suppressors. Tests showed that high in the atmosphere, CFCs and halons depleted the good ozone. In 1985, researchers led by Joseph Farman of Cambridge University in England discovered an "ozone hole" in the stratosphere of Antarctica. Situated above austral ice, the ozone hole did not threaten anyone, but if it kept expanding, the world would be imperiled by radiation no longer blocked.

In 1987, the Western nations agreed to phase out CFCs and halons. By 2012, every nation had ratified the protocol, making this the first universal treaty, on any subject, achieved on our pale blue dot. Stratospheric ozone depletion has now stopped, with the hole shrinking, presumably on its way to closing. Halons and CFCs were replaced with other chemicals that work just as well as refrigerants or in fire suppression but do not function as ozone depletion catalysts.

THERE IS AN INTERSECTION BETWEEN the ozone hole problem and the climate change problem. Technological dynamism coupled to political will repaired the ozone-layer problem: chemists found a solution, and nearly all leaders supported the necessary reform. This response differs significantly from the world's reaction to artificially triggered climate change. In the case of the ozone hole, it was open-and-shut that CFCs, compounds that do not occur naturally, were damaging the atmosphere. Equally clear was that the offending chemicals could be banned in ways that were economically practical. In the case of climate change, the primary offending chemical, carbon dioxide, occurs naturally in quantities vastly dwarfing human output, while fossil fuels cannot be phased out quickly in the way that CFCs and halons could.

The man-made rise in atmospheric carbon dioxide, from 300 parts per million in 1900 to 400 parts per million today, works out to one additional molecule of artificially generated carbon dioxide for each 10,000 molecules of everything else in the air. Many scientists thought that such a minor change could not affect a system as enormous, active, and crackling with energy as Earth's atmosphere. In 1991, this was a reasonable, mainstream view: the US National Academy of Sciences declared "there is no evidence" of human impact on climate. Then substantiation began to accumulate as research and experiments verified the counterintuitive notion that as little as one new molecule in 10,000 indeed can cause the atmosphere to retain more heat. In 2005, the National Academy of Sciences joined the science academies of Britain, China, Germany, and Japan in a joint statement declaring, "There is now strong evidence that significant global warming is occurring."

Because there was considerable initial doubt regarding climate change, and because global living standards would nosedive if society simply banned the combustion of fossil fuels the way it banned ozone-depleting compounds, the public discourse on global warming veered into partisan grandstanding. Just a generation ago, the US Republican Party supported science-based conservation: Ronald Reagan backed the CFC ban, and the elder President George Bush endorsed 1990 legislation to reduce air pollution. By the year of Donald Trump's presidential candidacy, Republicans had begun to shun conservation and the scientific method, while in the hyperpartisan politics of the moment, for advocates of every variety, "sound science" came to mean "whatever supports our donors' agenda." Trump would call climate change a hoax "created by and for the Chinese." This harebrained galimatias helped him win the White House. In 2017, China reduced greenhouse emissions by canceling construction of more than one hundred coal-fired power stations, leaving unclear why the Chinese government would fall for its own hoax.

EVERYTHING'S GOING TO RUN OUT, right? That seems to stand to reason as the Earth is finite, and though the galaxy above has immeasurable resources, centuries may pass before this matters to humanity. Because it seems to stand to reason that everything will run out, some view resource depletion as the dark cloud over nature.

A generation ago, commentators looked at rates of resource consumption, multiplied them by expected population increase, and foresaw a bleak future. This might be called the fallacy of the uninterrupted trend. If you'd taken the number of horses in New York City in the late nineteenth century and projected an uninterrupted trend, you'd have forecast Manhattan would become a giant stable. Instead, trends changed—partly because of technical innovation, and partly because market economics favor efficient resource allocation. The old Soviet Union granted bonuses to steel mills based not on production quality and not on the taboo concept of profit, but rather on how much ore, coke, and coal the mills consumed: the result was resource waste plus pollution. On the day in 1990 when the Germanys were reunified, East Germany's per-capita energy consumption was 25 percent greater than West Germany's, though living standards in West Germany were far higher; the Soviet-controlled Eastern system offered no incentives to limit waste. Market economics confers profit on those who reduce resource needs and pollution, both at the producer and consumer levels. Today's beer cans, for example, contain about 15 percent as much metal as cans of the past. This was not done to protect nature— lighter cans needing lower levels of materials make the selling of beer more lucrative. But though profit is the goal, less stress on the natural world is the side effect.

Finding ways to manufacture more from less has been a distinctive feature of recent decades of market economics. From about 1900 until the 1970s, per-capita consumption of metals, minerals, water, and energy rose in the United States and European Union. Had trends continued uninterrupted, shortages would have loomed. Instead, per-capita use of nearly everything has been declining in Western nations for a generation, even as living standards continue to rise. Today's new cars use considerably less gasoline per mile than did cars of the 1970s, even as they generate more horsepower (too much horsepower, if road rage is your guide). Today's refrigerators, with flat-screen displays and other frills, require only about one-quarter as much electricity as fridges of the 1980s. Manufacturing processes within factories, invisible to consumers but essential to production, require steadily lower levels of energy and metals and change ever faster in response to scarcity.

Morris Adelman, a Massachusetts Institute of Technology economist who was influential in the early postwar period, argued that no nature resource would be exhausted, at least for millennia, because price and technology would draw out more supply from a geological structure that is immense compared to human action. Experience supports this view. Beginning around a decade ago, as hundreds of millions of people wanted smartphones, there were shortages of the rare-earth minerals needed for miniature electronics. China, which produces rare-earth minerals, restricted their export, hoping manufacturers would locate in China to obtain supply. The result was that rising prices for rare-earth minerals made new production profitable. Australia began mining these substances and flooding the market, causing rare-earth minerals to cease being rare, even as Apple was selling iPhones at a record pace.

Adelman and other economists long have noted that resources may seem to be vanishing when prices are low because there's little incentive to search for new deposits, veins, or fields; when prices rise, finding more becomes rewarding, and suddenly the resource is plentiful. Or rising prices can offer an incentive to switch to alternatives. In 2016, Honda built a hybrid motor that does not require rare-earth minerals, pulling the rug out from under China's strategy.

The most striking example of resources not becoming exhausted is continuing abundance of fossil fuels (including too much coal, if greenhouse gases are your guide). A 1972 academic study titled *Limits to Growth,* which found considerable favor with intellectuals and editorialists, predicted that petroleum deposits could be depleted as soon as 1992; definitely, oil would be gone by 2002. During the Nixon and

Carter presidencies, it was commonly declared, including by academic and White House experts, that crude oil was on the way to $325 a barrel in current dollars.

In 2016, a barrel of petroleum was selling, not for $325, rather for $27. When *Limits to Growth* was published, the world was burning 55 million barrels of oil per day, a number the study, along with many other commentaries, declared unsustainable; now the number is 96 million barrels a day, yet the oil market is glutted. Adjusted for inflation, contemporary gasoline pump prices in the United States are about where they were when Dwight Eisenhower was president, saving consumers many billions of dollars annually. A geologist named King Hubbert is renowned for predicting in 1956 that the peak of American oil production would occur around the year 1970; then output would irrevocably decline as crude oil became exhausted. To the fringe aspects of environmentalism, Hubbert's forecast of "peak oil" was wonderful news—civilization will fail and we can say we told you so! Instead, US oil output has risen so much that America is on the verge of surpassing Saudi Arabia as a producer.

Limits to Growth was grounded in computer models, which either reach whatever conclusion their algorithms are written to produce or are limited by their data inputs, which may be fuzzy or simply wrong. Consider the polling models that in 2016 produced the conclusion that Hillary Clinton was sure to win the presidency. Some of these models were biased mathematically, others handicapped by data that was fuzzy or anchored in guesswork: and no matter how many advanced algorithms guesswork may be filtered through, it's still guesswork. Election models such as those posted by the popular website fivethirtyeight.com claim to forecast election results down to the decimal place; instead, in 2016 they couldn't even call the winner. Election forecasting should be seen as a form of entertainment rather than as statistically valid; environmental climate change forecasting should be approached with similar skepticism. Most contemporary doom predictions regarding global warming are based on computer models, which are much less persuasive than observational climate data.

Natural gas was thought in such diminishing supply that in 1978, James Schlesinger, secretary of the newly formed Department of Energy, said US natural gas supplies were nearly expended. That year Congress passed the National Energy Act, which required electric power utilities to switch from natural gas to coal. Essentially, Congress ordered utilities to increase their greenhouse emissions, since coal combustion results in roughly twice as much carbon per unit of electricity as natural gas. By 2016, natural gas prices had dropped to their lowest in twenty years, even as use increased, which other things being equal would cause higher prices. Abundance of natural gas led to falling electricity rates in many US states, again benefiting average consumers. John Holdren, whom Barack Obama would choose as his science adviser, in the early 1970s predicted natural gas would skyrocket in price, then be exhausted by about the year 2010. This proved the reverse of what actually happened—reserves rose dramatically, with the United States becoming a natural gas exporter.

The belief that oil and gas soon would be tapped out, followed by oil and gas reserves becoming so profuse Wall Street complains about falling prices, arose from several misunderstandings regarding nature. One concerns the immensity of geology. Even human actions such as burning 96 million barrels of oil per day—which would have seemed physically impossible to rationalists of the past—are minor compared to Earth's enormity, especially when one considers that almost all human activity occurs on the relatively thin surface of the planet's land, while most geology is deeply buried, or underneath seawater, or both.

Another confusion is the failure to grasp the economic dynamics that rising price draws out more supply by giving producers incentives to innovate, or to dig deeper, or both. One reason the US energy supply shortages of the 1970s occurred is that President Nixon placed price controls on oil and gas, thus discouraging production. Nixon also put controls on the interstate transmission of natural gas (which mostly moves by pipeline), discouraging states that generate supply (then, mainly Louisiana and Texas) from selling to states that need gas for heating and electricity (then, mainly New England). Buyer states employed political muscle to insist that producer states be hit with onerous price controls, which the buyer states of New England thought was a clever way to force the producer states of the South to provide a valuable commodity cheaply. The result was that producers stopped selling to interstate pipelines, hurting both classes of states: buyers could not get supply, producers could not make profits and so laid off workers. It took the political system several years to straighten this out.

Governments run by people who actively resist economics have done worse. Price controls in every application backfired in the Soviet Union, generating scarcity. Because Soviet government could never under any circumstances admit error, lack of natural resources was blamed, causing the Soviet Union to join the illusion of depleting oil. Once the communist monolith cracked and supply-and-demand was applied to Russian oil, there was ample petroleum in what's now the Russian Federation, which became a leading producer of crude.

Price controls and rationing that were emergency expediencies in the United States during World War II caused what looked like resource depletion. In 1943, Secretary of the Interior Harold Ickes Sr. wrote an article headlined (punctuation in the original) "We're Running Out of Oil!" At the Potsdam Conference in July 1945, Navy Secretary James Forrestal told Allied leaders to brace for the total exhaustion of petroleum by around 1960. Then wartime price controls were lifted, and soon there was plenty.

This lesson had been forgotten by the time of the oil crunch that began under Nixon. During the period most intellectual leaders believed fossil fuel resources were on the verge of exhaustion. Universities, grant-giving foundations, publishers, and the Department of Energy offered financial backing to those who reinforced this belief: for reasons that seemed strange then, and still seem strange today, elites considered it vital that average people be hit over the head with dire pronouncements that their fossil fuels would be taken away. Anyone who spent time with oil and gas wildcatters, as I did for a lengthy investigative project in the late 1970s, learned there was ample supply: the problem was not nature but political rules. An iconoclastic publication, the *Washington Monthly*, devoted much of a 1980 issue to the contention that far from being used up, as The Experts said, oil and gas were inexhaustible along the human time scale. In the issue, I wrote, "Natural gas is not depleted, [instead] so plentiful there is no reason not to use all we need." One did not need the CIA or FBI to figure this out—one had only to visit working oil and gas fields, and to interview hydrocarbon geologists. That Washington-based (and Brussels-based) ministries do not do this, rather, hire Experts who are paid to cry doom, places public comprehension of resources often in error.

Before leaving office in 1981, Carter, a pragmatic moderate, deregulated oil and gas. Supply increased so rapidly that the price-maintenance cartel of the Organization of Petroleum Exporting Countries broke, ending a monopoly that once seemed invincible. In years to come engineering advances such as three-dimensional seismology, horizontal drilling, and hydraulic fracturing ("fracking") would make production of oil and natural gas practical from shale deposits, which are common in North America, while exploration of the Bakken Formation of the Dakotas, Montana, and Saskatchewan led to discovery of substantial reserves. No government agency performed the research that led to these developments—which is why they happened! Government-led attempts to increase oil and gas supplies resulted in costly white-elephant facilities that spent vast amounts to produce mere drops of petroleum substitute. Any political science student wishing a tutorial in how not to address a problem should look up the Synthetic Fuels Corporation, created by Congress in 1980.

If a government agency had been created to develop three-dimensional seismology, the agency would have built imposing buildings, hired hundreds of deputy associate assistant administrators, lobbied for annual budget increases, and never produced any oil. Petroleum and gas output has increased in the United States and in other nations mainly because private initiatives ran rings around slow-moving political systems burdened by cronyism, special-interest grievances, and lack of a grasp of economics.

THE RESULT IS FAR FROM ideal. Ample fossil fuels equate to continuing greenhouse gases, fracking may contaminate groundwater; the excesses of Fortune 500 companies in the fossil-fuel order can be repellent. In 2016, Wells Fargo, the third-largest US bank and among the leading backers of oil and gas "plays," admitted systematically faking documents and fired John Stumpf, its CEO. On his way out the door, Stumpf, already paid

$19 million for the year in which he made the bank's once-storied name synonymous with fraud, was handed a $83 million bonus. Was his payday dictated by market forces, as the company contended? This requires you to believe Wells Fargo could not find anyone, not anyone at all, who possessed rudimentary banking skills plus was willing to work for less than $19 million per year. Yet however flawed the current global order of ample fossil fuel marketed by Fortune 500 firms, if petroleum and natural gas actually were depleted, society would be worse for this, with average people harmed far more than the rich.

In the 1970s, it was believed that no more than 500 billion barrels of petroleum remained in the ground. Since then, the world has burned roughly one trillion barrels, and today we know that at least 1.7 trillion barrels remain untapped. Though society has consumed more than twice as much as existed a generation ago, the reserve has gone up. Rather than a loaves-and-fishes intervention, these numbers reflect economic incentives, technological dynamism, and the enormity of the natural system.

"Peak oil" in production terms appears decades away, if the moment ever comes. In the end, of course the oil will run out. But society may move on to clean fuels well before that happens, especially since peak oil may be in the process of yielding to "peak demand"—energy efficiency reducing overall need for oil and gas. The International Energy Agency projects that oil demand will peak around 2040, at only about 10 percent more than today's consumption. That forecast could prove mistaken, as did many petroleum forecasts of the past, but suggests that the global craving for oil is currently moderating. From my 2009 book *Sonic Boom:* "Descendants of contemporary oil sheiks may wish their ancestors had sold every last drop of crude oil while someone still wanted the stuff."

BOTTLED WATER NOW COSTS MORE per gallon than gasoline, and water supply may matter more than petroleum supply. Back when oil seemed nearly finished, freshwater seemed copious, yet someday water may be a resource concern that exceeds fuel or minerals in significance. For now, as in other categories, trends are toward efficiency. In 2014, the US Geological Survey reported that per-capita freshwater use had fallen to the lowest level in half a century, though America had about 10 million more swimming pools and hot tubs than during the 1960s. Steinbeck's masterwork *East of Eden* begins by declaring California hopelessly overpopulated, because drought cycles have afflicted the Southwest for thousands of years. There are now four times as many Californians as when Steinbeck wrote: they drink and bathe and swim and water their orange trees, using efficiency engineering that did not exist in Steinbeck's time. California draws freshwater from snowpack: when, in 2011, a drought cycle began, the state's situation was depicted in the national media as hopeless. By 2016, the California snowpack had rebounded to normal, then 2017 brought torrential rains as snow covered Half Dome in Yosemite National Park.

THE AIR WE BREATHE IS the most intimate connection most people experience to nature. Smog is miasmic in Seoul, the capital of the otherwise developed nation of South Korea. Smog is so bad in coastal cities of China that raising children is not safe; in 2015, Beijing declared a "red alert" for smog, closing schools for three days. In 2016, flights in and out of Tianjin—15 million souls live in this metropolis, whose very existence is little known in the West—were canceled for several days because ground-hugging smog left the ceiling too low even for modern jetliners. On a typical Beijing day "particulates," tiny flecks of industrial emissions that can lodge in the lungs, are around three times the World Health Organization standard. Though, a decade ago, they were around four times that standard.

For a generation, the Chinese government maintained the fiction that air pollution is entirely natural in origin. (Some is; most is anthropogenic.) After the "red alert" episode, Beijing officials—worried, surely, about their own children—admitted that China is to blame for its air quality problems and pledged significant capital investment in clean technology. Admitting you have a problem is the first step to recovery.

Power plants in the United States have elaborate stack scrubbers that remove much of the facility's pollution from emissions; till recently, Chinese power plants did not. A typical coal-fired generating station in America turns nearly 40 percent of the energy value of fuel into electricity: in China, typical thermal efficiency is about half that amount, meaning more coal combusted and more pollutants per kilowatt-hour. The Beijing government purchases so much coal to fuel wasteful generating stations that often there are miles-long traffic jams at the country's border with Mongolia, where collier trucks carry their cargos into China. City-dwellers in China complain that centrally controlled coal-based heating renders their apartments far too hot; rural residents complain they shiver. One reason the Chinese government canceled those one hundred coal-fired stations was to reduce reliance on the nation's antiquated power-generating system—and to control smog, respiratory health being a more immediate concern than climate change.

Many cities in India have dreadful air quality, for smoke as well as smog; a 2017 study by the Boston-based Health Effects Institute found a rise in premature deaths in India caused by air pollution. One reason the Iranian government signed the 2015 nuclear agreement was air pollution in Tehran, whose basin-shaped topography creates the same smog-forming conditions as the Los Angeles Basin. Iran needed sanctions lifted so it could acquire modern products such as fuel-efficient cars and American- and British-built, low-emission, gas-turbine electricity generators. In Iran, India, and other developing nations, the same steps required to improve public respiratory health will have the bonus of reducing greenhouse gases.

Noise pollution is a developing world affliction too: anyone who's visited Cairo in the current century knows the Western big cities are quiet compared to the deafening clamor that makes average people's lives unpleasant in many developing world cities, to say nothing of rendering it hard to sleep or study. Developing-world clamor often is from diesel generators that are inefficient and dirty, as well as really loud, compared to electric power production in the West; in the West everyone has access to electricity, in developing nations the affluent buy diesel generators and the poor have nothing but the noise and fumes.

Developing nations can look to the positive examples of engineering and technology that reduce urban smog in the West. "Reformulation" of gasoline and diesel fuel removes many pollutants at the refinery, so smog-forming compounds never reach the tailpipe. Developed in the late 1980s by chemists at the Arco oil company, petroleum reformulation is a social boon most people don't even know occurred. Chemistry changes to alter the vapor pressure of gasoline also cut smog, as did improvements to the catalytic converters that are underneath cars and, increasingly, underneath trucks and buses. In early 2017, the inflation-adjusted gasoline pump prices that were about the same as the 1950s were joined by the chemistry of 2017 gasoline being significantly advanced—the same amount of money buying a much better product.

Those 125 "stage 1" smog alerts Los Angeles averaged in the 1970s? Today the City of Angels goes years between stage 1 announcements, while low-air-quality days are down to seven or eight per annum—still a concern, but no longer a threat to nature or public health. Air quality has improved considerably in Mexico City, whose advance from smog emergencies in the 1980s to reasonably clean air today shows the environment can be protected without crippling expense, even as population grows. Reformulation of Mexican gasoline to improve chemical quality while removing pollutants was an essential step.

While the Angelino love affair with cars remains passionate as ever, emission controls on any new make or model sold in the United States cut smog emissions by 99 percent compared to 1970s iterations. Emission controls are being mandated for aircraft, marine engines, construction equipment, locomotives, buses, snowmobiles, trucks, lawn mowers, and leaf blowers. (If adding emission control technology to leaf blowers strikes you as trivial, according to the California Air Resources Board, gasoline-powered yard equipment in Los Angeles generates more smog than all Los Angeles County cars combined.) Several automakers have pushed emissions down to the amusingly named "partial zero" classification, while electric propulsion continues to rise in practicality, promising net emission reduction when power plants and transmission lines are considered. Smog has decreased steadily in the United States, down 33 percent since 1980, even as standards have become stricter. A few decades ago, the Environmental Protection Agency's target for smog was 120 parts per billion of urban air. Today the legal limit is 70 parts per billion, and the observed actual average in American cities is 48 parts per billion.

In the last quarter-century, US air quality shows these trends: lead down 99 percent, carbon monoxide down 77 percent, sulfur dioxide down 81 percent, nitrogen oxides (another factor in acid rain) down 54 percent, industrial haze down 37 percent, and low-level ozone (the bad kind) down 22 percent. During this period, US population rose 28 percent while GDP per capita doubled, meaning air pollution per person decreased a great deal while air pollution compared to economic production declined spectacularly. The decline of nitrogen oxides (NO_x) is noteworthy: Volkswagen and Fiat Chrysler are known to have subverted emissions standards for this class of pollutants, yet despite this cheating, NO_x levels have declined. Cost-benefit studies consistently show that the expense of smog-reducing technology is justified in light of benefits such as longer life spans, less respiratory distress, and more enjoyable urban living. American cities have staged remarkable comebacks in no small part because their skies now are clear, which helps people appreciate life while property values rise. Except for greenhouse gases, environmental trends in the United States are solidly positive. The rest of the world can achieve the same.

Among the reasons for improved air quality in the United States is that electric utilities either are substituting natural gas for coal, or substituting surface coal from the Powder River region of Montana and Wyoming for underground coal from Kentucky and West Virginia. Powder River coal found in Rocky Mountain geology is inherently less polluting than the coal of Appalachian geology. Surface ("strip") mines also are safer for workers. Underground mines have hellish conditions; the dragline operators at surface mines work in fresh air and don't have billions of tons of rock perilously above their heads.

Here is the sort of conundrum observed across contemporary political economics. Making electricity from Powder River coal reduces air pollution and improves worker safety, creating broad social benefits, but ends jobs for underground miners, causing localized harm. During the 2016 presidential campaign, Donald Trump and Hillary Clinton made lavish promises about more coal mining jobs in Appalachia. The promises were blatant lies—though if they had been true, it would have been a terrible idea: society should abolish, not increase, underground coal mining. But politically it's easier to spin fantastical tales of obsolete jobs coming down from the sky than to deal with education and health care in communities that time has passed by.

Despite the widely held view that Europe is more enlightened than America, US air quality improvements lead the world—smog in Paris often is worse than anywhere in America. The world can follow the United States' lead and catch up, since nearly all US developments in air pollution control are either regulatory models where information is public or engineering ideas that are detailed in open-source technical literature.

THE OZONE HOLE CHALLENGE WAS straightforward compared to the greenhouse challenge, which a later chapter will address. Confusion is inevitable. In 2015, President Barack Obama said he became convinced of the need for global warming regulation because carbon dioxide emissions caused the asthma his daughter Malia suffered in childhood. Sulfur dioxide, not carbon dioxide, is the pollutant linked to asthma, and since the year of Malia's birth, airborne sulfur dioxide in the United States is down 64 percent.

Obama's seeming error regarding the chemistry of pollution may not have been accidental. The backstory of Obama's statement was that the Clean Air Act gives the US government broad jurisdiction over emissions that harm human health, but no mandate regarding greenhouse gases. If greenhouse gases were found to endanger the health of Americans, federal controls would be merited under existing Clean Air Act statutes. Politicians, the EPA, appellate courts, and the Supreme Court have been locked in inconclusive arguments regarding whether carbon dioxide endangers public health. The Republican Party wants carbon dioxide considered unrelated to health, since that would exclude greenhouse restrictions under the Clean Air Act. The Democratic Party wants carbon dioxide found to harm health, because then an entire sector of the economy—fossil fuels—would be transferred to the control of regulators.

US air quality laws have not been amended since 1991. Since then, urban air pollution has declined sharply while artificial influence on climate change has been proven. Yet US law still focuses on smog, a problem receding into the past, while not addressing climate change, the problem of the future. Most US environmental statutes—on water quality, toxins, species—are decades out of date, reflecting assumptions that no longer prevail. Partisan gridlock in Washington, DC, has prevented commonsense revisions of environmental law. This is one of the many instances in which Washington self-interest—partisans like endless gridlock, because promising to fight it is good for fund-raising—runs against national public interest.

If you don't believe most United States air is now clean, maybe that's because you don't spend enough time outdoors. Americans, even those who live in California, Colorado, and other states that offer both good weather and natural beauty, spend far too much time inside buildings and cars. Multiply your age times 0.9 to determine how many years you have been indoors. Go outside—it's good for you—and breathe deeply.

The summation of why nature does not collapse might be this: nature doesn't collapse because it can't. But nature can change in ways that are not friendly to any particular species. Most big land animals of the Pleistocene—the woolly mammoth, cave lion, dire wolf, mastodon, saber-toothed cat—vanished quickly when nature changed. Genus *Homo* rules today, but nature could change that too.

So food and resources will last, while reform can protect the natural world. But will the economy disintegrate?

Chapter 4

Will the Economy Collapse?

IN 2015, THE GENERAL SECRETARY of the Communist Party of Vietnam came to Washington, DC, not to negotiate a treaty, not to denounce Western imperialism, but to order jetliners. At a red-ribbon ceremony attended by American business executives and Vietnamese fashion models in bright national attire, the Capitol dome in the background, Nguyen Phu Trong signed a deal for the Boeing 787 Dreamliner, the world's most advanced passenger plane. Not long before, Boeing built the B-52 bombers that pulverized the Indochinese Peninsula. Today the company's factories turn out flagships of the Vietnam Airlines civilian fleet, gorgeous aircraft that carry former enemies, now friends, on their vacations.

This sort of change can be dizzying. We all seek a sense of security regarding employment and income, and instead the modern economy generates constant, jarring change. The economic system went off the rails during the Great Depression and again during the Great Recession: each time bouncing back, but with no assurances that another crash could be avoided. Experts can't see what is directly in front of their noses. (Shortly before the US housing market nosedive Alan Greenspan, chair of the Federal Reserve, said, "We don't perceive there is a national housing price bubble.") Predictions are useless. (In 2010, Treasury Secretary Timothy Geithner said there was "no chance" United States debt would lose its Triple-A status; a year later this happened.) Seemingly secure positions vanish. (Jobs building Westinghouse refrigerators or Smith Corona typewriters once were thought rock-solid.) New business categories come out of nowhere. (Sales of tablet computers rose from zero to 1 billion world-wide in five years.)

Such turmoil engages collapse anxiety. Someday there may be no products in stores, no food in markets, no fuel at filling stations. Shops, schools, warehouses, and hospitals will be shuttered. The global economic system will seize up and never run again. You worry about that, don't you?

So allow me to provide assurance by taking you behind the curtain. There is an elaborately guarded underground facility at a location I am not at liberty to disclose. Inside is a master control room more impressive than any ever constructed by the villain in a James Bond movie. Dials, switches, and monitor screens abound. Every datum of every manufacturing, financial, and consumer trend flows into the secret master control room, from which the global economy is run. Sitting in the big chair, in charge of it all, is—no one. The big chair is empty. That's why the facility is hidden, so people don't realize and panic.

No one runs the economy that causes Americans and Europeans such anxiety. Not the US president, not China's State Council, not the Bilderberg Group, not a shadowy conspiracy of international bankers, not even the CEO of Walmart. That the global economy functions without anyone in control is its greatest strength, as well as the paramount hope of avoiding a collapse. The Slovenian philosopher Slavoj Žižek, the leading contemporary Marxist, has noted with grudging admiration, "Capitalism is the sole social organizing structure in world history that is rendered stronger by its own instability."

There are multiple problems with the domestic and international economics of Western nations. But the empty control room is not one of those problems—rather, what a relief no one is in charge!

Suppose the president, or any individual, actually did control the economy. Today Americans would be driving 10-mpg finned cars without seat belts; auto technology would have been frozen at some point in the past, to preserve Detroit employment levels, ensure the United Auto Workers kept making donations to political incumbents, and to provide ample management positions for white Anglo-Saxon Protestant males whose fathers knew somebody who knew somebody. There would be no phone in your pocket: telecom technology would have been locked in place around the rotary-dial Princess in order to sustain the overpriced, consumer-be-damned Bell System monopoly. There would be no laptops or tablets: Silicon Valley inventions would have been stamped "classified" and reserved for the CIA, with an obsequious government official declaring—as Ken Olsen, founder of 1960s electronics giant Digital Equipment Corporation, actually did—"There is no reason for any individual to have a computer in the home." Only the rich would travel by jet: airline competition would be forbidden, pricing out average men and women in order to protect salaries at Eastern, Pan Am, and TWA. Standards of living would be far lower, since median household income of a generation ago, adjusted for inflation and household size, was less than half of today's.

There have been experiments with forms of economics that have someone in control—fascism, communism, feudalism, monarchy. These experiments were in every case dismal failures, except for providing luxury to a tiny elite. Fascism burned Germany and Japan to the ground. As practiced in Maoist China, the Soviet Union, North Korea, and Venezuela, communism conferred lavish excess on one person in a thousand while leaving everyone else despondent. Monarchy and feudalism slowed social progress to a crawl, showing themselves great at keeping women and minorities down, inept at everything else.

Indermit Gill, an India-born professor of public policy at Duke University, has noted that North and South Korea exemplify how economic systems help or hurt the average person. Starting with the same geography, resources, and people, the one using central control became an indigent nightmare, while the one letting the market decide eliminated poverty and achieved the world's highest rate of postsecondary education.

Gill further notes most developing nations that have followed the "Washington Consensus" policy prescription have raised living standards, increased education levels for girls and women, and held free elections, while most developing nations that cling to central economic control remain impoverished, backward, and under the thumbs of thugs and despots. Put together in the 1980s by an international team of economists, the Washington Consensus recommends that developing nations switch to free economies without central control, avoid debt, deregulate, create enforceable private property rights, liberalize trade going out and capital coming in, and have low marginal tax rates that they actually implement. (Troubled nations such as Greece post high tax rates, then allow the affluent to bribe their way out of taxes.) Some analysts scorn the Washington Consensus, which stands as the reverse of the prescription of absolute central planning—ministries and subsidies as far as the eye can see. That market-oriented economics usually (of course not always) helps the poor, while central planning usually harms the poor, does seem to settle the matter.

Nobody-in-control economics improves living standards for almost everyone while encouraging social progress, since even Fortune 500 types observe that shaking up the system is good. Based on what's known today at least, the average person is best served by an uncommanded system. But the thought that the big chair is empty is unsettling.

THE POWERFUL—PRESIDENTS, PRIME MINISTERS, central bankers— can influence a market economy of course, in leading well or poorly, but they don't have control. Many are the preposterous claims made regarding this on the presidential campaign trail: Hillary Clinton's declaration that she would be "commander-in-chief of our economy" ranks among them. Large blunders can harm the economy but absent their occurrence, "policy decisions at the top are a relatively minor factor," says Edward Lazear, a Stanford University professor who is a former chair of the White House Council of Economic Advisers. He contends, for instance, that the Great Recession "was mainly caused by the economy itself, and mainly cured by the economy itself." Most economic good and bad is mainly caused by, and mainly cured by, the economy itself—since no one is in charge.

Theorists call what happens in a market economy "distributed decision-making." No single entity dictates the course of events. That ensures turbulence, which is universally unpopular, but also reduces the odds of a colossal error. Vast numbers of distributed decisions about what people want, and how much they are willing to pay, flow into the system. These many small decisions generate a concurrence that usually represents the most efficient allocation of resources. Small distributed decisions may be wise or foolish: too many women and men fall for swindles, fail to save, buy high and sell low, commit other errors. Taken as a whole, the crazed, chaotic nobody-in-charge nature of a market economy leaves almost everyone better off.

This is different from saying modern economies are self-regulating. Such a claim was made before the panics of the late nineteenth century, before the 1929 Wall Street crash, before the 2008 credit crack-up that set the Great Recession in motion. During the Great Recession, Nicholas Sarkozy, then president of France, said the crack-up disproved "the idea of an all-powerful free market that is always right." No thoughtful person, including no thoughtful conservative, contends the free market is always right. Markets are subject to major malfunctions: legal standards are required. But we're all better off if no single person or entity is in charge either of the economy or of economic law. This formula accepts uncertainty in exchange for prosperity; higher living standards are likely, while collapse anxiety is guaranteed.

The functioning of market economies traditionally is attributed to an invisible hand, but that's the wrong analogy—implying an amorphous intelligence directing events toward a specific goal. The economy has no goal, simply reacts to changes in circumstances, including discoveries, inventions, shortages, shifts in consumer needs, and shifts in society's whims. Most of the time the result is most people better off. But there's no assurance this will happen, resulting in angst even when, objectively, times are good.

COLLAPSE ANXIETY IS HEIGHTENED BY the pace of change. Products and jobs flash in and out of existence like subatomic particles. A decade ago, Panasonic was expanding like crazy, and the company was a desirable place to be hired plus a strong investment for retirement savings. Then the company badly misjudged the emerging cell-phone market; the result was laid-off workers and stinging losses. By 2015, Panasonic had reinvented itself as the world's leading supplier of large-capacity batteries, a field with growth potential. Panasonic is building the futuristic factory in Nevada that will supply batteries for Tesla cars as well as a new product category, the home batteries that allow customers to store electricity during the wee hours when utility rates are low, for use in the afternoon when rates spike. Now Panasonic is again a fine place to be hired. But no one enjoys this kind of ride. Stability is what people want, and the modern economy does not produce stability.

For those who conceptualize the economy as a food chain with natural resources at the base, there is the fear of resource depletion, topped by fear about money itself. Nearly everyone in the West today relies on the fuzzy assumption that someone else—an employer, a customer, a bank, the Social Security Administration—will supply money. And just what is money? Once it was gold in your pocket; now ones and zeros in electronic files or on a chip on a plastic card. Once banks had currency in the vault; now banks have entries on hard drives. Physical production by the Bureau of Engraving and Printing of $1 currency notes peaked in 2006 and has declined since; printing of $20 notes peaked in 2005 and has since declined. Today, when the Federal Reserve "prints money," no printing may occur. The Fed simply declares that more money exists and often then (essentially) buys some of the newly declared money, paying with additional ones and zeroes.

Since money is only worth what someone else will offer in exchange, lacking any inherent value, in some ways money has become a consensual mass illusion. Should a crisis cause people to stop believing in money—instead, say, demanding barter for goods—the modern economy would unravel. That doesn't sound like a particularly steady situation.

Many think, "If only we could stop the crazed pace of change, forget information and intellectual property, return to a metal-and-wood economy, we'd get back to the old days when businesses were stable and jobs were reliable." This is a tempting line of thought, though it skips all the advantages the accelerated-pace economy provides. People wish they could restore an old-days economy without globalized change, but also keep the high living standards, advanced health care, cheap communication, and safe transportation the crazed accelerated-pace economy created. This can't happen—the bitter comes with the sweet.

There never was an economic golden age in which everyone had totally secure good jobs. Even during the early postwar expansion, when the union movement reached apogee because labor was in such demand, nearly all forms of employment paid less in real-dollar terms than to-day, benefits were marginal compared to today, factories were as likely to close, and no blacks or women needed apply. But millions of people in the United States and United Kingdom believe there once was an economic golden age—can't really say when, exactly, but, you know, it was back then, everything was better back then. Believing halcyon days were unfairly yanked away sounds like grounds to demand more government favors in the here-and-now.

THE UNFOCUSED BELIEF THAT THE economy was better in some unspecified past time produced millions of votes for Donald Trump, who was able to sell his declinist view in part because media coverage of the US economy unremittingly is downbeat. When employment rose sharply in 2016, the *New York Times* found the notion of positive economic news so outside the lines that the paper managed a disapproving page-one spin: "Jobless Rate Falls but Many Feel Passed By," a headline that might as well have read, "Utopia Still Not Achieved." In spring 2017, when US unemployment dropped to 4.4 percent, none of the three national big-network evening newscasts led with this fabulous news. All devoted less than twenty seconds to the story. *ABC World News Tonight* added a negative snarl by saying job creation could cause interest rates to rise; *NBC Nightly News* groused that even though this month's figures were amazing, last month's were "sluggish."

The larger reason Trump's negativity resonated with voters was the anxiety that is inevitable in an uncommanded economy. Social scientist Carol Graham of the University of Maryland has shown that most people base feelings about their economic situation not on what's happening now but what they anticipate for the future. Though things are mostly good today, we cannot be sure this will continue. Indeed we cannot, even if continued progress is the most likely prospect. Trump's subliminal message about the economy was, *You can't be sure the future will be good, therefore the present is awful.* This is nonsense, but 63 million voters believed it.

BUT THINGS MUST BE AWFUL since we know from the 2016 presidential campaign that "manufacturing has been destroyed." Some 85 percent of US jobs are in the manufacturing sector, where capital equipment is eliminating the need for labor and foreign competitors are entering US markets. Soon just 2 percent of US jobs will be in manufacturing, as "rusted-out factories" will be "scattered like tombstones" across the landscape, candidate Trump declared.

Actually, the above paragraph describes the year 1900, with the word "manufacturing" substituted for "agriculture" and "candidate Trump" substituted for "President McKinley." In 1900, 85 percent of US jobs were linked in some way to farming, where machines—tractors, threshers—were replacing fieldhands, and nations were beginning to produce surplus for the export market. Suppose there had been cable-news pundits in 1900. If you'd told one that by 2017 just 2 percent of US jobs would be in agriculture, economic collapse would have been predicted. But that's the figure for today, and everyone is better off, including farmers.

High-yield crops and mechanized harvests led to extensive disruption in farm country. By wiping out large numbers of field jobs, the 1944 invention of the cotton-picker caused millions of African Americans to move from rural parts of the old Confederacy to northern cities, seeking manufacturing employment. The changing sociology of Chicago's South Side, which would produce wonderful blues music, awful gun crime, and America's first black president, is recounted in one of the best books of the twentieth century, *The Promised Land* by Nicholas Lemann. As agricultural employment entered precipitous decline owing to mechanized harvesting, farm-country residents were viewed as without hope. Instead it turned out that manufacturing employment paid a lot better than farm work, while the new factory jobs opening up were closer to the educational institutions essential for modern self-advancement. The African American migration north for factory work helped spread the civil rights movement and reduce the black-white earnings gap. That gap persists: American whites on average earn a third more than American blacks. Nobody in her or his right mind would turn the farming clock back to 1900, or want the Mississippi Delta cotton crop once again picked by hand. Yet when beginning, the decline of agricultural employment seemed terrible.

Now with hardly any workers compared to 1900, US farm output keeps setting records. In the same fashion, with steadily fewer workers, US factories keep setting production records. Most Americans might guess the peak for United States manufacturing was in the 1950s or 1960s. Not so: the number-one year for US manufacturing output was 2016. Do you think factories were busier back in those hazy Good Ole Days, say, of the Ronald Reagan presidency? Since Reagan, US factory output has risen 83 percent. The single-generation almost-doubling of US manufacturing has been accompanied by a 30 percent decline in factory employment. Factory employment has hardly disappeared, as media culture likes to think: in 2016 there were 12.3 million US factory jobs, more than the number of jobs in food service. It's just that advancing technology means fewer manufacturing workers are needed—exactly the dynamic that overtook the farm.

Many, including Trump, blame global trade for fewer US factory jobs. Economists Martin Baily and Barry Bosworth of the center-left Brookings Institution calculate that most decline of US manufacturing employment as a share of GDP was already over by 2000, the year China joined the World Trade Organization, signaling the onset of full-bore globalization. Manufacturing jobs as a share of the American labor force peaked in 1953, when Japan was a bombed-out ruin and China was a closed-off provincial society, neither nation having any impact on goods, services, or employment in the United States. In 1960, manufacturing output was 11 percent of US GDP, while manufacturing jobs were 24 percent of the US economy. By 2013, manufacturing output was 12 percent of the US GDP—higher than in 1960—but manufacturing employment was down to 9 percent of the economy.

As manufacturing jobs decline, demand rises for teachers, engineers, nurses, and the skilled trades (electricians, welders). The dynamism view considers this normal—some sectors down, others up. Normal perhaps, though hard on our collective nerves.

Automation is one reason for fewer factory jobs compared to output, but only one. We're all familiar with the features of the products we buy: the features of the factories that make those products are just as important. My 2009 book *Sonic Boom* described in detail how General Electric took apart and rebuilt an Erie, Pennsylvania, locomotive factory, in order to manufacture railroad engines in shorter times at lower cost, producing more-reliable engines that burn less fuel and emit fewer pollutants. Rethinking the locomotive manufacturing process proved such a hit that General Electric, which Wall Street expected to drop out of the railroad business, instead opened a second factory in Fort Worth. Today China is the number-one customer for clean-running General Electric locomotives manufactured in Pennsylvania and in Texas.

In many product categories, improving the factory itself leads to lower prices and higher quality. The sprawling Renton, Washington, facility that assembles Boeing jetliners—40 percent of the commercial aircraft in the world's skies took off on their maiden flight from Renton airfield—builds the Boeing 737, a plane that debuted in 1967. That year Renton could manufacture one 737 per week. Now Renton turns out a much-improved 737 that's quieter, uses less fuel, and is equipped with advanced avionics, at a rate of about one per day. For faster production of a better product, the contemporary Renton facility has about half as many workers as in 1967, owing to improved internal factory engineering. The result is that some women and men who might otherwise have been employed building the Boeing 737 instead do not have such jobs. But everyone else—let's say 99.9 percent of Americans—is better off because improved manufacturing has led to safer, more affordable flights.

Rising efficiency in steelmaking, that quintessential industrial pursuit, has the same impact on society. Seeking the White House, Trump said, "We're going to put American-produced steel back into the backbone of our country" via "massive numbers of steel jobs." This was classic campaign moonshine—an ersatz grievance (American-produced steel never stopped being prominent) followed by a Santa Claus promise (adding "massive numbers of steel jobs" would require deliberate addition of wastefulness, such as tearing out modern furnaces and substituting antiquated ones). According to the American Iron and Steel Institute, 71 percent of the steel used in the United States is made here. Total US domestic steel output is down only somewhat compared to the postwar peak, while steelworker employment is down 75 percent, owing to production efficiency. An estimated fifteen times as many Americans have jobs at steel-purchasing firms—construction companies, appliance manufacturers—as at steel-producing firms. This suggests that more efficient steelmaking benefits dozens of other Americans for each one who might have been employed by an outdated, inefficient steel mill.

Broadly across modern Western economies, efficiencies that hold down prices help far more people than they harm. In the last five years, Canadian Pacific Railway has cut its workforce 40 percent while lowering freight charges and attaining higher average train speeds. Most Canadians benefit, while a small number are laid off. Society needs to find new roles for workers who lose jobs to efficiency. But to alter the economic dynamic that improves air travel or phone quality or freight service for most people would derail progress, if you'll excuse the pun.

Replacing labor with capital—people out, machines in—raises living standards for society as a whole while harming individual workers. Sometimes admirable, progressive ideas speed this sequence. In 2017, McDonald's, whose CEO is my distant cousin Steve Easterbrook, began installing touch-screen kiosks that replace some order-takers. McDonald's creates tens of thousands of jobs for the unskilled, including those who don't speak the local language. Legislatures and activists are pressing the company, and similar employers, to offer entry-level workers about $20 an hour in wages and benefits. This causes it to make sense for Easterbrook to substitute capital investments for entry-level employees, the least valuable kind. It's not just that machines don't go on strike. Machines don't picket outside places of business, as McDonald's workers did in many cities in 2016; machines don't file lawsuits. The rational incentives for Easterbrook and other business managers to lay off workers while investing in machines lie at the heart of the new-Luddite dilemma that will be taken up in a later chapter.

In 2016, the District of Columbia enacted legislation mandating that even recently hired employees receive two months of paid family leave annually. This sounded like a heartwarming achievement—what the writer Jack Shafer has called "therapeutic legislation." But the District's lawmakers might as well have purchased billboards reading: BUSINESSES: REPLACE WORKERS WITH MACHINES. The following year, Baltimore mayor Catherine Pugh, an African American Democrat, vetoed a $15-an-hour minimum wage. Editorialists expressed shock, but no one trying to create entry-level jobs in Baltimore—including the city's own payroll office—was shocked.

When agricultural employment began its nosedive about a century ago, the fear that farmhands would never again find jobs so good instead was supplanted by jobs with higher pay and better benefits. Today when steelworkers or railroad yardmasters are laid off, the fear is they'll never get another job as good. This is a legitimate fear for many. But it is dwarfed by the benefits conferred by improved production of goods and services. Consider the situation in Pittsburgh, long America's steelmaking capital. Today Steel City's current-dollar per-capita income is about double what it was at the peak of domestic steel output, while an urban renaissance is in progress: rising property values, clear skies, an arts scene, cutting-edge engineering research at Carnegie Mellon University, cutting-edge medicine at the University of Pittsburgh. Nobody in his or her right mind would turn the Pittsburgh clock back to the 1950s, even though economic trends have been unfavorable to some of the city's residents.

THE PHONY NOTION THAT THE United States no longer engages in manufacturing has been planted in the popular imagination in part because the news media report when old factories close but not when new ones open. For example, in 2008, Honda invested $800 million in Greensburg, Indiana, opening a state-of-the-art factory that employs 2,300 people to produce the high-mileage Civic, and uses internal recycling to such an extent that the facility sends no waste to landfills. This factory inaugural was shrugged at by the national media. A few years later, the closure of an obsolete auto parts factory in nearby Muncie, Indiana, received extensive media attention, replete with "dying Rust Belt" theatrics. Just as local-media emphasis on fires and murders creates the impression both are increasing when fires and crime are in long-term decline, national-media emphasis on factory closings creates the impression that US industrial production is a thing of the past.

Journalism as a profession is being convulsed by technological change in much the same way mining and manufacturing are being convulsed. Print newspaper circulation in the United States peaked in 1957 at one copy per day for every 2.8 people; today it's one per 7.7 people. Reporting pays steadily less in real-dollar terms, while journalism jobs that once offered security are becoming easily canceled independent contractor arrangements without benefits. This makes mainstream journalists an unhappy cohort, and they radiate unhappiness on all known frequencies. Yet just as there's never been a better time to purchase a product built in a US factory, there's never been a better time to be a news consumer. The advent of the Internet has increased the supply of news and opinions in the same way that open global trade has increased the supply of consumer goods. Writing and broadcasting respond to supply-and-demand like any other sector. The more datelined dispatches, opinion pieces, and on-air tirades there are, the less each sells for—making pundits and talking heads feel, just as factory workers feel, that economic change is out to get them personally.

Media negativity long predates the shift from newsprint to digital, but may be amplified by current events. One result of overlap between factory workers and journalists may be that the latter play up comparatively isolated instances of deleterious economic trends while playing down broadly positive developments in living standards, longevity, education, and liberty. A 2016 page-one *New York Times* story about unhappiness in middle America was datelined Paris, Kentucky—the heart of underground coal country. Appalachian coal production began waning when the Beatles were onstage together. Coal mining employment has fallen 80 percent in the last thirty years: the decline is nearly linear, regardless of which party is in power or which policies are in effect. Metallurgical-grade coal remains in demand, but merely since 2000, US domestic demand for the types of coal needed for power production, a sector unrelated to international trade, has dropped 37 percent. Of course people in Paris, Kentucky, would feel glum!

Unhappiness in coal mining is not unique to the United States. In 2016, Chinese coal miners went on strike to protest layoffs. Chinese miners were mad about trade competition—in their case, imports from Mongolia. Miners in Australia, England, Germany, and other nations are far from pleased regarding the inevitable fading of their livelihood. Yet the US press presents the decline of underground coal mining—great news for less air pollution and greenhouse gases, for eradicating black-lung disease—as a condemnation of the American economy. Not long after the Paris, Kentucky, dispatch, the *Washington Post* ran a harrowing page-one story about sickness and sadness in McDowell County, West Virginia, the county with the shortest life expectancy in the United States. McDowell is on the Kentucky–West Virginia border, deep in underground-coal country—a terrible place for jobs or health, which may justify special programs, but also an outlier, not representative of typical American experiences. The *Post* spun the story as the shocking truth about middle America.

Today a "mood of America" dispatch datelined almost anywhere in California or New England would be a chipper story; most stories would also be positive from datelines in Arizona, Colorado, the Dakotas, Florida, Georgia, Hawaii, Minnesota, New Mexico, Oregon, Tennessee, Texas, Utah, Washington, and the upper Rocky Mountain states. Because journalists feel beset by change in their own profession, they tend to gravitate to the places where economic change causes unhappiness.

Another factor is that every four years the industrial swing states—Indiana, Michigan, Ohio, Pennsylvania, and Wisconsin—receive outsized political and media attention. Those states contain a disproportionate number of voters harmed by globalization. New England, New York, Texas, and the West Coast are globalization beneficiaries. But these places are ignored during presidential cycles, since everyone knows in advance how they will vote. Several of the industrial swing states also are home to members of manufacturing and mining unions that are active donors to political candidates. Job losses in other sectors, such as department stores, reeling from Internet shopping, do not receive comparable attention because most workers do not belong to unions that have a role in labor lore and that transfer money to politicians.

During his presidential campaign, Donald Trump said, "Our trade deals with China are destroying this country.... There is total devastation all over the country from trade.... We need to start manufacturing again." Set aside that on the day Trump said this, American manufacturing output was at a record high. The New York University professors Pankaj Ghemawat and Steven Altman have shown that in 2016, the year Trump declared "total devastation" caused by imports, 84 percent of goods and services consumed by American citizens were produced inside the United States. Trump went on to declare that Japanese cars "just come pouring into the country." This statement was true in the 1980s, a period that both Trump and Bernie Sanders have extolled as a golden age— even though in the 1980s education levels and living standards were lower while disease rates, crime, and pollution were higher. By 2016, two-thirds of Japanese-marque cars sold in America were built in US factories staffed by US workers earning about $50 an hour in pay and benefits, about the same as UAW members for Detroit marques.

THE OLD "WHO LOST CHINA?" question is now joined by "who lost jobs to China?" Campaigning, Trump and Sanders told audiences that millions of American jobs had been "lost" to China. These jobs cannot be found in China, or anywhere, because they no longer exist—automation and productivity improvements are larger influences than trade in manufacturing employment trends, in Asia as well as in the West. The rise of manufacturing employment in China probably is over—Chinese econometric data is unreliable—with a drop in Chinese factory jobs likely soon, if not already in progress. If China had American-style elections, candidates there would shake their fists about jobs "lost" to the United States. Like farmhand work a century ago, the "lost" jobs in manufacturing never will come back. The challenge is to educate workers to take the jobs of the future.

Economist Michael Hicks of Ball State University calculates that about 13 percent of the decline of US manufacturing employment syncs to production overseas—the rest is caused by more-efficient production inside the United States, by product innovations, or by shifts in what consumers want. Should Congress and state legislatures pass laws to ban more-efficient production? Forbid product innovation? In 2016, Senator Susan Collins of Maine told Ryan Lizza of *The New Yorker* she has "become more skeptical about free trade than she used to be" because "Maine's paper mills have been closing in the past few years." Chinese production is not why US paper mills are closing—the reason is that Americans are buying less newsprint and glossy stock, reading *The New Yorker* in digital format rather than receiving issues in the mailbox. The era of morning editions that come hot off the presses then go *thud* on the doorstep had a romance that will be missed. But should Congress ban reading the news on smartphones and tablets? Outlaw the Kindle, Nook, and digital *New Yorker*? That would bring Maine paper mills back.

When Trump and Sanders made jobs "lost" to China a leading issue of the 2016 election, opinion writers and politicians embraced research by the economist David Autor of the Massachusetts Institute of Technology. His studies demonstrate that American manufacturing employment has declined by 1.5 million jobs because of international trade. That's about 13 percent of current US manufacturing employment, roughly the conclusion reached by the Ball State study. Autor got more attention because he focused on gloom, while Ball State highlighted the overall health of the manufacturing sector. Data in the MIT job loss study stop at 2007, which is significant because that is roughly when Chinese industrial employment, too, started downward.

The MIT research takes into account jobs subsumed by international commerce but not jobs gained. The Wilson Center, a nonpartisan think tank, in 2016 estimated that trade with Mexico adds about six million jobs to the US economy. Autor further has found that in parts of the United States where manufacturing jobs were lost to trade, the per-capita income reduction was $213. That's no fun, but no disaster either considering that the same forces that cost voters in Ohio or Wisconsin $213 per year held down consumer prices for all of the United States and the European Union. Autor is an accomplished academic: these paragraphs are not intended to chide him, but to demonstrate that the contemporary political and media systems seize on economic analysis that sounds negative, while ignoring troublesome positive complications.

A DEMOGRAPHIC MAP OF THE United States shows more prosperity and education along the coasts than in the interior. That does not mean Colorado and Montana are not wonderful, that Atlanta and Chicago are not great places, that Chattanooga and Provo are not hidden-gem small cities—only that outward-focused coastal regions are favored by economic tendencies. Broadly across the world, this is true: one reason China became prosperous while adjacent Mongolia did not is that China possesses a long coastal region while Mongolia is landlocked. "Comparative advantage," as well established as any idea in economics, benefits almost everyone in places that become trade partners, while exposing people to new ideas that lead to innovation. The role of trade, mainly across the waters, is embedded in history. A magisterial book, *The Sea and Civilization* by Lincoln Paine, shows that for three thousand years, regions, countries, and empires engaged in trading via ship developed faster than those that shunned exploration and exchange. Continuous economic interaction among different parts of the world through ocean commerce aided the rise of modernity, and now is a reason the global economy keeps pulsing.

But the bitter comes with the sweet: trade and interaction with distant nations bring about constant change and employment insecurity. As the economist Paul Krugman has noted, on each working day in recent years in the United States, about 75,000 people have lost jobs. Also in recent years, about 85,000 people per working day have found jobs, netting a steady overall employment gain. But no one wants to go through the stress and upset of being fired or laid off, even if there's another job on the other side. Trade and other factors drive this persistent change.

Countries, regions, cities, and individuals have been wishing for centuries that they could bring economic change to a halt. How the miners of the Cornwall area of southwest England wish large deposits of tin had not been found in South America! How my hometown of Buffalo, New York, wishes the failed Bethlehem Steel plant, the size of a city, had not faced competition from new ideas such as continuous casting, or that the towering grain silos of the city's waterfront, once pivotal to cereal markets, had not been bypassed in 1959 when the Saint Lawrence Seaway opened. How shipbuilders of Yizheng, on the Yangtze River, wish that super-sized container vessels had not reduced demand for more cargo ships. There are hundreds of similar examples.

The Yizheng dilemma leads to another aspect of contemporary economic turbulence. Competition not only is driving down the costs of goods, it is driving down the cost of transporting goods. Next-day and second-day shipping once were unknown, then solely for the wealthy: now average Americans and Europeans expect orders delivered to the door right away, at minimal cost. Bulk transportation of commodities, not evident in consumer markets but essential to production, keeps falling in price, which is good for standards of living while causing more change.

In the nineteenth century, bulk-transport ships traveled from the East Coast of the United States to China in about three months; now it takes about three weeks, and twenty-four-hour continent-to-continent air freight is no longer used just for tiny items but also for heavy shipments. Faster ships and smaller crews have cut the cost of transoceanic shipment to as low as $10 a ton. Container ships larger than America's nuclear-powered supercarriers have made transport affordable enough that cell-phone parts can be fabricated in a dozen places around the world, shipped to Asia for assembly, then shipped back for sale at ever-lower prices. Over the last roughly twenty-five years, China has built a sprawling infrastructure of docks and shipping cranes; the Panama and Suez Canals have been expanded to accommodate wider vessels; ports around the world have been dredged to allow deeper-draft vessels; a class of behemoth boats, the Malaccamax, has come into existence, measured to the meter to maximize container transit through the Strait of Malacca. The gargantuan Berendrecht Lock in Antwerp, completed in 1989, is one of many physical modifications of Earth's surface that accelerate trade while cutting costs. Almost everyone benefits from the lower prices made possible: but the same acceleration of change that improves living standards makes more insecurity inevitable.

Today crew members aboard container ships and crewing "bulkers" that carry ore and grain endure harsh conditions to support their families. Soon automated freighters will course the oceans which offer a favorable environment for silicon-chip conning. Then crew members won't be mistreated anymore because they won't have jobs, while the next round of lower retail prices leads to another improvement in standards of living. Should advances that eliminate crummy jobs be banned—or should the emphasis be on reforming the social order to offer a place to everyone?

Some of what put Trump in the White House was resentment in Midwestern swing states against trade agreements that favor other nations over the United States. Because Trump claimed this, establishment talking heads scoffed and contended it can't be true. But many US trade agreements do favor other nations over the United States—and this is something of which Americans should be proud.

The World Trade Organization regime the United States accepted in 2000 allows Beijing to charge three times the entry fees (tariffs and value-added taxes) that Washington may charge, in order to aid development of Chinese industry by legalizing protectionism for Beijing while banning the same practice for Washington. Brazil, India, and most of Africa can charge three and a half times what the United States is allowed to, again legalizing protection for them while banning the practice in the United States. Experts who thought middle America was too stupid or ignorant to catch on to this—the prevailing view among Washington, DC, elites— were shown to be wrong as middle America caught on and expressed its views by voting Trump. Overlooked is that Americans should be proud of slanted trade arrangements. Through the 2000 tariff concessions, the United States, long the most generous of nations, gave up some wealth to help others.

Angus Deaton, who won the Nobel Prize in Economics in 2015, has studied developing-nation inequality and concluded that the best coun-termeasure to global inequality is more trade between developing nations and the United States and Europe. Many aspects of globalization drive the middle class of the West crazy, but globalization is good for most of the human family. And globalization is just getting started—our planet is on the verge of becoming far more global.

If you told a worker who lost a job in the Muncie, Indiana, factory, "The same international trade that harmed you helps the majority of Americans and Europeans by holding down prices, while reducing world poverty at an amazing rate," the reply might be a colorful expletive. But this is the world's dynamic: relatively small economic concessions in the prosperous regions are coupled to huge gains in the places where most of humanity lives. This dynamic goes unseen in the West—but the result is the human family becoming increasingly better off.

THE NEWS WAS SHOCKING: IN the United States, the middle class is no lon-ger the majority. *CBS Evening News* opened a December 2015 broadcast with the story, accompanied by brightly colored pie charts drawn in such a way as to make the middle class seem to be vanishing. Backing up the charts was a study released that day by the Pew Research Center, a highly credible organization, reporting that the American middle class was "no longer the majority." Pew concluded that in 1971, 61 percent of Americans were middle-class; by 2015, just 50 percent were middle-class—no longer the majority. Broadcasts like this played a role in planting in the American public mind the "world is ending" sentiment underpinning the Trump victory the following year.

Those who dived into Pew's research saw that in 1971, 14 percent of Americans were in the upper bands of income, 25 percent in the lower bands; by 2015, 21 percent were upper-income, 29 percent lower. This meant more Americans going upward out of the middle class toward high income than going downward toward low income: more Americans were vanishing up from the middle class than were falling down. A subsequent Pew Research Center study would show there are more cities and counties in the United States where middle-class families of all races are going upward economically than are going downward. Most European Union nations exhibit similar numbers—headed-up exceeds headed-down. Positive details such as these tend to be skipped to focus on the scary tease that the middle class has stopped being the majority—though remaining the largest demographic, with the lock on political clout.

Stephen Rose, a labor economist at the Urban Institute, a center-left think tank, has for years been producing studies showing the middle class gets smaller mainly because people graduate in the direction of prosperity. Rose's 2016 data, released just as Trump was convincing the American body politic that "everything is down, down, down," and using somewhat different metrics than the Pew researchers, found that a generation ago, in 1979, 13 percent of Americans were in the upper income bands; 39 percent in the middle; 48 percent were low-income or poor. By 2014, Rose concluded, 31 percent of Americans were high income, 32 percent middle, and 37 percent low-income or poor. These numbers support the popular contention that the middle class is shrinking, but also, on the big picture, are almost entirely positive—a rising share of high-earners coupled to fewer low-earners. Which economy would you rather live in, the America of 1979 or of 2014?

The America of 2014 was not only more prosperous but more equitable. Consider another comparison to 1979. In that year the economy was stagnant yet inflation was high, a stifling combination; President Jimmy Carter gave a downbeat, nationally televised address known to history as the "malaise speech"; the most-talked-about serious book, *The Culture of Narcissism* by Christopher Lasch, bore the subhead *American Life in an Age of Diminished Expectations*. Adjusting to current dollars and for population growth, we would expect that today's US GDP would be about 40 percent larger than in 1979. Instead, the GDP has risen 165 percent—a fourfold increase during a generation supposedly plagued by "diminished expectations."

Setting aside all the progress against discrimination, crime, pollution, and disease, the economic numbers show the United States of the present day is a better place to be, in living standards, social mobility, and fairness, than the United States of a generation ago. Yet Americans speak of the present as bad, the past as preferable.

THE PEW RESEARCH CENTER METRIC for gauging the extent of the middle class took into account pretax income only. Citing income numbers alone is the approach employed by Senators Sanders of Vermont and Elizabeth Warren of Massachusetts, who are the left wing's most notable declinists, trafficking in anger and negativity. Income-only is the approach employed by Thomas Piketty of the Paris School of Economics and Emmanuel Saez of the University of California at Berkeley, who were favorite economists of the Obama White House. Piketty and Saez produced voluminous charts and graphs showing that because returns on capital exceed increases in wage income, the system is structured such that those at the top, who own the most equity (primarily as stock shares), will make out better than average people.

These conclusions take into account only pretax income, which the two economists call "the simplest and most powerful measure" of inequality. Inarguably, pretax income is the most powerful measure of inequality. That it is also the simplest does not make it correct; height is the simplest measure of a basketball player, but choosing up a team based solely on height would not be wise. No one in the United States or Europe runs a family on pretax income alone. Tax rates, government benefits, consumer prices, and household size must be taken into account too. Piketty's 2013 tome *Capital in the Twenty-First Century* was received by many editorialists and academics as having proven that rising inequality in pretax income means the Western economy is in an emergency situation. The book travels 704 pages without assessing how taxes, government benefits, and consumer prices impact the average people Piketty seeks to champion. Taxes, benefits, and prices are major factors in most people's lives: bringing this up makes the Western economic situation sound better than the income-only analysis. As a result, many economists and political figures fixate on pretax income, the negative indicator, trying to assume away the rest.

Income is worth less if heavily taxed or eroded by inflation. Income that is boosted by benefits is worth more, as is income spread across fewer people as households become smaller. What matters more than pretax income alone is buying power, which is shown by a (conceptual) five-term equation: income minus taxes plus benefits, multiplied to adjust for rising or falling prices, and adjusted for household size.

$$(I - T + B) \times CPI \text{ [adjusted for] } HS$$

Most Americans know that in recent decades taxes on the rich have been cut: there is a strong argument that taxes at the top should increase. Voters and pundits seem less aware that federal income taxes on the US middle class have been cut too, while in 2001, under legislation backed by the younger President George Bush, federal income taxes on the bottom fifth of households essentially were eliminated, a progressive step.

During both the younger Bush and Obama presidencies, as federal income taxes went down for nearly everyone, government benefits went up. In 2013, the Congressional Budget Office (CBO) calculated that a generation ago, the typical middle-class family paid more in federal income taxes than it received in federal benefits. Now it's the other way around: for the typical middle-class family, the value of federal benefits exceeds the cost of federal taxes by $7,800. As this has happened, households have become somewhat smaller. That rising buying power is, in the typical

American household, distributed across fewer people is a point almost always skipped in arguments that focus on rates of wage gain. Meanwhile, current-dollar prices for many staples have gone down. On the first day of the twentieth century, the typical American household spent 59 percent of funds on food and clothing. By the first day of the twenty-first century, that share had shrunk to 21 percent, mainly because the real-dollar price of food and clothes had declined, even as the quality of both increased.

Adjust for federal tax cuts in 1982, 1986, 2001, 2003, 2010, and 2012; for increasing federal benefits; for smaller households; for almost no inflation: what do we get? In 2014 the Brookings Institution economist Gary Burtless asked this question and found that since 1980, the bottom one-fifth of Americans saw their buying power advance 49 percent. The center fifth—the middle class—saw a 36 percent rise in buying power. Numbers for most of the European Union are similar. The improvements have been realized on a mostly steady slope, including during some years of the Great Recession. Of course this does not mean there's no one with money problems. But there will never be a situation in which no one has money problems. On the whole, buying power for average people is in good condition, and continuing a generations-long trend of improvement. The recent Congressional Budget Office statistics show that if lower taxes, higher benefits, and consumer prices are taken into account, since 2000 middle-class buying power has been rising somewhat, not falling as commonly assumed.

Presidential candidates, pundits, authors, and even entertainers constantly tell Americans and Europeans they are falling behind economically. Yet almost everyone in the United States and Europe is better off financially than a generation ago. Convinced they were worse off, 63 million Americans voted for Trump. The Democratic Party came within a few million popular votes of choosing Sanders to oppose him: a 2016 presidential contest of Trump versus Sanders would have featured both big-party candidates falsely telling voters they were worse off than in some largely imaginary Good Ole Days.

During his campaign, Sanders declared "the middle class is being squeezed" by "plummeting" wages. Like Trump's assertion that crime was rising when actually it is declining, Sanders's contention that wages are going down when actually they are going up fell into the puzzling category of negative claims that voters want to believe. The Labor Department reports that 2016 hourly wages rose at 2.9 percent, about double the rate of inflation, making 2016 a good year for wages. Spring 2017 saw nonfarm wages in the United States average $26.19 an hour, a record both in absolute terms and when adjusted to constant dollars. From 2007 to 2017, average hourly wages—an essential leading indicator for the middle class—rose 26 percent. There are millions of people who have trouble getting by. But that's a different issue from the strangely popular, and wholly phony, claim that wages are down.

A lengthy stretch of almost no inflation has caused people in America and Europe to take low inflation for granted. Inflation harms average people far more than any economic force other than unemployment, while doing little damage to the rich. Yet the extended period of low inflation—in buying power terms, a long boom—is all but ignored in Western public opinion. Senior citizens in the United States protest sullenly the several consecutive years with low or no Social Security cost-of-living adjustments (COLA). That's because there is almost no inflation: would seniors be better off with COLA bonuses but also higher prices? Policymakers of the past would reach for tranquilizers if told that central bankers of the present wish they could push inflation up. The bitter comes with the sweet: the same economic forces that make for turbulent change also constrain consumer prices, which is really good for average men and women.

Inevitably the economic efficiency that improves buying power for most average people harms some individuals whose jobs or specialties are phased out. Modern politics and media coverage tend to use the painful narrative of the small forgotten town as representing some kind of overall economic failure, skipping that every year most average people are better off than the year before. A reporter or politician visiting, for example, Johnsonburg, Pennsylvania, would find a dreary, fading industrial town where far too many don't spring out of bed in the morning to head for work or school. The dilapidated, century-old paper mill there, along the winding Clarion River, could be made to seem a symbol of American decline, since that mill can be seen, while the overall rise in prosperity cannot. Anyone with a good heart would care about Johnsonburg or any similar place—but that's not the same as thinking the nation would be better off by traveling back into the past when the town's paper mill was running two shifts but overall living standards were lower while discrimination, pollution, and disease were worse.

Perhaps so many voters and commentators fixate on the negative because it's part of human nature to want to feel self-pity. Others may simply close their ears against what does not support their agendas. Absent a second Garden of Eden, there never will be a moment when no one is hurting for money, health, love, or friendship. The larger picture matters more: the larger picture is mostly good, and mostly getting better.

The widespread belief that the Western economy is failing when actually living standards for almost everyone continue to improve is, best-case, a confounding indicator of human nature. Worst-case, it is the kind of dangerous misconception that elects crazed leaders.

BUT IS THERE HIDDEN UNEMPLOYMENT? On the Internet, one encounters elaborate rumors about crashed UFOs; on talk radio, a standby is that the impressive employment rates of the United States are instead a cover-up. The numbers, this conspiracy theory goes, are manipulated to mask labor-force participation, the fraction of prime-aged, healthy adults with jobs. In December 2016, just before Barack Obama left office, radio host Rush Limbaugh told listeners that labor-force participation "is at an all-time low."

The actual postwar low for labor-force participation came in 1966, when 60 percent of prime-aged, healthy Americans held jobs. In January 2017, 63 percent of prime-aged, healthy Americans held jobs. Adjusting for population growth, had the labor-force participation rate of 1966 been in effect in 2017, there would have been 117 million Americans employed; instead, the number for 2017 was 152 million with jobs. Compared to population increase, that's 35 million more Americans working than in those Good Old Days. Yet the talk-radio conspiracy world believes the shocking reality of unemployment is being covered up: a claim Trump echoed during his presidential campaign.

According to the Federal Reserve Bank of St. Louis, the labor-force participation rate for men has indeed fallen in recent decades, from

86 percent in 1950 to 69 percent in 2015. Simultaneously, labor-force participation for women has risen sharply, from 33 percent in 1950 to 57 percent in 2015. Summing these trends—moderate decline in laboring men, a larger increase in women working for wages—results in a solid employment picture for the United States, though of course improvement is needed. When commentators say that US labor-force participation is some kind of economic disaster, what they are saying in effect is that men having jobs is more important than women having jobs. Or that white men having jobs is more important than African American and Hispanic men working. Since about 2000, white male labor-force participation is down while African American and Hispanic male labor-force participation is up.

As the social scientist Charles Murray showed in his 2010 book *Coming Apart,* most movement in labor-force participation for men traces to unmarried white males dropping out of the working world. Some prime-aged white men stop working, Murray writes, not because they cannot find a job but because they do not want or need one. Why? They're not married. Susan B. Anthony proposed in 1877 that "an epoch of single women" was approaching. This epoch did arrive with the twenty-first century: in the United States, women who never married or are widowed or divorced are now more numerous than women with husbands. The rising numbers of unattached women bring with them rising numbers of unattached men—gay marriage is insufficiently common to matter in this context—and unattached men may not want steady work. Being a handyman or seasonal employee who's paid under the table, while drawing federal or veterans' disability checks, would not allow anyone to live well but may provide a prime-aged man with enough money for a room, food, and modest pleasures. Men with wives and children have no choice but to work, Murray notes, while unmarried males "are much less industrious than married ones."

The share of unmarried American men is increasing in part because men who never attended college are worth steadily less in the contemporary economy. The writer Anne Kim has noted that a generation ago men with a college diploma earned $7,000 more per year, in current dollars, than men without one, making high school and college graduates similarly appealing, economically, as marriage partners. Today a man with a college diploma earns on average $20,000 more than a man whose education stopped in high school. Men who were never Joe College are tumbling down the earnings ladder, becoming less attractive as mates. More end up unmarried, then not taking jobs.

Murray's spooky finding concerned how unemployed, single, prime-aged, white males use their bonanza of free time: they sleep late, play video games, and watch television. The advent of a sizable cohort of men who pull up the bedcovers to shut out the world, then waste the best years of their lives gazing at electronic screens, may be an indictment of American society. But don't blame the economy. At this writing, unemployment was 4.4 percent—most labor economists define anything below 5 percent as "full employment." Jobs are there for those who seek them.

SLOW GROWTH, ONCE ADVOCATED BY intellectuals, now is here, and not many like it. In the 1960s, the US economy grew at a blazing 5 percent per year. During the 1980s and 1990s, growth often hit 4 percent. Annualized, from 1950 to 2000 the US economy grew at 3.3 percent. Growth anywhere in these ranges means steadily rising household income, and restrains national debt. Expansion of the GDP in the United States and European Union slammed to a halt during the Great Recession. Since about 2010 the basics of economic life have been back to normal but growth has not, now annualizing at about 2 percent per annum in America, less in Europe.

Low GDP increase is the primary reason borrowing by government has quickened, and never mind that once, intellectuals and urban activists said what they dreamed of was slow growth. The growth trends can have an arithmetic impact. At the 1950–2000 annualized rate, household income doubles in about twenty-five years. At the current rate, household income takes much longer to double.

Phillip Longman has written, "The idea that Americans are bound by destiny to experience ever-greater affluence has been an article of faith since the Second World War." Western society has entered a phase of preoccupation with discovering previously unknown grievances, one of which is that because of slower growth, the next generation won't live dramatically better than the present one. Northwestern University economist Robert Gordon has won praise from pundits by producing studies and essays taking the view that the slowdown in growth is not just bad for the national debt but a calamity that ends the American Dream.

This aggressive claim can be disputed. The Pew Charitable Trusts found in a 2013 study that, adjusting for age and smaller families, 84 percent of Americans earn more than their parents did. Most US citizens in the top fifth for income grew up in homes that were not top-fifth, an indication that social mobility continues.

Complaining that household pretax income no longer increases as quickly as before is like complaining that airliner speeds doubled every generation in the early phase of aviation and now have gone a generation without any increase. Today's air service is fast, safe, and affordable, if cramped. There's no need to achieve supersonic or hypersonic velocity; the need is to sustain today's fast, safe, affordable air service for generations to come. The situation with the economy is the same. Whether contemporary economic standards can be sustained for generations to come is far more important than whether future generations will get absolutely everything imaginable.

Economist Martin Feldstein of Harvard University has argued that the formula of the Gross Domestic Product understates growth by measuring only output and prices, not quality of life. Here are two examples. Surgery of the 1950s is treated by the GDP formula as the same as surgery of today, though in almost all cases today's surgery achieves better results with less suffering. In the 1950s, a third of American retirees were impoverished. By 2013 the fraction was down to 9 percent, still too high, but a vast social improvement not reflected in GDP growth statistics. Feldstein contends that adjusting for rising quality of life and for products that are safer and more reliable—today's cars are much less likely to kill their drivers and passengers than cars of a generation ago, while more likely to start in the morning—the rate of growth in the United States is in good shape by every measure except one: pretax income. Since pretax income is the sole negative indicator, it is the one that dominates discussion.

The idea that slower growth of GDP and living standards ends the American Dream finds an audience since it is fashionably declinist. In

1960, 12 percent of US households had air conditioning; now, 90 percent do. The northern latitudes of the nation don't even need air conditioning; where do you go from 90 percent? The average new home in the United States in the 1980s was 1,680 square feet. The 2010 census found the average new home was 2,392 square feet, a 44 percent increase in a single generation. Would society even want the average new home to enlarge another 44 percent? That would be 3,450 square feet. Only a big family requires such expanse, and American and European family size is in long-term decline. Yet by the logic of declinism, if the next generation does not enjoy ultra-huge homes, that ends the American Dream.

To the extent public policy impacts economic growth—mostly the economy runs uncommanded, but policy does have an impact—recent legislation and regulations read as if intended to slow down growth. The Sarbanes-Oxley Act, signed by George W. Bush in 2002, and the Dodd-Frank Act, signed by Barack Obama in 2010, actively discourage the starting of new private enterprises, while placing roadblocks to the expansion of existing public firms. The Dodd-Frank Act runs 2,300 pages and has spawned 22,000 pages of federal rules, many of them intended to punish risk-taking while rewarding timidity, which reverses the traditional incentives regarding economic growth. The veteran investment banker William Cohan wrote in 2017, "The job of one out of every five people on Wall Street these days is to watch what the other four are doing." Some regulations produce benefits: those who object to environmental rules may slide glissando past the good they do, especially improvement of public health. But contemporary economic regulations impose dead-weight transaction costs that further the interests only of lawyers seeking billable hours and of federal, state, and local government officials seeking to protect their sinecure.

Studies by the nonpartisan Kauffman Foundation show that about 80 percent of new jobs in the United States are created by start-up firms. Yet Sarbanes-Oxley, passed by a Republican-controlled House of Representatives, treats those who wish to found a firm as guilty until proven innocent, raising costs and imposing delays. Existing big companies backed many of the laws and regulations that stifle innovation, because their legal departments could use the excruciating details to squash nimble new competitors not in a position to hire lawyers. "Everyone knows how to obey the laws against robbery, no one knows how to obey the 2,300-page Dodd-Frank Act," one analyst wrote. Existing firms have lobbyists who can finesse regulatory problems: start-ups are defeated, which is what the existing firms hope for, but then growth slows.

With each passing year in the United States, more actions are put under the control of laws or rules that vary from silly to progressive to anti-economy. Silly: it's a federal crime—not bad manners, a *federal crime*—to wear snowshoes in the parking lot of a national monument. Anti-economy: the *Code of Federal Regulations* now runs 178,000 pages, predominantly concerning economic activity. Yet politicians and editorialists feign surprise when growth slows. In 2016, economists at George Mason University estimated that by discouraging investment, federal and state regulations cause "an average reduction in the annual growth rate of the US gross domestic product of 0.8 percent." Add 0.8 percent per year to the GDP and wages would rise more, the deficit would decline, and there would be no fretting about slow growth.

In the initial decades following the devastation of World War II, the Western economy grew so much that it is unrealistic to think such growth would never end. Standards of living in the West are now sufficiently high that the challenge is to sustain these standards for generations to come, while ensuring that no one goes unaccounted for. That should be the New American Dream.

A SMALL CONCERN ABOUT THE American economy is the need for more bridges. Government cannot dial up growth or wages: often policymakers are little more than bystanders to economic developments. One reason cell phones and the Internet improved so rapidly, while prices fell so rapidly, is that both caught government unawares, establishing themselves before Washington could impose stifling restrictions.

There is one arena in which government action does amplify economic performance: infrastructure. In this arena, federal, state, and local governments have for a generation performed exceptionally poorly in the United States. Highways, bridges, and dams need repair; the population keeps growing, yet new roads and mass transit systems are few; subway and passenger train service is better in Europe than in America. German automakers have begun to design different suspensions for models sold in the United States, taking into account that US highways are in poor condition compared to autobahns. In 2016, the Department of Transportation found that 55,000 bridges in the United States need maintenance or replacement, including more than 20 percent of bridges in Iowa, Pennsylvania, and Rhode Island. Publicly funded sports stadia, which are popular with local politicians who want to pose for pictures with star athletes, are superfluous to economic growth: in a 2015 study, Ted Gayer and Alex Gold of the Brookings Institution concluded there is "no discernible positive relationship between sports facility construction and economic development." Roads, bridges, and bus rapid transit, by contrast, have clear multiplier effects. To take out loans to improve infrastructure can make good sense, in the same way that home improvement loans can make good sense. Yet while Washington borrows lavishly to subsidize interest groups, construction and repair are overlooked.

In 2014, President Barack Obama lamented of American infrastructure, "We are not spending enough." Rather, the United States spends plenty while getting little, since US infrastructure projects are overpriced, slow, and ill-administered. The ambitious high-speed Crossrail subway being completed underneath London is costing $285 million a mile; the world's longest and deepest rail tunnel, opened under the Swiss Alps in 2016, cost $355 million a mile; subway tunnels being bored beneath San Francisco and Seattle at the same time cost $1 billion a mile, far more in the United States than in England or Switzerland. Here is a Tale of Three Nations: in 2017, the bullet train from the capital of South Korea to the 2018 Olympics was costing $53 million per mile; the East London Line rail extension, being built in one of the most crowded places in the world, was costing $90 million a mile; a trolley project in the Maryland suburbs of Washington, DC, was costing $170 million a mile; a trolley project in Durham, North Carolina, was costing $185 million a mile. The US trolley projects are aboveground systems without complex engineering challenges. Yet the American trolleys are three times as expensive per mile as the Korean bullet train, and twice as expensive per mile as the British rail project that includes challenging engineering.

If only these were isolated examples—they are the norm. The Tappan Zee Bridge north of New York City was completed in 1955 at a cost of $700 million in today's money; a replacement expected to open in 2018 will cost at least $4 billion, six times as much as the original. The John Kennedy Memorial Bridge in Louisville, Kentucky, completed in 1963 for $85 million, is being replaced with a new bridge costing a dozen times as much. On a boulevard near Washington, DC, contractors are building a pedestrian underpass from a subway stop to Walter Reed National Medical Center. This short underpass is projected to cost $70 million and take four years to complete. In the bridge, trolley, and underpass projects, as in many other US infrastructure initiatives, the federal government provides large chunks of funding while state and local officials control the project: an incentive structure that rewards cost overruns and delays.

Because excessive regulation, dilatory litigation, and NIMBY (not-in-my-backyard) protests have become the US standard, public-investment projects now take too long, cost too much, and return too little value to the public. The North Carolina trolley is slated to require *fifteen years* from planning to open for business—a construction pace barely exceeding one mile per year—using the formula of federal funding plus local control equals dragging of feet. Many infrastructure projects contain giveaways to unions, which in turn donate to political candidates: all but formally a kickback system. Labor unions are standard in Western Europe infrastructure work, but the kickback mechanism to candidates is not.

The Ohio River has caused barge traffic bottlenecks since the Eisenhower presidency, owing to an antiquated lock. A federal project to replace the lock has been ongoing for *thirty years,* and trebled in inflation-adjusted cost, yet at this writing still is not complete. A larger lock under construction on the Ghent-Terneuzen Canal in the Netherlands is taking five years to build at a cost of about $1 billion; the US government has spent *thirty years* and three times as much on a river lock that still doesn't operate. If the US government wishes to stimulate economic growth, the answer is not giving state and local government more money to squander—the answer is making government construction managers accountable in the same way that private construction managers are.

* * *

A BIG CONCERN ABOUT MOST Western economies is national debt. Adjusted to current dollars, the public debt of the United States—the amount the nation owes to other nations or to investors, not the agency-to-agency bookkeeping involved with Social Security—doubled merely from 2006 to 2015. In a single decade, the United States took on more public debt than in the republic's previous 216 years of existence. During the 2006 to 2015 decade the White House, Senate, and House of Representatives alternated between Democratic and Republican control, making both parties equally culpable. The decade came just before the retirement of the Baby Boom, in other words, at a time the United States should have been saving against the certainty of rising pension expenditures. Instead the country was borrowing and spending like there was no tomorrow, and not even getting an upgraded infrastructure in the process.

Tomorrow has a way of coming.

Some economists view debt as an outdated concern. A school of thought called "modern monetary theory" contends that the hard-currency nations (Australia, Canada, the European Union, Japan, Singapore, Switzerland, the United Kingdom, and the United States) can borrow as much as they want and print money to make the payments. More precisely, they can declare additional ones and zeroes to make the payments. Maybe this theory is sound. Running the experiment to find out if modern monetary theory is correct would involve gambling with the bankruptcy of the Western world.

Among political strategists, the saying is, "Debt doesn't poll." American voters want higher benefits and more subsidies and don't give a fig about balancing the books. In the 2016 presidential campaign, Trump and Sanders did well by offering outlandish goody-bag promises (sweeping tax cuts in Trump's case, everything free in Sanders's) while saying little about how the goodies would be financed. Clinton unveiled a well-researched, intricate plan to fund her campaign positions so that the national debt would not rise. How old-fashioned! And we know what happened to Hillary Clinton.

Once government leaders felt that engaging more debt was irresponsible. George Washington insisted in 1789 that the first priority of the new nation be to pay off Revolutionary War debts, lest he and his contemporaries "ungenerously throw upon posterity the burden which we ourselves ought to bear." Presidents Reagan and the elder George Bush went against their Republican donor bases to increase federal taxes to hold down national debt, which they found worrisome at a fraction of today's inflation-adjusted level. In 2006, Barack Obama, a junior senator, voted nay on a $700 billion increase in the national debt ceiling, saying, "Washington is shifting the burden of bad choices onto the backs of our children and grandchildren." Once president, Obama added $7.3 trillion to the national debt—ten times the amount he said would be inexcusable.

In 2003, Congress, with the approval of the younger George Bush, passed a budget with a $500 billion fiscal-year deficit, then an unheard-of level of borrowing. Here is what happened: nothing.

Economists, and some on Capitol Hill, feared the big deficit would have devastating consequences, particularly following the budget surpluses recorded late in the Bill Clinton presidency. Instead, Congress dipped its toes into mega-borrowing and nothing happened. So the next year Congress borrowed anew—and nothing happened. Then borrowed more, and nothing happened. In 2009, the annual deficit had risen to $1.4 trillion. By Obama's final year in office, the $587 billion deficit was viewed with relief—though to all presidents before Obama and the younger George Bush, this amount would have seemed shockingly high, even if adjusted for population size.

Since government debt can resolve with strong economic growth, politicians claim to "fund" tax cuts, giveaways, and borrowing binges by assuming improbable future growth. During the 2016 campaign, Trump said future growth would average 6 percent per year; Sanders said 5 percent. Both projections exceeded observed growth by a hefty margin: from 1977 till the Great Recession began in 2008, US growth annualized at 2.8 percent. University of Chicago economist Austan Goolsbee calls campaign promises about growth "magic flying puppies." As soon as candidates obtain the power they sought, the magic puppies plummet from the sky. Shortly after being sworn in as president, Trump declared that addressing the debt "is no longer a top priority."

At the same time federal debt has distended, state pension accounts have gone into the red. The Pew Trusts has found that states have at least $1 trillion in unfunded liabilities, perhaps as much as $3 trillion. State pension funds make the unrealistic assumption their investments will post an average return of 7.6 percent, almost exactly the promise that Bernard Madoff employed to fleece his marks. Projecting unrealistic returns at unspecified future dates allows governors and mayors to pretend to be fiscally responsible and allows state and local pension fund managers to award themselves generous bonuses, while distributing current revenues as if they were investment yields—exactly the manner in which Ponzi schemes function. Connecticut, Illinois, New Jersey, and many California cities are among places with runaway unfunded liabilities to retirees: unfunded pension liabilities in Illinois equate to $22,500 per resident, and the state is not saving for ever-rising numbers of retirees. Dallas has unfunded pension liabilities equivalent to four years of the city's budget. Teachers' pension plans—which in many states justify big bonuses to fund officers by claiming excellent fiduciary performance—owe at least $500 billion they have not saved and in many states employ a Ponzi-scheme structure. Arizona, Illinois, Michigan, and Wisconsin are among states where public-school classroom spending has been cut to reallocate budget appropriations to pension accounts that supposedly were funded. A 2016 Manhattan Institute study found, "The vast majority of taxpayer contributions into teachers' pension plans are now used to pay down debt owed for past service rather than to save for benefits supposedly being earned by today's teachers," an accounting flimflam that ensures the situation will grow worse. The Social Security Administration is a model of probity compared to state and local pension plans. If such plans default, there will be pressure on Washington, DC, to borrow still more to cover state and local negligence.

The government debt spree that began early in the twenty-first century may have some relationship to slower economic growth, though nothing happened in terms of standard fears about public debt—no sudden inflation, no refusal of creditors to lend anew. This seems to have convinced the US Congress, and many European parliaments that the old rules don't apply anymore, and that borrow-and-spend can go on ad infinitum. The saying "we're all Keynesians now" once was meant to justify government borrowing to smooth out business cycles by firing up demand. But John Maynard Keynes's dictum had two parts: government should borrow and spend when the economy is slack, then in good times, cut spending to repay debt. Today Western and Asian governments are enthusiastic about the first half of the dictum, which rationalizes giveaways to appease interest groups, but ignore the second half, which demands self-discipline. We're all half-Keynesians now.

If governments borrow and nothing bad happens, why care? Let's invoke the spirit of Franklin Roosevelt, who liked to make analogies between the administration of the nation and running a home. Suppose a homeowner borrowed against the house to buy a Ferrari, take a first-class cruise, drink Cristal Champagne at breakfast. Initially nothing bad would happen; once the bills and credit charges came due, the home would end up repossessed. Congress, presidents, parliaments, and prime ministers of many nations have been acting like the prodigal homeowner. Greece and Spain are barely abovewater financially, Japan's debt exceeds GDP, China has been having municipalities sign what are really federal loans, hoping to mask the extent of the country's debt addiction. In 2017, the bond-rating firm Moody's Investors Services downgraded China's sovereign credit, warning that Beijing is veering into hock.

In 2017, Richard Samans of the World Economic Forum in Switzerland calculated that today, a world total of $70 trillion in pension obligations is unfunded: by 2050, the sum will rise to a breathtaking $400 trillion, most of this owed by governments, particularly of China and India. Four hundred trillion dollars is about five times the total current global economic production. The powerful 2012 book *The Reckoning*, by Michael Moran, argues that great nations of history failed not from overstretch, not from barbarians at the gate, but because they borrowed recklessly and then essentially were repossessed.

Debt creates funny-money for legislatures to shower on interest groups, which lavish campaign donations on them in return. It would be much cheaper to the taxpayer for the United States to provide public funding for elections, while banning donations, than to allow officials to squander large sums in return for the sliver that becomes the campaign kickback. Fresh debt allows government to put off uncomfortable political decisions. Because of the compounding effect, loan problems get steadily worse when action is postponed. Yet governments put off dealing with what they owe—"kicking the can down the road," as Obama said from the White House, and he should know, having taken more than a few swipes at the can himself.

The sheer magnitude of the national debt is not the issue—after all, with the population rising, the United States hits a record for nearly everything nearly every year. Debt is better understood on a per-capita basis, adjusting to current dollars and for the rising number of heads (the *capita* in per-capita). Here is the trend:

- In 1960, the US public debt was $12,800 per capita.
- By 1980, US public debt had fallen to $11,450 per capita.
- By 2000, US public debt was up to $27,700 per capita, more than double the debt of four decades before.
- As the Obama presidency ended in 2017, US public debt was $65,000 per capita; each American owed more than the median household income that year.
- Calculating from Census Bureau population projections and spending forecasts of the Congressional Budget Office, by 2047, US per-capita debt will be $235,000. Each American household will owe more than four years' worth of wages toward what previous generations borrowed.

That scary number for 2047 assumes interest rates stay low, and thus the government can borrow at low cost. The Federal Reserve cleaved to ZIRP—zero-interest-rate policy—for the entire Obama presidency. Had, under Obama, the price of Treasury notes been at the postwar average, his two terms would have added not $7.3 trillion but $10 trillion to the national debt. How interest rates stayed low for so long without triggering inflation is hotly debated by economists. Whatever the answer, if borrowing costs rebound from ZIRP toward the postwar pattern, public debt will multiply and fiscal irresponsibility in the United States—and Japan and other nations—will swamp all other domestic policy questions combined.

PERHAPS NUMBERS LIKE THOSE ABOVE cause you to think, "Then we must cut waste, fraud and abuse." Government could become leaner. Many federal, state, and local agencies are overstaffed with officials who spend their days in make-work or filing grievances against each other; fraud at the top is frequent. But waste, fraud, and abuse are comparatively minor elements of government appropriations. Invoking the phrase has become a handy way for politicians to change the subject from rash borrowing.

In 2017, the $4 trillion US federal budget allocated $3.4 trillion to entitlements, defense, and debt service, leaving $600 billion, just 15 percent, for all other categories. Suppose the complete sum of discretionary spending were eliminated—no FBI, no air traffic control, sell the national parks, no funding for education, roads, space exploration, or medical research, no State Department, no environmental agencies, no federal courts, no prisons, no border police. That would only slow the increase of national debt—not pay down what's already owed. Polls show Americans think about 25 percent of the federal budget is foreign aid; actually foreign aid is less than 1 percent of federal spending. On the theme that what matters in politics is not what's accurate but what people believe, Donald Trump said in 2017, "We are very concerned about the spiraling national debt and that's why we're cutting foreign aid." Eighty-five percent of the federal budget goes to defense, income transfers, and debt service. Blaming red ink on foreign aid plus waste, fraud, and abuse, as President Trump does, is a way to pretend to be facing the debt monster while actually doing nothing (other than golf, in Trump's case).

Perhaps the above paragraph causes you to think, "Then let's get rid of welfare and subsidies to illegal immigrants." Here is another juncture where politics is driven by what people want to believe. Americans want to believe that their tax money and public borrowing end up as handouts to illegals and welfare to people who ought to work. Some of both does happen, but the sum is diminutive compared to the federal budget. By far the largest share of the federal budget is subsidies to senior citizens that flow through Social Security and Medicare—$1.6 trillion for these accounts in 2017. America's native-born white majority wants to believe it is ruggedly self-sufficient while minorities and immigrants are living the life of Riley. Yet Social Security and Medicare, the king and queen of subsidies, go mainly to native-born white Americans. The third-largest transfer program, Medicaid, at $545 billion, does subsidize the poor and immigrants, but also provides nursing home care that is mainly for native-born whites. Federal welfare payments exclusively for the poor are not inconsequential, but pale before payments for the majority.

And though it's a pleasant fiction that Social Security merely refunds money the recipient saved, fiction this is. Today the typical Social Security recipient receives more than double what he or she paid in, plus interest. In order to pay retirees more than they saved, pretty much every penny Social Security obtains is spent that year on benefits, or used to reduce the federal deficit, with the "Trust Fund"—doesn't that sound reassuring?—an accounting fairy tale consisting not of money but IOUs issued from one government account to another. When Obama took office as president, the trustees of the Social Security Administration, who have a good track record in actuarial matters, said Social Security insolvency would come in 2037. By the time Obama left office, the insolvency year had moved forward to 2034. Medicare is on track to be depleted by 2029, with Social Security's disability fund failing in 2028. Preventing short-term insolvency of Social Security and Medicare would, the trustees estimate, require imposing a tax of about $1,400 per year on every household—and that's assuming use of soak-the-rich options, such as lifting the Social Security income tax cap.

As the share of retirees to workers (the "dependency ratio") continues to rise, Social Security, state-level pensions, and similar benefits will need ever-more cash. Medicare costs are likely to increase as Americans age and demand very expensive surgical interventions late in life, even if recovery is unlikely. Medicaid costs are going up rapidly, as the poor expect to receive the same extent and quality of treatment as others—previously, the poor expected to suffer in silence—while native-born Americans increasingly expect Medicaid, rather than their families, to pay nursing-home expenses. Half a century ago no American's nursing-home costs were picked up by federal taxpayers: by 2015, two-thirds of nursing home residents were being paid for by Medicaid, and the majority of beneficiaries were native born and not poor.

Society should have been saving, in anticipation of the demographic inevitability of an aging population that seeks pension checks, medical services, and nursing care. Instead we spent like tomorrow would never come. This was more than "ungenerous": it was the old, who dominate politics, awarding themselves money and expecting the young to pay.

Michael Mullen, a retired admiral who was chair of the Joint Chiefs of Staff and is now a professor at Princeton University, said in 2012, "Debt is the single biggest threat to US national security." He wasn't being cute, and the military had nothing to gain from this view. Nobody wants to deal with debt, which tells us that the subject must be faced—especially if the future holds big new expenses.

Considering this chapter just argued that national debt is the most worrisome aspect of the American economy, and of some other Western economies, big new expenses in the future may seem like the last thing a nation needs. But big new expenses may be unavoidable, and not for senior citizens, who are already the most subsidized segment of US society and of many European societies. The reason to reduce today's existing national debts is that, in the near future, all roads may lead to some version of Universal Basic Income. A coming chapter will address this concept. For the moment, what matters is that near-future economic growth and near-future social justice both may turn on some form of income guarantee, especially for those poorly educated men and women whose labor value can only go down. A Universal Basic Income might make the United States and some European nations freer and more fair places to live. But this reform won't be cheap—the first step must be to slay the debt monster that already exists.

THE SUMMATION OF WHY THE economy does not collapse is that no one is in charge.

With no one in charge, the economies of the West are in better shape than generally understood, and probably will stay that way—though we can't be sure, so unending economic anxiety is guaranteed.

What happens if crime or war wipe us out?

Chapter 5

Why Is Violence in Decline?

IN JANUARY 2017, THE WORLD Health Organization released a lengthy document that would have fascinated Frédéric Bastiat, the French philosopher who wrote the essay *That Which Is Seen and That Which Is Not Seen,* urging readers to contemplate what did not happen as much as what did. The WHO study reported that in the most recent year for which statistics were available, 54.5 million people died—more than the total number of people in France in the year Bastiat was born—and that heart disease, stroke, and respiratory failure were civilization's leading causes of mortality.

Bastiat would have noted that tuberculosis—which claimed his life in 1850, when he was forty-nine years of age—had dropped to the ninth cause of death overall. Surely that would have seemed to Bastiat a sign of progress: in many past centuries, tuberculosis was the number-one killer. Bastiat would have noticed that in the present day the three leading causes of death are age-related. Men and women of the twenty-first century live long enough to expire from the chronic conditions of old age because infectious diseases don't kill them first, as was the case in all previous centuries.

After mulling what was seen in the study, Bastiat would have been stunned by what is unseen. Violence, he would have exclaimed, is not in the world's top ten reasons for mortality. Since our ancestors fashioned clubs and spears in the antediluvian mists, murder and war have plagued humanity. Now they don't even register as leading causes of death. This is happening in a world under substantial population stress—and possessing plenty of guns.

Violence is not perceived as in decline. The impression given by national news is of a planet where mayhem is ubiquitous. Local newscasts emphasize killings, fires, robberies, and kidnappings, making life seem to consist of little else. New-media platforms react more to crimes than to social progress. Commentators speak of Armageddon approaching: the London-born foreign affairs observer Roger Cohen said in 2014 that people "have never previously felt so uneasy about the state of the world," not even during the Nazi horror. The impression given by the leadership class is of destruction abounding: "The world is in chaos," Henry Kissinger said in 2016. Political candidates speak of murder at unprecedented levels. Running for president, Donald Trump referred often to a "crime wave" making American cities "living hell."

Whatever else he may be, Donald Trump is a media president: he watches TV obsessively—five hours a day in the White House, if writer Elaine Godfrey is right—and tailors himself to others who do, while obsessively trolling social media. In the artificial universe of television, crime just keeps getting worse: decent citizens aren't safe in their homes with the doors bolted. Seniors watch more TV than the young, absorbing the false impression of rising crime, and seniors vote at a higher percentage. Politicians who declare that cities are hellishly dangerous are rewarded with the ballots of seniors who, in most cases, have not themselves experienced the urban revival of the past quarter-century: young people perceive contemporary American cities as safe, but vote in lower numbers than seniors. Speaking to the law students of the University of Chicago in April 2016, Barack Obama said, "No candidate has ever been punished by voters for seeming too tough on crime." Telling older white voters in the suburbs, exurbs, and countryside that downtown areas are nightmarish—"our inner cities are a disaster, you get shot walking to the store," Trump said during the campaign—is a way of appealing to prejudice without mentioning race. Minorities and the young, who have only themselves to blame for not bothering to vote, concede the content of political campaigning to the suburbs, especially, to suburban seniors. The result is that American national political campaigns are heavy on crime, crime, crime while light on issues such as eradicating poverty.

Television takes the same tack. Television news is pitched to senior citizens—that's why the ads are for prescription drugs—and seniors are easily frightened; emphasizing the grim keeps them watching. The entertainment aspect of television leads with violence too. Of top-rated US prime-time television in the 2015–2016 season, ten were crime shows, six were reality programming, four were the NFL, and five were all other categories. Formulaic "procedurals"—scriptwriters' code for the police dramas that dominate prime time—drastically overstate the frequency of murder of middle-class persons. Situations in procedurals may be absurd—young women in miniskirts walk alone down dark alleys. The absurd plots lead to explicit depictions of gore, projected directly into the home in high definition. Though crime dramas are labeled fiction, their proliferation fosters a belief that violent lawbreakers are running wild.

The historical trend is quite different: crime rising during Prohibition, then diminishing, then rising again beginning around 1960, then peaking in the early 1990s and declining since: in some cities, including New York City, declining to record lows. In 1990, some 2,245 people were murdered in New York City—about six homicides per day. By 2016, New York City murders were down to 335—fewer than one per day.

Data from the FBI show that in the United States 1993 was the peak year of the murder wave: from that point, gun homicides are down 49 percent, a figure that includes slight increases in 2014 and 2015. Since that peak year, all forms of violent crime are down almost 300 percent: the federal Bureau of Justice Statistics reports that assault, burglary, rape, and robbery declined almost every year after 1993. Some decline in gun homicide traces to lives saved by improved trauma response. Hospital emergency rooms and emergency medical technicians (EMTs) do a steadily better job. During Memorial Day weekend of 2017 in Chicago, forty-six people were shot, a frightful number, but forty-one survived. Shootings overall are down by almost 75 percent since 1993—a figure that, again, includes the slight increases of 2014 and 2015. Violent crime also is in decline in most places in the world, though horrible exceptions exist—the murder rate in Brazil is seven times that of the United States.

Progress against the scourge of murder may best be seen in the likelihood of a person becoming a victim. In 1990, during the crime wave, one New York City resident in 3,500 was murdered, reason to stay off the streets come nightfall. By 2016 the New York City murder rate was down to one resident in 24,000—in this context the larger the number, the better.

The long view shows that in 1900 one American in 17,000 was murdered. By 1990, the national murder rate had soared to one American in 10,000—roughly the murder rate of the Prohibition years. Since 1990, the US national murder rate has declined almost every year—in 2015 to one in 21,000. That represents a lower murder rate than the nineteenth century, when, according to our collective nostalgia, people were secure walking the street. Today, not only has homicide dropped out of the top ten causes of death in Centers for Disease Control statistics, but it is down to the seventeenth cause of death in the United States, trailing septicemia and "pneumonitis due to solids and liquids."

Yet Americans believe murder is rife, while only hospital personnel worry about septicemia. Gallup has for decades polled Americans on whether violent crime is rising or declining. For fifteen consecutive years before the 2016 election, the majority said crime was increasing. This misperception continued after Trump was sworn in. The Pew Research Center found in a 2017 poll that 70 percent of Americans thought crime was on the rise. To the extent American elections are decided by the seniors' vote, older people who have not themselves been in an urban center in years and who spend hours watching network television's methodical overstatement of criminality may constitute the locus of public belief that street violence is out of control.

As for war, isn't it raging out of control? That is the notion commentators and political leaders inculcate.

Four centuries ago, Thomas Hobbes said leaders want the public to believe war imminent because then people will cede more power to leaders. Variations of this view have been stated since Hobbes's day. Abraham Lincoln and Franklin Roosevelt were great presidents, but both utilized war as an excuse to claim for themselves extraordinary powers that most likely were not necessitated by the national interest, or at minimum, not necessary for the reasons Lincoln and Roosevelt invoked. John Adams, John Tyler, James Polk, William McKinley, Woodrow Wilson, Lyndon Johnson, Richard Nixon, Ronald Reagan, George W. Bush, and Barack Obama employed war or the prospect of war as rationalization for subverting law or Congress or both. Leaders of many nations, including of liberal democracies, have cited war or the prospect of war as reasons they should be granted extraordinary authority, or exempted from accountability. After the September 11, 2001, attacks on New York City and Washington, DC, military response against the government of Afghanistan was essential. But were extraconstitutional provisions really required? Were wiretaps, surveillance, and invasion of Iraq, which played no role in 9/11, really needed? Yet the younger President Bush asked for special authority that could not be reviewed by other branches of government. The assumption that war grows worse is to the advantage of leaders who seek more power or wish to divert public attention from corruption, bungling, and cronyism.

Like crime, war is in a cycle of decline. Horrifying scenes from South Sudan or Syria are atypical. The Conflict Data Program at Uppsala University in Sweden finds that over the last twenty-five years, the frequency, intensity, and harm of war have been diminishing. In the last twenty-five years, about two million people have been killed by all forms of organized battle—state-versus-state, nonstate violence by terrorists and warlords, and what Uppsala calls "one-sided" fighting, in which an armed group oppresses the helpless. Two million war deaths in twenty-five years is an awful number—but in the one hundred years of the twentieth century, 160 million people died because of wars. In the most recent quarter-century, then, people have been killed by wars at 5 percent of the rate of the twentieth century.

Taking into account population growth, if war deaths were as likely now as in 1960, about 400,000 people would have been killed by combat in 2015. Instead, about 100,000 perished. No one could think of this as a success story—the number is horrifically large. Yet it represents a step in the right direction. The 2015 statistic equates to one person in 70,000 globally dying because of combat, either directly as soldiers or civilian victims of fighting or indirectly because of embargoes and shortages caused by fighting. Figures for other recent years are about the same. One war death in 70,000 is among the smallest such rates in human history. The 2015 figure of a one-in-70,000 chance of dying because of war was much lower than that year's chance of dying in an automobile or bus crash. It is not hyperbole to say that in the current generation, roads have been more dangerous than armies.

Yet politics and public perceptions are more attuned to what people believe than to what is true. For example, in American elections, Democrats claim Republicans want to despoil the environment, while Republicans claim Democrats want military weakness. Neither is true, but both are believed, and so endlessly repeated. Because what people believe matters more than what is true, promoting claims that crime and war are rampant can be a means for political leaders to win votes while attaining the power and money so many seek to the exclusion of all else.

SO WHY *ISN'T* VIOLENCE WORSE? At his University of Chicago talk, Barack Obama said, "No one can fully explain the remarkable decline of crime." This is the consensus of law enforcement agencies and academic criminologists.

At the University of Chicago, the president, entertaining edgy questions from the nation's top law students, went into extensive specifics regarding public policy on crime, anti-terrorism, and combat. Obama was candid, but because he analyzed public policy rather than denouncing political opponents, most news organizations ignored the event: nothing bores media more than public policy. Had Obama insulted someone, every newscast would have led with that, while Facebook would have lit up. That both news media and social media prefer fist-shaking over reasoned discourse helped set the stage for the insult-a-matic Trump candidacy later that year.

No one can fully explain the remarkable decline of crime. Maybe the rise was caused by profusion of crack cocaine, whose users become dependent, vicious, and impulsive. Maybe the rise traces to lax handgun laws. Few crimes are committed with shotguns or rifles: the implements of crime are knives and handguns, the latter having two uses, as concealed weapons in felonies and as sidearms for law enforcement. (Soldiers are not fond of sidearms; extra rifle ammunition is more valuable to a soldier.) Maybe crime rose owing to welfare laws that had the unintended consequence of driving fathers out of the homes of poor families, depriving boys of role models other than the local drug dealer: young males without fathers present in their lives are more likely to commit acts of violence than other types of persons. Maybe crime rose in response to adulation of killing and rape in films and television marketed by Fortune 500 companies. (Cinematic producers stopped showing cigarettes because viewers are impressionable, yet increased glamorization of violence, including by posing stars with guns: the result was less smoking and plenty of shooting, exactly what Hollywood encouraged.) Maybe limousine liberals are to blame for coddling criminals. Maybe people simply were growing evil.

Reacting to the crime wave, police departments began to employ new tactics. Among them were CompStat, a system that assigns officers based on crime patterns rather than traditional beats. New York and other cities switched policing emphasis to enforcement of concealed-weapon restrictions, so street punks hesitate to carry. Following a ballot initiative, California, the largest state, made criminal sentences much harsher, adding a three-strikes standard; other states matched. Congress enacted mandatory-minimum laws; many states matched, and violent crimes generally are under state jurisdiction. A series of Supreme Court decisions ended most suppression of evidence: today prosecutors convict, or attain guilty pleas from, more than 90 percent of criminal defendants. President Bill Clinton backed 1994 legislation that expanded federal authority against lawbreaking, funded additional police, increased sentences, and applied capital punishment to more offenses. New technology, including DNA identification and cell-phone tracking, made catching offenders more likely. More people, especially minority males, went to the slammer, where they stayed longer. In 1970, one American in 500 was in prison. On the day the Clinton crime bill passed, one in 200 was incarcerated. By 2008, one American in 125 was behind bars—the highest incarceration rate in the world.

Stricter laws and more people jailed might seem an open-and-shut explanation of crime decline. Former New York City Police Commissioner Raymond Kelly contends that stop-and-frisk, a tactic employed by his department during the crime crackdown, saved about 7,000 African American and Hispanic lives, via the portion of the Big Apple homicide reduction that is attributable to confiscation of illegal weapons discovered during pat-downs. In 2016, Bill Clinton was jeered by Black Lives Matter activists when he defended the 1994 crime bill: Clinton responded by noting the legislation's leading impact was to save black lives, since African American are more likely to be murdered than whites. Not all steps taken against the homicide wave were harsh. The crime reporter Joseph Goldstein has noted that homicide has declined by a third in hard-bitten Camden, New Jersey, helped by a "Hippocratic ethos" of policing in which officers are tasked to protect suspects as well as victims.

Yet crime declined at about the same rates in cities that did not change policing tactics as in those that did. Crime has declined in cities that are about the same size and demographics as Camden but employ dramatically different police strategies. Crime declined at about the same rate in Canada as the United States, though Canadian statutes are relatively lax and Canada incarcerates only one person in 900. Crime continued to decline in New York City as, beginning in 2013, street stops by the NYPD went down about 85 percent. Homicide rates have been diminishing in most though not all of the world, regardless of laws, sentence severity, or policing tactics. Guatemala, Honduras, Mexico, and a few other nations have seen homicides rise: most nations have seen murder become less frequent, including El Salvador and Nicaragua, not long ago violent lands.

IS THE UNDERLYING REASON FOR less crime the reduction of lead in products and pollution? Lead is a potent toxin, associated with reduced IQ and loss of impulse control. Leaded paint can peel off walls and be eaten by children. Beginning in the 1920s, lead was blended into gasoline to boost octane. When consumer use of gasoline soared following World War II, lead levels of the atmosphere rose—and though most toddlers don't eat peeled paint, everyone breathes, rendering atmospheric lead an exposure pathway. Through the 1960s, the amount of lead in the air of most nations went up—and when children born into leaded air became teens, they committed violent crimes.

In 1976 the United States banned new cars that require leaded gasoline; in 1978 the United States banned leaded paint; in 1995 the United States banned leaded gasoline. Levels of airborne lead declined significantly—then when children born under clear skies became teens, they were less likely than their predecessors to commit violent crimes. During about the same period the European Union, and most nations, banned lead in fuels, paint, and many industrial applications: in almost every case, crime decline followed. As of this writing, leaded gasoline, the primary cause of exposure to lead, remains on sale only in Afghanistan, Algeria, Iran, Iraq, Myanmar, North Korea, and Yemen: all troubled societies. Most US and European residential buildings now are free of lead-based paint. West Baltimore is an exception, with many residential buildings where old leaded paint has not been removed: and West Baltimore has a crime rate higher than US averages.

If lead was the principal culprit in the increase of violent crime, the abolition of lead is exhibit A for the value of reform. Once, internal combustion engines required leaded fuel to function properly. Now they don't, owing to superior fuel chemistry, improved engine designs, better engineering of refineries, and the enactment of regulations whose benefits far exceed their costs.

As violent crime declines overall, it is persistent in some places. In 2016, Chicago had more homicides than Los Angeles and New York City combined. Chicago endured 762 murders that year, more than double the number of murders in New York City, which is far larger. Brooklyn has about the same population as Chicago, and about the same mix of ethnicities and incomes: yet Brooklyn has transformed from violent to tranquil, while Chicago's 2016 murder rate was quadruple that of Brooklyn. New York City boroughs have more police officers per capita than Chicago. Handguns are readily available in Indiana, a short drive from the Chicago city line: in New York state, a strong background-check regime catches most felons who attempt to purchase firearms, while there's no easily reached nearby state with an underground market for handguns. Perhaps most telling, the NYPD is renowned for high standards in hiring, training, and diversity, while the CPD does not excel in any of these categories. This suggests an obvious reform—raising standards for hiring, training, and diversity of a police force reduces crime.

Most Chicago murders are gang-related, with one-third of the city's homicides occurring in a few neighborhoods. Gang-infested neighborhoods and low-quality policing are a poisonous mix. In 2016, after Chicago police officials were compelled to admit that they and City Hall staged an elaborate cover-up of film of an unarmed seventeen-year-old African American being shot to death in the back by a policeman, CPD signed an agreement that essentially compels the department to make the same number of investigatory stops of white males as minority males. But as the policing analyst Heather MacDonald has noted, since 77 percent of homicide suspects in Cook County are African American, police there ought to be stopping more black males than white males. When a police department's standards are low and its record of performance is poor, racism is assumed, which further complicates protection of public safety.

A SURPRISING FACTOR IN THE crime decline may be the cell phone. Until recently, when a crime, fire, or injury occurred, bystanders had to either search frantically for a pay phone or pound on doors, hoping someone inside would be home and could call for help. Today when there is a crime or crash, the nearest police dispatcher knows in thirty seconds. The post-1990s crime decline is almost universal—what else has become almost universal during roughly the same period? Large numbers of men and women have begun to carry a device that allows instant contact with 911 or 999. Criminals are now more likely to be caught and taken out of circulation—or to be deterred by the knowledge they are surrounded by people who can summon law enforcement.

In the last ten years, the proliferation of the video-capable smartphone has changed the perception of policing. For generations, dark-skinned Americans have been saying police either do not protect them or treat them too harshly. As Paul Butler, a law professor at Georgetown University, has written, "The NAACP was founded in 1909 partly in response to the federal and state governments turning a blind eye to white violence against blacks." The front page of a March 1954 edition of the *New York*

Times carried a story about blacks being routinely abused by police, and not just in the South. Often there was little proof of mistreatment of African Americans by law enforcement. Now that practically everyone carries a video camera, visual evidence exists of police brutality. Eric Garner, the unarmed African American man choked to death by police in 2014 while shouting that he couldn't breathe; Walter Scott, the unarmed African American man shot to death in the back in 2015 by a policeman—filmed proof of outrages such as these cause some, especially those born after the homicide wave crested, to suppose that the crime decline has been caused, not by positive reforms such as lead elimination, but by oppression.

Even one unjustified shooting by law enforcement is a moral offense and a legal wrong. But cell-phone videos create the impression of a shootings-by-police rampage, when statistics tell a different story. Forty years ago, NYPD officers shot and killed about ninety people per year; as the crime wave crested twenty-five years ago, the NYPD was down to killing about thirty suspects per year. In 2015, the most recent year for which statistics are available, New York City officers killed eight people. In most cities, including Chicago, killings of suspects by police officers are in long-term decline. (Police in Dallas and Philadelphia are more likely to shoot to kill than officers in Chicago; why is another of the many puzzles on this subject.)

There is no unitary database of shootings by the many federal, state, and local law enforcement agencies of the United States—clearly, better data are needed. For 2016, the *Washington Post* assigned reporters to collect information about the use of deadly force by and against police. The *Post* found 963 Americans were killed in 2016 in confrontations with law officers. Most of them, 88 percent, were wielding a weapon when shot by police; 5 percent were known to be unarmed, making the shooting unjustified both by law and by law enforcement ethics; in the other 7 percent of instances, the situation was ambiguous.

That works out to forty-eight innocent Americans killed by police in 2016—a deeply troubling number, but not rampant slaughter. That year an unarmed American had a one in 6.5 million chance of being killed by a law enforcement officer, putting unjustified killing by police in the same risk-of-dying category as an American's risk of dying in a commercial airliner crash. Also in 2016, 64 of the nation's 900,000 law-enforcement officers were shot to death in the line of duty, a one in 14,000 chance of a police officer being killed by a civilian. Thus, in 2016, a law enforcement officer was fifteen times more likely to be killed while trying to keep the peace than a blameless civilian was likely to be killed by a bad cop. The numbers just don't show the innocent being gunned down left and right by out-of-control lawmen—which is what many Americans seem to think is happening.

About the same time the ubiquitous cell camera created a sense that police misbehavior was rampant, many, including federal judges appointed by Republican presidents, began to say that US sentencing and incarceration standards had become excessive: especially, were harsh on the sort of street drug crimes committed by the disenfranchised while forgiving of the sort of white-collar crimes committed by the privileged. In 2012, another California referendum softened the state's three-strikes law: voters rightly concluded that punishment had gone too far. In 2015, the Supreme Court ruled some aspects of mandatory-minimum sentencing unconstitutional. Conservative thinkers and politicians, including Bruce Rauner, the conservative Republican governor of Illinois, began to advocate shorter sentences; an end to the assumption—sometimes, the statutory requirement—that released felons not be hired; and relaxed parole and bail standards.

Today one American in sixty is under parole or another form of legal supervision, the highest rate in the world. Cash bail increasingly is seen as a way to ruin the life of someone who has not been convicted of a crime. A poor or working-class person who can't post bail may lose his or her job, or family, before the system gets around to saying the words "not guilty," small consolation at that point. Legislatures have been moving, haltingly, in the direction of more discretion for judges, owing to rising awareness that in a mandatory-minimum situation, how the prosecutor charges the suspect is more important than how the jury weighs the evidence. Gilad Edelman noted in 2017, "While legislatures write the laws and cops make the arrests, it's prosecutors who decide what a defendant will be charged with," and the charge, which in many cases the judge or jury cannot alter, determines the sentence. A prosecutor may throw the book at a disenfranchised person by piling on every obscure charge—there are 300,000 laws in the United States, many that a citizen would have no common-sense way of knowing exist—or may undercharge a well-connected person by allowing a guilty plea to a minor offense in exchange for dropping serious accusations.

Criminology studies consistently show that the likelihood of being caught and punished is a better deterrent than severity of punishment. That is, a person's belief, "If I rob this store I will be caught and sent to jail" deters better than a person's belief, "If I rob this store there is a tiny chance I will spend decades behind bars." The strong moral and religious arguments against capital punishment are joined by the practical argument, that its deterrent effect is slight compared to the deterrent provided by effective policing. That is, a person's belief, "If I commit murder I will be caught and spend the rest of my life in jail" deters better than a person's belief, "If I commit murder there is a tiny chance I will end up strapped to a gurney."

That potential criminals increasingly believe they will not escape judgment may in the end be the first reason for the crime decline. Closed-circuit cameras, tracking of cell phones, DNA matching, and other advances have made offenders more likely to be caught and convicted. If certainty-of-punishment has been increased, degree of punishment can be reduced, and rehabilitation efforts redoubled. In 2015, even the conservative heavyweights Charles and David Koch said they favored shorter sentences, less incarceration, and more emphasis on rehabilitation. Most reforms needed to control crime are already in place: what's needed now is reforms to help criminals straighten out.

TERRORISM IS A FORM OF crime that torments society. Sadly, this sin is not new—during the 1970s, terror bombings conducted by far-left fanatics were as common in Europe and the United States as are terror attacks conducted today by jihadist fanatics. Even taking into account the 2015 and 2016 attacks staged in France by jihadist hate groups, in recent years a resident of France has been less likely to die in a terror attack than in the 1970s and 1980s. Part of the intended effect of terrorism is to create the sense that sudden killing of the innocent is ubiquitous; objectively this is not true.

Present-day terrorism mainly occurs outside the United States and Europe: that doesn't make it any less bad, just belies the news-media and social-media sense that America and Europe are the places besieged by violence by jihadist hate groups. From January 2015 to summer 2016, 28,700 people worldwide died in terror attacks. Ninety-eight percent of the victims were in Africa, Afghanistan, the Middle East, or Pakistan.

At this writing, since the horror of the 9/11 attack, 123 people in the United States have been killed by terrorists. In the same period, 850 people in the United States were killed by lightning, rendering an American seven times more likely to die from a lightning bolt than a terrorist crime. As the social-justice advocate Nicholas Kristof has noted, since 9/11, some 16,000 American women (and a few men) have been murdered by their husbands, rendering American husbands 130 times as deadly as terrorists. Add the death toll of 9/11 and American husbands still are five times as deadly as terrorists. Starting at the year 2000, in order to include the horror of 9/11, and counting through 2016, about 530,000 people in the United States died in traffic crashes and about 3,000 in domestic-soil terror attacks, rendering an American 175 times more likely to be killed by a car than by a terrorist.

Of course, we choose our cars and our spouses, while terrorism is imposed by others, and there is a certain lucidity in fearing what we cannot control more than familiar hazards like the family sedan. Terrorism has the look of the demon in its eye, while natural threats like lightning operate without purpose, and most car crashes are accidental.

Still, terrorism as a menace is exaggerated in public understanding. Not only does the news-media–social-media nexus highlight terrorism to call attention to themselves, politicians do too. Shortly after 9/11, Rudy Giuliani, then mayor of New York City, said "dozens and dozens" of mass-casualty catastrophes on the same scale were sure to happen in the United States soon. His statement almost had a wistful quality, since if there had been additional attacks of the magnitude of 9/11, people like Giuliani would have received more power, prominence, and money. Thomas Hobbes would have understood.

*   *   *

WAR HELPS PUBLIC OFFICIALS ATTAIN more power, and pretending terrorism is everywhere helps public officials in a prosaic way—by justifying
the personal security they, but not taxpayers, now enjoy. When I lived
on Washington's Capitol Hill in the 1980s, it was easy to wander into
the US Capitol to knock on the door of a member of Congress. Women
and men ran the building's grand steps for exercise or took bag lunches
for picnics on those steps. Post-9/11, the US Capitol is ringed by fortifications, with casual access banned. Some statehouses and city halls have
become fortresses, while many federal, state, and even local government
administrative offices are elaborately defended. Ostensibly such measures
are to keep terrorists out; the primary impact is to keep average people out
so lawmakers and officials can interact exclusively with lobbyists, publi-
cists, and donors. Some of the rise in political anger since the turn of the
twenty-first century must trace to the barriers now interposed between
average people and the governing class.

Post-9/11 security buildups in the United States and Europe may have
saved lives; it is impossible to know what might have happened without
the new emphasis on guards, metal detectors, surveillance, and barriers,
which may have had the welcome side effect of also reducing street crime.
The political scientist John Mueller of Ohio State University estimates
that since 9/11 the United States has spent $1 trillion on security against
terrorism, most of the cost benefiting government insiders rather than
average people. Dana Priest, author of the book *Top Secret America*, believes that the post-9/11 enlargement of intelligence agencies and their
personnel—she calculates that the United States has 854,000 direct or
contractor employees whose work is classified—cost another $2 trillion.
The New Republic noted in 2010:

For security advice, the president now has a secretary of defense, a secretary of state, a director of national intelligence, a national security adviser,
a Central Intelligence Agency, a National Security Council, a President's
Intelligence Advisory Board, a National Security Agency, a Defense Intelligence Agency, separate Air Force, Navy, Marine, Army, and even Coast
Guard intelligence commands, a National Counterterrorism Center, an

FBI Directorate of Intelligence, a State Department Bureau of Intelligence and Research, a National Reconnaissance Office, and a National Geospatial-Intelligence Agency. Even the Treasury Department has an Office of Terrorism and Financial Intelligence.

The new headquarters in Springfield, Virginia, of the National Geospatial-Intelligence Agency (NGA) is the third-largest US government building. Most voters don't know the agency exists, let alone what it does. (The NGA makes hyperdetailed topographical maps, including of the private property of Americans, and at great expense compiles aerial and satellite photographs hauntingly similar to the ones Google Earth gives away free.) If security and intelligence investments have cost the United States a total of about $3 trillion since 9/11, that represents about 1.5 percent of GDP through the period. Add 1.5 percent to the US GDP, and growth would improve from pallid to bullish.

Martin Dempsey, a retired Army general who was chair of the Joint Chiefs of Staff and is now a professor at Duke University, said in 2016 that resilience against terrorism—not giving up the Western way of life—is more important than physical security. The mainstream media response to terrorism—endless-loop replays of sobbing victims, flashing red chyrons reading TERROR ALERT! TERROR ALERT!—is, as the Turkish-born social scientist Zeynep Tufekci of the University of North Carolina has written, "literally the goal of terrorists." In May 2017, after a suicide bomber from a jihadist hate group killed children at a pop concert in Manchester, England, BBC TV went round-the-clock with replays of bloodied victims fleeing the scene while major US networks flew anchors and production teams to Manchester to air the next evening's news from the attack site, all featuring multiple views of screaming crowds. There is tremendous emphasis in the West on physical security against terrorist violence, not as much emphasis on resilience. The resilient response in the aftermath of an attack would be a presenter staring forward, stating the hard facts, without sensationalist video—surely without images of panic that fairly plead with fanatics to strike again. Probably there is little relationship between public reaction and street crime, but public reaction is the purpose of terrorist crime. Resilience is the correct response.

There is strong desire for a clear explanation of why nearly all forms of crime have moderated: especially, for a narrative tied to single causes. But it may be that *no one can fully explain the remarkable decline of crime*—a frustrating conclusion unless the theories of the cognitive scientist Steven Pinker, to be addressed at the close of this chapter, ultimately will provide the explanation.

Why war is in decline seems, by contrast, straightforward.

JOSHUA GOLDSTEIN, A RESEARCHER AT the University of Massachusetts at Amherst, has spent years swimming upstream against conventional wisdom by documenting the decline of combat: there has been no direct great-power combat since the Korean War armistice of 1953, and no proxy great-power combat since the Soviet Union folded in 1991. Especially, Goldstein documents the unseen aspects of war—what has not happened. Since the close of World War II, atomic weapons have not been used. The last large naval battle was in 1944; the last large air battle was in 1972. Since the 1980s, there have been no naval battles and only a few brief air battles, though bombs continue to be dropped, mainly by the United States. A brief dogfight above Syria in 2017 was the first air-to-air combat in the world in the twenty-first century. Since the early 1990s, there have been no large battles involving tanks. The obliquely named "nonstate actors" continue to cause horrors, but combat between regular armies with tanks and artillery backed by air power—the most destructive kind of fighting—has nearly disappeared, a gigantic improvement compared to the period from 1914 to the 1991 Gulf War, when combat between regular armies with armor, cannons, and bombers was the norm across the world. And the Cold War never went hot: an achievement largely taken for granted, involving what did not happen.

Arms buildups are a danger sign: they preceded both world wars, the Polish-Soviet War, the Korean and Vietnam Wars, Arab attacks on Israel, and two horribly destructive conflicts little known in the West, the Iran-Iraq War and the three-way war among China, Cambodia, and Vietnam. In recent decades, arms buildups have become the exception, with the centuries-long international arms race seeming to wind down. The

Stockholm International Peace Research Institute, which tracks this issue, reports that since 1988, global per-capita military spending has declined 28 percent. Almost all nations today devote less than 2 percent of their GDP to arms and armies. Until the 1980s, the global average was 3.4 percent of GDP. In 2016, Americans spent more in restaurants ($780 billion) than their government spent on the defense budget ($610 billion). If only nations always viewed restaurants as more important than artillery!

Crime and war conjoin in being made, by improving communications technology, to seem more prevalent, even as they decline. The first news minicam was switched on in Los Angeles in 1974. Until then, television required elaborate laying of cables: this meant there were few live images of fighting or disasters. Today television has the ability to beam live images from whatever place in the world is plagued by combat, while hundreds of millions of people carry miniature video recorders that need mere seconds to broadcast images to social media accessible worldwide—a democratization of reporting that serves society in many ways but also emphasizes the negative over the positive. Not long before her 1989 death, the eminent historian Barbara Tuchman wrote, "After absorbing the news of today, one expects to face a world consisting entirely of strikes, crimes, power failures, broken water mains, stalled trains, school shutdowns, muggers, drug addicts, neo-Nazis and rapists. The fact of being reported multiplies the apparent extent of any deplorable development by fivefold to tenfold." Tuchman said this before the advents of the ubiquitous Web and tiny inexpensive smartphones with more capability than a dish-equipped news van of a generation ago. Imagine what she'd think today.

Rapid proliferation of live images of terrible things gives the impression that the scourge of combat is expanding, though society has been going through long stretches without the hands of militaries wrapped around each other's throats. In 2016, Colombia came to (uneasy) terms with rebel groups, ending a fifty-two-year civil war. A remarkable moment passed little noticed: there was no war anywhere in the Western Hemisphere. Juan Manuel Santos, president of Colombia, said that year, "Far from being a world at war as many people believe, we inhabit a world where five out of six people live in regions largely or entirely free of armed conflict."

*   *   *

THE DECLINE IN THE FREQUENCY and intensity of war, and of per-capita arms spending, is only about a quarter-century old, not enough to represent a fundamental shift. There were quarter-century periods of general peace in the past too, as well as past hopes, dashed, that great-power battle was no more. Yet several indicators suggest the arrow regarding warfare does point in a positive direction.

One is the dying gasps of colonialism. In addition to being morally wrong, colonialism bred violent conflict: today almost all former colonies are independent, which lessens war. Consider Asia, which for more than a century was in continuous conflagration, with a seeming knock-out tournament of colonial oppression, invasions, and counterinvasions in China, Indonesia, and the several nations of Southeast Asia by England, France, Germany, Japan, Russia, and the United States. Today, beyond the Demilitarized Zone between the Koreas, Asia is largely free of armed conflict. What's the difference? Colonialism in Asia has ended. Tensions remain, including in the South China Sea. But tensions are a lot better than air strikes.

The one-sixth of the world's population still plagued by war lives in a band stretching from Nigeria across sub-Saharan Africa through the Middle East to Afghanistan and Pakistan, plus the southeastern corner of the Balkans. These are the places where colonialism has not ended and where feudalism, a stepchild of colonialism, still obtains. They are also the places where advanced militaries (Russia in Crimea, Syria, and Ukraine; the United States throughout the Middle East; Turkey in Syria and Iraq) continuously make matters worse, whatever their intentions may be.

For a century, the Middle East and the Maghreb region of Africa have been locked in ceaseless cycles of colonialist violence stoked by American, British, French, Ottoman, and Russian meddling, cycles of violence that include, in Iraq since 1990, about the same explosive power from bombs, shells, and rockets as was used against the Axis in Europe in World War II. Yet American leaders cannot understand, just cannot fathom, why civil society does not develop in the Fertile Crescent of antiquity.

Constant outside military interference has prevented the Middle East and the Maghreb from entering modernity in economics, education, and democracy. Imagine if, beginning a century ago, great powers had dropped bombs and sent marines into the US Northeast at about the same rate as foreign militaries have flailed at the Middle East since the victors decided to carve the region up into spoils at the conclusion of World War I. Had the United States suffered the same degree of constant attack as has the Middle East, today New York City, Boston, and Washington, DC, would be pitted moonscapes without functioning schools, courts, or hospitals, and without legitimate employment. Gangs would roam the ruins, preying on those too poor to flee. Perhaps the gangs would spout some half-baked ideology to justify their depredations. The thugs ruling the remains of New York City would be akin to ISIS, just using a different acronym.

The departure of foreign powers was essential to the development of the young United States. For Americans to think the Middle East cannot make the same transition to self-government that the United States once made not only is paternalistic. It is futile, given Americans observe, after phenomenal expenditure of blood and treasure in Iraq, that our brilliant master plan for the Middle East does not work.

History shows that successful civil societies cannot take root until foreign powers depart. China, France, Japan, and the United States spent a century trying to control Vietnam; no matter what was blown up or who was bribed, no control was achieved and no civil society developed. What worked is when the colonizers left, America being the last to disengage: two generations later, Vietnam is prosperous, friendly, and on track to democracy. World War II showed the folly of wars of conquest; Vietnam taught the folly of thinking bombs can solve political problems; it is time these lessons were applied to the Middle East and the Maghreb. If the great powers simply were to stop interfering in these places, violence there might enter a cycle of decline. A fresh set of target coordinates is not the solution.

A FEW GENERATIONS AGO, WHEN war was rampant, most nations lacked government based on restrictive constitutions. Today most nations have constitutions—of varying qualities of course—and today prosperity mainly rises while combat mainly declines. The Yale University historian

Timothy Snyder has noted, "A common American error is to believe that freedom is the absence of state authority." So long as state authority is limited by constitutional law, the existence of government is a social good, advancing freedom. The contemporary nations with legally limited governments that protect individual rights and borders but do not seek conquest are the peaceful and prosperous ones. Those nations without stable governments, or with governments of men not laws, have always been, and are now, the unhappy places in the world.

"That government is best which governs least," the motto of Henry David Thoreau, is misinterpreted in American political mythology as longing for no government. The longing, rather, should be for restricted government controlled by laws that are clearly stated and may not be ignored by fiat. The Polish writer Stanislaw Lem introduced the concept of "warsphere," places where people endlessly fight because they don't know how to stop. The nations in the contemporary warsphere that stretches from Nigeria to Pakistan via the Middle East lack stable governments limited by constitutional law. Americans, Europeans, and others who enjoy the rights and protections of rule by laws not men must bear in mind, to twist on Ronald Reagan, government is not the problem—when properly restricted, government is the solution.

FOR THE LAST CENTURY, EACH time dictatorship and democracy went to war, democracy won. The shrinking of combat has happened at about the same time as the enlargement of democracy. Of course, the fact that two developments occur at the same time does not establish that one causes the other. But the twin trends of more democracy and less fighting seem too striking to be unrelated. The expansion of free-market/free-speech democracy diminishes war.

Family size has been in a century-long cycle of decline in nearly all nations and may relate to the fading of war. (Because of the very large number of young people in the world, global population is nearly certain to keep rising for at least several decades, even as average fertility goes down.) In 1800, there were seven live births per British woman and little public opposition to Britain's many wars and seizures of territory by force: England fought war after war after war with seemingly inexhaustible manpower. By 1900, live births per British woman were down to three and conscription to fight in World War I became controversial. Families with a lot of boys could lose one to combat; parents of small families might feel very differently. Today, in the Western nations, live births average a little under two per woman. Offspring are increasingly precious to parents, who don't want to hand children over to the state to die in some pointless battle staged so that some aging egotistical leader can shift blame. Fertility per woman remains highest in the warsphere nations. When families become smaller in central Africa and the Middle East and Pakistan, fighting will decline.

Nuclear deterrence mitigates against war and involves an obvious gamble with the fate of humanity. Europe, flashpoint of both world wars and of many prior armed conflicts, has known peace since the nuclear bomb. One might suppose that infernal device is the whole explanation for recent European amity. Yet most European nations do not possess nuclear weapons, and so most could invade neighbors without direct risk of ultimate retaliation. Unless Russia should be classified as part of Europe, in the last half-century the sole Europe-versus-Europe fighting was the 1999 NATO bombing of Belgrade, done to compel Serbian forces to stop the slaughter of innocents in Kosovo—the "one-sided fighting," in Uppsala terminology. The 1999 military operation was an effort by majority-Christian nations to save the lives of Muslims being persecuted by Christians; this never seems to merit mention in the Islamic world. Be that as it may, events of 1999 showed that conventional combat involving nuclear-armed states can occur in Europe without escalating to nuclear confrontation. That conventional military conflict remains possible in Europe, yet almost never happens, is one of the hopeful signs that, as Joshua Goldstein has written, society is "winning the war against war."

The declines of combat and of per-capita military spending go largely unremarked upon, which is a puzzling aspect of our moment. To future historians, the real puzzler may be that the decline of the Armageddon arsenal goes largely unremarked upon. The *Bulletin of Atomic Scientists,* founded by Manhattan Project veterans, calculates that 1986 was the summit year for nuclear warheads: there were 64,449, most held by the United States and Soviet Union. That was ample to end civilization, perhaps end human life: if most of those bombs had gone off, the nuclear-autumn effect would have caused mass extinctions too. As of 2016, the nuclear warhead count was down to 10,215. Since the initial START agreement took effect in 1994, nuclear-arms production facilities in the United States and Russian Federation have run in reverse, disassembling bombs and then melting the components, in view of the other side's inspectors.

The numbers convey that during the lifetimes of millennials, 85 percent of the end-of-days threat has been eliminated. The latest START agreement, ratified by the US Senate 71–26, mandates further reduction to about 4,000 total nuclear warheads in the world; that would reduce the end-of-days threat to 6 percent of a few decades ago. Few things more important have occurred in the lifetimes of recent generations. Yet the news media, social media, politicians, and intellectuals turn up their noses at nuclear deescalation—which represents the unseen, the Armageddon that does not happen.

Speaking in Prague in 2009, Barack Obama called for "a world without nuclear weapons." Would this be good? One need not be a Doctor Strangelove to suppose that for each great power to possess a few plutonium explosives reduces the chance of another world war. No rational leader would issue a nuclear first-strike order, which would consign his or her society to oblivion. The worries are that a maniac will come into possession of a crude atomic device, or that even a relatively constrained regional nuclear exchange will cause nuclear-autumn calamity across the globe. Troubling as these risks are, they represent a huge reduction in the jeopardy faced by Earth when there were 64,449 thermonuclear bombs, and nervous fingers on the triggers.

THE INTERNATIONAL ORGANIZATIONS SO DISLIKED by the political right may be reducing war. In 2016, the United Kingdom voted to withdraw from the European Union, which is notorious for bureaucratic featherbedding and ridiculous decrees: Brussels pronounced that eggs must be sold by the kilo, not the dozen. Yet since the 1957 founding of the European Union (under a different initial name), the 1999 bombing of Belgrade has been the sole Europe-on-Europe military conflict. In the centuries before 1957, there had been more phases with Europe-on-Europe war than without. Now sixty years have passed with one relatively brief battle, after which the victors claimed no territory or reparations. There must be some relationship between the arrival of the European Union and the departure of the European warsphere; our descendants may judge today's continent imprudent for taking the European Union for granted.

The World Health Organization, World Bank, World Trade Organization, International Organization for Migration, Organization for Economic Cooperation and Development, International Monetary Fund, International Federation of the Red Cross and Red Crescent, the fearless emergency-relief group Doctors Without Borders, and the noble anti-poverty group World Vision either came into existence or expanded significantly during the same period war has declined. There must be some relationship. There are plenty of reasons to scoff at the top-heavy administration and cinematic posturing of the United Nations: Americans have a valid complaint that they fund and protect the organization, receiving in exchange ritual denunciations. Yet the period of little great-power battle coincides with the existence of the United Nations. That statement cannot be just some fluke.

The former Pentagon official Rosa Brooks has written, "Today militarily powerful states are far less free than in the pre–United Nations era to use overt force to accomplish their aims." Until the United Nations, the state that invaded another state was opposed only by the other's allies, if allies there were. Now conquest of a neighbor—say, Iraq's 1990 invasion of Kuwait—may be opposed by all other nations. Franklin Roosevelt's vision for the United Nations was to remove the term "world war" from the human lexicon. FDR was no naïf; he knew that full eradication of violence is a dream for the far future. But eradication of world war may be a practical goal for the present. In the one-quarter of a century before establishment of the United Nations, world war happened twice; in the three-quarters of a century since, world war has not occurred.

As time passes, most categories of product rise in quality—stereos, down parkas, craft ales, practically everything is better than before. Diplomacy is rising in quality too. The past knew many diplomatic accords that appeared to resolve disputes, then provided pretext for more war. The 1887 Reinsurance Treaty between Germany and Russia supposedly ensured peace, instead helped start World War I; the Versailles Treaty and its many daughters, such as the Locarno Treaties, became synonyms for fiasco, setting in motion World War II. During the interwar period, treaties appeared to end the naval arms race that dominated great-power military spending, and appeared to ban Germany from militarizing the Rhineland. The former accord was abrogated by the United Kingdom, the latter ignored by France: this gave the signing of treaties a bad name. Many other treaties of the past were not worth the vellum they were written on, among them the 1928 Kellogg-Briand Pact, which claimed to outlaw war. Perhaps foul language and rainy days should have been prohibited too.

But as time passes, the quality of diplomacy improves. The United States and Russian Federation are in the twenty-fourth year of observance of the START agreements, which required both sides to give up the majority of the most powerful and costly weapons ever built. Imagine telling Bismarck or Metternich they'd have to convince kings and emperors to surrender their best weapons. Bismarck and Metternich would have laughed, yet American and Russian diplomats persuaded each other's leaders to turn swords into plowshares—or in this case, into fuel rods that only function in civilian power reactors. The advent of satellite reconnaissance and other advances in electronic intelligence have made it possible for nations to know if treaty partners are cheating; the result is less cheating. The rising quality of international mediation—better-skilled, better-informed diplomats who are painfully aware that major malfunctions of negotiations preceded both world wars—makes for treaties more likely to stick.

Of course, even well-thought-through treaties may fail or be manipulated: as Barack Obama left office, Moscow was weaseling around the rules of an agreement intended to restrict land-launched cruise missiles. In the main, diplomacy improves in quality, while having multilateral organizations lurking in the background gives nations an incentive to resolve disputes before they become international affairs. (Most governments would rather deal directly with another government than dial in the cast of thousands that is the United Nations.) Satellite reconnaissance, available only since the 1960s, and since the 1990s improved in resolution, adds "trust but verify" to treaties in a manner that is nearly impossible for an offending government to evade.

To some extent, the proof that treaties are increasing in effectiveness is seen where accords are absent. In diplomatic terms, World War II did not end until 1990, with the little-known Treaty on the Final Settlement with Respect to Germany. Signed by diplomats meeting in Moscow, this agreement allowed the two Germanys to unify; released claims on them by the Four Powers group of the United States, United Kingdom, Soviet Union, and France; and made the new Germany a liberal democracy, not a police-state. Cold War tensions went down, European prosperity rose, and the end of Soviet despotism was set in motion: after the 1990 agreement on Germany, Russians said, "Why can a nation we conquered have freedom but not us?" The absence of a treaty formally concluding World War II was a little-noted component of Cold War tension and risk; once the treaty was signed, conditions improved for all parties, and the Cold War wound down.

By contrast, the Korean War has yet to end in diplomatic terms: there is no peace agreement, just an armistice that resulted in a cease-fire but no resolution. North Korea remains a destitute dictatorship because its succession of addled tyrants can tell the populace the nation still is at war. The Koreas really need a peace treaty—a class of document that in recent decades has shown itself more valuable than generally understood.

FROM BEFORE THE COMMON ERA until Pearl Harbor, great powers competed at sea as much as on land. Carthage, Rome, and Troy fought regularly on the waters of the Mediterranean. Enormous fleets—the 1588 Spanish Armada boasted 130 ships—plied the oceans, fighting other fleets, seizing prizes, and staking claims to territory. Even in the days of sail, warships crossed the world: early in the sixteenth century, the Chinese and Portuguese navies clashed repeatedly near what's now Hong Kong. For millennia, nations sunk into their navies amounts that might have ended want, only to behold the investments literally sink. During the modern era, Argentina, Brazil, Britain, Chile, France, Germany, Japan, Russia, and the United States have expended groaning chests of treasure on warships. Naval rivalries between Britain and Germany helped ignite both world wars. The Pacific Theater fighting of World War II began in part because of America's 1940 decision to forward-deploy its fleet from California to Hawaii, closer to Tokyo, and in part because Japan placed an existential wager on the maritime theories of Alfred Thayer Mahan, a member of the society of famous persons who proved, following their deaths, to have been wrong about practically everything. Many centuries of an extravagant naval arms race culminated in the October 1944 Battle of Leyte Gulf, where 367 warships and 1,800 aircraft hammered at each other with cannon, bombs, torpedoes, and battleship shells weighing up to 3,000 pounds apiece.

Then the naval arms race stopped. So did naval fighting. The seas have been quiet for nearly seventy-five years, perhaps the longest stretch without bloodshed on the waters since first the sail was hoisted.

Some Argentine and British ships clashed during the 1982 Falklands conflict, and Iranian and Iraqi vessels scuffled around oil tankers during the mid-1980s, but big fights at sea have come to a halt, as has the great-power naval competition. The last time a major naval battle occurred, India was not yet an independent nation, the solid-state transistor had not been invented, and the Dodgers played in Brooklyn. Century upon century of great-power competition at sea ended with a final score of 10–0. That's the number of supercarrier strike groups possessed by the United States (ten) versus the number possessed by all other nations combined (zero).

World War II left the warships of the Axis powers in Davy Jones's locker. The Soviet Union tried to step in with bucket-of-bolts vessels that craved return to port; since about 1960, the US Navy has enforced hegemony over the blue water. "Hegemony" has a bad reputation in political science, assumed always to be undesirable. In this case, the size, power, and competence of the US Navy has banished fighting from much of Earth's surface.

For a half-century, no nation has even attempted to contest US naval dominion. The all-electric, stealth-hull cruisers the United States builds are so advanced—nicknamed "arsenal ships" for their firepower—that no other nation has even experimented with a vessel of this general type. The supercarrier strike groups that America deploys—full-deck, nuclear-powered carriers bearing long-range jets, protected by guided-missile destroyers and screened by nuclear submarines—are so potent, to say nothing of so expensive (naval hegemony cost the United States $155 billion in 2017), that no other nation has tried to build one. China and Russia possess no nuclear supercarriers, and have none under construction. The limited-deck, diesel-powered carriers China began laying down in 2015 will be suitable for patrolling coastal areas but not for the open ocean, while everything the US Navy builds is intended to travel beyond the horizon.

Because the US Navy operates far from the homes of Americans, many are not attuned to its size and might. Soldiers can march in Fourth of July parades, and Air Force fighters can perform Super Bowl flyovers; the Navy's boats can be observed only on the waves. Most who live in other nations are not attuned to the US Navy either. There's no compelling reason to think about a well-behaved military force stationed on the opposite side of the globe.

Under US Navy hegemony, piracy still occurs, but great powers have not seized merchant ships in three generations. That cargo ships whose decks are stacked with containers of valuable goods can steam anywhere without fear of being impounded by a warship is the unseen reason global trade took off, and global trade benefits almost everyone, while reducing war. The reality that the US Navy rules the blue water both reduces a historic cause of conflict and enables the prosperity of the contemporary era.

Speaking at West Point as president, Obama said that the United States does not use its might to acquire territory or seize resources. Instead, American might is employed to pursue what US leaders believe is best for the world. Such beliefs may be wrong, even tragically so. But has any other nation that possessed overwhelming military force ever refrained from using force for conquest or pursuit of riches? That is the unseen question of the oceans—unseen because fighting on the water has stopped.

MANY CONTEMPORARY TRENDS SUGGEST NORMAN Angell was right. Born in England in 1872, Angell was a Labour member of the Parliament who published a 1913 pamphlet—writing of pamphlets was the Instagram post of the time—proposing that economic interconnections of modern states make war counterproductive and futile. One year later the Great War broke out, and Angell was mocked as a false prophet.

But he did not say war would cease: rather, Angell said war had become counterproductive and futile. The Great War was one of conquest: the instigators—Germany, the Austro-Hungarian Empire, and the Ottoman Empire—wanted to steal, seize, and slaughter. Instead they harmed themselves, Germany reduced to starvation and foreign occupation while both empires dissolved, gone with the wind. That's pretty futile. The instigators of World War II, Germany and Japan, wanted to steal, seize, and slaughter. Ultimately they harmed themselves, losing millions of citizens while their cities and industry were bombed to rubble. That's pretty counterproductive. Since the conclusion of the Second World War, national leaders seem to have understood that war has become counterproductive and futile. Angell was right: the world just took longer than he expected to accept his analysis.

Until roughly the turn of the twentieth century, Angell contended, nations enriched themselves by appropriating territory and resources. Certainly Great Britain was enriched by military seizures of places and peoples across the globe. Once the industrial era began, Angell went on, nations could do better in terms of enrichment by manufacturing, growing, and trading than by attacking. To him, this was economics: in bygone times, the blood and treasure required for wars of conquest would pay back in spoils; now the same investment would yield higher returns in commerce. This economic transition makes war counterproductive and futile, except in self-defense, in which case there is no choice. And we observe that in the last roughly seventy-five years, even as population stress has risen and weapons have become easier to forge, wars of conquest have nearly ceased.

Mueller of Ohio State took up Angell's cudgels in an underappreciated 1989 book, *Retreat from Doomsday*, which presciently predicted the Soviet monolith was about to fracture. The Moscow dictatorship, Mueller said, was structured around the archaic concept of great-power battle, and "no society organized around war can endure any longer," a contention that so far has stood the test of time. Mueller proposed that nations trying to conquer each other through war is not an inevitable consequence of human nature, "but merely an idea, and a really bad idea, like dueling."

The economic interconnectedness Angell extolled becomes more deep-seated with each passing year. The predecessor of the European Union, the European Economic Community (EEC), initially was a common market for steel. By giving long-warring nations of Europe an incentive to work together rather than eye each other across gunsights, the EEC caused European states to learn how to cooperate. There had been European trade before, of course, but because barriers and tariffs were punitive, trade could not become a central aspect of an economy. In the years prior to Germany triggering the Great War, exports were less than 20 percent of GDP—the Junkers of that day could have told themselves that seizing what others possessed was more promising than legitimate commerce. Today, according to the World Bank, 47 percent of Germany's GDP is export of goods and services. This much higher rate of trade causes contemporary Teutonic society to be interconnected and peaceful, exactly as Angell dreamed.

The Harvard University political scientist Graham Allison coined the phrase "Thucydides Trap" to express that a rising power (Athens, in his analogy) inevitably comes into conflict with the existing dominant power (Sparta). With the United States today the existing dominant power, China, the rising power, might seem to be stepping into a Thucydides Trap. But Sparta and Athens had little economic interconnection, while there have never been two large economies as entwined as China's and America's.

Factory workers in the upper Midwest complain about how commerce with China disadvantaged them, and they have a point, but that commerce has not only reduced poverty for vast numbers, it may prevent the utter calamity of the United States and China going to war. No scenario can be imagined in which combat between China and the United States does not ruin the economies of both.

Norman Angell would argue that the Chinese have already come to this conclusion and already are determined to avoid the Thucydides Trap. Other than NASA's International Space Station, the most expensive engineering endeavor in history is the South-North Water Transfer Project, a $90 billion mega-aqueduct under construction to solve China's freshwater crunch. This magnificently fashioned system of canals, sluices, and pumps could be rendered worthless in a few hours by America's over-whelming air power. Chinese leaders endorsed the project because they believe war with the United States will not happen. American leaders should believe that too.

CAN WE REALLY BELIEVE ECONOMIC forces have shifted away from war? A leading voice of classical economics was David Ricardo, born in London in 1772. He maintained that at bottom, wealth was control of land, and feared that as the number of people kept expanding but the acreage of land did not, the world would go haywire. Living before the development of high-yield farming, Ricardo assumed a rising population could be fed only by tilling more land; knew the wealth and privilege of the European aristocracy was based on land; knew wars were fought either over land or over access to sea lanes. Aristocrats held land and extracted rent, doing nothing of value themselves, then passed the land to their descendants. The terms "idle rich," "landed family," and "landed gentry" reflect this system, which had been the basis of the European and Asian economies for centuries.

In the Europe of Ricardo's day, it was next to impossible for the average person to acquire land, severely limiting social mobility—which was just the way the aristocrats wanted things. Americans like to think their ancestors came to the New World seeking political and religious liberty: many did, but many sought the chance to own their own land and thereby acquire wealth. To quote again *East of Eden*, of the arrival of white settlers to California, Steinbeck notes that many "had filaments of memories of feudal Europe where great families became and remained great because they owned land," and so kept moving west until reaching a place where they, too, could stake title to large tracts.

In the period before the American Revolution, each year England found itself with more aristocrats but a fixed supply of land for them to be lords and ladies of. As with average people, the solution for aristocrats was the New World. I live in Maryland, whose counties are named for the English nobility receiving tracts of land there: among them Calvert County, for Cecil Calvert, known to history as Lord Baltimore, and Anne Arundel County, for his wife, the Baroness Baltimore. Such awards of land were in effect awards of wealth, because control of land was the primary path to riches. European arrivals and Native Americans clashed over this concept, as the latter did not recognize private ownership of land. The Cherokee leader Sequoyah, who studied and admired the US Constitution, proposed a Cherokee constitution that would shadow America's founding document in every respect except stipulating that land could be owned only by peoples, not individuals. Of course it was not long until settlers and American Indians were fighting, mostly over land.

Because land meant riches, warlords, princes, kings, queens, kaisers, czars, and emperors long waged war for this form of plunder. Unceasing combat for land was a theme of the nineteenth and early twentieth centuries. To cite a few of many examples: the Tonkin War between Qing China and France in 1884 was over who would control the land of North Vietnam; the Balkan Wars that preceded World War I were about land; through World War I, Germany and France fought over control of tracts in East Africa and in Alsace-Lorraine; Austria attempted to seize Mexico in 1864 to expand its land holdings; England's brutal suppression of the Boers in South Africa was mainly about land; Japan and Russia went to war in 1904 over which would possess parcels of land in coastal China; and other wars over land were fought, using modern names, by Algeria, Armenia, Australia, Austria, Bangladesh, Bosnia, Canada, Croatia, the Czech Republic, Egypt, England, France, Georgia, Germany, Greece, Hungary, India, Israel, Lithuania, Macedonia, Morocco, New Zealand, Pakistan, Palestine, Poland, Russia, Serbia, Slovakia, Spain, Syria, Turkey, Ukraine, and the United States.

By the onset of World War II, *lebensraum*—land acquisition—was the openly stated goal of Nazi invasions of Poland and Ukraine. Yale's Snyder has written that Hitler "thought existence meant a struggle for land and for the riches of nature." In the final year of World War I, famine struck the Central Powers as naval blockades prevented food shipments, and Germans lacked sufficient acreage to grow their own. Believing possession of acres the sole means to increase crop production, Hitler wanted more land to produce spätzle and schnitzel for Germany's growing population, saying, "I need the East (Poland and Ukraine) in order that no one is able to starve us again like in the last war." He praised America's "wide-open spaces," noting in a prewar speech that Germany's population density was thirteen times that of the United States. America had enough land to feed its people, Hitler maintained, while Germany did not. This rationalized the quest for eastern lebensraum, which had been a goal of German leaders for decades before the Nazi stain.

Since the middle of the twentieth century, the Green Revolution has decoupled crop production from acreage, followed by the intellectual property revolution decoupling wealth from the riches of nature, and war has declined. Today Germany's population is 20 percent larger than during the Nazi era, and no German worries about where the next meal will come from or eyes the territory of neighboring nations.

In recent generations it has become cheaper to buy than to conquer. Holding land is today just one of many paths to wealth—a longer, winding path compared to investing in start-ups—and while lush topsoil always will be in demand, the politics of scarcity do not apply to food supply, and may never again. Nations that eye each other warily can compete economically to their hearts' content, compiling reserve accounts to purchase equity or real estate in a world where goods move without restraint on the waters and capital can, in most cases, cross borders to a fare-thee-well. Exactly why the United States invaded Iraq in 2003 has never been clear: we can only be sure this was not a war of conquest, as it would have cost noticeably less to purchase all the oil in Iraq than to seize by force that godforsaken country. Broadly across the globe, buying is now cheaper—as well as a lot more practical—than attacking. And war has declined.

At this juncture, it is essential to reiterate that positive trends in lesser frequency and intensity of war and in acquisition of national-scale wealth by economic production rather than conquest are only a quarter-century on. That is not long by the standards of history. Some awful reversal of fortune may be in our future; worse, one of the nuclear powers may make The Big Mistake. For now, we live in a world where all forms of violence are in at least mild decline—some in sharp decline—compared to population rise. And that leads to the theories of Michael Tomasello and Steven Pinker.

*   *   *

Tomasello studies social cognition at Duke University and at the Max Planck Institute in Leipzig. His research finds that although human beings are perceived as insensible to the needs of their fellows, men and women have incentives to behave altruistically: this not only makes for an improved society; it also increases the individual's chance of getting ahead. Tomasello's 2009 treatise *Why We Cooperate* might have been titled *Selfish Reasons to Become a Better Person*. Young children naturally assist each other, his studies show: later, the adult world trains them to focus on themselves. Why must the natural inclination to cooperate be conditioned out of us? The school of thought Tomasello embodies says the world is not fated to perpetual strife: people from many classes and cultures can achieve harmony, or at least stop fighting over every damned thing.

The parallel is to misperceptions of the natural world. People assume nature is a battle to the death of all against all; learning of the wolf who devours the lamb, we imitate this in statecraft, business, dating. But nature is not exclusively predators stalking prey. Many life forms are interdependent, or at least do not interfere with each other. Sugar maples have deep roots that pull up more groundwater than the tree requires, then discharge the water to the surrounding soil, allowing plants such as goldenrod, which has short roots, to live nearby. The presence of goldenrod holds soil in place around the sugar maple. There are many similar examples. "Survival of the fittest" is misunderstood as asserting, "Nature expects the strong to kill the weak." What "fittest" actually means is "best suited to flourish." In this sense, cooperation can be as potent as sharp talons.

Pinker, like Tomasello a psychologist by training, studies cognition at Harvard University. He offers a larger thesis: just as the devices we make gradually improve in quality, morality gradually improves. With each year that goes by, a greater proportion of the human family realizes that crime and war are morally wrong.

"That the Cold War ended without the Soviet Union attacking Europe, despite having the power and opportunity for gains, is one of the bright moments in history," Pinker says. Because the Cold War turning hot did not happen, it falls into the category of unseen, but the didn't-happen aspect should be contemplated. Pinker continues, "The desire for a single narrative makes it hard for people to think about the crime decline, or accept that war is diminishing, because experts cannot in either case create a single narrative around one cause. Another world war could happen of course, but I don't see any fundamental clash of civilizations. And there is no conservation of conflict."

The principle of "conservation of energy" holds that in a closed system, the form of energy can change but not the amount. Until roughly the past half-century, human society behaved as though there were conservation of conflict—the types and locations of disputes and wars might have changed, but the total amount of ill will remained the same. Pinker thinks no. "There is some degree of directionality in the increase in morality—society moving toward more moral awareness," Pinker says. "Sympathy has been looked down on as a secondary emotion, but is the essence of a less violent future. Sympathy is based on understanding that others suffer. This kind of understanding long has existed within families or local groups, but can expand to larger communities, then to the nation, then to humanity as a whole."

Today politicians and commentators are obsessed with driving wedges between identity factions. Pinker views that as a passing fad, inflated at the moment because leaders, entertainers, and the news media have not figured out where they fit in the new globally connected world. "As communication keeps improving and travel grows cheaper and easier, people will expand their circles of sympathy. We won't become kinder to each other because we fear getting caught and punished if we cause harm. More people will accept that causing harm is simply *wrong*."

Views such as these may seem excessively optimistic, and optimism can appear naive. Nightmare scenarios are unnervingly easy to imagine: Japan rearms to counter North Korean missiles, African civil wars intensify, India and Pakistan engage in the misnamed "limited" nuclear exchange, the United States decides to force the budding Chinese fleet back to port, a religious fanatic gets his hands on an atomic bomb. Even if Pinker is right, generations will pass before we may be sure that human morality is increasing. But if the world does embrace the ethical view, rules against violence we impose on ourselves, of our own volition, will be stronger than any rules imposed by courts, police, or armies.

THE SUMMATION OF WHY CRIME and war are in decline must be stated tentatively, so as not to add a jinx: human beings are finally beginning to wise up.

But what happens if our own technology is our undoing?

Chapter 6

Why Does Technology Become Safer Instead of More Dangerous?

MANY REMEMBER CARL SAGAN, a Cornell University astronomer who died in 1996 after becoming, in the United States, the best-known serious academic of his day. Sagan led an accomplished life that included helping design the Voyager project, humanity's first attempt to propel an object beyond the solar system. As *Voyager One* departed our neighborhood for the cosmos, Sagan persuaded NASA to turn the probe's camera back toward Earth. The result was "Pale Blue Dot," perhaps the most striking photograph in the annals of science. From 3.7 billion miles, our home is a faint pinpoint visible in the blue spectrum owing to its unusual—so far, unique—atmosphere of oxygen and nitrogen. Oxygen is highly reactive, so probably oxygenated air will be found only in the presence of a generating process: life, in Earth's case.

Once, Sagan and some colleagues employed a radio telescope to transmit a broadcast asking any distant aliens who heard the message to contact Earth. He believed this would be a wonderful event, because a civilization sophisticated enough to travel the stars would have matured beyond belligerence. Sagan worried about climate change and nuclear brinkmanship, but in the main was an optimist, believing the human adventure has barely begun. A lot's been discovered since 1996 that suggests the adventure will be grand. Were he still alive, Sagan would need to change his signature saying—that there are in creation "billions and billions" of stars—to "sextillions and sextillions."

About the same time the Cornell astronomer was offering optimistic arguments regarding technology, Ulrich Beck, a sociologist at the University of Munich, achieved, in Europe, a similarly high public profile by issuing pessimistic warnings on the same topic. Beck expounded the notion that technology would grow ever more dangerous, inevitably increasing risk, wiping out individuality, and perhaps wiping out life. Technology, Beck contended, was in thrall to the desire of corporations and governments to expand their power using machines, electronics, and chemicals. He thought the term "progress" belonged in quotation marks as the enemy of everything human: science and engineering would be threats even if philosophers controlled them. Beck had a haunting point, that risk, like money, is unevenly distributed—the poor and working class are much more likely to be harmed than the well-off. Before his 2014 death, Beck cheered up a bit, noting the fact that almost seventy years had passed without Europeans massacring each other, which suggested perhaps all was not lost.

Not many decades ago, Beck's view of technology seemed more likely to prove correct than Sagan's. Industrial production choked cities with smog while fouling water. Food products were stuffed with unpronounceable artificial compounds, while toxins leaked into the environment or were deliberately dumped. Doctors' offices—doctors' offices!—contained high-dose X-ray machines that caused birth defects. Children's pajamas were treated with the chlorinated compound TRIS, a carcinogen. Foot travel and horseback had given way to average people owning two-ton projectiles that could accelerate in a blur and be aimed at anyone or anything. At the beginning of the twentieth century, the land speed record was 66 miles per hour; today teenagers regularly exceed that velocity, while listening to music and checking text messages. Millions of people were taking to the air—wouldn't crowded skies translate to mayhem? Crops were doused with pesticides, herbicides, and fungicides; insecticides sprayed willy-nilly over neighborhoods by low-flying planes.

And that was just in civilian life. In military affairs, where danger is the whole point, technology grew steadily more destructive. Fighter planes got faster, tanks more powerful, bombers could carry greater tonnage over longer distances. The firearms possessed by individuals evolved from short-range, single-action revolvers firing low-energy rounds to large-magazine semiautomatics whose bullets fly at 2,000 miles per hour. It seemed technology could only become more dangerous. Perhaps a return to a small-village lifestyle based on horse-drawn plows and smithy shops would save us.

Instead, for the current generation, technology grows safer and cleaner by nearly every measure. Let's start with the greatest technological threat the typical man or woman ever faces—the automobile.

TRAFFIC ACCIDENTS KILL TWELVE TIMES as many people per year, globally, as war. That data point is a recent development in two respects—war deaths are down while exposure to road death is up because worldwide ownership of cars, pickup trucks, and SUVs has increased rapidly. To the extent the automobile has become a leading mortality factor, nations eagerly compete to manufacture this self-propelled pathogen.

Most of the harm done by vehicles—in addition to killing, traffic crashes injure about 50 million people annually—occurs in the developing world, where shabby roads and unmarked intersections increase accident likelihood. Developing-world traffic is made even more hazardous by people driving old cars and trucks that lack safety features, and driving them poorly. Traffic deaths are five times higher, per mile traveled, in Algeria, the Dominican Republic, Gambia, and Thailand than in Italy (known for fast cars), four times higher in India than the Netherlands, three times higher in Jordan than in the United States and Canada.

Safe driving requires self-restraint. Only in the current generation have large numbers of developing-nation citizens attained access to cars, and for many, it is the first time they have felt power in any context. Many don't handle this well, nor do their societies reflect the understanding, established in most Western civic cultures, that voluntary self-restraint is in everyone's interest. For instance, in India and Pakistan—I have driven in both nations and don't recommend the experience—flashing one's headlights does not mean "you go first," but rather, "I would sooner I and my family die a pointless death than yield one inch to you." Broadly across the developing world, roads are more dangerous than in the West, and when a crash occurs, ambulances do not arrive quickly. Fast-growing cities such as Lagos, São Paulo, and Seoul are so paralyzed with traffic that sometimes ambulances cannot reach crash locations.

So is technology or culture to blame for traffic deaths? Technology is the villain if by this is meant the technology that manufactures automobiles and trucks in huge numbers. Global production rose from 8 million in 1950 to 25 million in 1971, to 68 million in 2014—nine times as many cars and trucks were produced that year as in 1950, during a period in which global population trebled, equating to a big increase in the cars-to-people ratio. (The world also makes ten times as many bicycles as in 1950.) For the last several years, China has built more automobiles than the United States. A generation ago in China, only the Party elites rode in cars; now cities experience such gridlock from average people's cars that engineers have been tinkering with buses that travel on stilts suspended above traffic jams. Culture rather than technology is the villain if by culture is meant the modern urge to be somewhere else. Much of the world wastes time racing from Point A to Point B and then back to A. There is a moment in many couples' lives when they say to each other, "Where did the years go?" Increasingly the answer is, "We spent them in the car."

Yet the cars, trucks, and buses themselves become steadily safer. Automobiles in the United States were not required to have seat belts until 1968; using the belts was not mandated until years later. The epidemiologist Devra Davis has documented how, until around 1980, automakers resisted the addition of shoulder harnesses, which are much more effective than lap belts, then resisted the addition of air bags. Automakers also spent a long phase refusing to disclose miles-per-gallon numbers, calling them "trade secrets." Survival, she has shown, was a taboo subject in auto advertising, crashes considered acts of God, not blunders by people or through absence of safety engineering.

How that has changed. Today every make and model of new car sold in North America and western Europe, and most new pickup trucks, has antilock brakes, air bags, and an advance invisible to buyers—a body and frame redesigned to absorb impact without the steering shaft being pushed into the passenger compartment, once the cause of many traffic fatalities. Further invisible to buyers, but present in most new cars and trucks, are pretensioners, originally developed for combat helicopters. When an accelerometer senses the rapid speed decrease that occurs during a crash, a device snugs the shoulder harness against the driver's or passengers' chests, preventing hard jerking motions. Some studies suggest that pretensioners, which are cheaper and simpler than air bags and do not pose the air bag's slight but real possibility of explosion, have made air bags irrelevant.

Many cars now incorporate backup cameras; blind-spot monitoring; traction control and stability control to reduce the odds of spinouts and rollovers; lane-departure monitors that warn the driver about drifting; and automated emergency braking that is activated if tiny radar dishes spot a vehicle or pedestrian to be hit unless the car slows. Like other aspects of technology, radar began as exotic and expensive and now is incorporated at low cost into consumer products. Many new cars have post-collision systems that keep a damaged vehicle moving in a straight line—careening into oncoming traffic changes a fender-bender into a fatality—while using any smartphone aboard to send a crash report to 911 or 999. New cars in the European Union have headlights that illuminate what's around corners; American cars will have them in 2018. Under development are sensors that notice if the driver is drowsy and pixel-beam headlights that function like full-time high beams without dazzling the eyes of oncoming drivers. A gizmo at the bench-test stage called V2V—vehicle to vehicle—will allow cars and trucks to report their positions and speed to computers of nearby cars and trucks.

One of Beck's assumptions about hazards caused by technology was that regulation would not be the antidote, because wealthy corporations would coopt the regulatory process. Once this was true of automakers, who spared no expense to lobby against seat belts and emission standards. Volkswagen tried to dupe government on tailpipe rules, gimmicking supposedly "clean" diesel engines so they would pass regulatory tests and then pollute in daily use: this boomeranged when the company was caught, assessed about $20 billion in fines, and lost market share. Today many automakers instead try to get ahead of regulators. Radar-equipped automated brakes were designed by automakers on their own and began showing up without fanfare. My wife's 2015 Honda has automated brakes—not a fancy car, a

Honda. Toyota has said it will install radar-equipped automatic brakes in all cars, including budget models, by 2018; other automakers say by no later than 2021.

A watershed was the 1994 introduction in the United States of government star rankings for car safety, which changed the sales dynamic. "Automobile manufacturers said star-ranking systems for crash safety would never work," says Stefan Duma, a professor of engineering at Virginia Tech University. "This turned out completely wrong. Star ratings communicate to buyers in a clear, simple way. The ratings caused automakers to rethink engineering, with the goal of getting five-star safety they could advertise. The result is that driving is less dangerous than it used to be."

In the United States, traffic deaths, both per miles traveled and overall, have declined steadily for two generations. Highway deaths peaked in 1973 at 52,000, dropping to 39,000 in 2016. Had highway deaths risen from 1973 to 2016 in sync with population growth and miles traveled, US traffic crashes would have claimed 150,000 lives that year, four times the actual number. Stated the opposite way, today driving in the United States is one-fourth as dangerous as in 1973.

Fatalities are still too high, as are injuries: roughly four million Americans are injured in road crashes annually. An earlier chapter noted the riddle of why ever more Americans receive disability payments even though improved medical science ought to be reducing the ranks of the incapacitated. One reason may be that car safety advances and better emergency rooms save victims of traffic crashes who in the past would have died; then they are discharged from the hospital as disabled persons. Both the personal anguish and the economic harm may go unnoted.

Drunken driving has declined but distracted driving has risen; in 2013, more American teenagers died from texting and driving than from drinking and driving. The National Highway Traffic Safety Administration finds that at least 90 percent of crashes involve an impaired driver, and increasingly, phones and in-car electronics are the impairment, with 3,500 Americans killed, and 400,000 injured, by cell-phone-caused distracted driving crashes in 2015. Had a terror attack in 2015 killed 3,500 Americans and injured 400,000 more, the country would have demanded all-out retaliation: the slowly growing casualty toll linked to Verizon and

T-Mobile was met with a collective national yawn, as there is no single scary episode. Studies show smartphones that work through a car's sound system are just as dangerous as the handheld type—the content of the call, not holding a brick to your ear, is what distracts the driver. A 2016 survey by the State Farm insurance company found 36 percent of drivers admit to texting behind the wheel: that's the number who *admit to an insurer* they do this. Many new cars have the equivalent of a television in the dashboard, able to play images from music videos and, in some cases, movies. Automakers call such devices "infotainment systems," using this term not in their internal marketing memoranda, rather, in the sales pitch.

This leaves little mystery regarding why traffic deaths have not declined even more. While automakers and regulators have made society safer by emplacing in vehicles safety tech such as antilock brakes, both groups have taken the see-no-evil monkey's position regarding smartphones. Most new cars and pickup trucks integrate smartphones into dashboard electronics, enabling distracted driving. Some new cars read text messages aloud; the driver can dictate a response. New cars and pickups with Apple's CarPlay or Google's Android Auto permit users to text while driving by typing messages onto the dashboard touch screen. This madness will end when automakers begin losing liability suits over deaths caused by dashboard infotainment in moving vehicles.

Why the same automakers that have shown commitment to physical safety, such as impact-absorbing frames, are oblivious to electronic risk is something of a conundrum, beyond that buyers are in love with smartphones and want their cars to make the affair a threesome. Government's failure to keep cars from becoming the enablers of texting tragedy is another matter. While both regulators and legislatures have done nothing to prevent mobile texting, government puts its foot down on one electronic option. The dashboard GPS systems of contemporary cars and trucks could warn of ticket-issuing cameras ahead, but they don't. Drivers who want ticket-camera warnings must purchase an after-market device, such as a Garmin, from a vendor with no legal relationship to the automaker. Since the stated purpose of ticket-issuing cameras is to get drivers to slow down—"traffic calming," to European regulators—warnings from the dashboard GPS would seem agreeable, and drivers would respond by slowing down. But local governments would lose revenue. So no built-in ticket-camera warnings that imperil government revenue but plenty of built-in texting tech that imperils lives. Yet despite this, driving gets ever safer.

As cars become safer, they grow cleaner and less wasteful. Ulrich Beck assumed that machinery could gain power—an obvious goal of engineers and corporate managers—only through increased danger and resource waste. This turns out not to be true. Compared to 1970, the typical new-car engine generates significantly more horsepower and torque while using less gasoline per mile and, as an earlier chapter showed, emitting far less smog-forming pollutants. Owing to California's aggressive campaign against smog, and to the Clean Air Act granting the Golden State a trump card versus federal sovereignty, California has been the leader in cleaning up vehicles: when New England states match California rules, as they usually do, that swings the national car market toward clean. In 2017, with just 1 percent of national car sales at zero-emission all-electric, California's Air Resources Board mandated that 15 percent of cars sold there in 2025 must be zero-emission. That makes it likely 15 percent of all cars sold in the United States in 2025 will be zero-emission: Porsche has already gone California one better and said that by that year 50 percent of its California sales will be electric cars. Had Beck lived in California, the leader state in US progressive politics, he might have taken a different view of regulatory power.

Petroleum use by automobiles—these paragraphs concern the United States, world capital of car culture—is in steady decline, though not by enough. In 2015, the US government claimed the fleet average was 34.5 miles per gallon. At the 2015 greenhouse gas negotiations in Paris, Barack Obama boasted about that magnificent 34.5-miles-per-gallon number; EPA regulators and members of Congress, including Representative John Conyers of Michigan, the auto state, joined in the Paris boasting. Researcher Michael Sivak of the University of Michigan found that in 2015 the average new car sold in the United States got 25 miles per gallon, while the fleet average that includes cars, pickup trucks, and SUVs was 17.9 miles per gallon. This is clear progress—a generation ago, new cars sold in the United States averaged 14 miles per gallon and the fleet average was 10 miles per gallon—but hardly the numbers government asserted. The phony achievement Obama boasted about was almost double the actual achievement.

Back when oil imports were a national worry and the mileage performance of Detroit-marque cars was awful, Congress created a regulatory regime that had two goals: the positive goal of pressuring automakers to do better on gas mileage and the deleterious goal of generating a political cover story about progress being greater than it actually was. In 2015, when the official average gas mileage of new US cars was 34.5, a buyer who visited the showroom of any brand would have been hard-pressed to find even one model whose window sticker stated fuel economy of the number that supposedly was the national average.

The US fuel-economy regulatory regime was intended to be incomprehensible, and achieved that end. In 2011, Obama brought top automaker executives to the White House to agree to a fleet average of 54.5 miles per gallon beginning with the 2025 model year. If that level of fuel economy were achieved in the real world, global oil prices would plummet as petroleum demand declined. But since the actual fuel economy of new 2015 US vehicles was 17.9 miles per gallon, raising average performance to 54.5 miles per gallon in 2025 would require a 210 percent improvement in a decade. Considering the 80 percent improvement observed in the previous forty years, this seems pie in the sky.

Sivak's research suggests the 54.5 miles per gallon political hocus-pocus target for 2025 would translate to an actual new-vehicle performance of about 36 miles per gallon. If achieved, such an average would cause major reductions in US oil use, while cutting US greenhouse gas emissions about 10 percent. (In vehicles, carbon dioxide output is proportional to fossil fuel burned.) A big improvement in gas mileage also would offer fuel-purchase savings for consumers. In 2017, Fiat Chrysler unveiled a Pacifica minivan with a plug-in hybrid powertrain: an electric engine that can be recharged plus an internal combustion engine fueled by a gas tank; the vehicle can travel indefinitely on long trips. The car is fast (zero-to-sixty in eight seconds), roomy, has every creature comfort and safety device the mind can imagine—and gets 84 miles per gallon. At

$45,000, the Pacifica is beyond most budgets, and even at that price, Fiat Chrysler takes a loss on each one sold: the new Pacifica is not, in itself, the answer to the 2025 gas mileage target. But the car's existence shows that a big, fast, roomy, high-mileage vehicle is possible on a technical basis. High-mileage, comfortable, safe cars will be a welcome addition to society, especially if Sivak is right that what he calls "motorization"—the combination of how many vehicles are on the road and how many miles they are driven—has peaked, gradually to decline.

CARS ARE NOT ALONE: ALMOST everything—aircraft, ships, locomotives, home appliances, office lighting systems, industrial equipment, factories, power plants themselves—grows more energy-efficient.

Appliance makers in the United States and European Union complained mightily in the early 1970s when government began to impose efficiency standards for refrigerators; just as automakers claimed environmental standards would make cars unaffordable, manufacturers asserted the same about the icebox. The typical new refrigerator sold in 2010 uses 40 percent as much electricity as a 1970 model, while having twice as much storage space and costing one-third as much in current dollars, according to US Department of Energy figures. Gradual replacement of energy-hog iceboxes with efficient models cut people's power bills while, from 1987 to 2011, reducing US electricity demand enough to avoid the need for thirty-one new large power plants that otherwise would have been constructed, with the bill sent to ratepayers.

Among the most influential pieces of serious writing in the postwar era was a 1976 *Foreign Affairs* article, by Amory Lovins, warning that the US electric power grid was about to become overloaded. National-level energy demand is measured in "quads," or quadrillions of BTUs (British thermal units). Taking existing trends and projecting them out to the twenty-first century, the 1976 analysis said that, by 2011, the United States would need 200 quads of electricity annually. The actual number for 2011 was 98 quads—efficiency technology, including some advocacy by Lovins, had made the much lower amount feasible, even as many energy-using products, including refrigerators, rose in size and quality. In 1975, President Gerald Ford said 200 new nuclear power reactors would need to be built by the year 2000; instead, 19 were built, and today electricity is in oversupply. The idea that energy use was growing more wasteful, when the reverse was happening, continued to dominate public thought, perhaps because, being negative, it was what people wanted to believe. In 2001, Vice President Dick Cheney declared that unless the United States built at least 1,300 additional power plants by the year 2021—a number that would mean 150 new generating stations in California alone—there would be permanent rolling brownouts across the country. As of 2018, only a handful of new power plants had opened following Cheney's decree, and electricity was in oversupply.

Technology-boosted energy efficiency initiatives are many, partly because they are encouraged by market forces. In recent years, seagoing container vessels have added "sails" in the form of scoreboard-size kites on long tethers and rotors that look like standpipes: both cut fuel need. Automakers have taken steps as well, including Ford's development of pickups that weigh less because a new form of aluminum substitutes for steel. Aircraft are mainly made of aluminum, which is light compared to steel, placing less demand on engines, but aluminum long has been considered too expensive for any vehicle that doesn't fly. Ford Motors found a way to alloy aluminum at an affordable price, an impressive engineering feat that resulted in the company's F-150 pickup truck, the best-selling vehicle in the United States, getting about 20 percent better fuel economy than the previous steel-based model. Other automakers are researching affordable aluminum and new forms of window glass that weigh less. For decades, cars and small trucks have run on 12-volt electrical systems. In the works are 48-volt systems that will allow air conditioners and heaters to be powered by the battery, not the engine, cutting gasoline need. Electric cars continue to improve in range and practicality, swapping oil use for electricity from central generators that, ideally, rely on clean power or nuclear power, neither of which props up Persian Gulf dictatorships or causes greenhouse gas emissions.

The one move to reduce oil use that automakers don't want to discuss is horsepower reduction. Today's internal combustion engines are far more efficient than yesterday's, but most efficiency gains have gone into horsepower and torque, not fuel savings. In 1980, the average new car sold in the United States had 110 horsepower; by 2015, the average was 245 horsepower. Output-to-displacement is the measure of efficiency for internal combustion engines. The 1982 Ford Mustang GT employed a V-8 engine that generated 32 horsepower per liter of displacement; today's Mustang has a turbocharged four-piston engine that makes 135 horsepower per liter, a fourfold rise in efficiency compared to the 1982 motor. Such advances have allowed absurd levels of power to become commonplace. American taxpayers bailed out General Motors; the company thanked them with the 640-horsepower Cadillac CTS-V, a rich person's plaything so overpowered as to be socially irresponsible.

Road-rage behavior became a concern in the United States about twenty years ago, just as typical cars were acquiring sufficient oomph that typical drivers—not owners of hot rods, but those behind the wheels of family cars—could drag-race at stoplights and cut others off. Electric cars have many desirable properties, but may make the stoplight drag-race situation worse. In cars and trucks, torque overcomes inertia to cause primary acceleration, then horsepower adds speed. Because electric motors are good at torque, battery-powered cars can be really quick off the line. The 2018 Porsche Panamera hybrid does zero-to-sixty in three seconds, versus seven seconds for the 1964 Pontiac GTO, storied muscle car of the 1960s pop hit *Little GTO*. Before the driving environment becomes even more hectic, electric motor output should be regulated just as gasoline-engine horsepower should be.

Engineering trade-offs that reduce power in exchange for higher gas mileage, or more battery life in the case of electric cars, would cut greenhouse gas emissions (directly from cars or indirectly from power plants) while mitigating against the highways being road-rage ecosystems. Automakers are in an arms-race situation regarding power: when competitors add acceleration, they must follow suit. If Congress restricted engine output, cars, pickups, and SUVs would become safer and cleaner, while driving would be less crazed. Some like to think, "If I want a high-horsepower car, no one can tell me what I can buy." This is not true, at least as regards American roads. (Private racetracks are another matter.) Courts repeatedly have ruled that what's allowed on public roads may be regulated for safety, environmental impact, and effect on the public square. But the fact that Americans like to think there exists some kind of right to overpowered vehicles is a barrier to reducing traffic death risk, petroleum consumption, and driving stress.

IF PEOPLE ARE RESISTING MORE sensible cars, let's get people out of the loop. Before too long, the autonomous car is likely. Computer-driven cars will reduce accidents: the computer won't get drowsy or try to cut another computer off. They will reduce traffic jams: traffic would flow more smoothly if cars employed uniform speeds and didn't make needless lane changes, jockeying to get a few seconds ahead. Studies by researchers at the Massachusetts Institute of Technology suggest that an all-autonomous-vehicle system would reduce traffic jams 80 percent— traffic would flow freely even in the Manhattan tunnels.

The three-car suburban family—about one-third of American households own at least three vehicles—will become a one-car family, the vehicle driving itself to wherever the next pickup or drop-off is required by a family member. Offices, schools, and entertainment destinations won't need parking lots by the doors: cars will drop off their masters and mistresses, continue on to remote parking facilities, then come back when summoned. Groups of friends will get together to purchase one shared self-driving car, rather than each person owning a car: all members of the group will save on car and insurance expenses, resulting in another increase in standards of living. The horsepower arms race will end, since a car that refuses to violate the speed limit—this is going to please some people while driving others to distraction—would not benefit from prodigious power output.

Automakers have opened research offices in and around Palo Alto, California, seeking techie-wizard input into self-driving designs. Ford Motors expects by 2021 to be selling fully autonomous cars—no steering wheel—designed for group ownership. This would seem the fulfillment of a Summer-of-Love hippie whimsy were it not the marketing strategy of a Fortune 500 firm. Once cars become safer through computer control, more affordable through group ownership, cleaner through lower oil consumption, and less of a source of urban headaches through the end of the rush-hour traffic jam—then we'll never be rid of car culture, which will exist for decades or centuries to come, if not until the sun explodes.

The computer-controlled car will take the fun out of driving in exchange for convenience and reductions in the cost and stress of everyday life. Perhaps future curmudgeons will extol the Good Old Days when families spent time together stuck in traffic. Senior citizens will become more active once they need only tell the car where to go, while the sorrow of roadside crosses where a teenager was lost in a crash may recede into the past. Computer-controlled cars will reduce the worst form of unnatural death in today's world: cars are much more treacherous than most of us care to think about. Our descendants will say, "Grandma, you used to *drive*? Wasn't that awfully dangerous?" Yes.

Cars, SUVs, and pickup trucks with electronic minds will have downsides beyond that no amount of cursing and pounding on the dash will cause the vehicle to speed. They will create elaborate records of where they've been and when; government will claim not to eavesdrop on the records, but it will. Malfunctions will be a source of terror to anyone who owns or shares the same model. Since we all have confidence in our skills behind the wheel—83 percent of Americans say they are above-average drivers—today hearing of a wreck makes us think the cause was some idiot's carelessness; that will be impossible to think about a computer-car wreck. Hacking into a computer-driven vehicle's software will create a precision-guided urban weapon; no degree of car-code security can rule this out. If future autonomous cars really don't have pedals and steering, just seats for passengers, a cyberattack that cripples GPS signals will bring society to a halt.

Buses and trucks will be driven by computers too. Long-distance truck drivers often are overworked and sleepy; far more people die in collisions caused by trucks than in airline crashes, and the rate of truck-caused fatalities has been rising in recent years, even as other forms of unnatural death moderate. For most families, the chief benefit of autonomous vehicles will be convenience. For trucking companies, the autonomous vehicle will replace wages, benefits, and workplace litigation with a capital cost that can be depreciated. Already the truck division of Mercedes-Benz has prototype autonomous trucks operating on German roads. Labor economists who deride long-haul trucks as "sweatshops on wheels" want better pay and shorter hours for drivers. What they are going to get is the elimination of long-haul driving as a profession.

Taxi, Uber, truck drivers, and bus drivers will lose their jobs; car dealerships will become fewer, salespeople and mechanics losing jobs as families own one car, or half a car, instead of several cars; many other kinds of change and dislocation are coming. Unless you really think legislatures can outlaw change in transportation technology—and thank goodness they did not when there were no seat belts—this future will arrive: safer, cleaner, more convenient, and fewer roles for those without college degrees.

FLYING KEEPS BECOMING SAFER, MORE so than even aviation enthusiasts might have expected. Civilian airliner crashes peaked in 1972 and have declined steadily since. In 2013, 462 people worldwide died in air crashes, making flying through a thunderstorm less dangerous than riding a bicycle in a park on a sunny day. The odds of being killed during a major-airline scheduled flight have fallen to about one in 20 million, compared to about one-in-6-million odds of dying during a car ride. Flying has grown safer through improved electronics, better engine reliability, and more knowledge of the sky. For example, the standard escape maneuver for wind shear changed when meteorologists developed data maps of what happens inside this phenomenon: the result is wind shear claiming fewer aircraft. As fatalities decline, pilot error remains about three times as likely to cause a crash as mechanical failure. You don't need to belong to an airline pilots' union to see that points toward increased use of flight management computers.

Or perhaps toward autonomous planes. The celebrated journalist James Fallows, an instrument-rated pilot and author of two books on aviation, believes automated aircraft will be right behind automated vehicles. Small jets operating without the expense of flight-deck personnel and with no need to wait for them to arrive at the field would allow convenient, low-cost air taxis, beckoned by smartphone as is Lyft today. Perhaps you're thinking, *I ain't getting into no flying machine that does not have a pilot.* Generations to come may do so without reservation, if you will excuse the pun. The chess grandmaster and Russian dissident Garry Kasparov noted in 2017 that people once refused to get into elevators that did not have operators.

PRETTY MUCH EVERYTHING RELATED TO technology, science, and engineering becomes safer. The shift from blue-collar to white-collar careers, combined with the arrival of the Occupational Safety and Health Administration (OSHA), improved factory and warehouse designs, and improved construction equipment, has caused workplace fatalities to go down. In 1970, one full-time worker in 4,800 was killed on the job. The death rate has declined almost annually, to one in 29,600 in 2016. Reporting for work is today one-sixth as dangerous as in 1970.

Fire, and deaths from fire, are in long-term decline. In 1977, there were 1.1 million structure fires in the United States, causing 6,505 deaths. Both figures have waned almost annually—by 2015 to 501,500 structure fires and 2,685 deaths from fire. In absolute terms, that represents a 55 percent decline in fires and a 59 percent decline in deaths from fire. Considering the population was rising during the period, as well as the number of buildings, the declines are even more striking. Fire death has grown less common owing to built-in sprinklers, fire-resistant building materials, and the inexpensive smoke detector, one of the top bang-for-the-buck developments of technology.

Today many urban fire departments are more like ambulance agencies. Owing to the conspicuous heroism of New York's Fire Department on September 11, 2001, politicians like to wear FDNY hats and campaign with firefighters: running for president in 2004, John Kerry often appeared with uniformed firefighters at his side, extolling his plan for a national expansion of fire departments. Yet the nation needs fewer firefighters, not more. This is still another area in which jobs will decline, though with an aging population, jobs for EMTs—the ambulance-agency aspect of the fire department—will rise.

OPPONENTS OF CAPITAL PUNISHMENT (count me among them) grimace on hearing that drugs used for executions must meet the legal standard of "safe and efficacious." How can substances whose purpose is to cause death be classified "safe"? This leads to a paradox: modern high-tech weapons are becoming more effective and less deadly at the same time.

From the nineteenth-century development of breech-loading rifled cannon through the earthshaking artillery barrages of World War I trench warfare, through the World War II leveling of whole cities from the air, to the debut of bloodcurdling "steel rain" rockets in the 1991 Gulf War, combat has been a matter of ever-faster shells and ever-heavier bombs causing destruction over ever-wider areas.

In 1996, Ruth Sivard, an economist who worked as a Department of State arms control analyst, calculated that major twentieth-century wars involved the detonation of 11 megatons worth of explosives, about one hundred times the blast yield of the Hiroshima atomic device. The 11 megatons destroyed most of the urban centers of Germany and Japan, with grave damage to Bulgaria, Cambodia, China, England, Hungary, Iran, Iraq, Italy, the Koreas, Malaysia, Myanmar, the Netherlands, North Africa, Poland, Romania, Russia, Sicily, Ukraine, Vietnam, and Yugoslavia, killing somewhere around 40 million civilians. Because most of the bombs and shells of the twentieth century missed their targets, civilians were more likely to die than combatants, schools and homes more likely to be destroyed than armories. Air raids staged against Iraq by the United States and United Kingdom during the Gulf War involved jets flying a lot faster than aircraft of World War II, but the results were little different. Most of what was dropped in 1991 was large (500 to 2,000 pounds), unguided "dumb bombs" that missed what they were aimed at, causing ghastly devastation and civilian casualties while achieving limited military effect.

When global positioning system (GPS) guidance was perfected just before the turn of the twenty-first century, this premise of warfare changed. Relatively small, precision-guided munitions became weapons of choice. In 1998, with the world's attention on the Bill Clinton impeachment scandal, US warplanes attacked the atomic weapon facilities of Iraq using new GPS-guided munitions—and bombs hit exactly what they were aimed at. Five years later, as the United States invaded Iraq, ostensibly to halt Saddam Hussein's atomic weapons program, no such program was found. Inspectors realized the 1998 operation blew up Iraq's weapons of mass destruction facilities, while inflicting relatively few civilian casualties. The surgical strike, long a White House fantasy, actually happened.

The GPS-guided munition that debuted in 1998, with the Pentagonese name JDAM, changed air strikes from vast tonnages causing mass devastation to effective with relatively small numbers of relatively light munitions. Large bombs had been standard so that blast radius would compensate for lack of accuracy. Once bombs were hitting where aimed, planners realized smaller munitions were called for. Today the basic bomb carried by Air Force jets has GPS guidance and a 250-pound warhead, smaller than basic bombs of World War II and the Korean, Vietnam, and Gulf Wars (smaller both in size and in blast yield, considering the chemistry of explosives has improved, if that's the right word). The new relatively small bombs are deadly for what they hit, but not for whatever is nearby.

When the United States used large dumb bombs against Cambodia during the Richard Nixon administration, an estimated 500,000 civilians were slaughtered. When the United States used small guided munitions during the 2003 Iraq invasion, the civilian casualty toll, Barack Obama said in 2016, was "tens of thousands"—still an appalling number, but much lower than in similar air campaigns of the past. As the political scientist John Tirman of the Massachusetts Institute of Technology has written, Americans feel fury, with reason, over innocent life taken on 9/11, yet act as though innocent lives taken in subsequent retaliatory actions somehow don't count. The Pentagon acknowledged in 2017 that a US airstrike in a crowded section of Mosul, Iraq, killed at least 105 civilians; the target of the strike was two ISIS snipers. The deaths of many innocents in an attempt to kill two combatants did not so much as make the front pages of American newspapers, let alone become a subject of general controversy. Had 105 Americans died because of an Iraqi bomb dropped on an American city, the United States would have experienced a paroxysm.

At least the smaller, accurate weapons now employed by the United States and other militaries reduce civilian dead. If the choice is the lesser of evils—widespread devastation or precision targeting—which would you select? In 1982, Israeli soldiers invaded Lebanon, supported by air strikes using large dumb bombs. In 2006, Israel staged the same invasion in the same place, supported by air strikes using small-warhead GPS weapons. Whatever one thinks of the ethics of these actions, the 1982 big-bomb invasion killed about 10,000 Lebanese civilians, while in 2006 the small-bomb death total was about 1,000. In 1918, during fighting for the French village of Le Hamel, some 3,000 American, Australian, British, and German combatants died in just two hours. In Western fighting for Afghanistan—2018 will mark the year this forever-war exceeds the duration of the Second Punic War—some 800 Afghan, American, British, and Pakistani combatants died during a nearly decade-long battle over Sangin, a village that is about the same size as Le Hamel. The difference was not ferocity of combat, dreadful in each instance. The difference was that in 1918 both sides employed "indirect fire," unaimed weapons that strike the wrong targets and cause large blasts, while a century later in Afghanistan both sides employed precision arms.

Modern missiles with what engineers call the "hawk" property— "*h*oming *a*ll the *w*ay to *k*ill"—employ radar, lasers, television, GPS, or digital terrain-following to hit exactly what they are aimed at, which furthers the progression toward smaller explosions. During World War II, when British bombers struck German fortifications on the island of Heligoland, 5,000 tons of unguided explosives were dropped. In 2017, when the United States launched highly accurate cruise missiles at a Syrian airbase, an installation roughly the size of the Heligoland fortification, 30 tons of explosives were used for about the same effect as 5,000 tons in World War II. Some modern weapons are big: in 2017, the United States unleashed, in Afghanistan, a bomb larger than any from World War II. In general, the trend is toward less destructive munitions. In Serbia in 1999, the United States employed "soft bombs"—which do not explode but disperse clouds of graphite filaments that disable a power grid without blasting or smashing anything. If an opponent yields following a soft-bomb raid, electricity can be restored quickly.

Increasing use by the United States of drone aircraft to fire upon persons whom Washington believes to be terrorists raises a cascade of moral and legal questions. What happens when the button is pushed? Most of the drones that American forces fly above the conflict zones are mini-aircraft launching the bull's-eye-accurate AGM-114, whose warhead weighs 18 to 20 pounds. This amount of explosive will destroy a vehicle or part of a building, but not an entire building; usually there is little of the blandly named "collateral damage." Early during America's forever-war occupation of Afghanistan, US officers realized the munitions at their disposal, designed for use against Soviet armor, were destroying too much. The result was a relatively little precision missile, the AGM-176, first deployed in 2008, which has a 13-pound warhead that does no collateral damage.

At the University of Chicago, Barack Obama was asked about the morality of the United States arrogating a right to use drones to kill in the poor and defenseless nations of the world. He dodged that question, just as the question was dodged by the younger George Bush, first president to command drones. Obama did say that since there will be US air strikes, they must be conducted with the least destructive weapons that can be developed.

MODERN MILITARIES ARE BECOMING LESS dangerous in ways beyond the relatively small guided munition replacing the large dumb warhead. The United States is down from tens of thousands of heavy bombers during the 1940s to about two hundred bombers total, no longer a large enough force to stage the sort of unyielding aerial bombardment to which the Axis, Cambodia, and North Vietnam were subjected. Russia and China possess only a handful of heavy bombers; France, Germany, and the United Kingdom possess none. Today's modest numbers of combat aircraft delivering precision munitions are a keener threat to valid military targets than were the immense "bomber streams" of World War II, but less of a threat to civilians, because the explosions are fewer and smaller. What bombers remain are not on nuclear standby anymore, while the US B-1 supersonic bomber has been retrofitted to carry only conventional munitions.

Warships of all navies are fewer than in the past and pose little threat to targets on land, where the civilians are. The world's major militaries have fewer artillery pieces than in the past, and while flashy jets receive the attention, often cannons and howitzers are the primary instruments of combat harm. During World War II, 60 million pounds of explosives were fired into Sevastopol by artillery. Today no army on earth could deliver such a barrage, though the satellite-guided rounds employed by America and Russia are much more effective against military targets than World War II artillery that blasted everything in the general direction of the adversary.

Most nations ratified a 1993 treaty banning chemical weapons: as of 2016, 93 percent of the global stockpile had been burned. One reason the 2017 use of sarin gas in the Syrian civil war led to international condemnation is that governments have forsworn such weapons.

The United States and Russian Federation have disassembled and melted most of their city-busting nuclear bombs, the ones with a megaton or more of yield. A megaton is around fifty times the blast power of the Hiroshima bomb; at the height of the Cold War, hundreds of megaton-plus monstrosities were aimed at the world's cities. The newest US nuclear bomb, the B61–12, has a yield only a little more than the Hiroshima device. (In this sense, "only" and "little" are strange qualifiers.) The B61-12's and their relatively low-yield Russian equivalents are not targeted at cities. In 1994, London, Moscow, and Washington agreed to remove target coordinates from recently built nuclear-tipped missiles. Rendering such missiles capable of striking an enemy, by loading in coordinates, will create a pause that may allow cooler heads to prevail. In 2010, Defense Secretary Robert Gates revealed the three governments further agreed that older nuclear missiles equipped with earlier forms of guidance will be targeted to the open ocean, so that one fired by mistake will fly into the sea.

Studies by the Federation of American Scientists show that, as recently as 1990, Washington and Moscow had thousands of nuclear warheads deployed on surface ships and submarines, where individual officers might end up making launch decisions. Today America's only nuclear-armed vessels are *Ohio*-class submarines, and *Ohio*-class subs, the Federation calculates, depart on patrol at "their lowest rate ever," while Russia's similar boats rarely leave port.

The most dangerous machine that humanity has constructed is the *Ohio*-class strategic missile submarine. At one point the United States sailed eighteen of these apocalypse horsemen, each armed with twenty-four ballistic missiles bearing twelve nuclear warheads apiece. That was enough on a single boat to obliterate a nation, and enough aboard the underwater flotilla to end human life. Today some *Ohio*-class submarines have been converted from nuclear to conventional weapons. The whole category is scheduled to be replaced with *Columbia*-class submarines, of which there will be at most twelve boats, each with sixteen nuclear missiles rather than twenty-four. Fewer strategic submarines with fewer missiles will represent a roughly 60 percent reduction in the ultimate-weapon inventory of the United States. Russia retired the last of its *Ohio*-equivalent nuclear missile submarines in 2012. There will be at most eight boats in Russia's *Columbia*-equivalent class, netting about a 70 percent reduction in Moscow's undersea ultimate-weapon inventory. Militaries remain capable of awful devastation, but the trend is toward fewer nuclear weapons and less destructive conventional arms.

JESSE AUSUBEL, THE ROCKEFELLER UNIVERSITY researcher, made his academic reputation in the 1980s by predicting resource use would decline even as living standards rise. At the time, this seemed fanciful. Now it is established that resource exploitation can go down as living standards go up. Studies at UCLA have found that designing buildings for energy efficiency lowered electric power consumption in the Los Angeles area by about 20 percent, a reason the City of Angels can have more people, an improved standard of living, and less smog. The Cornell University extension campus under construction on an island in the East River adjacent to Manhattan will power itself, via solar panels and a geothermal facility; these are expensive options, but as architects gain experience with such methods, the price should fall. Since Ausubel has been right before, I asked his predictions today.

"Broadly speaking, efficiency wins," he says. "Mineral, metal, paper, and water use per capita peaked in the 1970s or 1980s and has declined, causing technology to be less harmful to nature while soft demand reduces price. The next generation will see building materials become lighter, lowering costs and resource use, even as buildings get stronger and a lot less likely to burn. Chemical batteries will not improve much. The potential is in reducing power requirements so less battery capacity is needed; reducing power requirements will go really well. Sound pollution of the seas will be acknowledged as an important issue. The oceans are a hundred years behind the land in terms of governance. Large ocean 'parks' should be established with rules against poaching and other abuses. Ocean rules could be enforced by drones, which can cover a lot more area than the Coast Guard.

"Agriculture has become so effective that we're producing too much calories and protein for our own good. The rich nations would be better off with 25 percent less food. Top yield in farming may be close to maxing out, but average yield can improve a great deal; reducing waste and improving distribution is more important than increasing production. We've adapted so rapidly to population growth that if the global count stops at nine or ten billion people, the world should be okay. Twenty billion people would be different.

"Car sharing will have more impact than expected. The United States has 200 million cars, SUVs, and pickup trucks, each driven an hour per day, parked for the other twenty-three hours. If we get use up to two hours per day, then we only need half as many vehicles. Keeping airplanes in the air earning revenue, rather than sitting on some field, is what cut the cost of flying—the same basic idea is coming to ground vehicles. Right now cars are about 30 percent efficient in terms of converting energy into motion. Soon they will reach about 50 percent efficiency at the same time that we only need half as many of them. Resource demand will go down, living standards will go up, and urban living will be less crazed."

Ausubel thinks there is a lot of urban living ahead: the move from the countryside to cities will continue to accelerate, making most men and women better educated, more tolerant, and accustomed to being around people who are different from them—the last effect being perhaps the great virtue of the city.

Speaking at the University of Glasgow in 2016, Ausubel showed a series of slides demonstrating that since antiquity, human beings have been in motion on average seventy minutes per day. Whether on foot or horseback, in carriages, streetcars, or personal cars, for seventy minutes a day we roam. "This is some deep optimization caused by hundreds of thousands of years of evolution, a daily inspection of our nearby territory," Ausubel says. As means of travel become more rapid—autonomous jets, maglev trains, perhaps the extremely fast "hyperloop"-style subway—people will continue to roam for seventy minutes a day, while increasing their range. "In Europe since 1950, the tripling of the average speed of travel has extended personal area tenfold," he said. "This is going to happen for the whole world, and will be safe."

THE SUMMATION OF WHY TECHNOLOGY grows safer instead of more dangerous turns on a combination of liberal ideology (regulation), conservative ideology (market forces), military needs (precision guidance replacing huge explosions), and manufacturing pragmatics (reducing resource and fuel use makes products more valuable). Genus *Homo* is good at making things efficient: increasing the efficiency of technology will cause us to be safer, while less threatening to nature.

But what happens to a safer, cleaner world if dictators take over?

Chapter 7

Why Don't the Dictators Win?

PICTURE SUMMER 1940. NAZI DARKNESS covers Europe, imperial Japanese darkness has fallen over Asia. The vast Soviet Union, comprising fifteen modern nations, is under the heel of a police-state that starves its own citizens and summarily executes any dissident. China is torn by a three-way war that will end badly, with the government-imposed misery that is the trademark of communism. Central and South America and Spain are in the hands of tinpot military oppressors whose trademark is the temper tantrum followed by disappearance of opponents and academics. Poland, Ukraine, and the Baltic states are repressed by Nazis and Communists simultaneously. India, Indonesia, Southeast Asia, and most of Africa are exploited by colonialism. Backed by industrial-scale weaponry and the newly developed mass propaganda—before radio, political decrees could be heard only in person—fascism and communism seem impossible to overcome: since they allow no rights and torture anyone who criticizes their Big Brother figures, how can revolution happen? The light of democracy still shines in only a few places—Australia, Canada, the United States, and the British Isles, though the latter light flickers, considering Britons brutally subjugate India for the personal profit of the English aristocracy. Matters get so bleak Franklin Roosevelt suggests to Winston Churchill that the Royal Navy abandon a doomed homeland and sail west to assist in making North America the final redoubt of human liberty.

Now picture the present day. The German and Japanese forms of fascism have been blasted to kingdom come. The thought-police form of communism is nearly gone, defeated in Russia by a once-unimaginable movement: internal activism for consent of the governed. Imperialism is nearly gone, with an independent India the largest democracy in history. More nations hold multiparty elections than do not. Freedom of speech has expanded, if fitfully, across the globe. All manner of political problems persist, and more are coming. But the dictators didn't win, while the United States, for its many failings, employed the core ideal of the Enlightenment—that the individual is more important than the state—to become the strongest and most prosperous nation the world has ever known.

Dictatorship in its many forms is immoral and coldblooded, democracy in its many forms, jumbled and nebulous. Yet since 1940, whenever the two philosophies clashed, either democracy won outright or the result was stalemate. (Details of this contention are in the notes.) Technology has not made Big Brothers bigger: rather, increasingly free flow of information has shifted power toward average people, everywhere except the Middle East, North Korea, and a few other holdouts. And while there has recently been what Larry Diamond, a Stanford University professor, calls a democracy recession—backsliding in China, Russia, Thailand, and Turkey—in the main the good guys keep beating the bad guys.

As a young academic during the early 1980s, Diamond made the distinctly minority prediction that democracy was about to put dictatorship to rout. At the time, his view was seen as nonsense. Communism was viewed as monolithic and indestructible, while military regimes were considered too entrenched to change. Jeanne Kirkpatrick, Ronald Reagan's ambassador to the United Nations and a favorite of hard-liners, maintained America might as well sidle up to authoritarian governments: dreaming of democracy was naive. But Diamond was fascinated by an event most of the West missed: the Carnation Revolution. In 1974, Portugal peacefully converted from tinpot dictatorship to democracy, then granted independence to colonies in Africa and Asia. Diamond thought Portugal, not the Soviet Union, was the leading indicator. He was right.

In years to come the Iron Curtain fell, with most Warsaw Pact nations switching to elections. Indonesia, South Korea, Spain, Greece, South Africa, and most of Central and South America became democracies, in most cases making peaceful transitions from dictators to elected officials. Max Roser, of the University of Oxford, calculates that today 55 percent of humanity lives under true free-elections democracy, a percentage that would have seemed inconceivable to kings and kaisers of the past. Most free societies have achieved liberal democracy, the best kind—liberal in the sense that America's Framers spoke the term: broad rights to personal and religious freedom and to ownership of private property.

"Nothing like the current generation's continuous growth in democracy has ever been seen before," Diamond says. Why did he feel this was coming? "A generation ago, there was a tendency to write off poor people as not concerned with freedom. I taught in Africa in 1980, then did a lot of travel. When I traveled the world, I was struck by how badly the poor longed to be free. Liberty is not a luxury for the well-off, it's something people really want—in China, in Cuba, everywhere. Today polls show even Arabs in the Middle East badly want their dictators replaced with democracy."

As free elections increase, military coups decline. Jonathan Powell of Central Florida University and Clayton Thyne of the University of Kentucky study coups. They calculate that from 1950 to 1990, on average, military plotters seized power somewhere on ten occasions per year. Since 1990, the average is down to three coups per year. Enthusiasm for democracy and increasing prosperity in Africa and Latin America have made it harder for the coup d'état to be taken seriously.

We'd like to think democracy wins because of ethical superiority: in an ideal world, the ethical superiority of representative government might be the alpha and omega of this issue. In the real post-1940 world, what matters foremost is that democracy is better than dictatorship at money and at war.

THE RECENT PAST CAN SEEM incalculably distant. Only two generations ago, intelligent people in the West actually believed Nikita Khrushchev's "we will bury you" boast—that the communist working class would overawe the free-market world economically by outproducing the West. Did not historical determinism mandate this result? Was not communism elaborately organized around industrial production, while the

Enlightenment system was organized around the frail notion of personal happiness? In 1961, Paul Samuelson, the first American to win the Nobel Prize for Economics, predicted the Soviet economy would pass the US economy by the 1980s at the latest. Around the same time, John Kenneth Galbraith, Samuelson's rival as highest-profile American economist, began to say that an evolving "technostructure" of huge, impersonal factories would blow American-style entrepreneurs out of the water. Weren't huge, impersonal factories just what communism was good at?

The Soviet economy did not pass the American economy in the 1980s, or ever: when the Soviet Union crumpled in 1989, the US economy was twice as large as the Soviet economy; today the US GDP is fourteen times that of the Russian Federation. The United States outproduces China and Russia combined, with an ample margin to spare. Per capita, today's American is seven times as productive as today's Russian or Chinese citizen. So much for "we will bury you."

Money has mattered at least since the ancient Greeks began hammering coins on anvils. With each passing decade in the modern world, money matters more: democracy's gift for producing money becomes increasingly important relative to other features of systems of government. Because land no longer is essential to generation of wealth, with the result that most of the time it's cheaper and more effective to purchase than to conquer—whether by force or by altering public opinion—the increasing import of money, joined to decreasing roles of natural resources and sheer manpower, works in favor of free societies.

Another reason for the rise of free societies is that the tumultuous nature of market economics—the very aspect of the American and European systems that makes Americans and Europeans insecure—rewards creativity. Authoritarian systems punish creativity. As Deirdre McCloskey, an economic historian at the University of Illinois at Chicago, has written, "liberated people are ingenious," while those oppressed by dictators, communism, or feudalism cannot express inventiveness. Russia long has produced top-notch scientists, while its focus on education for girls and women meant Russia enjoyed twice the supply of ideas as some other nations. Yet the Soviet Union, and later the Russian Federation, never succeeded in commercializing ideas regarding lasers, computers, aviation, and rocketry, which are strengths of Russian science. In authoritarian regimes, ideas are seen as threats, not as opportunities. Controlling what already exists is the backward-focused goal of tyranny: creating what will exist next is seen as a subject that should not be discussed.

Through most of the twentieth century, land, labor, and natural endowment were the crux of economic production; as the twentieth century drew toward a close, capital, information, and intellectual property became more important. The zany, uncommanded systems of the West were able to adjust—made stronger by their own instability—while grim, frowning dictatorships were not. Today's world wants dollars, euros, and yen and maybe a little digital currency. No one in the entire expanse of the Milky Way wants rubles. Iran is spoken of as if a potent nation, but its economy is a Dumpster fire: many workers never receive pay, and a simple transaction, such as buying a bag of groceries, can cost 10,000 *tomans*—hyperinflation that makes the Weimar Republic seem a Harvard Business School case-study success story. In early 2017, the market capitalization of Apple reached $800 billion, versus the Russian Federation's GDP of $1.3 trillion. Just one American company is nearly as valuable as Russia's entire country! This money edge increases over time, giving democracy an ever-bigger lead in money.

In the renowned 1961 drama *Judgment at Nuremberg*, Burt Lancaster, portraying a Nazi on trial, tells the judge, portrayed by Spencer Tracy, "When Germany was a democracy, we had nothing. Once she became a dictatorship, Germany got whatever she wanted." Similar to actual testimony at a Nuremberg tribunal, this statement encapsulates what, a century ago, could seem true—people could believe that placing a tyrant upon a throne serves the national interest, because dictatorships are better than representative government at giving the people what they want. Even if that was true once, no longer is it so.

FREEDOM OF THOUGHT CONFERS ON democracy the education edge. Most of the world's great colleges and universities are in the United States; a handful are in Europe and Japan; the rest of the world combined cannot match even one top college or university in America or England. With each passing year, colleges and universities matter more while mineral deposits and animal husbandry matter less.

Approaching the turn of the twentieth century, democracies strengthened themselves by embracing the movement toward universal public education. Germany, initially the leader of this movement, sabotaged itself by imposing thought-control on schools and universities. In the early postwar era, the United States made an expensive commitment to expanding universities and helping average people attend via the GI Bill and the California public university system as well as the "public Ivies" in Colorado, Illinois, Michigan, North Carolina, Pennsylvania, Texas, Vermont, Virginia, Washington State, and Wisconsin. During the same period, dictatorships of the left and right were shutting universities down. The US investment in public universities has been repaid many times over, while the folly engaged in by anti-education dictatorships is punished daily. By 2006, researchers led by Jon Miller of Michigan State University would show there was nearly a one-to-one relationship between education and economic output: the better a nation's education, the greater its GDP.

Dictatorships cannot produce free-thought education because dictators oppose the very concept: in this, authoritarians concede an ever-larger advantage to democrats. If you could live in a country with great colleges, lots of money, and lots of uncertainty, or a country with a great secret police force, lots of fossil fuels, and the assurance next year will be the same as this year, which passport would you choose? Steven Radelet of Georgetown University has noted that developing nations that do not have dictators are working to improve their higher education institutions—India is staging a significant push for better colleges and universities—while countries led by despots don't want an educated populace. This keeps dictatorships backward and weak compared to democracies.

Another reason democracy is more productive than dictatorship is less wasted motion by average people. A properly functioning rule-of-law democracy allows citizens to ignore politics and go on about their lives. All forms of dictatorship demand constant obeisance, that citizens pay undivided attention to the state and to the irrational pronouncements of some cult-of-personality figure. Donald Trump's election cast fear not so much owing to his platform or curious roster of advisers, but because he forced Americans to fret about politics and about his random mood swings, diverting effort from their jobs, families, and pursuit of happiness.

A generation ago, the leaders of China grudgingly accepted that free enterprise is better at prosperity than state control; China's economic output since then proves the point. In the current generation, the Red Dragon grudgingly acknowledged that America's colleges are vastly better than China's; elites began sending their children to the United States to receive real educations. Will democracy in China follow, as the night the day? Beijing's recent relapse toward censorship shows that its leadership class considers clinging to power more important than consent of the governed—China is staging a "Great Leap Backward" in which "dissent is not permissible," *The Atlantic* said in 2016. China will grow much stronger if it becomes a democracy rather than stays mired in its current amalgam model of economic freedom without political freedom. Mikhail Gorbachev, who presided over the dissolution of the Soviet Union, said in 2016 that the next step for Russia should be switching to democracy, "not in the future but right now." We'd like to think Gorbachev made this statement for moral reasons. Maybe he was looking at economic data.

THE GUNS OF AUGUST THAT sounded in 1914 matched the autocracies of Germany, Bulgaria, and the old Ottoman and Austro-Hungarian Empires against the democracies of the United Kingdom, French Third Republic, Canada, United States, Australia, Italy, and Japan, with monarchist Russia and Serbia as wild cards. World War I is little studied in today's politics because every aspect of the conflict seems irredeemably sordid. Yet in this dreadful clash, democracy prevailed by a clear margin. There was bitterness, especially in the United States, when World War I did not prove to be a war to end all others. What was proved was that (reasonably) free societies, assumed to be weak and indulgent, could defeat autocracy, assumed to be invincible. When the democracies fought the dictatorships at the start of the twentieth century and the democracies won, this planted a seed in social thinking: people admire winners.

By 1940, the two basic philosophies of government were at war again, this time with everything at stake. Democracy carried the day again, and by a much larger margin than in the previous world war. The initiators of World War I were left damaged; those who started World War II were left smoldering. Note that when Italy and Japan fought in World War I as democracies, they came out ahead; when they fought in World War II as dictatorships, they were thrashed. As dictatorships, Germany and Japan were devastated; when, following World War II, they became liberal democracies, both thrived. In the Second World War, Russia again was the wild card, having replaced inherited despotism with communist despotism. After the fighting ended, Russia remained a dictatorship—its corrupt leadership class stridently ignoring the good things happening in democracies—and so remained an unhappy, deprived society.

In military terms, the lesson of World War II was that democracies are significantly better at fighting than dictatorships. George Marshall, chief of staff of the US Army, said in 1944, "We are determined that before the sun sets on this terrible struggle our flag will be recognized throughout the world as the symbol of freedom on the one hand, of overwhelming power on the other." Many are aware that World War II showed "the symbol of freedom" superior to any symbolism of tyranny. That World War II concluded with democracy possessing "overwhelming power" is less acknowledged, but as imperative.

Perhaps soldiers of democracies fight well because they believe in what they are fighting for, while soldiers of dictatorships fight because they are compelled to do so. Military historians tend to conclude that soldiers of every nationality are motivated not by the flags they represent but by desires to live, to demonstrate courage, and to protect fellow soldiers. In this sense, solders' motivations may be roughly equal: Germans and Russians fought valiantly in World War II despite loathsome governments.

Material production is another matter; here democracy is hands-down superior to tyranny. As the historian Jay Winik has written, during World War II "the United States produced two million trucks, 300,000 warplanes, more than 100,000 tanks, 87,000 warships, 5,000 cargo ships, more than 20 million rifles, machine guns and pistols and 44 million rounds of ammunition—the equivalent of building two Panama Canals per month." On the morning of the D-Day landing, the United States moved the equivalent of the populations of Baltimore and Boston "in total darkness over 112 miles of choppy water in 12 hours," sending along hard-to-fathom quantities of munitions and medical supplies, plus 100,000 packets of gum and 6,200 pounds of candy.

A German tank called the Panther was the best armored vehicle of World War II, superior to the US tank called the Sherman. Germany was able to manufacture 6,000 Panthers and had trouble supplying them with gasoline over short distances; the United States built 49,000 Shermans, and their fuel tanks were full thousands of miles from home. During World War II, the United States outproduced Germany and Japan between three-to-one and ten-to-one in aircraft, ships, tanks, tank destroyers, field pieces, radars, squad weapons, and bazookas; built the Manhattan Project, the most complex undertaking any nation had ever attempted; supplied much of the military matériel employed by the Red Army; completed the Grand Coulee Dam to generate the electricity needed for unprecedented amounts of aluminum for the heavy bombers that only the Allies were able to manufacture in number; erected the world's two longest pipelines to move fuel to the East Coast for shipment to the European Theater; and built refineries for 100-octane aviation gas, which during the war American made more of than the rest of the world combined. In the final year of the war, the US staging base on Guam was receiving 120,000 barrels of high-octane aviation fuel per day. The entire Japanese military was down to 21,000 barrels per day of avgas, low-quality fuel that often caused engines to sputter during battle.

The fleet of fascist Japan was outgunned in its home waters by a democratic force that had to travel the length of the Pacific Ocean. No Axis soldier ever stood on American soil, nor did any Axis aircraft enter continental US airspace. By contrast, the United States and England dropped 3.4 million tons of bombs on Axis territory, while from the west—the zone of fighting run by democracy—4.5 million soldiers entered Germany, backed by 17,000 tanks, 28,000 aircraft, 65,000 artillery pieces, and about a million trucks and jeeps.

One might wonder if democracy produced so much more than dictatorship during World War II because the factories and refineries of the

United States were protected by oceans, while air strikes disrupted the infrastructure of tyranny. But even when aerial bombardment was not occurring, democracy far out-produced dictatorship. Strategic bombing of Japan did not begin until summer 1944. From the attack on Pearl Harbor until that summer, American shipyards christened seventeen fleet-class aircraft carriers, the most valuable vessels of World War II, while Japanese shipyards produced six. In the same period, the United States launched almost one hundred escort carriers; Japan launched twelve. As the analyst Daniel Yergin has noted, when in 1926 Japan ended suffrage to become a fascist state, the Japanese upper class "rejected liberalism, capitalism and democracy as engines of weakness and decadence." Japan was burned to the ground by a weak, decadent system that could build aircraft carriers with far greater efficiency.

Free societies hold an edge in fostering inventions and inventiveness, which closed societies discourage. In an irony, free societies also are better at organization than closed societies. As World War II began, Germany and Japan relied on disjointed manufacturing systems that produced a large range of aircraft and armored vehicles that were hard to maintain, because each model required specialized spare parts, and hard to train for, because there was little uniformity. In *Why the Allies Won,* historian Richard Overy called the fact that the Luftwaffe had 425 aircraft types while the US Air Force (then with a different name) had fifteen one of the deciding aspects of the war. What in the nineteenth century was dubbed the "American system of manufacturing" focused on standardized machine tools and jigs that rolled out products with interchangeable parts. By the onset of World War II, democracies had switched to this system; Germany did not adopt American-style manufacturing until 1943, when it was too late; Japan did not adopt standardized manufacturing until after the war.

As the Northwestern University historian Michael Sherry wrote in 1987, "Fascist totalitarianism produced far less centralization than the Allies achieved." Nothing's perfect, but for the most part, citizens of democracies voluntarily discipline themselves, which is good for organization and teamwork; fearing punishment, citizens of dictatorships rarely show initiative. Free economies reward whatever is most efficient, which for war footing is centralization. Communist governments and South American militarism seemed as if they should be good at centralization, but in practice lagged behind free societies in this element of manufacturing output.

Democracy holds the ethical edge over dictatorship; holding the money and battlefield edges as well does not hurt.

THE ETHICAL CASE FOR DEMOCRACY is tainted in many respects. In the United States, slavery and then Jim Crow laws, as well as atrocities against Native Americans, along with violation of treaties they signed and the Senate ratified; British, Spanish, Portuguese, and Dutch participation in the slave trade; British, French, Spanish, Portuguese, Belgian, and Dutch colonial oppression. Many other democratic nations and cultures have committed grave offenses.

Contemporary Americans tend to think of slavery as a moral outrage that was corrected by the Thirteenth Amendment and of segregation as a political outrage that was corrected by civil rights legislation and affirmative action. As the writer Ta-Nehisi Coates has noted, slavery and segregation also were economic institutions, and these legacies are far from corrected. "The ghettoes of America are the direct result of decades of public-policy decisions: the redlining of real-estate zoning maps, the expanded authority given to prosecutors, the increased funding given to prisons," Coates wrote in 2017. Until 1968, real estate redlining was not something shameful the Federal Housing Authority did in secret but formal FHA policy that was instrumental in shifting net worth from African Americans to whites.

The fantastic productive output of democracies happened in part because African and American Indian slaves, and oppressed Africans, Asians, and subcontinental Indians, and the indentured of many ethnicities, labored against their wills to generate wealth for governments that promised liberty. History offers a succession of enigmas, among them that the economic power the democracies employed to stop twentieth-century dictatorship, benefiting the world, was grounded in mistreatment of peoples whose freedom was denied. This should not prevent anyone from thinking democracy is the best social order available today. Rather, should remind that even in democracies, aftereffects of exploitation are all around us.

DICTATORSHIP HAS NO CHANCE OF defeating democracy at war, at economics, for that matter at movies, popular music, or pizza delivery. Perhaps dictatorship can gain by eroding democracy rather than by competing directly.

Most of history's leading nations collapsed from within, not in response to external factors: Russia's leaders, who were young when the Soviet Union collapsed from within, know this well. Shortly before the inauguration of Donald Trump, the outgoing director of national intelligence, James Clapper, a retired Air Force lieutenant general, said, "Russian efforts to influence the 2016 US presidential election represent the most recent expression of Moscow's long-standing desire to undermine the US-led liberal democratic order." At this writing, the extent to which Moscow may have influenced the 2016 US presidential election was unclear. Moscow's desire to do so was not.

Wall Street speculators try to short-sell stocks: today Russia and other authoritarian regimes are trying to short-sell democracy. Russia never will beat democracy in a fair fight. But dictatorship can short-sell those governments that protect freedom of speech and civil rights by planting rumors, inveigling citizens to question the legitimacy of free elections, and making democracy seem to be falling apart. Planting rumors to cause firms to appear to be falling apart is the technique of stock market short-selling: if the stock price then tumbles, the short-sellers benefit. Totalitarian governments are hoping the "stock price"—the reputation—of the United States will tumble, allowing them (keeping the metaphor) to snatch up assets at a bargain. If Russia did assist Trump in gaining the White House, the impact on the United States—a vain, incompetent president who is unprepared and acts befuddled, distracting his nation—was exactly what a short-selling strategy would seek.

DURING THE SAME RECENT PERIOD when democracy expanded, two counterweights arose. One is the Internet. Initially, web access was the bane of dictators. George Orwell thought Oceania, his *Nineteen Eighty-Four* dystopia, would use electronics to prevent citizens from knowing what was really going on; during the initial spread of the Internet, it turned out electronics worked the other way around, allowing average people to know what's happening. Dictators have begun to respond: for instance, China strengthening the Great Firewall to impede Internet reporting of corruption by local party hacks, Turkey blocking access to Wikipedia to prevent citizens from accessing information about genocide against Armenian Christians. But even in Western nations, where web use is unfettered, the second phase of the Internet has a corroding impact on democracy.

The second counterweight is that fast-rising affluence in the nations that hold free elections, or at least allow free economics, creates a tempting goody bag to steal from. William Galston, a US Marine who became an academic and then a senior White House official during the Bill Clinton presidency, wrote in 2016, "The crucial question is whether elites rule in their own interest or for the common good." In a successful society, elites rule for the common good. In a society that yields to corruption, not so much.

"When a poor man steals he goes to jail, when a rich man steals, he becomes a government minister." So said Luiz Inácio Lula da Silva, and should know: Lula went on to become president of Brazil and looked the other way on perhaps the worst corruption scandal in the tawdry annals of this topic. By 2017, Lula had been sentenced to prison for stealing public funds; another president of Brazil had been impeached for embezzlement; dozens of mayors were in prison for graft; Brazil's equivalent of the FBI was serving search warrants in the homes of the "Brazillionaires" who use helicopters to fly over the country's epic traffic jams; and Marcelo Odebrecht, CEO of Brazil's largest construction company, had been sentenced to nineteen years for bribing government officials. (Odebrecht admitted to paying $350 million in bribes in Brazil and $100 million in bribes in that worker's paradise, Venezuela.) Stealing from the public had replaced soccer as Brazil's national sport. Brazil has the most commodity-dependent large economy—ore, soybeans, sugar—and commodity accounts lend themselves to pilfering, a reason the commodity-dependent oil economies of Russia and the Persian Gulf dictatorships are rife with sleaze. During the Brazilian scandal, Fabiano Silveira, an official with the Hogwarts-like title Minister of Transparency, resigned when caught covering up corruption. His job was to expose corruption.

The US Justice Department led the investigation of graft in Brazil and succeeded in, among other things, getting Rolls-Royce, which manufactures aircraft engines mounted on the Embraer jetliners built in Brazil, to pay an $800 million fine for bribery there and in other South American nations. The FBI established a division with the actual name Kleptocracy Asset Recovery Initiative, which has frozen $3 billion stolen by foreign government officials and stashed in US accounts.

In just the last few years, Malaysia's prime minister was caught with at least $1 billion that he claimed was campaign donations but which was taxpayer money. The top central banker of Bangladesh resigned after $81 million in his nation's funds vanished—that deposit slip must be around here somewhere!—from an account in New York City. A top official who had just left the Argentinian government was arrested while throwing bags of money over a wall into a monastery, in the belief that stolen funds would become exempt from the law there. Gulnara Karimova, daughter of the late president of Uzbekistan, was found to have $830 million though she was unemployed. Pavlo Lazarenko, former prime minister of Ukraine, had at least $250 million in the bank though his sole source of income was a civil servant's salary. Joseph Kabila, dictator of the misnamed Democratic Republic of the Congo, was believed to have stolen at least $95 million from the public.

Recent corruption scandals have hit Afghanistan, where much of the $115 billion in US reconstruction funds has been stolen. Embezzlement of public funds and kickbacks on public works either happened or were alleged recently in Angola, Australia, Cambodia, China, Egypt, Israel, Mexico, Nigeria, Pakistan, Peru, the Philippines, Romania, Russia, Slovakia, South Africa, Spain, and Uganda. The scheme in Romania was particularly ingenious: the government enacted a law exempting officeholders from prosecution for larceny; Boss Tweed would have been impressed. The president of South Korea was impeached for stealing from taxpayers, and the head of Samsung, the country's corporate giant, was taken to jail in chains for the same offense. The 2015 agreement to restrain Iran's nuclear-weapons program included the United States returning about $400 million in Iranian deposits from American accounts, where the money had been immobilized for decades. Iran wanted the return not as checks or wire transfers but in dollar and euro notes: the cargo hold of a sizable US military plane was required to fly eighty pallets of cold cash to Tehran. Why did Iranian government officials request small bills rather than electronic transmissions? So they could steal without leaving a digital trail.

Milan Vaishnav, a researcher at the Carnegie Endowment for International Peace, has shown that the net worth of the typical state or federal lawmaker in India triples during his or her first term of office—not, pretty obviously, from guessing right on cattle futures, as Hillary Clinton once claimed, with a straight face, about a sudden rise in her net worth. The 2015 discovery of the Panama Papers showed that government officials in China, Iceland, Russia, and Saudi Arabia were using shell companies to hide stolen public funds; today referring to Russia as "Nigeria with snow" is an insult to Nigeria—and to snow for that matter. In 2017, François Fillon, former prime minister of France, was found to have his wife and children on the public payroll, which was not the problem, since nepotism, like practically any consensual behavior, is legal in France. The problem was that Fillon put his family on the public payroll for no-show jobs for which they received salaries without performing any work. The French far right's Marine Le Pen was funding her 2017 campaign for president by filing fake expense accounts and using other gimmicks to defraud the European Parliament. France's top official tasked with catching wealthy tax evaders—the upper crusts of France, Greece, and other European nations brazenly cheat on taxes—was sentenced to three years in prison for hiding his own assets offshore in order to dodge taxes.

Global Financial Integrity, a nonpartisan think tank, estimates that in the decade from 2004 to 2013 about $7.8 trillion was stolen from the public by government officials, representing about 2 percent of global GDP during the period. Diamond has written, "When most of the opportunities in life, including the chance to become rich, are controlled by the state, it is difficult to get politicians to play by the rules of the democratic game." Thank goodness the United States, leader of the free world, does not sink to these depths. Except…

*   *   *

EVERYONE KNOWS RICHARD NIXON HAD to resign for committing crimes and cover-ups of crimes. Less known is that Nixon's vice president, Spiro Agnew, also resigned for commission of the crime of corruption; he had accepted about $750,000 in bribes. In a maneuver that would have impressed Al Capone, the vice president of the United States was charged with tax evasion for not declaring bribes as income.

At least when Nixon was caught he had the dignity to say, *I give up*—words too many leaders, once caught, refuse to pronounce. Large numbers of federal, state, and local US officials are joining Nixon in being caught for crimes committed while in office. In the same recent period as the international government corruption just noted, there have been public fraud scandals in Alabama, California, Georgia, Illinois, Maryland, Massachusetts, Michigan, New York (state and city), and Washington, DC. Puerto Rico defaulted on $73 billion in government-administered bonds, some of whose proceeds mysteriously vanished. The mayor of Detroit was sentenced to twenty-eight years in prison for expropriating state money. The mayor of New Orleans was sentenced to ten years for stealing money that was to have prepared the city for storms such as Hurricane Katrina.

The mayor of Baltimore stole boxes of gift cards intended for distribution to the poor, then spent the cards on herself. (She resigned in return for no jail time and keeping an $83,000-per-year pension—essentially, the mayor of Baltimore was rewarded for corruption.) A Pennsylvania government official was indicted for accepting bribes. The official was the Philadelphia district attorney, who prosecutes government kickbacks and fraud. In the nation's capital, several city council members have recently been convicted of corruption, including one for stealing government funds from a youth sports league he bragged about running as a public service. Next door to the capital, the chief executive of Prince George's County was imprisoned for taking kickbacks. When the FBI announced a search warrant at his door, his wife tried to stuff $80,000 cash into her clothes.

In New York, Alan Hevesi, the state comptroller, was sentenced to prison for taking $1.5 million in bribes. A state comptroller's role is to safeguard public funds. The speaker of the New York State Assembly was sentenced to twelve years in prison for seeking kickbacks. (At this writing, his case was on appeal.) Utica, New York, got a $585 million state grant that was supposed to create 1,000 jobs—at $585,000 per job, an overpriced public investment. The result was no jobs other than for prosecutors who filed bribery and bid-rigging charges following disappearance of the money. A New York City official admitted using public funds to pay his personal meal bills. The official was the Brooklyn district attorney, whose duties include prosecuting misuse of public funds.

In Illinois, where four of the last eight governors have been jailed for corruption, the state auditor, whose job is to prevent theft of public funds, was accused of corruption. The case had not gone to trial at this writing; prosecutors alleged $247,000 missing from an expense account was listed as "auto repairs." The former head of the Chicago public school system was sentenced to four years in prison for taking kickbacks for steering a $20 million no-bid contract: this, at a time classes were being canceled because funds were short. A Chicago official was sentenced to ten years in prison for accepting bribes to steer a contract to a company that operates red-light ticket cameras. Lights next to the cameras were calibrated to show yellow for only two seconds so that even careful drivers could not avoid tickets. This was double corruption—kickbacks on a deal whose purpose was to swindle taxpayers. Say what you will about the Windy City, at least the grift is entertaining.

In California and in New York, managers of pension funds for retired state workers have been convicted of taking bribes. Pension funds long have been a favorite of organized crime, since no individual pensioner has any way of knowing what's happening with the ledgers; now the organized-crime approach to pension funds extends to state government. California state senator Leland Yee was imprisoned in 2015 after pleading guilty to racketeering. Yee helped enact strict gun laws for San Francisco and then, having created a shortage, engaged in gun-running, which would be entertaining were it not so serious.

At the federal level, in 2016, Representative Chaka Fattah, a longtime member of Congress, was sentenced to ten years for corruption that included stealing from a "charity" he ran. Many celebrities and politicians seek donations for "charities" or "foundations" that exist to fund their lifestyles and, to boot, provide a vehicle for claiming tax deductions for routine expenses average people pay out of pocket. Presidential candidate

Hillary Clinton and former president Bill Clinton took an estimated $156 million in donations for a "foundation" they employed partly to flatter their egos; some of the donations appeared to have been conferred in exchange for government favors and State Department entrée. (The Associated Press tried without success to establish direct quid pro quo, though in regard to the *Citizens United* Supreme Court decision that allowed corporate donations to candidates, Hillary Clinton declared that quid pro quo need not be shown because any sizable transfer of money to a candidate perforce buys access.) The nineteenth-century sociologist Max Weber proposed that government seeks a monopoly on the power to use violence. A twenty-first-century Weber might say government officials seek a monopoly on the power to reach into other people's pockets.

John Mikesell, a professor at Indiana University, estimates corruption in government construction contracting costs taxpayers up to $1,300 per person annually. The Istanbul-born economist Daron Acemoglu of the Massachusetts Institute of Technology has written that government corruption "empowers unrepresentative elites while shutting out the rest of the country." To the extent candidates in democracies make Santa Claus campaign promises, then once elected use their positions to benefit themselves, democracy may seem disturbingly like organized crime. Vaishnav, the Carnegie researcher, contends the leading threat to freedom in India—owing to the country's size, the democracy experiment in progress there is more significant than events in the United States—is that local and state candidates openly present themselves as gangsters, because voters think they need gangsters to get things done with India's notorious calcified bureaucracy.

Pilferage by government officials does more than waste taxpayers' money—the more troubling impact is that it diminishes the legitimacy of democracy. The Roman Empire's worst adversary was not Huns on horseback galloping across the steppes, rather, corruption within. On the flip side of this coin, Singapore is more affluent than nearby societies with about the same geography, resources, and people because the government is both democratic and incorruptible.

Increasing availability of information via the Internet may create an impression that government venality is out of control, when what's really happening is that long-standing practices finally are being exposed—if the latter, a healthy development. But the same digital and economic forces that improve the Internet are harming newspapers and local news broadcasters, whose cutbacks on coverage of city halls and statehouses have opened the door to the next round of graft. Whatever the underlying situation, there is no doubt the same candidates who stab their fingers in the air about street crime don't want political crime prosecuted.

IN PAST CENTURIES, AUTHORITARIAN REGIMES and monarchies did not so much as pretend to possess the consent of the governed: czars and strongmen were essentially crime bosses. After World War I increased the appeal of democratic institutions, some nations took to holding fake elections in which victory for the top dog was assured; afterward he would say, "See, the people chose me." The crime-boss mode of government controlled Germany under Hitler, the Soviet Union under Stalin, and China under Mao—they were not in office for twelve, thirty, and thirty-one years, respectively, because they were loved. Today, crime-boss government has controlled Cuba and North Korea for more than half a century, while fake-election mode continues in Africa, Russia, and elsewhere. Muammar Gaddafi was a crime-boss ruler of Libya for forty-two years, until his assassination in 2011. Omar Torrijos was a crime-boss dictator of Panama from 1968 to 1981; he awarded himself the title Maximum Leader. When Fidel Castro died in 2016, he had run Cuba for fifty-seven years, staging ersatz elections so that he could pretend to have popular support—that is, to flatter himself. Yahya Jammeh became crime boss of Gambia in a 1994 coup and stayed in office until 2016. After Gambians demanded a real election and voted him out, Jammeh refused to leave office, until a West African international military force massed at the border, threatening him with physical eviction. Then he departed, taking along tens of millions of dollars' worth of gems and original art he had acquired with looted public funds. Hafez al-Assad ruled Syria in thug style for thirty years; his 2000 death set in motion the Syrian civil war, which is about who would get to be the new dictator. At this writing, Robert Mugabe has been the Big Brother of Zimbabwe for thirty-seven years. His style of campaigning is to have opponents arrested.

In 2016, Scott Anderson, for twenty-five years a roving international correspondent, wrote a reminiscence of his experience: "By 2011, any Egyptian younger than 41—and that was roughly 75 percent of the population—had only ever known two heads of state, while a Syrian of the same age had lived his or her entire life under the control of the father-and-son Assad dynasty." Anderson found the crime-family and fake-election premises of rule, utilized in many nations but most pronounced in Africa and the Middle East, a recipe for "utter stagnation."

Honest leaders chosen by free election are the best option for any society. The difficulty liberal democracies, including the United States, are having with the "honest" part is more than disquieting. Please don't, if a Republican, blame voter fraud or, if a Democrat, blame voter suppression. Voter fraud and voter suppression are the Loch Ness Monsters of contemporary political special-pleading—they always vanish back into the lake before witnesses arrive. Voter fraud and voter suppression may alter low-turnout local races for sheriff or county council; studies consistently show neither has any impact on national elections. Republicans cry voter fraud, and Democrats cry voter suppression, to avoid facing that the public did not like their candidates or policies. Blame must be shifted.

That many nations have changed, since the 1940 low point, from authoritarian to democratic affords hope that every nation will make this transition. In Africa, China, the Middle East, Pakistan, and elsewhere, citizens want free elections and freedom of speech; governments of their countries strive to prevent both. For a century, those who long to be free have looked to the United States as their exemplar. Will this continue?

"THE MOST WORRISOME DIMENSION OF the democracy recession has been the decline of democratic efficacy, energy, and self-confidence in the West, including the United States," says Larry Diamond. "There is a growing sense that democracy in the United States has not been functioning effectively enough to address the challenges of honest governance. As I travel the world, I see that people everywhere pay tremendous attention to events in the United States. When they observe a bigoted plutocrat succeeding here, this gives cheer to the world's dictators."

Diamond is no street-theater agitator. His office is at Stanford's Hoover Institution, a mostly conservative public-policy study center that is the right's answer to the mostly liberal Kennedy School of Government at Harvard. And he finds the winner of the 2016 American presidential election a "bigoted plutocrat." Defenders of democracy must accept that Trump was chosen—there's no assurance that free elections will produce good leaders. But those who are chosen must be held to high standards. Before becoming secretary of defense, James Mattis, a retired Marine general, said, "America has two fundamental powers, intimidation and inspiration." Of the two, inspiration is both preferable and more effective. This works only when the United States, and its president, sets an admirable example.

Donald Trump comes from a TV-show background in which it's normal to look directly at the camera and lie. Make-believe stories and fictitious statements are perfectly reputable in the cinematic and theatrical arts, so long as presented to the audience as such. President Reagan came from an acting background too. But prior to seeking the White House, Reagan was governor of California and studied public policy extensively; by the time of the 1980 campaign, he had become a statesman. Trump ran for president before holding any office or spending one minute studying civics and took the helm of the United States while still at the stage of thinking that, like an actor, his job was to deliver lines.

Office-seekers have told lies before, and will again. The issue with Trump is that once in the White House, his constant lying continued, giving "cheer to the world's dictators." When Trump fired FBI director James Comey in hopes of stopping an investigation into his ties to Russia, then publicly warned Comey not to speak out, dictators nodded in approval. How could the United States continue to preach representative government to the rest of the world when its own leader thumbed his nose at the standards of democracy?

Those standards, based on the US Constitution and the legal framework that descended from the triumph of 1789, are elaborately designed to resist aspiring tyrants. Odds are the Constitution will prevail over whatever the forty-fifth president dishes out. Nevertheless, it is disturbing Trump has such a gift for telling lies that he convinced 63 million voters

America is in terrible shape and needs its governing institutions destroyed, when the country has never been in better condition, and its institutions, if balky and expensive, are the most successful of any nation's—there are two hundred countries that wish they were the United States. And it is disturbing that Trump makes America seem dazed and confused before a world looking for democratic encouragement. These aspects of the forty-fifth presidency will be disconcerting long after Trump has consigned himself to the dustbin of history.

PERHAPS ONE POSITIVE EFFECT OF the Trump election will be to convince the young to vote. Turnout in 2016 was 71 percent for senior citizens and 46 percent for those age twenty-nine and below. The young have an easier time reaching the polls than seniors, but the latter group is the one that makes the effort. By not voting, the young allow the old to demand extra subsidies, with the invoices handed to their juniors; years along, saddled with other people's debts, those now young will rue their mistake.

The top three of the 2016 presidential race—Donald Trump, Hillary Clinton, and Bernie Sanders—were Social Security recipients. In that year those serving in the House of Representatives, in the Senate, and on the Supreme Court had their highest average and median ages ever. One reason American politics is gridlocked is that elderly leaders restage disputes that are decades out of date, like high school reunion couples arguing about who should have gone to the prom with whom. Fresh thinking is needed, which means young people running for office and the young voting. Presidents need not be old and out of touch: John Kennedy was forty-three when sworn in, Barack Obama was forty-eight, Franklin Roosevelt was fifty-one, the younger George Bush was fifty-five. As happened in 2016, elections will produce leaders who are old and out of touch if the young do not cast ballots.

DIAMOND, WHO THINKS TWO-PARTY DUOPOLY is the worst aspect of US politics, offers this reform prescription for reviving the country's "democratic efficacy, energy, and self-confidence": open primaries, repeal of laws that prevent primary losers from filing for the general election, an end to gerrymandering, resolution of the lobbyist revolving-door problem, rank-choice voting, and presidential election via popular vote. Let's examine each of his ideas.

Open Primaries. Fewer than half of America's states hold open primaries in which voters may cast ballots for any party. The others allow only registered party members to vote, and only for their party. This is done to discourage third and fourth parties; those who seek a voice in primaries must declare as a Democrat or Republican. In New York State one can declare as a Conservative, and in Minnesota as a member of the Farmer-Labor Party, but these are exceptions; as a practical matter, in most states primary voters must consent to the party duopoly. Closed primaries meant that a Democrat or independent who wanted to vote against Trump in early 2016 had to change his or her registration to do so, while surrendering the chance to vote for or against Democrats and independents. The Framers, who did not anticipate the development of a party system, would be shocked to learn that the last president who was not either Democratic or Republican was Millard Fillmore in 1850. Because under the Constitution the states control their voting rules, states must act to fix this problem.

(Aside on primaries) Most states hold primaries that feel like the general election—same polling places, same machines, same poll judges. This makes it seem the existence of Republicans and Democrats is somehow mandated by law—and that's what the party duopoly wants voters to think. Dressing up primaries to look like general elections is rationalized as helping voters rehearse for the big event. The real purpose is to create an illusion that the Democratic and Republican Parties are formal aspects of government. If states no longer sanctioned primaries, this illusion would end, giving new political parties a chance.

(Aside on states) Few pieces of legislation are more cynical than the 2002 Help America Vote Act. The bill, whose ostensible purpose was to require states to install voting machines that do not cause spoiled ballots, also requires states to collect data on voters' lives and electoral habits. In many instances, only political parties and political action committees can access the data; the duopoly uses the information to sustain its

stranglehold. Neither Democrats nor Republicans in Congress want to repeal the bill, which has been manna from heaven for incumbents.

(Aside on voting by mail) When the United States limped in with 61 percent turnout for the 2016 presidential ballot, Oregon, which votes by mail, achieved 79 percent. Turnout at that level—nearly the 81 percent turnout in 2017 national elections in the Netherlands, a global leader in civic participation—would make American presidential choices more representative, while raising the odds that whoever wins has a mandate to govern: clear-cut victors are good for democracy. There are proposals for voting by laptop or phone, but the hacking hazard is obvious. Oregon's rule achieves an ideal balance between ease and civic participation: voters must have a physical address in the community, not just a web address.

Repeal "Sore-Loser" Laws. Forty-five states prevent a candidate who stood for a Republican or Democratic nomination from filing for that year's general election as an independent. This is why Sanders was not on the ballot in November 2016: technically he gave up, but he knew most states would bar him in any case. Sore-loser bans are another manner in which states treat the primaries, which ought to be private events, as if they were decreed by the Founding Fathers; such laws exist to protect Republicans and Democrats against those who challenge the two-party cartel.

End Gerrymandering. In 2016, polls showed a meager 11 percent approval rating for Congress—and who were these 11 percent kooks who thought Congress was doing well? Yet 97 percent of incumbents in the House of Representatives were reelected, with an average victory margin of 37 percent—almost everyone from an extremely unpopular House of Representatives was reelected by a landslide. This happened because most House districts have been gerrymandered to manipulate results. Gerrymandering has been an issue in politics of the House of Representatives since Elbridge Gerry, elected governor of Massachusetts after the 1810 census, jiggered districts to create safe seats for cronies. A 97 percent reelection rate for an extremely unpopular House would cause even Gerry to think his own idea has gone too far. Because the Senate cannot be gerrymandered, in 2016, the incumbent reelection rate was 87 percent. Apply this rate to the House, and many more newcomers would have won.

Though gerrymandering is an old problem, recent developments have made this a stronger tool to protect incumbents who, facing little threat at the ballot box, devote their time to selling the public down the river to lobbyists and interest groups. Those developments include zip code analysis and block-by-block or apartment-building-by-apartment-building "microtargeting" of voting patterns, using data gleaned from surveys, the census, and the Help America Vote Act. I live in Maryland's Sixth Congressional District, an incongruity that begins in bright-blue Montgomery County near Washington, DC, then stretches 178 miles west along a narrow band to the deep-red rural boundary of the state. Following the 2010 census, this district was created by the Democratic-controlled legislature to keep conservatives out of the Maryland congressional delegation. In other states, Republican-controlled legislatures create equally absurd districts to keep liberals out. Dirty pool is dirty pool, no matter who does what to whom, and the effect in most cases is to ensure reelection of incumbents regardless of how poorly they perform.

In 2017, a federal court in Wisconsin ruled that gerrymandering intended to allow a political party to cartelize seats violates the one-person-one-vote premise. The Supreme Court is expected to issue an opinion on this case in 2018. Gerrymandering has ended in California, the largest state and, perhaps, another instance in which California will be at the forefront of American social change. Golden State voters approved a ballot initiative creating a neutral commission to reapportion California following the 2010 census. The commission had bipartisan backing from the Democratic-controlled statehouse and the Republican-controlled governor's mansion. The reform has worked well. Are you listening, other forty-nine states?

No matter how carefully composed, any commission someday may engage in hanky-panky regarding lines. If algorithms drew congressional districts, arm-twisting could be eliminated, while disclosure of the code would make the process completely open. Google "impartial automatic redistricting" to see such a proposal and test-drive the effect on your state. Note the algorithm creates districts that not only are politically non-aligned, also do not have byzantine elongations that separate racial blocs or pit identity groups against each other.

Reform Lobbying. Lobbyists exert too much sway in Congress and state-houses, while too many officials leave office and go through the revolving door into this world's third-oldest profession. Federal legislation enacted in 1995 appears to regulate lobbying, but is toothless. At election time, the political parties make a great show of promising tougher standards but by the strangest and most amazing happenstance never follow through. Democratic Senate majority leader Tom Daschle denounced lobbyists, then after leaving office in 2005 became a lobbyist. Republican Donald Trump promised strict binding prohibitions against his top officials becoming lobbyists, then once in the White House quietly amended the standard to a voluntary pledge with no enforcement mechanism. The Constitution's assurance of freedom to "petition for a redress of grievances" protects the basic activity of lobbying, as it should. If disclosure rules and revolving-door prohibitions were substantive, voters would know who's paying whom for access and whether interest groups across the spectrum, from oil barons to teachers' unions, are really writing the legislation that lawmakers claim serves the public.

Rank-Choice Voting. The duopoly system often forces voters to make queasy choices, as in 2016, when the only meaningful general-election options were the odious Trump and the oleaginous Clinton. The devil's bargain enjoining Democrats and Republicans is that both make sure no party but one or the other attains office, while true independents are frozen out. In rank-choice voting (sometimes called "instant runoff"), voters order multiple candidates by preference; the result can be that independent or third-party candidates stand a better chance. Maine and San Francisco use versions of rank-choice voting in state and local ballots; Australia and New Zealand employ the system for national elections. Rank-choice voting does not guarantee the best candidate wins—no method offers that. But in the United States, rank-choice would break the headlock the Democratic and Republican Parties have on what the Framers intended to be an open election system.

Popular Election of the President. Two of the five most recent US presidential elections (2000 and 2016) concluded with the popular-vote loser taking the White House via the Electoral College. The total was nearly three of five: in 2004, George W. Bush recorded a comfortable margin in the popular vote, but had the result in Ohio differed by 2 percent, John Kerry would have been president. Whatever one thinks of the 2000 balloting—some studies found Bush the true winner in Florida, others, Al Gore the true winner—the fact that the recount-of-a-recount-of-a-recount mess could happen in the first place was made possible by the obsolete Electoral College structure. Popular vote would have meant no hullabaloo and no uncertainty regarding who belonged in the Oval Office.

By calling into question the legitimacy of the US president—even if he was the true winner, Bush's stature irrevocably was damaged—the Electoral College in 2000 fashioned the current situation in American politics in which whoever's out of power endlessly rehashes what happened in the past rather than addressing what needs to occur in the here and now. More rehashing followed the 2016 ballot: had popular election been in effect, there would have been no controversy, rather, a clear result. As microtargeting of voters grows more effective, the risk intensifies that popular winners will be White House losers, triggering unending controversies, hamstringing national leadership, and mortifying democracy.

Electoral College rules are well known, and candidates ignore those rules at their peril. Trump campaigned with the College in mind; Clinton's head-scratcher decision to focus on Arizona and North Carolina, while shunning Michigan and Wisconsin, was the political equivalent of booking passage on the *Hindenburg*. But the Electoral College rules being well known does not prove them relevant to the present day.

Steve Silberstein, an official of the advocacy group National Popular Vote, has argued, "The Constitution asks us to elect a president of the United States, what we get is a president of Ohio and Florida." He notes that from the point at which Trump and Clinton became the 2016 nominees, they made 228 campaign appearances in Florida, North Carolina, Pennsylvania, and Ohio compared to a total of two appearances in California, New Jersey, New York, and Texas. Those four states, ignored in presidential politics, have almost twice the population of the four states showered with attention. And America lectures the world on democracy!

At the founding of the United States, the House represented the people by popular vote, the Senate represented the states by appointment, and the president was chosen following debate among a small assembly of electors. The first five chief executives, George Washington through James Monroe, received no popular votes; their campaigns occurred entirely in the Electoral College. In 1824, states began to stage beauty-contest ballots for electors; gradually the process morphed into today's system, in which voters check-mark the president they want but do not actually cast a ballot for that person. The winner-take-all criteria employed for electors in states other than Maine and Nebraska created the 2000 and 2016 situations in which large margins in major states were overcome by lots of tight margins in midsize states. This is a worst-of-both-worlds outcome from the perspective of 1789—the majority does not rule, but the Electoral College does not debate the qualifications of candidates either.

No one supposes the 1789 voting system inviolable. In 1868, the Constitution was amended to extend the franchise to former slaves; in 1912, to begin direct popular election of senators; in 1919, to extend suffrage to women; in 1962, to forbid poll taxes; in 1971, to extend suffrage to any person at least eighteen years of age. That's five significant reforms of the manner in which the United States stages national voting. Replacement of the Electoral College with popular election of the president is the amendment needed today.

If in effect now, direct election would boost the Democratic Party, owing to its strong position in California. But a generation ago, Republicans held the strong position in California, and a generation hence, may once more. Future political affiliation cannot be foreseen. In my lifetime, seven national electoral realignments have occurred: in 1964, 1968, 1974, 1980, 1994, 2008, and 2016. That realignments happen quickly shows the unpredictability of voter sentiment. There's no knowing which party popular election of the president may favor in the future—or even if that party exists today.

Sparsely inhabited states don't want to abolish the Electoral College because they would lose clout compared to populous states. But the small states already have extra sway in the Senate, which since 1912 has stopped embodying statehouse-versus-federal concerns (the Senate's original constitutional function) and now serves primarily to overrepresent sparsely inhabited areas. Wyoming gets two Senate seats for 590,000 people, and California gets two Senate seats for 39 million, which equates to sixty-six times as much Senate representation for the Wyoming resident as for the Californian. The twenty-two smallest states have the same population as California, but twenty-two times as much power in the Senate. Those twenty-two small states are disproportionately conservative, placing the Senate well to the right of the polity as a whole.

When America was mainly wilderness, much of the nation lived far from cities and communication occurred via mail pouch carried by riders; the Framers had good reason to fret that the needs of the countryside would be overlooked in the capital. Those reasons have expired. Today 79 percent of Americans live in cities or counties that are contiguous to cities, while communication with farm and mountain areas, and with Alaska and Hawaii, has become instantaneous. Today the political concerns of the many should outweigh the political concerns of the few, bearing in mind that the Bill of Rights safeguards the individual under all circumstances. That means no more Electoral College with its weird impact of causing circumstances and political attitudes in the large cities of California, New York, and Texas to become irrelevant during presidential elections compared to a roadside diner in Pennsylvania or a county fair in North Carolina.

Because thirty-eight states would need to ratify a constitutional amendment to replace the Electoral College with popular vote, the task is not easy. What task worth accomplishing is easy? Overcoming gerrymandering in California was supposedly impossible for the same reason that overcoming the Electoral College supposedly is impossible—that those favored by the existing system would block change. Arnold Schwarzenegger, a conservative Republican, pushed California to end gerrymandering by framing the issue in terms of the public good. Acting on concerns of the public rather than of interest groups and lobbyists has fallen out of favor in US politics—one reason for voter disgust regarding elections. "Reform can never happen" has been argued many a time, and this argument usually proves wrong. What American democracy needs most is a revival of the sense of public spirit. People might respond.

THE SUMMATION OF WHY THE dictators don't win is that democracy is better at money and war: democracy can deliver the carrot while threatening the stick. That democracy also is ethically superior to dictatorship is a nice bonus. But democracy needs to clean up its own house regarding corruption and favoritism to insiders. There's no law of nature that says the postwar movement toward freedom cannot reverse.

Democracy is the best form of government for the better world we hope to live in. But a better world is just a faraway dream, right?

Part II

∞

The Arrow of History

Chapter 8

How Declinism Became Chic

PREPARING FOR THIS WRITING PROJECT, I read an unsettling book. The author, a highly sophisticated observer, warned that American society is spiraling out of control. Expanded international trade is costing jobs; change comes so fast the head swims; improved communication will accelerate change still further; new views on race, gender, and sexuality are upsetting hallowed traditions; Old Europe is exhausted and sagging; China will take over the world. Worst, the American educational system cannot keep pace. Deficient regarding mathematics, technology, and science, American schools do not teach the young what they need to know for a globalized environment.

Then I read another disturbing book. This one warned that waves of dark-skinned refugees who adhere to strange religions are pouring into the United States and western Europe—just pouring in! Unless borders are closed and towering walls constructed, Nordic-descended white people could vanish from the Earth in as little as a few decades.

A third troubling book drew my attention. This volume declaimed that Anglo-Saxon civilization has entered a final phase, "wintertime," inevitably to be absorbed by the higher fertility rates and warlike societies of the developing world. The Enlightenment was a promising idea, but doomed: kaput, finis, *hasta la vista*.

Seeking relief from such gloom, I bought tickets to the theater. I saw one of the most-performed plays in American drama: twelve men argued about illegal immigrants ruining the nation as crime turned inner cities hellish. I walked across Broadway to another playhouse to watch the work of a winner of the Pulitzer Prize for Drama. The subject was how illegal immigrants are tearing the United States apart.

Perhaps the movies would divert me. I attended a top-grossing film in which a Hollywood star declared, "This used to be a hell of a good country. I can't understand what's gone wrong with it." Perhaps song and dance would lift my spirits. I took a seat for the best-known American musical, which was about how outsiders were pouring in—just pouring in—and ruining everything, even demolishing that most cherished of daydreams, young love.

So I retired to my den with a novel by one of the few Americans to achieve the Nobel Prize in Literature. The novel told of a United States entering an ultimate cycle of deterioration, undone by greed in big business, corruption in government, plagiarism in academia, and inaction against illegal immigrants.

Every work mentioned above is between fifty years and a full century old—so surely the United States and Europe must have failed by now!

The first book is *The Education of Henry Adams,* published in 1918. Grandson of President John Adams, Henry Adams led a favored life of affluence and connections: among many celebrated persons, he knew both Charles Darwin and Charles Lyell, central figure of modern geology. The author was so sure the United States was headed to hell in a handbasket that he left instructions that the manuscript for *The Education of Henry Adams* not be conveyed to a publisher until after his death, to spare himself the melancholy of encountering public endorsement of his assessment of the impending crack-up of Western society.

The second book is *The Passing of the Great Race* by Madison Grant, published in 1916. Grant declared government-imposed eugenics the last, desperate chance to sustain the United States and Europe. The third book is *The Decline of the West* by Oswald Spengler, published in volumes from 1918 to 1923. The United States and Europe are about to join Babylon and Pharaonic Egypt on the scrapheap, Spengler contended; don't even bother trying to save freedom, whose time has passed.

The first play was *Twelve Angry Men* by Reginald Rose, initially performed in 1954 as a drama, then a famed 1957 movie starring Henry Fonda. Twelve jurors known only by their numbers debate the effect of illegal immigration on the United States and whether what's now called stop-and-frisk policing is public safety or racism. The second play was Arthur Miller's *A View from the Bridge,* which premiered in 1955, just before Miller wed Marilyn Monroe. The illegal immigrants believed by the play's protagonist to be ruining America are not from Syria or Yemen, rather, from Italy. The movie was *Easy Rider,* premiering the same month as the Apollo 11 moon landing and starring Jack Nicholson. The musical was *West Side Story,* which premiered on Broadway in 1957. The Jets gang wants the Sharks gang out of New York City. Members of the Jets consider the Sharks encroaching foreigners, though the latter are from Puerto Rico, where, since 1917, anyone born is a US citizen. The novel was *The Winter of Our Discontent* by John Steinbeck, published in 1961. Students know Steinbeck's *Grapes of Wrath,* which presents working-class Depression life as an indictment of American society. *Winter of Our Discontent* presents postwar white-collar life as an indictment of American society.

About the Henry Adams contention that Americans fail to grasp science: since the establishment of Nobel prizes for physics, chemistry, and medicine, there have been more winners from the United States than from the next five highest-winning nations combined. About those immigrants "just pouring in" (Donald Trump's mantra from the 2016 presidential campaign): in 1946, there were 10 million immigrants in the United States; today there are 39 million and the country is richer, stronger, more fair, and more free than ever. Why use 1946 as base year? That was the year Trump was born, as the grandson of an immigrant.

In the many decades that incorporate the above works, levels of income, health, freedom, and education have risen steadily for typical Americans; discrimination, poverty, and pollution have diminished. By every objective measure, through the period in which writers and artists thought the United States would disintegrate, instead America became the most successful nation ever. Old Europe hasn't done too badly either. Many millions of people want to get into the United States and European Union; hardly anybody wants to leave. Yet Americans and Europeans continue to believe their societies are declining.

*　　*　　*

PANICS REGARDING DECLINISM HAVE A long tradition in the United States, despite the country's seemingly divine endowments of resources and geography. Increase Mather, born in 1639 in what was then the Massachusetts Bay Colony, wrote jeremiads declaring North America was already waning; his pulpit-pounding sermons about imminent ruin were quite popular. Former Colorado senator Gary Hart noted of negativism in American annals, "Thomas Jefferson was sure the country was going to hell when John Adams supported the Alien and Sedition Acts," an event that occurred in 1798.

Down through the decades, many circumstances that ought to have been seen as setbacks instead were pronounced utter calamities. The 1957 launch of *Sputnik* caused CBS News to bulletin "a national emergency," while *Life* magazine, then a leading US print publication, said the Soviet Union was about to pass the United States in global power. *The Atlantic*'s 1994 cover story "The Coming Anarchy" basically declared the world about to end, with developing nations swirling into apocalyptic brutality while Western economies and governments would cease functioning. Anyone can be wrong with a prediction—I have some experience in this regard—but *The Atlantic* is the world's best magazine, and the author, Robert Kaplan, is a skillful writer; both embraced the most outlandish possible interpretation of declinism, as did President Bill Clinton, who praised the article from the White House. Had the magazine made a mainly positive forecast, while the cover read "The Coming Gradual Improvement," the article would have proven analytically correct, but the sense of dreadful decline would have been missing.

Donald Trump's daffy statements about American decline are troubling; bear in mind that daffy statements about American decline are time-honored, and as likely to come from Democrats as from Republicans. Following *Sputnik*, Lyndon Johnson, soon to be president, took to the Senate floor to deliver a speech asserting Moscow had a secret plan to control Earth's weather from outer space. In 2012, Barack Obama's National Intelligence Council produced a report declaring that by 2030 the United States would no longer hold great-power status, while China's GDP would exceed America's. For this declinist forecast to come true,

China must more than double its GDP in just twelve years, which is all but physically impossible. (China's economy does rival America's on purchasing power parity, a measure different from GDP.) And if you want to mess with America's military in 2030, be my guest.

Intellectuals embrace declinism because other views are looked down upon as Pangloss or Pollyanna. In contemporary US academia, the idea that the United States has been a net positive for humanity is close to a forbidden thought. David Brooks wrote in 2017, "Starting decades ago, many people, especially in the universities, lost faith in the Western-civ narrative. Now students are taught that Western civilization is a history of reactionary oppression." American history is indeed full of acts of violence against minorities. But had Western civilization never occurred, the academics who now condemn it would not have comfortable positions at universities. Much more important, would today's world really be a better place?

Research centers and government agencies lean toward doom predictions because they justify more funding: scientists may be truth-seekers but also are grant-seekers. Political interest groups lean to doomsday and devil-figure claims in order to support their fund-raising. Rising prosperity creates both more money to give as donations and a larger donation-seeking class with ever-more-specialized grievances. The George W. Bush presidency was a heyday for donation-seekers who call on wealthy liberals, the Obama presidency a blissful time for donation-seekers whose mailing lists tilt right. The Trump presidency has been a godsend for television news ratings, newspaper circulation, late-night comedians, and fund-raisers of all stripes. If Trump were an honest, reasonable man, fund-raisers would be inconsolable.

Driving the process is competition to see who can announce the most exaggerated alarums. During his presidential candidacy, Bernie Sanders said American government "serves only the one percent." Sanders made this claim a short time after Congress enacted ObamaCare, an income-transfer program that was funded by capital-gains taxes on top earners and projected by the Congressional Budget Office to redistribute $1.3 trillion from the wealthy to the working class in its first decade alone. Sanders further said, "Our country today faces a series of unprecedented crises." This wasn't true in any meaningful sense—but was what audiences expected to hear.

Choosing the month of June 2016 arbitrarily, I tracked occurrence of "crisis" in the *New York Times,* excluding instances that required the presence of the word, such as quotations. In June 2016, the *New York Times* used "crisis" 914 times, or 30 instances per day. To the most important newspaper in the world, every event was an unprecedented crisis.

The United States hardly is alone in being afflicted by overblown negative claims, nor is our moment distinctive in this respect. Two thousand four hundred years ago, Plato mused that the sweetly ordered world of his youth was going to hell in a handbasket, though did not use the Greek word for "handbasket." Had Plato attended a Donald Trump rally, the philosopher would have stroked his beard, adjusted his sandals, and nodded sagely as Trump declared, "It's always bad, down, down, down"—a sound-bite-length version of the ancient Athenian opinion of directionality.

WHY DID PLATO THINK IT's always down, down, down? The first reason is that, like every woman and man alive during the period of organized societies, the founder of the Platonic Academy was descended from the wary of the far past. Natural selection preferred the watchful over the unworried: the former scanned the horizon for predators, the latter stopped to smell the flowers and got eaten by something. Our bodies produce spikes of adrenaline during danger; slow-flowing cortisol, the stress hormone—a sort of junior adrenaline—raises acuity and muscle response during uncertainty. There's been a lot of uncertainty through history, and there's more coming. Since time immemorial, those whose bodies were good at producing adrenaline and cortisol were more likely to reproduce than others. Genes are not destiny, but do tell us about ourselves: what they tell us regarding declinism is that we are descended from ancestors who had pessimistic mind-sets and stressed-out blood chemistry. Maybe we're better off this way: Bertrand Russell said, "The more you complain the longer God lets you live." But if natural selection causes men and women to be wary, along with that comes negative worldview.

The second consideration is that, like everyone past, present, and future, Plato was getting older, not younger. Psychologists and philosophers have noted that the Garden of Eden account is a metaphor for the passage from youth to adulthood. Most children (obviously, and very sadly, not all) awake to a world that seems sweetly ordered by benevolent parents who provide for their needs. As time passes the parents stop providing, the youthful sense of unlimited promise is lost; childlike wonder is replaced by disappointments, betrayal, and unsatisfied wants. During youth, an incomprehensible amount of time lies ahead; once midlife begins, the time to come palpably shrinks. Aging is not a curse: many older men and women acquire wisdom and an awareness of well-being that are as satisfying as the avid visions of younger years. But getting older puts everyone into the mind-set of decline. From middle age forward, decline colors every condition a human being can experience.

We project this mind-set onto our societies. Right now the demographics of the United States and European Union are shifting toward age; the result is declinism projected onto these societies, whose aging members perceive an approaching endpoint even if, overall, most things are getting better for most people.

FEARS OF DECLINE HAVE BEEN rally cries for centuries. In many cultures at many times, people have felt mysterious forces are robbing them of their due, trusting exhortations about the Good Old Days. Trump's 2016 campaign avowal, "I love the old days," appealed to the hazy—and factually untrue—belief that things were better once. Most of what happens is not driven by mysterious forces, but rather by the inevitability of change, which usually improves life but is stressful, nerve-racking, and impossible to predict. People don't want to hear that change either cannot be stopped (the usual case) or should not be stopped, any more than people want to hear that aging cannot be stopped. People want to hear that what they once had was stolen away, and they've been wronged. The sweetness of youth is always stolen away, for all persons; good-old-days arguments in politics seek to apply this sense of loss to society as a whole, even if society's become better than it was when we were young. Donald Trump would not have convinced American voters their nation is in the throes of decay unless they were already inclined to think so. This incongruous condition—the United States has never been better off, yet voters perceive disaster—was reached for reasons unrelated to Trump. In the same sense, the equally incongruous condition of the United Kingdom on the 2016 day of the Brexit referendum—never better off and voters mad as hell—was reached for reasons unrelated to the prime minister and Parliament of that year.

One aspect of declinism looked the same in both nations in 2016: the new notion of majority victimhood. Roughly a generation ago, national leaders, along with colleges and public schools, began to come clean about disgraces in the American and British heritages. Disgrace in the United States included slavery, segregation, and policing abuse of African Americans; mistreatment of American Indians and Asians (the Chinese Exclusion Act of 1882 is a little-remembered lowlight); refusal to admit Jewish refugees until late in World War II (a dreadful failing of the otherwise noble Franklin Roosevelt); discrimination against women and gays. Disgrace in the United Kingdom included slave trading, imperialism, millions murdered for profit in colonies; jailing of the poor and gays; refusal to help Jews flee Hitler (look up the 1938 Évian Conference and feel sick to your stomach); repression of Ireland. These and other instances of American and British behavior had been airbrushed out of history. Roughly a generation ago was the juncture at which, finally, leaders in the United States and United Kingdom began to acknowledge the shame that came with greatness. Public schools and colleges made teaching social shame a point of emphasis, as well they should have.

Somewhere along the way, that groups should receive recognition for suffering was transformed into a notion that such recognition should be sought-after. Minorities have obvious reasons for seeking acknowledgment for their suffering; what happens if the majority feels itself mistreated too? White majorities in the United States and United Kingdom (and some other nations) began to long, in George Will's memorable phrase, for "the coveted status of victimhood."

At face value, it can seem absurd that anyone would covet victimhood. But if being perceived as a victim leads to benefits, there may be a logic to desiring this station. After all, schools were teaching that society abuses all who lack wealth, so why shouldn't whites, the majority of whom are not wealthy, be seen as victims? Schools and employers were granting special treatment to favored groups through affirmative action and other programs—why shouldn't whites seek special treatment?

Perhaps the swearing-in of the first African American president allowed American whites to begin to think of themselves as, for the first time, on the short end of the stick. In the hands of the white majority, the notion of victimhood has proven powerful, simply because, in the United States and United Kingdom, there are more whites than other types of people combined. The majority's message in 2016 might have been, "You're a victim? Two can play at this game." Trump seemed to appeal because he was the first major candidate of the coveted-victimhood era who explicitly told whites they are exploited when special favors are granted to minorities. "I am your voice," Trump told campaign audiences—the voice of grievance. Trump's constant recitation of the terms "unfair" and "rigged" was what political consultants call a "dog whistle"—a way of encouraging white voters to apply to themselves the vocabulary of victimhood and of racial grievance, without actually mentioning either.

The issue is not whether a white-victimhood worldview is true: what matters is that large blocs of voters believed it to be true. White Americans and Britons have experienced many hardships, including sacrifices in wars to protect the freedom of those who didn't fight. But white men could tell themselves that no matter how hard times might get, at least society made people like them kings of the hill. Increasingly, American and British whites do not perceive society as ordered for their benefit. African Americans and members of other minority groups long have known that society's deck is stacked against them and have learned to live with this while struggling against it. The sentiment is new to whites, who, because of their numbers, gave victimhood status the largest voting bloc it had ever achieved in the American and British votes of 2016.

Perhaps you are thinking, "Wait a minute, everybody can't be a victim." But every man or woman can view himself or herself as a victim. We all know people with good looks and money or both who nevertheless wallow in self-pity. If everybody's a victim, someone or something must be to blame. This leads to a larger question beyond Trump and Brexit.

*   *   *

IN THE 1950s, AS RONALD Reagan was shifting from Hollywood to politics, he traveled the country greeting staff and presenting lectures at the factories and offices of General Electric, sponsor of his anthology series *General Electric Theater*. His standby talk was titled "Our Eroding Freedoms." This was during one of the periods now enshrined in mainstream collective nostalgia as Good Old Days, yet Reagan warned of loss and deterioration. The 1950s—a decade of stifling conformity, much lower living standards, and discrimination against blacks, women, and gays— were not the Good Old Days in any respect, except perhaps for Kiwanis recruiting and drive-in movies. Nor was freedom eroding, rather, about to expand in dramatic fashion with the Civil Rights and Voting Rights Acts; with the admission of women to elite colleges and universities; with *Times v. Sullivan* and *Times v. United States* (better known as the Pentagon Papers case), court decisions that liberalized news reporting; with the *Gideon* case (in which the Supreme Court ruled that poor people accused of crimes must have counsel); and with other advances. But Reagan told audiences their liberty was being taken away, and they clapped warmly.

The best of Reagan's many biographers was Lou Cannon, who, being a California Republican, understood the fortieth president in a way many on the East Coast did not. Cannon reports that as Reagan traveled the United States in the 1950s developing the political lines he would use in his ascent to the White House, he discovered that people wanted to blame whatever they didn't like, or whatever was wrong in their lives, on the federal government. They did not want to blame their families, friends, or communities, and despite the American ethos of self-reliance, they emphatically did not want to blame themselves. Washington, DC, made the perfect fall guy. Distant, furtive, expanding—extension of federal power was essential to US victory in World War II—denounce Washington and listeners will nod in approval, the aspiring president found. So Reagan, whose politics then were center-left—at the time he was pro-union and advocated an open border between the United States and Mexico—began taking potshots at federal government, and his popularity grew.

Reagan's embrace of a blame-Washington worldview set the tone for an American political discourse in which blame-Washington would become the theme many politicians and lobbyists employed to obtain lucrative sinecure in the place they pretended to despise. Ritualized denunciation of federal government helped elect recent presidents Reagan, the younger George Bush, and Trump. By early 2017, both residents of the White House (Trump and Vice President Mike Pence), the speaker of the House of Representatives (Paul Ryan), the majority leader of the Senate (Mitch McConnell), the White House chief of staff (Reince Priebus), many dozens of members of Congress, and two Supreme Court justices (Samuel Alito and Clarence Thomas) had secured for themselves Washington opulence by unremitting censure of Washington. Al Sharpton once said, "Fundamentally, life is a hustle," and Sharpton knew whereof he spoke. Through the past half-century, blaming Washington has been the most effective hustle in American national politics.

Regardless of whether blaming Washington was a self-promotion tactic or a genuine philosophical position, sinecure-seekers in politics and media have persuaded large numbers of voters to believe the analysis, with its concomitant illusion of a nation headed down. In recent decades, polls have shown that Americans hold steadily lower regard for their capital. Americans hold ever-lower regard for much of what occupies the national and international stages, while thinking their own communities and schools—the places they see with their own eyes—are shipshape. Gallup polls find it has been a generation or more since Americans felt "a great deal of confidence" in big business, Congress, courts, health care, the press, public schools, and organized religion. All could stand improvement, but have all really gone into death spirals? Americans think the distant national institutions with which they rarely interact are in dire debility, yet simultaneously say they like the clergy, doctors, schoolteachers, local officials, and businesspeople they know personally.

Federal agencies need streamlining, and some of the regulations they impose are ridiculous. But the United States is the strongest, most powerful, and richest country, the best in creativity—science, business, art—the country that every other government in the world envies. Washington,

DC, and the laws the capital enforces have *nothing* to do with this—American exceptionalism is just some weird coincidence that happens in spite of the federal enterprise being rotten? How could the nation be such a success if its capital city really is, as Trump claimed, in thrall to shady incompetents?

Many in the American polity further believe Washington is squandering their money while their statehouses and city halls are not. In the United States, about 40 percent of state and local budgets appears to be raised locally but actually originates with the national debt—borrowed by Washington, then transferred to states, counties, and cities. The result is a bookkeeping switcheroo that allows state and local leaders to seem a lot better than they are while making Washington seem worse.

If states paid their own way, state and local taxes and debt would rise while federal taxes and debt declined—by large amounts in each instance. Voters would fulminate against governors and mayors while praising Washington. This gives state and local politicians, who outnumber national politicians by a substantial margin, a stake in promoting the "Washington is awful" story line, which protects them while feeding the narrative of declinism. Having the capital borrow so that states and cities can appear to be funding themselves promotes a second false narrative—that Washington is giving away money to the poor and to immigrants that was earned by the hardworking majority whose communities would be self-sufficient were it not for federal handouts. American states and cities emphatically are not self-sufficient, but the national bookkeeping switcheroo makes them look that way.

Americans seem to derive an odd comfort from assertions that whatever they don't like is Washington's fault rather than the result of interwoven forces that offer benefits as well as costs, or the fault of neighbors and communities, or simply their own fault. Wanting to believe the worst, Americans get worked up about small failings while taking large social and technical advances for granted, as if they fell from the sky. Campaigning, Trump seemed to many voters a breath of fresh air because he promised to tear down Washington institutions. Most likely actually doing so would leave average people worse off. But lots of people believed tearing down institutions would be good because decades of false alarms and blame-Washington poseurs had sold them the illusion of decline.

REFLECTING ON SUMMER DAYS AS a lifeguard when he was a young man, Reagan said he was surprised to learn that people became angry when rescued. Those pulled from the water were not appreciative, rather, incensed at the lifeguard, because everyone along the beach saw them struggle and knew they had failed to look after themselves. By the same token, many voters are not grateful to federal programs for assisting them but cross, since needing assistance implies they are at fault. During the 2016 Brexit referendum, areas of the United Kingdom that are net recipients of European Union subsidies voted to leave, while areas that are net taxpayers to Brussels voted to remain. During the 2016 presidential election, in general the states that receive more in subsidies from Washington than they send in taxes voted for Trump—who promised to destroy the source of their subsidies—while states that pay more to Washington than they get back voted against Trump.

Some interpreted this behavior as ignorance. A *New Yorker* cartoon showed sheep grazing by the campaign billboard of a Trump-like wolf, whose election slogan was I AM GOING TO EAT YOU. But most likely the 2016 instances of American and British areas voting against the sources of their subsidies reflected a desire to have it both ways—people sought to receive money from government while at the same time shaking their fists regarding handouts. They didn't want anyone to observe the lifeguard assisting them to safety.

Government had little impact on our grandparents' fates, unless conscripting them for battle. How much you made, how you spent what you made, how you lived—that was on you and on whatever private organizations you decided to join. As recently as the Great Society phase of the mid-1960s, Americans expected little government assistance in their lives until retirement age was reached. No more. As the economics writer Josh Barro has noted, in 1960, 23 percent of the US GDP flowed through local, state, and national government: today 41 percent does, and nearly all the increase is transfer payments and entitlements. Figures are higher still in contemporary Europe. All the levels of government in Germany control 44 percent of GDP; in the United Kingdom, 48 percent. In Belgium, Denmark, Finland, and Sweden, there is now more GDP controlled by government than by individuals and the private sector.

As the government's slice of GDP widens, so does awareness among voters that complaining is a path to special dispensation. This incentivizes complaining, generating more declinism—along with its sibling illusion, that reforms won't work.

FOR DECADES, GALLUP HAS CONDUCTED a monthly poll on this question: "In general, are you satisfied or dissatisfied with the way things are going in the United States?" The last time a majority of Americans deemed themselves "satisfied" was winter 2004. Since then, the majority response has been negative—at this writing, negative for 161 consecutive months. In recent years, an average of 70 percent of Americans have pronounced themselves "dissatisfied" with the circumstances of their country. Beyond the Gallup metronome swinging from positive to negative, another thing that happened in the winter of 2004 was that Facebook opened for business. Of course, the fact that two developments happen synchronously does not establish one caused the other. But in this case there may be a connection.

With blistering speed even by the standards of digital tech, Facebook would acquire 200 million regular users in the United States. As Facebook's public profile increased, satisfaction with the nation declined. Facebook would prove a versatile, well-liked platform for practically anything users wanted to share and also would refine the art of accentuating the negative. Since Gutenberg's printing press, headline writers have known that if it bleeds, it leads: the communications business has been highlighting bad news for centuries. Facebook found ways to push the envelope. Birthdays and cuddly kittens have roles on Facebook and similar social media, but claims of racism, sexism, conspiracies, sorrow, and the scandalous are what punch above their weight.

Facebook would steer the evolving social-media world toward the negative: to go viral, social-media posts, whether brief tweets or rambling diatribes, need three-second "WTF!" shock value. Suggestions of horrifying abuses, plus a blurry picture that could be anything, inspire a "WTF!" reaction. There's no shock value to "Living standards, education levels, personal freedom, and longevity gradually improve," which is what the United States has accomplished since 2004. Pew Research Center national satisfaction polling has, since 2004, been showing the same result as Gallup. Pew finds that on political topics, angry, downbeat Facebook material draws more likes and shares than complimentary or neutral material. The phenomenon is not confined to the United States. Researchers at the University of Canberra found that, beginning around 2007, when broadband became common in Australia, Aussies started to say that their nation was in decline, though by any objective metric, conditions down under are the best they have ever been.

By the 2016 presidential election, Donald Trump openly would endorse unfounded innuendos and crackpot conspiracy theories that voters encountered mainly via social media. Before the arrival of Facebook and related new enterprises, learning of a crackpot conspiracy theory required trekking to a dingy underground bookstore to purchase some dense, smudgy, self-published volume. By the 2016 election, all that was required was a brief glance at a device in your pocket or purse. Two generations ago, according to Pew Research Center studies, 75 percent of Americans trusted government to be honest and do what is right in most cases. By the 2016 election, just 12 percent held such trust. Is this because they were at last beholding the long-hidden truth? Perhaps, or perhaps they had become surrounded by unfounded innuendos and crackpot theories with a low burden of proof—usually, zero. The University of Rochester historian Christopher Lasch, who died in 1994, wrote that in contemporary American culture, "the important consideration is not whether information is true but whether information sounds true." In an amazingly short time, Facebook and similar social media doubled the firepower of "sounds true." Simultaneously, American perceptions of the United States went downhill.

FACEBOOK ORIGINALLY WAS INTENDED FOR laptops and the old CRT-display desktop computers. The initial purpose was for members to post pictures and accounts of themselves that friends would view on desk-bound technology. (The name comes from mugshot "face books" of fellow students that freshmen were given when arriving at university.) The first iPhone went on sale three years after Facebook debuted. Few guessed how rapidly smartphones would improve in quality and expand in popularity. As the writer Timothy Noah has noted, by 2007, Americans sent more text messages than they made voice calls. By 2011, as iPhone sales passed the 100 million mark, Facebook and other new-media endeavors migrated from people's desks to their pockets as social-media platforms became more likely to be accessed by mobile phone than via stationary devices.

It is a remarkable technical and economic achievement that just a decade after debut of the iPhone huge numbers of average people around the world carry affordable communication devices any one of which exceeds the total computing power available to NASA during the moon landings. Today 80 percent of Americans and Europeans have smartphones; about 40 percent of the entire world has a smartphone. Facebook has about two billion daily users. Was there ever a point at which two billion people bought a newspaper or walked into a post office on the same day?

The proliferation of smartphones loaded with social-media apps changed the physical relationship between people and news. A newspaper or magazine rests on a table, the television sits on a cabinet or hangs on a wall—if you walk away, they do not follow you. As smartphones improved, people began keeping their phones with them constantly, even when moving from room to room. There was no walking away. To employ a smartphone for social media entails holding the device up near your face. The face part of Facebook acquired an unexpected meaning—in your face, physically close.

Film students and fledgling stage directors are taught the concept of "comic distance," which in one interpretation says the nearby seems tragic while dialogue taking place in the distance is more likely to get laughs. This is why sitcoms typically have a large set—a living room, a headquarters—where several people are seen at once, while tear-jerkers feature close-ups of faces. When social-media posts are viewed on smartphones held a short distance from the eyes, what is beheld loses comic distance and leans tragic.

Holly Shakya and Nicholas Christakis, sociologists at the University of California at San Diego and Yale University, respectively, found in a 2017 study of Americans that the more time they spent on Facebook the worse they felt, even if looking at cheerful posts. Some of this effect probably stemmed from what social media calls FOMO—Fear of Missing Out, the sense that everyone except you is invited to a party. Women and men have experienced FOMO for generations: when you've got nothing to do on a Saturday night, you imagine others are off somewhere having a great time. Facebook and similar social-media sites amplify FOMO by flooding your mental inbox with images that give the impression everybody except you is indeed having a great time—regardless of whether this is true, since people always smile when they know a picture is being taken. Shakya and Christakis determined that updating one's Facebook status and clicking "like" to Facebook content posted by others are associated with "a decrease of five percent to eight percent of a standard deviation in self-reported mental health." Glancing at social media now and then is a good way to stay informed about friends and current events, but devoting significant attention to smartphone screens appears to have roughly the same depressive effect as drinking too much. Americans increasingly devote significant attention to Facebook, then feel bad.

Going into the 2016 election, Pew Research reported that Americans' leading sources of national-condition information were social media and cable news, both of which relentlessly overstate discord. Newspapers and network newscasts, though hardly free of bias, in most cases impose professional standards—they acknowledge the competing sides to a story, attempt to be fair, and engage in efforts to determine if assertions can be confirmed. Social media has no professional standards. The computer code, and sometimes people, behind Facebook, Google, and similar popular social-media and new-media sites weeds out vulgarity and explicit bigotry, but doesn't care if material is fact-checked or attempts to be fair, while pure fiction must be totally obvious to be filtered out. The result is that on people's phones are unending streams of a blubbery information-like substance "that doesn't distinguish between the fake and the real," as Robert Thomson has said.

Just as in daytime television shouting and weeping cause people who are doing something else to look up at the tube, on social media wild exaggeration and contrived fabrication get people to look. What they see when they look is an imaginary world in which everything's getting worse. (I have labored for years on this book keenly aware that *Doomsday 2020!* is what would suit contemporary expectations.) A generation ago, men and women got two injections of bad news per twenty-four-hour news cycle: when morning newspapers arrived and when network evening newscasts came on air; some days they had a third injection if the postal carrier placed a serious magazine in the mailbox. Now bad news is ratta-tatta-tat the day long via smartphone and other screen devices, the news cycle measured in minutes. Every time you look at your phone, you see dozens of just-posted hurtful reports and irate claims. Many posts don't withstand scrutiny or are abject forgery. But who has time to analyze the sources? Statistics say most things are getting better for most people, yet right here on the phone are these indignant anecdotes—in your face in a literal sense.

IT'S BECOME COMMON TO HEAR that contemporary electronic expression causes polarization. In 2006, the year before arrival of the iPhone, a political science textbook, *Red and Blue Nation,* said:

> A lot of what looks like rising polarization actually is society becoming more opinionated. A generation ago it was considered good manners to avoid expressing strong opinions, especially regarding politics and religion, while the media restricted opinion to quotations from experts and to clearly labeled editorial pages. In recent decades, such restraints have weakened. Once teachers wanted to hear students recite the opinions of great writers, discouraging students from expressing their own viewpoints: now teachers hector students who do not have their own views. We not only expect talking heads on television to have instant opinions on anything and everything, we expect the person on the street to have strongly held opinions on any topic raised.

The strongly stated judgment—the 2006 textbook called it "the opinionization of America"—came into fashion roughly around the time the arrival of social media began to enable fast, inexpensive dispersal of opinions. This conveyed the sense of a sudden explosion of anger, which in turn suggested society must be far worse than society seems. What really was happening was a sudden explosion of opinionization—women and men expressing in strong language feelings they'd long held, but kept to themselves because keeping one's opinions to oneself was seen as good manners.

Now shaking one's fist is seen not only as acceptable but obligatory. In the current generation, American society has grown more open, tolerant, and respectful of differences. Today it is viewed as shameful to speak to others who are present in racist or sexist language or to disparage the ethnicity or sexuality of anyone within earshot. Simultaneously, society has opinionized: it is expected that all will possess strong views. Opinions require outlets. As Americans treat each other personally with rising respect, they get angrier and angrier at persons they've never met, whom they know solely as far-off figures in politics and entertainment or as handles on social media.

It has also become common to hear that contemporary electronic communication creates an echo chamber in which people are exposed only to points of view they already agree with. This is not a recent development. In our parents' generation, most American and European cities had at least two newspapers, one with a conservative/management slant, another with a liberal/labor slant. Many would subscribe to, or purchase at newsstands, the paper whose worldview they liked. Thought journals of earlier periods had open predispositions: rare was the Republican who took the *New York Review of Books* or the Democrat who relished *National Review*. Back further, when exposure to ideas and opinions involved attending political speeches or Chautauqua-style lectures, men and women were more likely to go out of their way to hear those they already agreed with than those who would challenge their assumptions. The echo-chamber problem 'twas ever thus.

The difference under Facebook is that the echo chamber is generated automatically. Social-media sites use algorithms that channel liberal comments to liberals, conservative comments to conservatives. This piles mechanized predisposition atop the observer expectations that human nature already has, replacing the previous information world—in which, via the publications and channels you selected, you'd encounter what you actively chose to agree with—with a new information world consisting of what you agree with but did not choose. The sifting happens in the background, unbidden, and can seem not to be happening. The impression created is of a world gone mad.

NEWSPAPERS AND MAGAZINES OF THE 1980s and 1990s invested in various attempts at zoned or specialized editions that would deliver content optimized to specific parts of the nation or specific areas of large cities. The costs of printing and distribution frustrated these efforts. Freed from such expense, social media can offer a hyperzoned edition on every subject.

Because there will always be more going on than any one person can grasp, and because their algorithms are efficient, Facebook and similar platforms can project many hyperzoned worlds: a world in which the alt-right is running wild, a world in which the academic left is out of control, a world in which crime and illegal immigrants are unrestrained, a world in which evil tycoons scheme to destroy jobs. Name the world you want to live in—or that you want to complain about being victimized by—and a social-media algorithm will generate that world. Dozens of mutually contradictory feeds can be assembled, all compelling, all based on what's happening at exactly that moment and thereby making the user feel she or he must check the phone continuously. And ratta-tatta-tat, all bad.

The electronic ease and constant updating of the contemporary echo chamber differentiate today's observer bias from this effect in the past. Because in most cases the social-media user is only glancing at web material while doing something else, most takeaways are superficial—and that makes it easier to generate bogeymen. Devil figures long have been essential to political or interest-group fund-raising but until recently have been hard to sell, requiring arduous campaigns of direct-mail and planted stories. Now devil figures are easy to sell—social media aggregator algorithms practically create them automatically.

This is not a Good Old Days contention regarding communication. The contemporary order of weak revenue for serious news organizations but ready access to thousands of such organizations around the globe, plus searchable laptop retrieval of government, research, and historical documents, is superior to the prior order of strong revenue for a few big-media stalwarts but none of the rest. If the stalwarts are maddened by the attention paid to Silicon Valley upstarts—"I have no information that supports these tweets," FBI director James Comey actually said in a congressional hearing in 2017—disruption always was inevitable whether social media came along or not.

But by boosting the negative, then presenting the results ratta-tatta-tat on a device physically close to your person, Facebook and kin push the United States and Europe further toward belief in their own declines. This aided Brexit and helped Donald Trump, Twitter addict, become president, decrying an "American carnage" that was occurring almost exclusively in his own mind and in cyberspace. Nobody planned it that way. A lot happens that is not planned.

THE WIDER BELIEF THAT SOCIETY is headed down, along with wider claims of victimhood, has grown in the United States at approximately the same time as claims for liability and compensation have increased. Liability litigation sometimes receives short shrift: the law behind such suits may prevent corporations and others in power from harming those not in power, but whenever something goes wrong—and even in the Garden of Eden, things went wrong—society now wants blame assigned and settlements awarded.

Americans, especially, don't like to contemplate that life outcomes are influenced by luck and other impersonal forces: Americans want to presume merit and effort always explain success, while societal unfairness or sloth always account for failure. The psychologist Amos Tversky, who died in 1996, thought the human brain is wired to impose causality—to think "A caused B" rather than "B happened for a web of complicated reasons that no one controlled." The assumption of causality allows the well-off to believe they own more and earn more because they personally are deserving, not because their merit was aided by good luck while others' was not. Luck in this sense rarely means at the roulette wheel but more often genetics. Those born smart or athletic or attractive or artistic tend to think this shows innate personal worth, though such qualities, however admirable, are assigned largely as biological coin tosses. No one would say, "Because I flipped heads five straight times, I have been chosen." Many tell themselves, "Because I am intelligent/handsome/sexy/gifted, I am chosen." Whether we work hard and act responsibly is under our control; whether we are born with intelligence, looks, and talent is fundamentally luck.

If many outcomes are impersonal, no one is to blame. If, on the other hand, someone or some organization is to blame, compensation is deserved—and the wronged should be angry. Since the people immediately around us don't seem so bad, the someone to blame must be those we do not know—the other political party, the insiders in Washington, the dangerous illegal immigrants said to be pouring into the country in army-sized numbers though we never see this occur, the sexual predators said to be lurking everywhere, those with different religions or ethnic backgrounds. Research by Edward Mansfield and Diana Mutz at the University of Pennsylvania has shown that most Americans now think their own identity groups are hardworking and deserving, while other identity groups are spoiled and subsidized. As the lawyer and legal analyst Philip Howard noted in 2001, the assumption there is always someone to blame has made Americans more suspicious of each other, always "expecting a den of thieves, or worse." Much of what appears on the smartphone reinforces the den-of-thieves conception.

NOBODY PLANNED THIS EITHER, BUT the information-like substance that constitutes so much of contemporary communication reinforces fixation on anecdotes rather than on the larger picture. Anecdotes personalize events, and it's always more interesting to hear about a person than about a study debated at a roundtable hosted by a think tank. But just as the Bible is so long one can find a verse that appears to prove any contention about theology, the United States has 320 million residents: one can find an anecdote that appears to prove anything.

Politicians, commentators, and social-media voices rely heavily on anecdotes, often anonymous. Stories of individuals matter, but should be balanced against larger trends. Increasingly, the worlds of mainstream media, social media, politics, and academia—where anecdotes receive the glorified label "stories"—present the single instance as more revealing than the larger arc, though the reverse is true.

In his 2011 State of the Union Address, Barack Obama quoted "a struggling small business owner" and a "woman who said she felt the pain of recession." Both were conveniently nameless, and as journalists long have known, people who don't exist do not complain about being misquoted. Suppose the two persons to whom Obama alluded do exist. Like most anecdotes in policy debates, their stories have a negative flavor; Obama would not have quoted an unnamed "woman who said she felt her life was going really well." As the Florida State University psychologist Roy Baumeister has shown, the greater likelihood of listeners retaining negative than positive information biases media coverage—and political anecdotes—toward the unhappy.

Even if most things get better for most people, there will always be individuals and families with many types of serious problems, as well as places where conditions may constitute a valid need for assistance from society. Fixation on such instances rather than on the larger picture, however, undercuts the case for the next round of reforms by making it seem the ship is sinking.

Yes, this book contains anecdotes, and here are a few. As this project progressed I found, when talking to audiences, that discussion of increasing longevity coupled to reduction of disease rates always caused someone to raise a hand and object, "How can you say that, I have a friend who has cancer." Discussion of rising living standards and improvement of net buying power for average people always caused someone to raise a hand and say, "But I have a family member who is unemployed and says there are no jobs." Other indicators of social improvement always caused someone to raise a hand and say, "But I know a person who..."

At first I thought that for some convoluted psychological reason, good news scares people; after all, we are trained to expect the worst, and seldom disappointed. Eventually I came to feel that single anecdotes have acquired the same standing as large bodies of fact. Everyone knows the latter are more significant, but large bodies of fact are hard to fathom while anecdotes are self-explanatory. The trend toward ratta-tatta-tat of anecdotes on the phones we hold up close to our faces pushes us toward disconsolate views. Some questions do not have answers; what to do about fixation on anecdotes may be such a question. At the least, Americans and Europeans should be aware of the phenomenon and guard against the thought formula that boils down to, "I saw this terrible thing on Instagram and therefore everything must be terrible."

SOCIAL-MEDIA, CABLE-NEWS, AND TALK-RADIO JUDGMENTS without fact-checking or sourcing create a milieu in which overstatement may be carried to the absurd. Trump claimed during his campaign that the government was covering up the fact that 42 percent of Americans were unemployed, a number that would be possible only if senior citizens, infants, and the incarcerated were included. Stumping for Hillary Clinton, former attorney general Eric Holder declared that a "new Jim Crow" stalks America. The new Jim Crow turned out to be North Carolina's reduction of the early-voting period, used by a higher proportion of African Americans than whites, from seventeen days to ten days. A generation ago, no one in North Carolina could vote early; now a partial reduction in preferential treatment is said to be as horrible as turning police dogs on demonstrators. Conservatives spent years describing ObamaCare in apocalyptic language, though the program extended medical insurance to 14 million people previously not covered and helped moderate the growth of health care's share of the GDP. Liberalism went see-and-raise, the civil rights leader Andrew Young asking in 2014, "Has the world ever been in worse shape?"

Preposterous statements are a staple of politics: the Lincoln-Douglas debates and many other past political clashes contained hefty servings of hyperbole. In daily interactions within communities, the person who makes preposterous claims to family, friends, neighbors, and coworkers will lose face. Yet the same sorts of statements that cause loss of face when made to those whom we know personally cause attention and celebrity when made on television and, now, on social media. This is an aspect of the vexation that Americans say their own immediate communities are fine, but the nation is not: by and large the people immediately around us are not engaged in making preposterous claims, while politicians, cable-news guests, social media, and new-media outlets are.

The nonsense that swirls onto our smartphones and other screens can seem aimless. But as Emily Bazelon wrote in 2017 of Trump's calamity pronouncements, "a vision of a nation besieged provides justification" for extremist policies. This brings into domestic policymaking Hobbes's admonition that leaders like war because more power will accrue to them: leaders may like crises, or the perception of crises, in domestic affairs as well.

Trump's swearing-in assertion of "American carnage" was preposterous, but perfect for social media: short, snappy, anger-stoking, factually meaningless. Trump employed the buzz words to justify extremist policies. Eight years earlier, when Obama was sworn in on the same steps, he too declared the nation "besieged" and immediately asked Congress for special powers—in his case, authority to award $800 billion to Democratic Party interest groups. Officially this was to counter the Great Recession; the real purpose was to grant Obama more clout, since his advisers knew (or "should have known," as prosecutors say) that federal appropriations placed in the pipeline in 2009 would not impact the economy until the recession had already cured itself anyway. In his second term, Obama tried to award himself more power by writing executive orders rather than consulting Congress, making the preposterous claim that climate change justified bypassing legislative channels. Eight years further back, and before the 9/11 attack, George W. Bush claimed an energy-supply "emergency" justified special powers for the White House. Since Franklin Roosevelt, every newly elected president other than Dwight Eisenhower has pronounced that some kind of emergency validates extra power for the White House. Today social media amplifies such claims, and in so doing advances the sense of declinism.

Nazi analogies are by nature extreme, but that does not necessarily make them unfitting. Timothy Snyder of Yale University, among the leading historians of our day, finds Hitler believed in catastrophism—the reverse of the dynamism this book advocates. Hitler, Snyder has written, realized that conflating Big Lies, ludicrous gibberish, pseudo-science, and Judgment Day predictions "creates a rapturous sense of catastrophic time and thus the potential for radical action."

For centuries royalty and despots have wanted the public to believe the worst so that those at the top will receive more power; today this viewpoint has expanded to a broad range of officeholders, officials, lobby-ists, fund-raisers, and attention-seekers. If the public can be persuaded the situation is really bad, Trump and his advisers today, or the next president and her or his advisers tomorrow, will be treated with deference, while political organizations will command larger sums of money. Most worri-some, extremists, whose greatest desire is to sit in judgment of how others live, will have reason to impose their views on others.

THE CONTEMPORARY BELIEF THAT ONE'S immediate community is fine while the nation is in crisis may be strengthened by the drop in worship-service attendance, which began in Europe after World War II and now manifests in North America as well. The writer Peter Beinart has noted that a striking segment of Trump voters, those who bought the "Ameri-can carnage" line, share a trait: they describe themselves as evangelical Christians, yet do not attend church. "Rates of religious attendance have fallen more than twice as much among whites without a college degree as among those who graduated college," Beinart writes. Considering yourself strongly religious without being present at worship services may confer the judgmentalism that can be the worst part of religious observance—I am blessed by God, others are damned—without the sense of fellowship that can be the best part. Those present at Christian churches are reminded Jesus said, "This is my commandment, that you love one another." Those who view themselves as saved yet do not participate in worship services may find it easier to believe the worst about others whom they imagine to be terrible miscreants but never personally encounter. More time with the algorithm-generated hysteria of screens and less with the serenity of worship services of any faith may edge Americans toward accepting pro-nouncements of decline.

Increasingly, Americans reside among others of the same educational and class backgrounds, which social commentator Bill Bishop calls "the Big Sort." Freedom of association is a right—but what impact does this right have on declinist thinking? Bishop contends the United States is in the second generation of creating networks of communities in which liberals encounter only other liberals, conservatives encounter only other conservatives, and evangelicals encounter only other evangelicals.

Communities of the like-minded tend to be upbeat about local circumstances and downbeat regarding the national situation, Bishop reports. Rarely meeting and interacting with those who think differently can foster fake-news-style beliefs: liberals can think conservatives are the enemy, conservatives can think liberals are unhinged, evangelicals can blame the godless. Being in like-minded and like-educated communities eases one's thinking that far-off, never-actually-encountered people with different views are the cause of every ill.

Linked to Big Sort place-of-residence choices is what contemporary sociologists call homogamy, borrowing from botany a term to describe how, increasingly, the educated marry the educated, then become isolated from the views and concerns of the poorly educated. In 1960, 3 percent of US marriages involved both spouses having bachelor's degrees; by 2010, both spouses had a college degree in 25 percent of US marriages. Because parents' highest degrees earned are the best predictor of a child's highest degree earned, the offspring of a college-college marriage has a much greater likelihood of wearing a robe on a college commencement day, then going on to a good job, than the offspring of a marriage of two people who stopped at high school. Like freedom of association, freedom to wed is axiomatic, but both push society away from melting-pot mixing and toward homogenized groups that know of other groups mainly through alarmist drivel on cell phones.

Big Sort communities of left and right, less churchgoing, assortative marriage—these entirely voluntary forces, which may accentuate the perception of decline, meet at the point where liberty increases. There cannot be too much liberty, but there can be consequences. A 1992 book titled *The End of Equality* made a series of forecasts relevant to our moment. Written by Mickey Kaus, whose ideology defies categorization, *The End of Equality* warns that breaking down barriers of segregation and prejudice—and how could anyone be opposed to that?—will lead to a situation in which the downtrodden are no longer seen as harmed by society, but rather as getting what they deserve. Before *Brown v. Board of Education* and the civil rights acts, America actively worked to impede black citizens, who therefore could not be blamed if they failed in life. Once the school doors were open, young African Americans who refused to do their homework, or parents or guardians who refused to take away the video-game controllers to facilitate homework, had only themselves to blame. When colleges shunned the white working class, America actively worked to impede poor whites; once college admissions offices sought out the poor, white young people who did not strive for college had only themselves to blame. Kaus contends that since today's society no longer sabotages minorities or the poor, if you fail, you can't point the finger at society—you have to point the finger at yourself.

Kaus described this line of thought in order to reject it, but warned that such thinking could hold wide appeal. People will believe, he cautioned, that the segments of society with problems deserve those problems, that losers deserve to lose. Trump's go-to pejorative is "loser"—to hear the forty-fifth president talk, every third person he has ever met is a loser. We'd like to think Trump's affinity for this word arises only from his character defects. But *The End of Equality* forecast in 1992 that the word "loser" would enter an American lexicon once centered on optimism and hope. Now "loser" is here—as is the inexpensive, convenient means, via smartphone, to hurl such accusations, and other claims of negativity, at persons you've never met and never will.

"Many Americans now believe their children will not live as well as they themselves do," the investment whiz Warren Buffett said in 2016. "That view is wrong: the babies being born in America today are the luckiest in history." Time will tell what luck will be theirs, but his was not Nebraska cornball philosophizing, but rather, a sophisticated view. Deirdre McCloskey, the Illinois economic historian, has said, "People like to hear the world is going to hell, yet pessimism has consistently been a poor guide to understanding the modern world."

Things can go wrong of course, but things can go right. In 2003, Massachusetts became the first US state to recognize gay marriage. By 2014, two-thirds of American states were issuing same-sex licenses, and in 2015 a Supreme Court decision legalized the practice nationally. There may be philosophical objections to gay marriage, but pessimism regarding reform was "a poor guide" to approaching this issue. As Patrick Sharkey, a professor of sociology at New York University, has written, "The measures of dysfunction that stirred such alarm in the 1990s have declined noticeably. Welfare receipt has plummeted, the teen birthrate has fallen by half, the percentage of students who drop out of high school has diminished steadily and the homicide rate is the lowest it has been in 50 years." Pessimism was a poor guide to crime, pollution abatement, disease control, poverty reduction, food supply, safety, the prevalence of war, the spread of democracy, protection of natural resources—pessimism is almost always a poor guide. Americans think their nation is in decline. We're just getting started!

Let me end this chapter with another century-old American book, *My Antonia* by Willa Cather, published in 1918. In *My Antonia*—a solid contender for the Great American Novel—the protagonist must learn to let go of the longing for return to an imagined halcyon past. One hundred years ago, Cather felt Americans failed to appreciate how good they have it, or to focus on how much better life may become. She was right then, and still is right today.

Chapter 9

The "Impossible" Challenge
of Climate Change

IF YOU DOUBT GOD HAS a sense of humor, consider the Arctic ice cap. The artificial aspect of global warming is softening northern polar sea ice, which is down about 28 percent since 1980. The melting will make possible drilling for the large deposits of seabed petroleum thought to lie beneath the North Pole. That will mean more oil for cars and trucks, which will put more carbon dioxide into the atmosphere, resulting in more climate change.

God may be chortling as well over warming of Beringia, the corridor of permafrost from Siberia through Alaska to the Mackenzie delta of western Canada. The warming of Beringia is turning soil from the consistency of pavement to soft and wet enough to support crops that will feed the growing human family. But as the Russian researcher Sergey Zimov showed in 2006, the unusual soil found in Beringia—anyone visiting the outback of Alaska wonders, *What is this stuff I am standing on?*—contains more carbon than Earth's forests, though the latter cover a more extensive landmass. Thus the same warming that could make the permafrost tillable could accelerate carbon buildup in the atmosphere. Men and women would have plenty of gasoline to drive to stores with plenty of food on the shelves, even as the climate changes in ways that foul up everything else.

God may be having a few laughs over the changed politics of nuclear power too. In the late 1970s, Jerry Brown became governor of California largely on his opposition to nuclear power, particularly the Diablo

Canyon reactor station under construction near Los Angeles. By 2016, Brown was once again governor of the Golden State, and Diablo Canyon, having completed its planned service life, was slated to close. Brown, who failed to stop the reactor from opening in the late 1970s, failed again in 2016—this time in his campaign to keep the reactor from being scheduled for shutdown. Brown switched sides, from opposing reactors to favoring them, because nuclear power generates electricity without emitting greenhouse gases. Many former opponents of electricity from uranium now support the idea: reactors put no carbon into the air and, in American applications at least, have operated safely. (The antiquated reactors of Japan and Russia are another matter.) The impacts of Artic melting and the reversal of fortunes of nuclear engineering are amusing from a divine perspective—though the climate change joke is on us.

THAT THERE IS SOME KIND of climate change is irrefutable. The 2005 National Academy of Sciences finding of "strong evidence that significant global warming is occurring" was based on extensive analysis of decades of air, ocean, and land temperature records, and ruled out natural variation, however significant, as sole cause. In 2014, the National Academy of Sciences concluded that burning of fossil fuels was producing "clear evidence that humans are causing the climate to change." Through roughly the last decade, the American Association for the Advancement of Science, the American Geophysical Union, and the American Meteorological Society have found compelling markers of human impact on climate. These organizations are red-white-and-blue, not parts of the United Nations' Intergovernmental Panel on Climate Change (IPCC), which does good science in the background but is politicized at the top. The case for climate change can be made, convincingly, without reference to the IPCC or anti-American political theatrics of the United Nations. (The United Nations is credible on agriculture and population demographics but less so on climate because some member nations demand greenhouse-justified payments from the United States, essentially giving the General Assembly a financial interest in what is supposed to be an impartial scientific debate.) The case for rising temperature trends can be made, convincingly, from the Climate Change Science Program supervised by President

George W. Bush, which in 2006 declared "clear evidence of human influences on the climate system."

The existence of a scientific consensus is not the same as the assurance of truth. Scientific consensus has been wrong before and will be wrong again. Thomas Kuhn's 1962 book *The Structure of Scientific Revolutions* is well known for introducing the term "paradigm shift," less known for warning that scientists may endorse whatever viewpoint will maximize their incomes. Climate researchers are more likely to be funded if they cry apocalypse, and act accordingly. But though not proof, the scientific consensus on climate change is a strong indicator.

Much public debate regarding climate change is conducted in extreme forms of language that reflect current political schisms, as well as the location of fund-raising ahead of other concerns. To Energy Secretary Rick Perry—placed in charge of American nuclear laboratories a few weeks after appearing as a contestant on *Dancing with the Stars*—climate change is a "contrived phony mess" concocted by activists who for some unfathomable reason want everyone to freeze in the dark. To Bernie Sanders, global warming is "already causing devastating problems in the United States and around the world…if we do not act boldly the situation will only become much worse." To Jill Stein, the 2016 Green Party presidential candidate, a "climate state of emergency" should be declared; conveniently, such a declaration would give government absolute control over industry and consumer products, cherished Green Party goals. To Noam Chomsky, a favorite of academic alarmists, global warming is "the most important question in history," now "accelerating the race to disaster." To Paul Krugman, a favorite of media alarmists, Republican policies regarding greenhouse gases "may end up being a civilization-ending event."

In some ways climate change is the ideal issue for contemporary huffed-up public debate, being a blank slate onto which practically any view, from any ideology, may be projected, while no refutation (scientific, economic, or political) is possible with current knowledge. There's tremendous greener-than-thou temptation—elites in Hollywood and Manhattan and on the soiree circuits of Brussels and Washington, DC, can wag their fingers about how other people are destroying the planet, without making any sacrifice or hard decision themselves. There is equal propaganda temptation—shortly after becoming president, Donald Trump told executive agencies to stop using the phrase "climate change," which to the far right is code for socialism. In 1990, John Sununu, White House chief of staff for the elder President George Bush and holder of a master's in science from MIT, instructed executive agencies to use the phrase "climate change" because it expresses the totality of the issue better than "global warming." By 2017, the very accuracy of "climate change" was viewed, by propagandists, as objectionable.

Senator James Inhofe, until early 2017 the chair of the Senate Environment Committee, has called global warming "the greatest hoax ever perpetrated on the American people." From the opposite side, anyone who does not accept that climate change imperils civilization, if not life itself, is a "denier." Campaigning for the White House, Hillary Clinton blasted "the climate deniers in Congress," a statement that doesn't even make sense—no one denies there is climate. When the conservative attorney Scott Pruitt became Trump's EPA administrator, mainstream news organizations, including CNN and *USA Today,* scorned him as a "denier" based on a nuanced statement that may or may not prove correct but was hardly zealotry. (Pruitt said carbon emissions from US power plants are "not a primary contributor to the global warming that we see," the nuance being *primary* since less than 1 percent of atmospheric carbon dioxide originates with American electricity generation.) An earlier chapter noted that in modern politics, "sound science" has come to mean "whatever supports our donors' agenda." When Clinton declared on the presidential campaign trial that global warming must be real because "I believe in science," she was making a statement that served as a political cue card to Silicon Valley donors, in the same way that calling global warming a fraud is a cue card to the Mister Moneybags set.

Political cue cards have different meanings to different generations. Once, the Republican Party advocated research-based energy and conservation policies while the Democratic Party railed against calls for study as a delaying tactic. Today Democrats celebrate research (on sexuality as well as the environment), while Republicans cover their ears against its conclusions. At some future juncture, the positions may switch again.

Science is not necessarily correct, but on some issues is the best guide available, and in the main, science currently supports climate change concern.

UNLIKE THE POLITICAL CLAIMS MADE regarding the issue, the research consensus on climate change is real but limited. As described by Robert Stavins, director of Harvard University's Environmental Economics Program, the consensus is: that the Earth is warming; that at least some of the warming is caused by human action; and that further climate change has a small chance of being good, a likelihood of being bad, and a small chance of being terrible.

On this first point of consensus—that the Earth is warming—the US National Oceanic and Atmospheric Administration (NOAA), whose track record is excellent, has determined that for many recent years the global mean temperature has been about 1.5 degrees Fahrenheit above the average of the past century. Gradual warming has been happening for decades, except following the 1991 eruption of Mount Pinatubo, which clouded the upper atmosphere with heat-reflecting smoke and ash. Changing climate is seen in spring coming steadily sooner, in different rainfall patterns (more downpours, fewer light showers), in amended migratory patterns of some birds, and in acceleration of the melting of sea ice and land glaciers. (Some of this melting occurs naturally since, when the industrial period began, Earth already was in the rebound phase that follows an ice age.) Talk radio likes to assert a mystifying global warming "hiatus," but NOAA does not detect any hiatus in data regarding either air or sea-surface temperatures, both of which have been rising consistently. NOAA and other research centers further find that climate change is less rapid than expected. Air and sea-surface temperatures are increasing more slowly than forecasters expected; sea level rise is happening at a lesser pace than expected.

Despite the common assertion, changing climate is not seen in the frequency and intensity of hurricanes, typhoons, and tornadoes. The continental United States experienced little hurricane activity from 2006 to 2016, an unusually long calm spell, then powerful hurricanes Harvey and Irma struck in 2017. If Harvey and Irma proved artificial climate change, as some claimed, then the unusually long calm spell in previous years must have disproved climate change. The Geophysical Fluid Dynamics Laboratory, a division of NOAA, said in 2017, "It is premature to conclude that human activities, and particularly greenhouse gas emissions that cause global warming, have already had a detectable impact on Atlantic hurricane or global tropical cyclone activity." Nor do trends in property damage prove climate change; rather, the popularity of littoral homes and hotels has placed more property in the path of coastal storms.

Research suggests that downpour-style hard rains and increased incidence of flooding will imperil the near future more than the spectacular swirling tropical cyclone image beloved by cable news. "Anthropogenic warming by the end of the 21st century will likely cause tropical cyclones to have substantially higher rainfall rates than present-day ones," the Geophysical Fluid Dynamics Laboratory warned in 2017. The high water in Houston caused by Hurricane Harvey was joined, the same year, by an unusually severe monsoon-season flood in Mumbai. Simple rain—but of Noachian proportion—may be in store.

The second point of consensus, that human action must have something to do with observed changes in climate, is as strong as any contention in contemporary science. The third point is where the controversy resides—how harmful will climate change become? Whether artificially triggered global warming will imperil society or merely have minor effects, or even on balance be advantageous, remains an unknown.

The last century's mild rise in global temperatures has had positive consequences, extending growing seasons and moderating energy demand. (Globally, more power is used to heat buildings against the cold than to cool them against the heat, though that could change.) Additional mild warming could make Alaska, Canada, Russia, and Scandinavia more valuable: by accident of geography, almost all high-latitude land—frozen regions that would benefit from warming—is in the Northern Hemisphere. Some species would be harmed by polar warming (the Pacific walrus), while some may prosper as never before (the bowhead whale).

There is a poorly understood equilibrium between carbon dioxide, the primary artificial greenhouse gas, and water vapor, a greenhouse gas that occurs naturally. Carbon dioxide does not condense under atmospheric pressure; water vapor does. Water vapor that condenses into droplets forms clouds that reflect sunlight back into space. This natural feedback may be a reason carbon emissions from human activity so far have not led to the degree of warming many researchers expected. But there's no way of knowing how long the cloud-regulation effect may counter rising greenhouse levels.

SOME ADDITIONAL RISE IN TEMPERATURE is close to certain, owing to the amounts of artificially emitted carbon and methane already in the atmosphere and to the feedback impacts from melting of sea ice and glaciers. Melting replaces a reflective surface—snow and ice tend to bounce back sunlight—with dark colors that absorb heat.

Warming of the oceans, a larger effect than ice melting, may be the most worrisome feedback. Because most of the surface of the Earth is deep water that holds quite a bit more mass than the atmosphere, and because mass resists temperature changes—a stone house is cool inside on a hot day—the oceans are important to air temperature trends. The meteorological event known as the Little Ice Age lasted from about 1300 to about 1850 and left the seas relatively cool when the run-up in artificial greenhouse gases began. Cool on the 1848 day when the first modern oil well was drilled, in Azerbaijan, the oceans have been resisting warming of the atmosphere, another likely reason climate change has not taken off as predicted.

Once the relative coolness of the oceans is overcome by rising air temperatures, the seas will cease resisting global warming and begin to amplify the effect. In 2017, researchers led by Zeke Hausfather of the University of California at Berkeley showed that sea-surface temperatures have entered a cycle of increase. That suggests the oceans will be relatively warm for at least many decades to come—the phase of relatively cool waters lasted more than a century—even if greenhouse emissions yield to clean tech.

THE PROGRESSION OF ENERGY SOURCES from wood and agricultural wastes (very dirty in terms of both smog and carbon dioxide) to coal (cleaner than wood but still dirty) to hydroelectric dams (clean but approaching maximum output in most of the world) to petroleum (medium dirty) to natural gas (clean in smog terms but still contributing to the greenhouse effect) to uranium (very clean but very expensive) to solar and wind (very clean and potentially not expensive) shows society moving in the green direction. So too do conjectural clean energy sources such as harnessing tidal motion, collecting sunlight in space (where it is much more intense), and converting hydrogen into electricity and water. In 2017, British power companies got through an entire day without burning any coal for electricity. This happened during a delightfully temperate spring interlude when power demand was unusually low, but was a milestone nonetheless. England is on track to eliminate coal use by 2025, which would have seemed inconceivable in 1952, when British power and heat came from coal and a thick inversion of coal pollution killed 4,000 people in London.

Most of the world is on a similar trajectory, away from dirty energy toward clean. During the 2016 election season, Trump said he would bring back coal-mining jobs, speaking as though coal jobs were synonymous with economic success. That same year a Department of Energy study found solar energy production in the United States already creates more jobs than coal production. Political phonies resist information like this, being more concerned with what people believe than with what's true. Eventually the economic value of clean energy will be widely understood.

But even if industrial and agricultural emissions of greenhouse gases go down, the planet is fated to a phase of rising temperature—barring some sudden variation in the sun, which we really don't want to root for. The challenge of climate change is not so much to prevent global temperatures from rising—if the Earth only gets a little warmer, that will be manageable. The challenge is to control or adapt to the subsidiary impacts of greenhouse gases.

Rising sea levels could inundate many coastal cities. In 2016, Robert DeConto of the University of Massachusetts at Amherst led a team that calculated that during the previous "interglacial" period—about 115,000 years ago, the prior time, before our moment, that Earth was naturally warm—the oceans were twenty to thirty feet higher than now. Both liquification of land ice and thermal expansion of the oceans (warm water takes up more volume than cold water) are likely to raise sea levels at least three feet by around 2100, DeConto's research suggests, with sea-level increase continuing through the twenty-second century even if artificial greenhouse emissions end. Already some coastal cities of China are experiencing flooding during strong rains, perhaps a precursor of sea-level rise. Lakes will not be immune: Lake Ontario has been rising, at least in part owing to thermal expansion of its lambent waters.

Changing rainfall patterns could melt snowpack at high altitudes and make today's breadbasket regions arid. The freshwater now flowing down to the oceans could alter their currents, which, among other things, warm western Europe, most of which is north of Maine. The European Union could become cold even as median temperatures overall are rising.

The computer models employed to make climate change predictions provide little more than educated guesses, since computer simulations on any subject—climate, elections, sports—come to whatever conclusions are programmed into the model. Climate models predict the atmosphere will warm by another 4 degrees Fahrenheit, which would represent a global red-alert. Under such conditions, the Beringia region and a few other places would be better off. The near-Equator developing world would be worse off—a heat wave reaching 114 degrees Fahrenheit killed 1,200 people in Karachi in 2015, so imagine if it's even hotter—and the hot nations are, by and large, the poor nations, the ones least able, economically, to respond to climate change.

Models can be useful, but should not be mistaken for data. James Hansen of NASA, perhaps the world's most proficient climate modeler, declared in 2016 that his computers say dangerous global warming is about to begin. Hansen first said this in 1988 and has repeated the statement many times since, on each occasion predicting a different start year. Society simply does not know if global warming will become dangerous, or if so, when.

Not knowing what the climate future may hold really doesn't matter. There is plenty in what we do know to render climate change a vital concern for our world, considering climate will vary at the same time as population continues to rise and the economy continues to be turbulent. But should we feel frightened, as so much popular commentary suggests?

Stavins says, "I have two children in their twenties, and climate change is not high on the list of issues that I worry about for their futures. Climate change can be fixed. In the history of environmental protection, almost all challenges have been corrected more rapidly than expected and at lower cost."

HUMANITY COULD ADAPT TO THE difficulties of a warming world. Coastal cities could be abandoned; entire new farming regions could be plowed; health care and pension spending could be diverted to construction of enormous desalinization plants; European life could move indoors, as parts of Finland and Scandinavia already live. Wouldn't it be a lot more practical to control greenhouse gases?

The US Energy Information Administration (EIA) projected in 2016 that by 2040 global energy demand will rise 48 percent. About a decade ago, the projection was that global energy demand would rise about 100 percent. But even if global energy demand rises by a lower amount than once expected, a 48 percent increase is a formidable undertaking—one that must be achieved so that the developing world can live as well as does the West.

Jesse Ausubel, the Rockefeller University scholar quoted earlier, helped organize one of the first big scientific events on global warming, the 1979 World Climate Conference in Switzerland. Ausubel, you'll recall, in the 1980s made the crazy prediction that resource use would go down as living standards went up. Around the same time he made a second crazy prediction. Atmospheric carbon dioxide then was at about 335 parts per million (ppm); some analysts said reaching 350 ppm would cause human society to disintegrate, perhaps even trigger a mass extinction. Ausubel forecast that 400 ppm could be reached without notable impact on the world—and 400 ppm is the atmospheric carbon dioxide level today. Ausubel added a third crazy prediction: that carbon dioxide buildup in the atmosphere would continue until cresting at around 450 ppm, in around 2040, and then the buildup would stop, because clean energy would pass fossil energy around that juncture.

"I am still not much concerned with total emissions—they have either peaked or nearly peaked," Ausubel told me in 2016. "Emission levels are not the question, the question is whether the natural system is a dial or a switch. If it's a dial, and New York City gets the climate of Baltimore while some plants blossom sooner in the spring, that's manageable. If the natural system is a switch that's either off or on, there will either be no trouble or big trouble. Attempts to model this question produce whatever answer you build into the model. There's only one way to find out for sure, and we'd be a lot better off if we never found out."

Researchers who prefer five-dollar words call this the "linearity" issue. Is climate linear? That is, do slowly building greenhouse gas levels equate to slowly rising temperatures? If so, the impact of climate change sounds wieldy. Or does climate have tipping points? Say, a sudden alteration in ocean currents that leads to rapid transitions over broad areas. Should that prove to be the case, well, the sentence finishes itself. One need not endorse fashionably bleak views in order to want reforms that head off any tipping-point aspect of climate change.

Greenhouse gases are an air pollution problem. Previous air pollution problems—smog, acid rain, airborne lead, industrial haze, emissions of the chemicals that harmed stratospheric ozone—have been "corrected more rapidly than expected and at lower cost," as Stavins says. The fix for smog combined new technology (catalytic converters on cars, reformulation of gasoline and diesel fuel) with strict regulation. The fix for acid rain was a business model: "cap and trade," free-market exchange of emission certificates that decline in value until the underlying problem is corrected. The fix for airborne lead was an outright ban, as was the fix for chemicals that deplete stratospheric ozone. The fix for haze was engineering improvements at industrial facilities and construction sites. Because greenhouse gases are the biggest environmental challenge to date—the Super Bowl of pollution control—some combination of all these reforms will be required. All have worked before and can work again.

THE TIMING IS MORE FAVORABLE than might seem from the tone of climate change commentary. At this writing, for three consecutive years the world's emission of greenhouse gases has not increased, even as global GDP rises; in other words, global levels of greenhouse emissions already have begun to decline relative to economic output. American greenhouse emissions began to shrink a decade ago when the Great Recession started, then continued a trend of mild decline during the boom that followed. China—which emits about 50 percent more carbon dioxide than the United States—has shown a mild trend of greenhouse gas decline since 2014.

These decreases are not flukes, rather, harbingers. Oxford University's Institute for Energy Studies has determined that global per-capita carbon dioxide emissions peaked in 1979 and have been declining since, even as most of the world exhibits economic growth. The nonpartisan World Resources Institute calculated in 2016 that many of the world's advanced economies have already "decoupled"—their output of goods and services can increase, and their miles traveled by citizens can rise, as their carbon emissions go down. The United States, Germany, France, and United Kingdom are on the decoupled-economy roster, along with most of Scandinavia. The EIA reports that in 2010 the American economy needed 60 percent less energy per unit of output than in 1950 and, for reasons of market forces, is on track to need 75 percent less by 2025, even should government take no action. The advanced economies, including the car-centric United States, are learning to grow while becoming cleaner in greenhouse terms; if they can do this, eventually all nations will. The peak of artificial greenhouse emissions may not be in some distant future, rather, happening right now.

EVEN IF THE GREENHOUSE GAS peak has already come, the climate change issue will endure at least through the twenty-first century, as carbon continues to accumulate in the atmosphere—if you slow down the rate at which you pour wine into a glass, the glass still keeps filling. Carbon dioxide molecules take decades to cycle naturally out of the atmosphere, such that even if artificial greenhouse gas emissions stopped altogether, global warming could continue for a long time.

Yet optimism is justified. There is today, depending on the nation, little to no greenhouse gas regulation, and yet carbon emissions are declining relative to economic output. Market forces already favor greenhouse gas reductions, especially through efficient or clean uses of energy.

Green energy forms such as wind and solar are only a small percentage of the world's supply, but their share is rising steadily. As recently as 2005, in the United States hydro power generated about ten times as much electricity as wind: by 2016, US megawatts from wind power exceeded those from hydro power, and not because hydro decreased. Researchers led by physicist Nancy Haegel of the Naval Postgraduate School in Monterey, California, concluded in 2017: "The annual potential of solar energy far exceeds the world's total energy consumption." Currently the world uses about 15 terawatts of power annually. Deriving two to three terawatts from solar is a practical goal for the current generation, the researchers found, because photovoltaic modules have fallen in price by about 90 percent since the 1970s and appear on their way to being as cost-effective as burning natural gas, today's go-to source for new electric power capacity. Ultimately 15 or more terawatts of power could be attained from solar— at a vast capital investment. But from then on, no fuel supply would need to be purchased and no greenhouse gases would be emitted.

Improved forms of agriculture may reduce greenhouse emissions, as may clever ideas for energy infrastructure. In the latter category are the stove-sized lithium batteries that store electricity when kilowatts are plentiful, for use during high-demand periods. Offices, schools, and even some homes in Arizona and California are installing such batteries, as are some farms in Germany; they will lower the need for fossil energy in frigid or sweltering weather, further cutting greenhouse gases. Today the batteries are too expensive to be practical in most cases. Perhaps they will join the list of products that begin as playthings for the rich and later become affordable.

Another up-and-coming clever idea is local, distributed power production. Not that long ago, homes and schools did not have individual furnaces: an innovation of the late nineteenth century was steam made centrally and piped, a system that not only was inefficient but engaged a Goldilocks problem, as buildings were either too hot or too cold. (Parts of New York City and New Hampshire still employ central steam heat; much of urban China still is heated in this manner, with some buildings so hot the windows are kept open in winter while shivering occupants of nearby structures plead with the landlord for warmth.) When individual furnaces became the norm, comfort increased while total energy consumed for warmth moderated. Individual electricity production house-by-house—not just a solar boost but miniature power cells running, perhaps, on hydrogen—isn't practical yet, but may get there. Individual electricity production for small structures such as schools and stores is not cost-effective yet either, but can be described on an engineering basis, and the history of engineering is that once an idea can be described, implementation becomes a matter of ironing out the details and obtaining funding. Someday we may all kiss the central power utility good-bye. The result will be the end of the grid-failure power blackout, along with lower greenhouse emissions.

In the United States, California and most of New England have state-level partial restrictions on greenhouse gases. California imposed state-level automotive smog standards, other states matched, and smog-caused emissions declined nationwide. The Golden State lately has been imposing greenhouse gas standards. If other states match, this may tip the United States toward national greenhouse-gas control—without Congress or federal courts ever getting involved. And note: having America's strictest smog and greenhouse rules has not harmed the California economy, which continues to boom.

Beyond state initiatives, the United States has no national carbon-reduction program; at this writing, an Obama-era federal plan for reducing carbon from power plants was on thin ice, both with Trump and with courts. The European Union has a carbon-trading system modeled on successful acid rain trading programs; the permits have mildly reduced greenhouse emissions, but the European Union system is rife with loopholes. At a 2015 conference in France, most of the world's nations agreed to future reductions of greenhouse gases, though no enforcement mechanism was appended. (When, at a 1992 heads-of-state summit in Rio de Janeiro, the elder President George Bush endorsed nonbinding greenhouse goals, he was widely mocked by editorialists; when, in 2015 in Paris, President Barack Obama endorsed nearly identical nonbinding goals, he was praised as a visionary.) Trump said he would withdraw the United States from the Paris Agreement, though at an unspecified future date; at this writing, his gyrations on the question were too many to track. Considering the Paris deal has no enforcement rules and differs little from the 1992 Rio deal, whether the United States stays or goes may seem to matter little. The central achievement of the Paris negotiators is that most of the world's nations are now on record as accepting that greenhouse emissions must be reduced, a proposition many major nations denied until recently. Another positive sign is that China, India, Brazil, and Indonesia now talk to the West on climate change issues and exchange engineering information. Any area in which major nations cooperate builds trust in other areas.

The next step should be the policy that dare not speak its name: a *tax*.

THE WORD "TAX" HAS BECOME unutterable in American politics, where voters demand from government that they pay less and get more. More precisely, American voters demand: "Slash other people's benefits while increasing mine." A bill titled the Other Districts Budget Cuts Act would do well in today's House of Representatives.

"Tax" is not a hugely popular term in any democracy. Many modern political leaders won't say the word: the Western political class employs euphemisms such as "resources" and "revenue" to avoid speaking of the policy that dare not say its name. But a tax on carbon emissions could be just what the doctor ordered to create a profit incentive for inventions and innovations that constrain greenhouse gases.

Today the United States and European Union assess duties on labor, capital, and commerce, through income and corporate taxes, sales and excise taxes, and value-added taxes. In most instances, pollution and waste are not taxed. Yet labor, capital, and commerce are good for society, while pollution and waste are undesirable. Neoclassical economics teaches that whatever you tax, you get less of. The Western tax structure results in less commerce and investment than otherwise might occur. Taxes on labor discourage hiring (employers must cover half of a worker's payroll tax and in most cases provide health care insurance, effectively a tax against hiring), while taxes on capital discourage economic growth. If instead pollution and waste were taxed, maybe we'd get less of those.

After Trump was sworn in as president, a coalition of conservative establishment figures, including James Baker (secretary of state under the elder George Bush) and George Shultz (treasury secretary under Richard Nixon), proposed taxing greenhouse gases, then rebating the gain to consumers, which would have the effect of reducing taxes on labor, capital, and commerce. ExxonMobil, General Motors, Johnson & Johnson, PepsiCo, and other corporate titans endorsed the idea. Shultz said a carbon tax "would achieve substantially greater reduction of greenhouse gas emissions" than any proposed regulation, while "being best for economic growth, which explains why prominent companies are backing the idea." Such a proposal coming from elder statesmen would, under forty-four of America's forty-five presidents, have been received with deep seriousness. Trump was too busy playing golf to evince interest in eminently sensible public policy. But Trump and his well-dressed lightweights will run their course: then, a carbon tax should be a priority.

Not only would a carbon tax discourage something society does not want (pollution) rather than something society needs (labor and capital), but would do so without adding yet another layer of government. Various schemes to reduce greenhouse gases via regulatory oversight might work but would require more agencies, rules, and administrators. There are plenty of these already.

No one wants to pay taxes—I certainly don't—but taxes have the virtue of distributed decision-making. When a tax is imposed, companies and consumers decide for themselves whether to make no change in their behavior and pay up, or change in ways that lessen or eliminate the tax impact—in this case, switch to clean fuels, invest in efficiency technology, and live a greener lifestyle, all of which become more practical each year. Having Congress dictate the precise steps needed to reduce greenhouse gases is a recipe for snafus: distributed decision-making is more promising.

THE CARBON TAX CONCEPT HAS drawn support from the right as well as the left. Greg Mankiw, chair of the Council of Economic Advisers under the younger President Bush, is a longtime proponent of the concept. Jerry Taylor, head of the libertarian Niskanen Center in Washington, DC, for years was derisive of global warming claims, then, when the science came in, switched to supporting carbon taxes. The Fortune 500 is on board because, as Amy Harder has written, "Major oil companies like ExxonMobil and Royal Dutch Shell have increasingly invested in natural gas, which emits 50 percent less carbon than coal when burned." Companies that own natural gas reserves stand to gain from carbon taxes, which, by favoring natural gas, will enhance quarterly returns.

A carbon tax also would create a profit incentive for inventions and business models that reduce greenhouse gases. Ideologues want to punish organizations and people whose actions cause greenhouse emissions, skipping that those actions usually are beneficial: farming, electricity generation, and so on. Forward-thinking leaders want to reward innovations that reduce the problem. The history of reform shows that rewarding success is more effective than punishing failure.

URBAN AIR POLLUTION, ACID RAIN, and airborne toxic chemicals have declined sharply across the developed world and are in moderate decline in most developing nations, though no international treaty governs these problems. The inventions and business ideas that reduce smog and its cousins have spread globally without the United Nations, or anyone, in charge of their proliferation: countries have switched to pollution-reducing technology and policies because doing so is in their national self-interest. Supposing a carbon tax, or similar policy, brings about inventions and cost reductions that allow affordable controls of greenhouse gases, nations will go in this direction for self-interest reasons too. Should climate change become dangerous, no one will be able to hide. That's all the incentive any nation needs for greenhouse progress. Even China, hub of headlong greenhouse gas growth, now acknowledges this.

Sometimes it is objected that because any individual action regarding greenhouse gases has scant relevance on the global scale, progress is pointless. But this is like a police officer saying, "Even if I arrest that bank robber, other people will try to rob banks." In 2015, EPA administrator Gina McCarthy told a congressional hearing that if a proposal to reduce carbon emissions from American power plants worked as planned, warming of the Earth was projected to lessen by only one-tenth of a degree Fahrenheit. This information was mocked as showing an exercise in futility. But if a reasonable business-as-usual expectation is 4 degrees Fahrenheit of warming, and if there is a decent chance that number would harm human society, then reducing warming by a tenth of a degree—by 3 percent of the projected problem—is worthwhile.

Any greenhouse gas innovation, business model, or regulation will, in and of itself, have at best a slight impact on a system as gigantic as Earth's atmosphere. But lots of ideas and initiatives may add up to problem solved, as innovations attempting to meet one goal end up applying to others.

A generation ago, analysts became concerned about mercury residue from coal combustion. Fund-raisers declared the end of the world, while business lobbies countered that any action would be regulatory overkill. When initial attempts to deal with airborne mercury reduced power-plant emissions only by about 10 percent, this seemed insignificant. But engineering knowledge gained in the initial attempt is now being employed for the near-elimination of mercury emissions from power plants and municipal incinerators, without cost escalation.

The Paris accord on greenhouse gases would, if enforced, allow China to increase its carbon output by about 20 percent by the year 2100. To some, this represents an intolerable exemption. But a decade ago, China was on track to double its carbon output by 2100. Already China's worst case is much less bad, and the knowledge being gained during the country's current mild decline in greenhouse production may lead to preventing big future increases—even though the current decline is minor compared to the overall problem. A broad lesson of reform is that small initial steps can create the know-how that leads to major strides.

Should greenhouse innovations succeed, the climate change problem may turn out to be addressed more readily, and more affordably, than now assumed. But even if innovations reduce greenhouse gases to the point where they no longer accumulate, society must prepare for the warming that is nearly inevitable, given built-up momentum in carbon levels and climate feedbacks. That suggests seawalls and other hydraulic protection for many cities; breeding of new crops that thrive in different ranges of temperature and moisture; public health initiatives to prevent expansion of equatorial diseases (a warmer world will have a larger equatorial band); more electricity production in developing nations, where the world's poor lack so much as fans for summer heat waves. Rather than wring our hands over what may be coming with climate—this is unknowable—society should start working on climate adaptation right now, and fill in the blanks later.

PERHAPS CLIMATE CALAMITY AWAITS, BUT more likely, the global warming threat will be looked back on as one that was managed without sacrifice of living standards, even as the global population grew and poverty continued to decline. What a disappointment for the instant-doomsday crowd!

This favorable forecast will prove out only if society chooses reform, which leads to the question of what other areas need this balm.

Chapter 10

The "Impossible" Challenge of Inequality

HERE'S A THOUGHT EXPERIMENT. SUPPOSE you could choose between a country where the majority dwell in grinding poverty, desperate for food, shelter, and medicine, but no one is rich, and a country where the majority live a decent material existence but inequality is high and the moneyed class roar around in Lamborghinis, laughing at average people. Where would you want to live?

As perhaps you have surmised, the circumstances in this thought experiment are real. The above paragraph compares China of the year 1990 to China today. In 1990, some 67 percent of Chinese citizens lived in misery by the World Bank classification—less than $1.90 per day to spend. Today only 1 percent of Chinese are impoverished by the same definition. That equates to about 750 million people lifted out of destitution in a single generation. Few human achievements hold a candle to this—750 million is more than the total number of people who were alive in the entire world on the day the Declaration of Independence was announced.

The same economic and technological forces that helped vast numbers of men and women in China escape the curse of poverty also made small numbers filthy rich, generating more inequality. This has been the pattern of many developing nations: the dynamics that improve living standards and social conditions, allowing longer lives, more education, and at least some freedom, also enrich a minority. Benjamin Friedman, an economist at Harvard University, contends economic growth based on global trade is generating "greater opportunity, tolerance of diversity, social mobility, commitment to fairness and dedication to democracy" in the developing world. At the same time, people at the top go from riding in horse-drawn broughams to boarding private jets.

So would China have been better off remaining in the year 1990? Ideal would have been the same reduction of poverty minus the inequality, but this may not be possible, at least in today's world. Branko Milanovic, a Serbian-born economist at City University of New York, whose academic specialty is inequality research, says, "In China, less poverty and more inequality were part and parcel of each other. Probably there would have been no way to get the economic growth without the increased inequality and opportunities for corruption."

Perhaps there would have been no way to achieve the rising living standards that are benefiting most of the world without the insecurity that market forces generate, or without the side effect of an outsized One Percent whose opulence is offensive and whose political influence distorts every system of government.

Inequality could be eliminated by confiscatory public policy, but that would stop the global economic system from reducing poverty. In this sense, inequality is not necessarily a net negative, so long as average people become better off—which for several generations has been the result of free-market economies and global trade. The bitter comes with the sweet: the same system that funnels too much to the top also causes living standards to rise for almost everyone, including the poor. The effects are interrelated.

AVERAGE AMERICANS ARE DOING PRETTY well on the buying-power scale, as a previous chapter showed. Because this point is almost totally overlooked in public debate, a brief recapitulation is helpful. Taking greater buying power—lower federal taxes, higher benefits, declining consumer prices—into consideration means average people are gaining from contemporary economic forces even as the lion's share goes to the top. Adjusting for inflation, today's typical American worker earns three times as much, in pay and benefits, as a typical worker in 1950. Poverty-line calculations take into account income only: adjust for higher entitlement payments and long-term favorable trends in the Consumer Price Index, and US poverty has declined 40 percent in the past half-century.

Judged by income only, there's runaway inequality. In 1929, as Wall Street crashed, the top 5 percent in the United States commanded 30 percent of pretax income. This figure declined to 15 percent by 1950, then began to rise again, to 21 percent in 2000. Since that juncture, the top's share has zoomed, with the highest 5 percent of households in 2015 garnering 35 percent of the nation's income, more than the comparable figure for 1929. In the United States and European Union, top earners command a disproportionate share of income—disproportionate both in absolute terms and compared to their production. This causes anger at the bottom, renders the middle unhappy, and, most important, may be unjust.

Why was inequality high in the 1920s, then declined, then rose again? Consider how two trend lines would look for the United States.

The first trend line would show federal policy. The United States did not assess a national income tax until 1913. Until roughly the 1920s, federal revenues were employed solely to fund government activities such as defense, diplomacy, courts, and flood control; no federal monies went to income transfer. Some cities had a patronage-controlled "poormaster" to whom those down on their luck could beg; most citizens obtained their means solely through labor, business, private or religious charity, or families, not through government. The New Deal introduced the notion of income-transfer programs, principally Social Security, enacted in 1935. (Canada already had a similar system; today all developed nations do.) New Deal legislation transferred money in other ways, including the National Industrial Recovery Act, whose primary purpose was to raise prices—today this sounds daft, but made sense for the conditions of the time—plus the 1935 bill that created the Works Progress Administration and the 1939 food stamps legislation. Federal intervention in the marketplace both helped the economy recover from the Depression and put inequality on a slope of decline, by transferring income toward the lower quintiles.

By the 1960s, inequality was rising again and government intervened again, through enactment of Medicare and Medicaid, plus a range of social welfare programs, including cash payments, housing vouchers, and federal, state, and local funding for construction of low-income housing. As Robert Samuelson has noted, in 1962, only 2 percent of the federal budget was for health care, with individuals paying almost all such costs; today, 31 percent of the federal budget is spent on health care, with taxpayers picking up a sizable share of the invoices for hospital and physician services to individuals. Medicare for seniors and Medicaid for the poor were founded to improve medical outcomes; their equal impact was as income transfers, sparing seniors and disadvantaged persons most of the costs they might have borne.

Today many recipients take the income-transfer aspect of Medicare and Medicaid for granted, complaining vociferously about copays, as if there ever had been a Good Old Days when health care was at contemporary advanced quality yet everything was free. Single-payer medicine such as in France, which has high-quality health care, is not free, as often said: it's just that there are few fees to patients at the point of service, because taxpayers cover the invoices. "Free" and "somebody else pays" commonly are confused in public debate. Single-payer may be the long-term solution for US health care conundrums: the money saved on administration would finance expanded coverage and continued research, and the stress of health insurance uncertainty would be eliminated. European Union nations spend less per capita on health care than the United States, yet achieve as good or better outcomes, in part because their systems are less stressful, and stress does medical damage.

Whether single-payer could happen under US political conditions is a book unto itself. But however desirable, single-payer emphatically would not be "free." There was never a Good Old Days when health care services were both high-quality and cost nothing, and there never will be, unless a post-scarcity economy someday can be achieved.

Today's Medicare and Medicaid, financed mostly on the "somebody else pays" premise, may be what keep their recipients alive to take Bertrand Russell's advice and complain. In 2017, the *Wall Street Journal* quoted seventy-nine-year-old Carole Siesser of Delray Beach, Florida, who needs a specialized drug, saying, "They really take advantage of seniors" because she must cover $5,600 of the drug's annual $26,000 price. Siesser had outlived her birth-year life expectancy for American women by nineteen years, probably in part because of transfer payments through Medicare, yet considered 20 percent of the price of a life-sustaining medication to constitute society taking advantage of her. Many contemporary social welfare programs have this result—voters want both low taxes and expensive benefits that from their point of view are free or nearly so, resulting in voters showing anger toward government even as life gets better.

During the Barack Obama presidency, the Affordable Care Act sought to expand health insurance support to the working class and lower middle class; like Medicare and Medicaid, functionally ObamaCare was an income-transfer program in which the wealthy are taxed so working-class and lower-middle-class persons can avoid an expense. Little commentary took into consideration that the economic role of ObamaCare was to increase the buying power of the working- and lower middle classes by covering a cost they previously paid. Under Obama, eligibility for food stamps and disability subsidies was broadened, transferring more income; a 1994 requirement that welfare recipients make a bona fide attempt to find work was suspended; federal subsidies for unemployment compensation were increased, while the benefit period was extended from half a year to two years, a major act of assistance to the working class that many Americans don't even know occurred. By the end of the Obama administration, according to the Congressional Budget Office (CBO), transfers through government—whether as cash, as benefits, or as costs paid by someone else—averaged approximately $14,000 per household.

ALL THESE ACTIONS MITIGATED AGAINST inequality. Good Old Days thinking sometimes is applied to the New Deal years to argue that America was more generous then, and many appear to believe this. There seems meager public awareness that Medicare and Medicaid, both substantial subsidies to individuals, were not Depression-era programs, rather, created during the Lyndon Johnson presidency, long after the New Deal. Nor does there seem much awareness that the modern, monetarily significant version of federal housing subsidies for minorities began in 1970, under Richard Nixon, who also expanded eligibility for food stamps, raised welfare benefits, and extended disability payment eligibility to all Americans. Prior to Nixon, millions of the disabled were on their own.

Adjusting to current dollars and for population growth, contemporary income-transfer programs—including Social Security, Medicare,

Medicaid, ObamaCare, and the alphabet soup of TANF (Temporary Assistance for Needy Families), SNAP (Supplemental Nutrition Assistance Program, formerly the food stamps program), CHIP (Children's Health Insurance Program), SSDI (Social Security Disability Insurance), SSI (Supplemental Security Income), and EITC (Earned Income Tax Credit)—mean Washington transfers about four times as much, per recipient, as was transferred during the New Deal. It's good that government aid to individuals is greater today than in the past—no one should live as many did during the Depression. But US federal spending for the poor, the working poor, the lower middle class, the disabled, and the retired is more substantial than generally understood. That federal entitlement spending is backed by two sources—taxes on the affluent and borrowing from the young through the national debt. Both are income-transfer mechanisms.

Yet income inequality still is high. The Belarus-born economist Simon Kuznets, who won the Nobel Prize in Economics in 1971, showed that industrial development first increases and then decreases inequality. This formula has held since 1971 in most nations: if Kuznets continues to be correct, inequality in China soon will moderate. But inequality currents of the past century in the United States and Europe have been more like rolling waves than Kuznets expected, even discounting for the world wars. This brings us to the trend line in America since the 1920s, which shows what the economy values most.

One hundred years ago, access to natural resources was the first element of economic growth, while most labor was unskilled and thereby had relatively little value: this tended to concentrate wealth with the robber barons. Then the big expansion of manufacturing and construction that occurred after World War II—after the war, not during the war; whatever Marxists may claim, combat is terrible for business—caused employers to compete for workers, putting labor in the driver's seat and pushing down inequality. High rates of union membership were among reasons for rising hourly wages, but labor-market conditions were more important.

By the 1990s—obviously this is a simplified narrative—information and intellectual property had risen in value compared to commodities, while the combination of more-efficient production and higher-quality, longer-lasting products cooled the labor market. This began a trend of increased inequality. Even as entitlement payments expanded, the economic forces that concentrated income upward swamped government's attempts at redistribution. The result was the present situation: aristocratic profligacy at the top; most people, including the middle class and the poor, somewhat better off; and everybody in a foul mood, even the wealthy, who feel themselves ill used. The economies of contemporary developed nations value information and intellectual property a lot more than resources or labor. Perhaps some future condition will change this, but for the moment, America, China, and parts of Europe are generating income inequality.

YET BROADLY ACROSS THE WORLD, inequality is decreasing, not rising. Milanovic calculates that beginning in 1988—roughly when China and India liberalized and free-market international trade began to surge—the overall inequality of the world has declined about 10 percent. Economists measure inequality using the Gini coefficient, a scale on which the lower the number, the better. "Since 1988, the global Gini coefficient has fallen from 0.69 to 0.63," Milanovic says. "That represents the first overall decline of inequality during the industrial era. The reason is the amazing decrease in poverty. Since 1988, the world's real income has risen more in a single generation than that number had ever risen in a full century. Because inequality has increased in the United States and some other developed nations, there's an assumption it's increasing everywhere. Globally this problem is in remission."

If ire regarding inequality makes you want to rip down the stanchions of the global economy, bear in mind that this very system has resulted in the human family's typical income increasing "more in a single generation than that number had ever risen in a full century."

Milanovic's research shows that from 1988 to 2008, real income of the world's impoverished grew 20 percent. Real income of the world's lower middle class—the majority of humanity—grew 50 percent. Real income of the world's wealthy grew 60 percent. There are about sixty-five lower-middle-class people for each wealthy person, so the total amount of new income attained by the lower middle class rose by more than new income attained by the wealthy, though the wealthy got the big houses and flashy cars. The only income stratum that did not do really well from 1988 to 2008 was, Milanovic calculates, the main middle class, which he defines as the seventy-fifth to ninetieth percentiles of global income. That class is well-off compared to the world, but saw a 1988–2008 income gain of only about 5 percent. "These are the nucleus of the Western voting public, and feel left behind by events that are aiding the top, as is very well known, and also aiding the bottom, as is barely known, but not aiding them," Milanovic says.

A society that is unequal but treats most average people well—the contemporary condition in the United States and European Union—is preferable to no inequality but low living standards. Could a golden mean be achieved? One possible reform would be income limits; another, higher taxes on the well-to-do; another, Universal Basic Income.

INCOME LIMITS SEEM APPEALING BECAUSE top executive windfalls give capitalism a bad name. In 2015, the CEO of Valiant Pharmaceuticals, Michael Pearson, paid himself $143 million even as the company was having a terrible year; the CEO of heavily subsidized Solar City, Lyndon Rive, paid himself $77 million even as the company was preparing to lay off thousands of employees; the CEO of heavily subsidized Lockheed Martin, Marillyn Hewson, paid herself $28 million. In 2016, CEOs of large North American companies took home an average of $16 million, about 270 times the average pay of workers at their firms, according to the Economic Policy Institute, think tank of the US labor movement.

Why CEO bonanza numbers like these are not viewed as white-collar crime is hard to fathom. Most CEOs' paydays are rubber-stamped by highly obedient boards of directors staffed with chief executives of other companies, who have an intense self-interest in driving up typical CEO pay. Boards don't use the word "pay"—pay is for the unwashed—rather, speak loftily of "compensation," as if the CEO were a philanthropist honoring the firm by reporting to the executive dining room. In 2016, Leslie Moonves, CEO of CBS, paid himself $69 million, though the company's dividends had been down in recent years and many employees were laid off. The CBS news division (via *CBS Evening News*) and entertainment arm (via *The Late Show with Stephen Colbert*) regularly denounce wealth and privilege in the Trump administration, yet CBS itself is organized to generate wealth and privilege for a tiny few at the top. In 2017, athletic apparel firm Nike began an advertising campaign, oriented around the word "equality," that hectors others about disparity in income. Nike pays the Indonesian workers who sew the company's sneakers $3 a day, while in 2016 Nike CEO Mark Parker stuffed $48 million into his own pockets, according to the corporate-board analysis firm Equilar. Hectoring others for what you refuse to do yourself is hypocrisy. Nike took its game up a notch by pretending to believe in social justice.

Wretched excess for CEOs and similar high executives not only gives capitalism a bad name but also generates resentment on the part of average people against top earners. But colossal paydays can be too alluring even for self-proclaimed progressives to resist. Former Yahoo CEO Marissa Mayer, who spent a lot of time patting herself on the back for enlightened views, awarded herself $35 million in 2015 even as the company was losing money and laying off workers.

Suppose top pay at public corporations were capped at $1 million per year, which still seems like plenty of incentive to get up in the morning and go to the office. (Assume for the sake of argument there's a loophole-resistant way to establish the cap—pro sports leagues have shown that salary caps can be enforced—and set aside for another day whether private corporations could be so regulated.) This would be healthy for democracy and for the reputation of market economics, eliminating the dander caused when capitalists game the system to screw average people. But this reform would do little to ameliorate income inequality. If the top CEO pay average had been capped at $1 million, with the savings uniformly distributed, each American household would have received $25. In 2015, Honeywell CEO David Cote paid himself $36 million. Suppose he'd earned $1 million, with the yield evenly distributed to Honeywell employees. Each would have received $268.

There just isn't enough in CEO windfalls to alter the basic equation of equality. Until such time as there may be a fundamental breakthrough in the structure of economics, such as a post-scarcity economy, market forces are in everyone's interest, which may mean tolerating a few individuals who end up with far more than they've done anything to deserve.

So if executive pay restrictions won't solve inequality, what about taxing the rich?

THE US UPPER CLASS, THE top quintile, received 53 percent of the nation's income and paid 69 percent of the nation's federal taxes; the poor and working class, the bottom quintile, received 5 percent of the nation's income and paid just shy of nothing in federal income taxes, according to Congressional Budget Office data on the most recent year for which statistics are available. Combining federal income taxes (channeled largely to entitlements), payroll taxes (channeled exclusively to entitlements), and other levies, the top 1 percent of American earners paid an effective federal tax rate of 34 percent, while the middle class paid an effective federal tax rate of 14 percent. These figures show the US federal tax system is already progressive—which many don't believe, and others don't want to believe. The current federal tax system, the CBO concluded, is "the most progressive it has been since at least the mid-1990s," with tax rates high for top earners but for all others "significantly below the average rates over the 1979–2013 period." State and local taxes often are not progressive; in the current generation, state and local governments have been a burden on the poor while federal government has been an aid.

As president, Barack Obama often said federal taxes on the affluent should be higher still. Then he and Michelle paid an effective federal tax rate of 18 percent on the final IRS forms they disclosed—a notably lower federal tax rate than the 34 percent paid by most in their income category. Obama made a show of saying other rich people should not take every deduction, then took every deduction for himself. Maybe while he did his taxes he was wearing Nikes.

Even if the US federal tax system already is progressive, there is a strong case for raising marginal rates. People at the top benefit extravagantly from contemporary economic forces: they should show gratitude to society by paying larger tax bills. The problem is that even a steep increase in rates at the top—or elimination of deductions, which would be the same as raising rates—does not generate enough to do much about inequality.

In 2015, economists led by William Gale of the Brookings Institution calculated that raising the top federal tax rate to 50 percent, then redistributing new revenue entirely to the bottom quintile, would have an "exceedingly modest" effect on inequality. The higher rate would increase federal revenue by about $95 billion; transferring the sum to the bottom would remit about $2,000 per year to poor and working-poor American adults, money that would be welcome, to be sure, but would not alter the basics of social equity.

During the 2016 presidential campaign, Bernie Sanders and Hillary Clinton advocated federal tax increases at the top. The Sanders plan would have raised an added $150 billion per year, though the Vermont senator proposed to distribute most of the revenue not toward the bottom, rather, to senior citizens, who are already society's most-favored group economically, and to the middle class, which already is fairly well off. Sanders styled himself as a justice crusader, but knowing seniors and the middle class go to the polls while the poor vote in low numbers even in states that have arranged ballot systems for their convenience—the poor not voting is the most exasperating aspect of American democracy—he proposed that added tax revenue be received by Sanders supporters rather than by the needy. Clinton's plan would have raised about $110 billion per annum in additional federal revenue, all of which she proposed to spend on new programs that may or may not have been worthy ideas but would not have placed cash in the hands of the desperate.

However meritorious the Brookings, Sanders, and Clinton tax-the-rich plans may be, they wouldn't alter the underlying momentum in American inequality, whose impetus comes from economic forces that are much stronger than government tinkering. There may be too many rich people for society's comfort, yet there are not enough of them for soaking the rich, alone, to be the inequality solution. Soaking the middle class would be required too, and find the candidate who backs that plan. Which leaves us with Universal Basic Income.

EVERY LOW-INCOME INDIVIDUAL SHOULD RECEIVE a guaranteed annual wage conferred in cash without strings attached, for the recipient to use as she or he sees fit. Who proposed this: Elizabeth Warren, Cornel West,

Leon Trotsky? The proposal came from Milton Friedman, crown prince of free-market economics, in his 1962 treatise *Capitalism and Freedom*.

Friedman favored ending corporate taxes, with unrestricted capital movement across borders; he opposed most regulations on business and was ahead of the wave in blasting "powers concentrated in Washington." If people voluntarily agree to work for peanuts in exploitive sweatshops, he said, government should not interfere with that choice: Nike paying $3 a day in Indonesia would have been fine with him. No one did a better job than Friedman in espousing the Chicago School notion that economic freedom and personal liberty are the same thing. Yet Friedman also thought that because market-based economies are tempestuous, there should be income guarantees to ensure that a job loss, illness, or other set-back would not bring poverty at the low rungs of the ladder. Every adult, Friedman supposed, should receive $2,500 per year as an income floor. The bottom quintile of households should receive $25,000 per year—"in the form most useful to the individual, namely, cash"—in order to elim-inate poverty.

In 1796, Thomas Paine, one of the Founding Fathers, proposed that federal revenue (then drawn solely from tariffs) be redistributed by award-ing each adult male 10 pounds per year, roughly $2,000 today. Paine's view was that monies collected by government belong to the public, not to federal or state agencies, and the highest use of public resources is elimina-tion of poverty. American prosperity has increased perhaps tenfold since the eighteenth century; a modern Thomas Paine might propose $20,000 per year per adult, sufficient at today's cost of living to end impoverish-ment and money desperation.

Versions of this concept have bounced around public policy circles for many decades. President Richard Nixon asked Congress to legislate what he called a Family Assistance Plan, an annual cash income guarantee: the House and Senate, then both Democratic, said no. A reader of Fried-man, Nixon thought eliminating the complex War on Poverty regulatory bureaucracy and simply giving cash to the disadvantaged would end de-pendency while encouraging new businesses in run-down urban areas. At the time, big cities were viewed as about to become ungovernable, if not uninhabitable, owing to crime, drugs, unemployment, pollution, and the continuing influx of rural residents who were leaving the countryside as automation in agriculture eliminated farmhand jobs. Through the 1960s and early 1970s, Presidents Johnson and Nixon had, at the ready, declarations of martial law to be imposed on urban areas: both presidents thought frenzied rioting just around the corner. That cities such as Cleveland and Pittsburgh would stage enormous comebacks, and that by our moment urban living would be seen as highly desirable, is another positive trend that would have seemed incomprehensible not long ago.

When the Family Assistance Plan failed on Capitol Hill, Nixon rebranded the proposal as a "negative income tax"—Friedman's word choice. The Democratic Congress rejected that too. Today the idea goes by the name Universal Basic Income.

THE MANY FORMS OF INCOME-TRANSFER assistance that already exist in the United States include classical welfare, which since 1997 has been known as Temporary Assistance for Needy Families. Another program, the Earned Income Tax Credit, sends Treasury checks of $2,000 to $5,000 to working-class women and men who owe no federal income taxes: EITC is a social-justice initiative that many Americans don't know about. (Transmitting a Form 1040 to the Internal Revenue Service activates the EITC: low-income persons who think they are outwitting The Man by not filing a 1040 often are making a mistake.) Minors from poor families receive free care via the Children's Health Insurance Program; some states provide free hospital care for low-income persons of any age. Public housing vouchers pay most or all of the cost of basic housing, though only when vacancies exist. Many cities now require that new high-end housing developments include underpriced units reserved for the working class; as of the Obama presidency, this standard applies to any development receiving federal support. The food stamp program provides coupons that can be exchanged only for groceries, but since the stamps replace an expected expense, they might as well be cash. Social Security's fast-expanding disability programs confer payments roughly equal to working forty hours a week at the federal minimum wage. In 2015, the United States spent $878 billion on subsidies exclusively for those with low incomes. That was one-quarter of the federal budget, dramatically exceeded the $582 billion spent on defense that year, and was essentially identical to the $882 billion cost of Social Security. It simply is not true that the contemporary United States does not help the economically disadvantaged, however much some may long to believe this.

But that help could become more effective. For millions, federal disability now functions as an inefficient, humiliating form of income support. To obtain the payments, recipients must make themselves enfeebled, claiming chronic pain, severe depression, "mood disorders," or other conditions impossible to evaluate objectively—essentially, begging to the poormaster. Veterans' disability programs are similar. Former Republican member of the House and cabinet secretary Jack Kemp, who died in 2009—Kemp was a saint compared to today's callous GOP—said, "The measure of a society is not how many receive public assistance but how many do not need public assistance." By this gauge, federal disability assistance is demeaning. Once eligibility is obtained, few return to work; their fear of being tossed out of the program is an incentive to remain in dependency.

Universal Basic Income would replace all public assistance with a cash grant to adults regardless of whether working or not, whether healthy or not. Most proposals involve a grant of $1,000 a month—about what federal disability programs pay, but without the strings attached. Every adult would receive Universal Basic Income, not just the head of household or primary wage-earner. Demonstration programs for Universal Basic Income concepts are in progress in Canada, Finland, and Kenya.

Universal Basic Income could offer multiple advantages over current structures. Unlike welfare (TANF) and disability programs, work would not be discouraged: adults could receive both wage income and Universal Basic Income. Unlike those who administer public housing vouchers, social service officials would not exert control over recipients' lives; adults could pool their Universal Basic Incomes and make their own housing choices. When life setbacks like job losses occur, there would be income for essentials, without having to grovel at unemployment or social welfare offices. Making the month's rent or paying a sudden expense like a new water pump for the car no longer would be the terrible misfortune that such moments can represent to millions of people. Assured of some income, those lacking educational degrees, who have little value in the current economy, would become attractive as marriage partners, which is deceptively important.

There are, of course, drawbacks to Universal Basic Income. The expense would make the national debt worse, while social service bureaucracies, and their political lobbies, would generate substantial resistance: like wars, government programs are much easier to begin than to end. Using federal disability plans as a pricing guide, extending Universal Basic Income to every American adult would cost about $3.5 trillion a year, a staggering sum. That's before savings from eliminating the maze of social service hierarchies: the federal Department of Housing and Urban Development could be closed, along with dozens of state and city welfare and housing agencies. Thousands of officials would lose their jobs, while state and local governments and congressional committees would lose control over pots of funny-money that are prime sources of kickbacks and "consulting contracts"—those are scare quotes—to relatives and cronies. The lobbies involved would not quit without a fight.

Elimination of social service bureaucracy would reduce the cost of Universal Basic Income to about $2 trillion a year—still a giant number, but getting within range of the roughly $1 trillion annually already spent in this area. In 2017, the Organization for Economic Cooperation and Development calculated that Italy could offer a Universal Basic Income payment to every adult for less than the country now spends on entitlements, if Italy closed its welfare enforcement offices and simply handed out cash. About 80 percent of low-income Italians would end up with more money under such a plan, the OECD found, while the country's budget deficit would decline.

Friedman's negative income tax concept relied on replacing all forms of entitlement subsidies with cash grants, in order to allow individuals to make their own decisions about how to lead their lives and to save enough on administration to afford the grants. Fifty years ago, Friedman noted that benefit programs with complicated restrictions require expensive welfare bureaucracies that divert spending from the needy into overhead; show soft racism, by assuming the poor don't understand money and are "shiftless," a racial code word; and push recipients toward a dependency mind-set. Just give people cash and let them live with their choices, Friedman contended. The point is as valid today as half a century ago.

The conservative social scientist Charles Murray has proposed a Universal Basic Income, which he believes, taking after Friedman, is essential to correct economic injustice, especially the low earnings potential of those without college diplomas. Murray would replace the entire menu of entitlement programs, including Social Security, with $1,000 per month tax-free to every America adult. Replacing Social Security with Universal Basic Income—needless to say, easier said than done politically—would cut the net cost of income guarantee programs to around $1 trillion annually, while fixing the looming insolvency of Social Security. Because the money would come throughout adult life, each person would save some for retirement—Murray asks, are people really so foolish they won't know to open a savings account? By promoting self-reliance, this approach, Murray has written, will improve personal responsibility: once everybody knows everybody else has an income stream, "It will be possible to say to the irresponsible what can't be said now, 'Don't try to tell us you are helpless, because we know you aren't.'" "Woe is me" won't work anymore as an approach to life.

Obviously there would be problems: what happens to the person who blows through a UBI check, then says, "Where's my free housing and food stamps?" But the Universal Basic Income concept offers at least a conceptual way to think about a society in which inequality does not cause injustice—and surely represents a better use of social resources than yet another round of tax cuts for the rich. Tax cuts for the rich are justified with the "magic flying puppies" claim that they will trigger vast economic expansion in far-off future years. Spending whatever government borrows on average people makes a zillion times more sense than spending on the top quintile.

A STEP IN THE DIRECTION of reducing inequality would be a higher federal minimum wage. If the 1970 federal minimum wage had kept pace with inflation, the standard would now be $10.50 an hour. Instead, the federal minimum is $7.25 an hour, one-third less in real dollars. Some inequality is caused by concentration of earnings at the top; some is caused by the

United States welcoming (as it should) large numbers of immigrants, who both reduce household median earnings and create downward pressure on wages; and some is caused by the low minimum wage, which zings entry-level workers. Several states have minimum wages that do keep pace with inflation: California's is $10.50 an hour. High state minimum wages do not seem to spike unemployment, as sometimes predicted. California's unemployment with a high minimum wage is fourth-tenths of a percent above unemployment in Texas, which has a low minimum wage.

The twin goals of reducing unemployment and promoting social justice suggest that anyone working forty hours a week at the federal minimum wage should be able to support a small family. At $7.25 an hour, forty hours of work for fifty weeks produces about $13,500 in after-tax income, enough to support only one person. Returning the federal minimum to its 1970 value would produce about $19,000 a year, after payroll taxes, for a forty-hour week. Inequality would decline; legitimate employment would become more appealing compared to crime; justice would increase.

Inequality could be reduced further by altering public policies that favor owning a home, apartment, or condo over renting: the mortgage interest deduction and federal backing of mortgage loans.

When the mortgage interest deduction began about a century ago, the goal was to encourage average people to own property, then viewed as a moon-shot idea. For several generations, the interest deduction aspect of the federal tax code helped all average people build net worth, since renters who borrowed to pay the rent could deduct their debt costs. In 1986, federal tax codes were amended to confine consumer interest deductions to mortgages. From that juncture, the deduction specifically aided homeowners while harming renters by omission. Beginning roughly around that time, federal subsidies extended below-market (or below-credit-rating) interest rates to many mortgage holders; no comparable program assisted renters. The social goal of encouraging average people to own property remained valid, as in generations past, but since 1986, federal policy has concentrated net worth toward homeowners and away from renters, while driving up home prices in a manner that hinders aspiring first-time buyers; federal policy now also tends to cause urban rents to rise, preventing many men and women from living in the cities, where the best jobs are. Perhaps, then, it should be no surprise that since 1986 inequality has increased.

The more expensive the home, the greater the value of the mortgage interest deduction and the greater the advantage to the ownership class, even when federal housing assistance to the poor is taken into consideration. By 2017, the typical homeowner had about thirty times the net worth of the typical renter. Some of this difference is explained by homeownership pushing couples toward long-term relationships, legitimate employment, and fiscally sensible living—all valid policy goals. But some is explained by government policies that channel net worth from renters to owners.

Since roughly the 1980s, owning a home has been seen as an investment, not as a way to get a place to live. The Case-Shiller Index of home values shows that US homes have appreciated 248 percent since the 1986 tax law change, a run-up that rivals some growth stocks. Baby boom Americans fume if the value of their home doesn't increase annually, though to their grandparents homes were places to live, not anchors of investment portfolios. Renters who are on their own in the Darwinian ecosphere of landlords and annual increases must wince when contemplating the manner in which public policy aids homeowners but not them.

The tax code could be rendered neutral to the rent-or-own equation by eliminating the mortgage interest deduction while increasing the standard deduction. The affluent would lose a tax break, but the affluent should be society's last concern. Low-income and most middle-class homeowners, and nearly all renters, would opt for the standard deduction, leveling the field. Such a tax change should reduce inequality, with the side effect of stimulating rental construction: many cities and a not-insignificant number of suburbs and exurbs have apartment shortages.

A COUNTERINTUITIVE RESPONSE TO INEQUALITY is tax code changes to urge people to move. Milanovic says, "Most of one's lifetime income is determined at birth," because the place where you live means far more to your income than any other factor. As much as 80 percent of lifetime income is determined by where you are. No one person, Milanovic notes, can alter the economic growth rate or the job market of a country, city, or county. What one person *can* do is move from a bust place to a boom place.

This straightforward consideration holds tremendous implications for the migration debate. Today the African Union has a somewhat higher population than the European Union, and tens of thousands of Africans risk their lives to reach Europe, doing what Milanovic's studies recommend: leaving a low-income and low-freedom environment for one with high marks on both scales. Many Africans also wish to emigrate to Australia, Canada, or the United States, and these lands should accept more arrivals—immigration has always made the United States stronger—but many Africans lack the means to reach North America or Australia; Europe is more attainable. If current population trends continue, by around 2050, the African Union will have treble the population of the European Union. "The wealth differential from the northern to southern coast of the Mediterranean is the largest in history," Milanovic says. "Who or what caused this is beside the point from the perspective of the individual. The incentive to cross that water and get north will only become more intense."

Americans like to think their ancestors traversed the waters seeking political and religious liberty. Many did; many were seeking economic opportunity, leaving the stagnation and social failings of the bust places where they were born for a new land with unlimited boom potential. So why don't more Americans pull up stakes today within their own still-very-large, still-booming nation?

Tyler Cowen, an economist at George Mason University, notes that although conventional wisdom says Americans move constantly, the reality is otherwise. "Americans traditionally have thought of themselves as the great movers, and that was true in the nineteenth century and through most of the twentieth," Cowen has written. "Since the 1980s, Americans have become much less restless in movements across the country. The interstate migration rate has fallen to half its 1948–1971 average. If we look at the rate of moving between counties within a state, it fell 31 percent. The rate of moving within a county fell 38 percent." According to the Census Bureau, fifty years ago, some 20 percent of Americans moved each year. That share has declined steadily since, to 12 percent in 2014—believed to be the lowest mover rate in US annals.

When US unemployment started to drop sharply in 2014, signaling a strong labor market, many employers, including manufacturers in the Midwest, said they could not convince workers to move into their areas to take good jobs that were unfilled. Contrast this to the late 1970s, when the first automaker retrenchment began in Detroit: some who lost Michigan jobs pulled up stakes and moved to Arizona and Texas. In the Lone Star State, they were known as "black-taggers," for the white-on-black Michigan license plate of the period. Black-taggers helped fuel the economic boom of the Southwest and often ended up better off than those who remained in Michigan. Black-tagger opportunities remain: the unemployed or underemployed could pull up stakes and move to New England, the West Coast, or the Dakotas, where good jobs go begging. By 2017, the unemployment rate was below 3 percent in much of the Rocky Mountain region, particularly Colorado and Utah, yet Americans were not moving to those states—employers reported trouble filling entry-level jobs paying $25 an hour in wages and benefits.

In the United States since the 1980s, the period of less moving coincides with the period of more inequality and rising discontent. How many who voted for Trump in 2016, expressing anger about economic currents, were willing to pack their belongings and move to a place where the job market is better, as opposed to demanding subsidies and trade protections? Cowen suggests that the lower, middle, and upper classes have been joined by a new "complacent class": Americans—predominantly white—who won't take action to look after themselves but demand that others provide for them. Public policy that moderates urban rents and helps people change locations in response to economic changes might be more effective, and less expensive, than border taxes and trade wars.

Do all roads lead to Universal Basic Income? Some form of Milton Friedman–style income regime might head off the looming situation in which only the educated have realistic hope of bettering themselves.

The Universal Basic Income concept is superior to how any nation's entitlement system functions at present. Replacing the dependency mindset of social welfare and retirement programs with an idea that rewards self-sufficiency, while preventing a sudden expense or job change from becoming personal ruin, would make society more just and be a positive for economic growth.

The government debt situations of Western nations make Universal Basic Income unaffordable right now. This is another reason why national debts must be addressed—to clear the financial decks for some kind of universal income in the near future. Today's entitlement distributions paper over problems, while today's pension programs postpone wrenching decisions; replacing both with Universal Basic Income, while eliminating rules, bureaucracies, and officialdom, could put Western society on a sounder footing for generations to come. As an ideal, Universal Basic Income is superior to contemporary programs: universal income might solve social problems, rather than slow the rate at which they increase.

If the value of inventions and intellectual property continues to rise while the value of unskilled labor continues to decline, Universal Basic Income may become vital for justice. As time passes, expect this reform to sound better.

Chapter 11

We'll Never Run Out of Challenges…

THE WORLD HAS MANY PROBLEMS: there is temptation to become discouraged. No one, not even a benevolent philosopher with an unlimited budget, could fix every problem. Yet this knowledge should not cause loss of spirit. Our ancestors did not give up—and they faced daily struggles worse than all but a few of those faced today. We mustn't let them down.

With that in mind, let's turn to other areas where reform may succeed.

SOME PROBLEMS CAN BE FIXED via legislation, others cannot. Laws can bar segregation by race or by gender but cannot end bigotry or sexism, which can be addressed only through the advancement of social attitudes. In these categories, trends are positive—all Western nations have been evolving away from biases against minorities, women, and gays. But there's one heading under which societies could benefit by evolving back in the direction of old assumptions: marriage, which is good for health, economics, and children.

William Farr, one of the founders of epidemiology, showed in 1858 that the wedded live longer than the unwed. This finding still holds in the twenty-first century: spouses (whether heterosexual or same-sex) suffer fewer heart attacks and strokes than the never-married or separated. But the well-being benefits of marriage apply to an ever-smaller segment of the Western population. On the first day of the twentieth century, 80 percent of American households were headed by a married couple; on the first day of the twenty-first century, 53 percent were. In 2014, the Pew Research Center found, "a record share of American adults have never been married." Among men, the 10 percent who had never been married in 1960 had grown to 23 percent by 2014.

Education level and class background have become predictors of marriage likelihood. A few generations ago, most Americans of the working and lower-middle classes got married and stayed married: today most either never wed or their marriages fail. In the upper-middle and well-off classes of the United States, wedding bells are common and divorce courts are not. Despite the stereotype of the rich walking out on spouses while humble working people honor their vows, in contemporary American society it's the other way around. The 2010 census showed that the majority of women whose education ended at high school either never marry or become divorced, while the majority of college-educated women marry and remain married.

Many marriages lead to unhappiness: the wedded state can be romantic but should not be romanticized. But all marriages are an economic contract, allowing the couple to live better by combining resources, and improving children's odds of success in life. In a 2010 study, the Pew Research Center found that since 1970 the household income of married people has steadily risen, by about 50 percent adjusted for inflation, while the household income of the unmarried peaked in about 1990 and has fallen since.

The marriage gap—the well-off married, the working class not married—helps explain much of the money gap in the United States. Gary Burtless of the Brookings Institution has determined that at least 10 percent of US income inequality is caused by educated people marrying each other. A generation ago, according to the National Center for Marriage and Family Research at Bowling Green State University, one-third of women who did not graduate from college were unmarried when their first child was born. By 2010, the majority of women who did not graduate from college were unmarried when their first child was born. Children raised by married couples, whether opposite-sex or same-sex, have better prospects in education and employment, while being less likely to get into trouble with the law.

Ron Haskins and Isabel Sawhill, also at the Brookings Institution, have found that contemporary Americans from any background can avoid poverty by observing a traditionalistic formula: graduate from high school, wait until at least age twenty-one to marry, and marry before having children. "Of American adults who followed these fairly simple rules, only about two percent are in poverty and nearly 75 percent have joined the middle class," Haskins has written. The pandemonium that is modern life may appear to have changed everything, but traditional standards like those noted by Haskins and Sawhill still obtain.

In the European Union, marriage as an institution has been giving way to long-term partnerships that function like marriage, except no one ever walks down the aisle; long-term partnerships seem to work in European societies. In the United States, there remains a clear societal distinction: the wedded do notably better than the unwed. This can be a source of personal sorrow for those who wanted to get married but never found the right partner; just as luck is a larger force in economics than most care to contemplate, luck is also a huge element of dating. In 2015, when gay marriage was legalized across the United States, there was an outpouring of wedding celebration events and stories. But gay marriage will matter to 2 or 3 percent of the population at most; imagine how the wedding celebration coverage of 2015 must have affected the far larger share of the population composed of those who would like to wed but have no partner.

Though laws cannot make people decide to marry each other, or to tough out the inevitable disputes and hard times in any marriage, laws can impact this issue by making partners more attractive in economic terms, and unions more likely to be successful. Such reforms include Universal Basic Income; a higher minimum wage; reducing the costs of public universities, community colleges, and junior colleges so more can afford to attend; and better child care to improve educational outcomes. Reforms such as these could encourage marriage, especially below the level of the college-graduated cognitive elite.

Early in the postwar era, intellectuals denounced marriage, which was depicted as a prison for women. When same-gender couples wanted to marry, the intellectual world suddenly pivoted and praised the wedded state. Public policy must take into account that despite many drawbacks, families formed around couples should be the organizing basis for society, today and through any likely future. If encouraging marriage sounds old-fashioned, so be it.

EFFORTS TO IMPROVE PUBLIC SCHOOLS by injecting money have in most cases come to naught. The home and peer-group environments, which public schools cannot control, may be more consequential than the classroom, in part because most people's IQs are established by around age six (first grade) and vary little after that, regardless of school quality. Research by economist James Heckman of the University of Chicago has shown that home child-care help for families during the toddler years—when IQ levels are fluid and improve in response to a child being read to rather than being plunked down in front of a television—results in better educational outcomes for children, higher family incomes, and fewer crimes by male children. Assistance to families with toddler-aged boys and girls may prove more cost-effective than yet another round of funding for school districts. Data from New York City suggest a broad pre-K program would cost only about 5 percent as much as a public school system in toto, thus representing a smart investment. And if you're tempted to think, "New York City isn't a good example, New York City is run by those liberals," bear in mind that New York City also is an economic powerhouse the whole world envies.

For generations, the ideal of American education has been to send everyone to college, and perhaps someday this ideal will be realized. At present only about 40 percent of American high school seniors score well enough on the SAT or ACT to show they are prepared for college. Whatever one may think of aptitude tests, their findings cannot be wished away, as the tests reliably predict college attainment.

In the United States, 41 percent of adults hold a college degree, a fraction that, among the world's highest, should be a source of pride. But on a practical basis, there may be a ceiling to the bachelor's degree share of the population, especially if the United States continues, as it should, to admit large numbers of immigrants. In a non-native-born family, the third generation generally does well in school, but the first and second do not. Studies of the 2016 graduating class from the Los Angeles Unified

School District, where many high school students are first-generation immigrants, show only 47 percent averaged at least a C in required courses—this is the average after adding grade inflation—while typical scores on college aptitude tests were nothing to write home about. It is fair to suppose that around half of Americans are long shots to complete a four-year college education, even if tuition were no object; most likely the share in Europe is similar.

David Freedman has written, "Smart people should make the most of their gifts, but they should not be permitted to reshape society so as to instate giftedness as a universal yardstick of human worth." In many nations, culture assumes the smart are more admirable than others: as Don Peck has written, "Among the most pernicious aspects of the meritocracy is the equation of merit with test-taking success." People of average educational aptitude have the same social value as smart people. Because smart people can in most cases look out for themselves, public policy should focus on supporting vocational schools as well as two-year community and junior colleges that serve the needs of average people; helping parents with toddlers during the IQ-in-flux period; and adding vocational skills to public high schools.

Not that long ago, most public high schools offered shop classes that taught mechanical skills, woodworking, and metalworking to prepare students for employment in factories, in construction, or as mechanics. These offerings have tended to fade as public school systems began to feel that most teens should focus on college prep; as a result, students whose odds of college success were low would graduate from high school without a marketable skill. In recent years, auto dealerships have struggled to hire service technicians: high schools don't teach students how to fix cars anymore. Construction and repair firms have trouble hiring electricians, plumbers, locksmiths, carpenters, and welders. Businesses complain of the lack of applicants for good jobs that are available in the skilled trades. Schools must adjust.

BEYOND THAT, THE EVER-ACCELERATING PACE of economic change should prompt a reassessment of how education is structured. Since the late nineteenth century, the structure has been to focus on learning during childhood, the teen years, and early adulthood, followed by, after either high school or college graduation, total cessation of learning. The sixty-eight-year-old private equity billionaire David Rubenstein said in 2017 that since leaving college he has cleaved to a personal rule of reading one book per week, which puts him at nearly 2,500 books read. By contrast, one-third of American college graduates never read another book after walking to "Pomp and Circumstance," while most Americans, after either high school or college commencement, enter educational cessation for the remainder of their lives.

Not only is this a recipe for closing inquisitive minds, it is a recipe for becoming obsolete in a fast-changing global economy. As recently as a generation ago, most people who went into a line of work expected to stay there until retirement. Now, one, two, or several line-of-work changes are becoming the rule. Those higher education institutions geared to twenty-year-olds—why are they not responding?

Suppose the current standard of school-school-school followed by no school at all gave way to one along these lines: work for five years, then spend a year back in college or vocational school learning about the latest economic and research developments, then work for five years, then return to school for another year, and so on. Colleges need to cease being places almost solely for those about to launch into the world and instead become places where men and women of all ages are present on a regular basis. College instructors should look out, not at classes consisting solely of beaming youth, but at classes with a mix of young, middle-aged, and seniors. This not only would help Americans and Europeans adjust to the inevitability of economic turmoil: it would serve inquisitiveness of the mind as well.

IN ADDITION TO NEW VIEWS of education, as longevity increases, societies will need new views of what aging means. In 1940, the typical American lived 7 percent of life retired; now the figure is 23 percent of life in retirement, well on its way to one-third of a lifetime. As the population ages, so do the powers that be, and they're aging in place. When the seventy-year-old Trump took the White House, surrounded by cabinet members who were not exactly spring chickens—average age, sixty-two—the top figures in the opposition leadership were, in spring 2017, Charles Schumer (age sixty-six), Hillary Clinton (age sixty-nine), Bernie Sanders (age seventy-five), Nancy Pelosi (age seventy-seven), and Steny Hoyer (age seventy-seven). Over at the Supreme Court, seven of the nine justices were eligible for Social Security, and four of the nine were above the mandatory retirement age for judges in many states. A graying government would be expected to be concerned foremost with protection of the status quo—just what is observed in the politics of Japan and, increasingly, of the United States.

Government is growing sclerotic at the very time when the aging of the populace demands new ideas. "There's already a tremendous advantage to incumbency," one experienced political operative told me. "As people live longer, incumbents will become more entrenched. Strom Thurmond might not be unusual anymore. Many from both parties could cling to power too long, freezing out fresh thinking. It won't be good for democracy." The speaker was no starry-eyed radical, rather, Karl Rove, chief political strategist for the second President Bush.

Reforms of the political system could make Congress less like a nursing home. A constitutional amendment is needed to eliminate lifetime tenure on the Supreme Court. The first nine justices served an average of nine years each; the most recent nine to leave the Court served an average of twenty-three years. At this writing, Justices Anthony Kennedy, Clarence Thomas, and Ruth Ginsburg are in their twenty-ninth, twenty-fifth, and twenty-fourth years, respectively. The Framers, who could not have anticipated the degree of increase in human longevity, would be scandalized to learn they unintentionally created a system in which a handful of unelected, unaccountable grandees lord it over the body politic for decades. An amendment to limit Supreme Court justices to a single ten-year term would prevent the Court from becoming smug and out of touch; prevent confirmations from being life-and-death partisan struggles; place a new justice on the Court roughly once a year, bringing in fresh thinking and diversity; and create a cadre of former justices who are young enough to take cabinet posts or travel the country explaining how the American legal system works. This would be highly preferable to the current arrangement of deceased justices dragged off the bench by morticians, as if they had been royalty who expired on a throne.

SOCIAL SECURITY REMAINS STRUCTURED AS if longevity were still at the level in effect when the program came into existence in the 1930s. The early retirement option, added by Congress in 1961—start drawing at age sixty-two, though with lower benefits—is appealing if life is short but backfires as life spans extend. People who opt for early Social Security may fly through their savings and reach their eighties facing years of living on a smaller amount than they would have received if they had not filed for early benefits. Polls show that Americans consistently underestimate how long they will live—a convenient assumption that justifies retiring early and spending now, while causing dependency over the long run.

James Vaupel, the longevity demographer noted earlier, has warned that society's reluctance to face the policy choices of rising longevity "distorts people's decisions about how much to save and when to retire... [and gives] license to politicians to postpone painful adjustments to Social Security." Ronald Reagan was the last president to take constructive action on the long-term financing of US society—his administration raised the Social Security tax and enacted a slight increase in the age of full Social Security benefits. Today most members of Congress would agree in private that retirement economics must change again; in public hardly any will touch this third-rail topic. Because of the compounding effects in pension funding, with each year that reform is put off, problems grow worse.

Retirement economics needs to change via means-testing of Social Security (the well-off old should not receive this income transfer from the money-tight young); trimming of cost-of-living formulas; and easing access for average people, and small businesses, to 401(k)-style plans that are owned by the individual, not anchored in political promises. Such reforms could stabilize future national budgets and are more easily achieved now than after the crunch hits. The on-off concept of retirement needs to change—from work-work-work followed by no work at all to many years of gradual downshifting toward part-time and volunteer roles. In the brief lives of most previous centuries, it was all a man or woman could hope to accomplish to bear and raise children; enervation followed. If life spans keep extending, after child-raising, a phase of decades of friendships and experiences could await—one potentially more fulfilling than the emotionally charged but fast-burning friendships of youth.

PERHAPS REFORMS WILL COME TO naught if the robots take over. Trends in manufacturing point toward factories with almost no workers. Bemoaning this won't change the inevitable, any more than 1850s attempts by railroad laborers to destroy standard-gauge tracks prevented the end of the multiple-gauge system that required more navvies, stevedores, and switchmen. A century ago, when agricultural workers began to be replaced by machines, there was a sense of dread, which was forgotten when factory employment became more desirable. Today, as manufacturing workers are replaced by machines, there is a sense of dread, even as careers in teaching and health care expand. Someday machines may fulfill jobs in hospitals—at the current economic pace, "someday" could mean next year—while other sectors expand.

What if the machines start to think? Electronic brains and muscle-like servomotors are advancing so rapidly that one can imagine robots walking down the street to meetings where they decide to rebel and wipe out their human creators. This is not the elevator pitch for a Will Smith movie, rather, a description of the 1920 play *R.U.R.* by Czech writer Karel Čapek, who coined the word "robot." In the play, robots become self-aware and exterminate people; the last man alive witnesses two androids falling in love as Adam and Eve of the species that replaces *Homo sapiens*. For years I've dreaded a big-budget Hollywood version of *R.U.R.* replete with starships, time travel, swimsuit scenes, and explosions. The original is far more haunting than any major-studio version might be. A century ago—before anyone had heard the words "silicon chip"—people worried about robots taking over.

There are small and large concerns. The small concern is the New Luddite fear that machines will lead to general unemployment. Two hundred years ago, Luddites, whose livelihoods depended on handlooms, began smashing stocking frames and other powered devices for knitting.

Parliament responded with one of history's strangest pieces of legislation, the Frame-Breaking Act of 1812, which imposed the death penalty on those who destroyed industrial mechanisms. In the Napoleonic Wars raging at the time, machines killed people, yet people were forbidden to kill machines. The Luddite vision proved to be wrong. Since 1812, living conditions, pay, and benefits for working people have improved steadily, while unemployment has almost always been lower than when Luddites met on the moors to plan attacks on the hated weaving contrivances.

Just because the Luddites were wrong then doesn't mean they'll be wrong in the twenty-first century. Already automation has replaced many factory workers. Automation in this sense is not bipedal robots with shiny metallic faces, rather, the contemporary answer to the stocking frame: powered arms that perform repetitive motions, sensors that inspect assemblies, lifts that move weight. Factory automation unquestionably has made factory workers less important, though has also reduced harm to people in manufacturing. The old steel mills and auto plants that commentators and politicians inexplicably sentimentalize were dirty, loud, hot, soul-crushing, and most of all dangerous.

The wave of agricultural automation that began a century ago made farm workers less important, and today everyone is better off, while unemployment remains low. Exactly when the industrial era began can be disputed, but let's say the starting point was James Watt's steam engine of 1763. Since then, material standards and adjusted-currency pay for most average people have improved in most generations.

Today's attempts at mobile self-guiding robots tend to result in loud crashes into walls. Once autonomous small and midsized devices can move around well, they will replace hospital orderlies, construction-site journeymen, pizza delivery personnel, and some kinds of soldiers; they will also provide routine assistance to the elderly and disabled who live alone or have special needs. A Japanese company has marketed a creepy robot-thing called Pepper that provides assistance to the elderly in Japan, the nation with the longest life spans, where many older people live alone. Which is creepier—having a robot-thing nearby or having no person or thing available if you need help? The probability is that improving automatons will have the same effect as other advances in engineering and technology: economic disruption, some jobs lost while others are gained, and higher living standards for almost everyone.

Most likely robots, no matter how advanced, never will do any more or less than they are designed to do. The Boeing 747 is an astonishingly complex mechanism with six million parts and state-of-the-art electronics. Of the 1,500 that fly the skies of the world, not a single one has become self-aware and turned on its creators nor performed any action unrelated to flight engineering. A person, company, or government could design a robot whose purpose is to harm or dominate people. But that's the same problem as with weapons, whose purpose is harm. Your toaster does not suddenly turn itself into a hand grenade; industrial automatons won't turn themselves into sinister, glowing-eyed beasts.

The large concern is that some form of electronic intellect will come into existence. Quantum computers fantastically more powerful than today's mainframes are under development: in principle, such devices could perform stupendous computational tasks, such as guessing all possible passwords to a bank account, in seconds, rather than the years the best current computers need. The Yale University computer scientist David Gelernter forecast in 2016 that inexpensive chips functioning with the equivalent of a 5,000 IQ will go on sale fairly soon, resulting in your phone, your car's dashboard, and your dishwasher control panel being smarter than you. Already some new-chip design is done by existing chips: programmers don't really know what's going on. Once it's inexpensive to string together a bunch of 5,000-IQ chips, the only leverage men and women will have over whatever results is the ability to switch the power off. And as happened in a classic *Star Trek* episode, intelligent computers may figure out how to prevent their power supply from being interrupted. That's the fear, at least.

At one level the notion of artificial consciousness is far-fetched. Considering researchers, philosophers, and theologians have been unable to agree on what human consciousness is, how can there be an artificial version of something whose natural version defies comprehension? But even if we don't understand what human consciousness is, we know it exists and is, at bottom, electrical in nature: death happens not when the heart stops (that can be reversed) but when electrical patterns in the brain end.

One does not need a sci-fi script to imagine that if electronic minds come into existence, they might perceive the march of evolution as: microbes, multicellular life, plants, mammals, great apes, people, chips. Taking into account how we treat the evolutionary step prior to ours, the great apes, how might chips treat the evolutionary step that came before them?

Electronic intelligence might not care about humanity, considering that the silicon equivalent of the seven-billion-person human population could reside in the dimensions of a peanut butter jar. Or electronic intelligence might permanently be constrained to running whatever people allow such devices to be connected to. But danger is real. Three generations ago, the advent of thermonuclear explosions appeared to doom humanity; instead, the world has grown more peaceful since then. In the next generation, artificial intelligence may become an existential threat. In 2015, Elon Musk, Martin Rees, Francesca Rossi, Steve Wozniak, and other luminaries of the tech and physics realms warned that artificial intelligence could be a great benefit but also could cause society great harm. The time to impose regulation on artificial intelligence, they said, is now—before chips are capable of thinking for themselves. Laws have mandated basic safety for a range of products, including cars and flying machines. Laws that mandate kill switches for electronic devices are in order.

EVEN THOUGH MOST INDICATORS ARE positive, there are still overarching fears of possible events that would make life drastically worse. One is that an atomic bomb will explode in a city. Nuclear-armed nations never have fought, as deterrence logic dissuades anyone who is rational—including bad, but rational, dictators. Irrational leaders are not unknown in the histories of nations, and among nonstate actors, the raving lunatic seems to be the one most likely to end up in charge. It is common to hear that anyone can download a diagram of an atomic bomb from the Internet. This is like saying anyone can download a diagram of a human heart: having the diagram is not the same as being able to perform cardiac surgery. It takes more than a diagram to build an atomic bomb, especially since fissile materials are hard to fabricate or steal. But though these and many other factors render a crude atomic explosion in a city unlikely, they do not render it impossible. The blast would kill thousands. The retaliation would kill many millions, if bomb materials could be traced to a specific nation—the electronic signatures of atomic bombs allow their origins to be determined. Global commerce might come to a halt for decades, creating a second Great Depression.

Even if no maniac ever gets his hands on a crude atomic device, society is foolish to take for granted several initiatives, including the blandly named Cooperative Threat Reduction Program, that track and seize atomic components while converting weapons-grade fissile material into substances that can only be used as fuel for the generation of electricity. Many in politics have been lukewarm to the Cooperative Threat Reduction Program because the initiative involves working with the Russians; many activists are lukewarm because the initiative has the effect of keeping civilian nuclear reactors humming. The program should be expanded.

The world's nuclear arsenal has contracted, but the risk remains grave. Researchers Alan Robock of Rutgers University and Owen Toon of the University of Colorado calculate that even a limited nuclear exchange (another strange qualifier) between India and Pakistan "would produce so much smoke that temperatures would plunge around the world, threatening the global food supply." The global cooling that followed the 1991 eruption of Mount Pinatubo made researchers realize that smoke pumped high into the atmosphere lasts much longer than low-altitude smoke, and Mount Pinatubo emitted a fraction of what might be caused by a "limited" nuclear exchange. Early in the atomic era, radioactive fallout from the bomb seemed an existential threat to civilization—smoke in the stratosphere might be as bad. The trouble is that it's not clear what can be done to prevent nations from losing their collective minds and using nuclear munitions—other than continue the ongoing global project of making humanity understand that war has become counterproductive.

Volcanoes pose a natural threat that could manifest at any time. The most recent supervolcano explosion, Mount Tambora in Indonesia—a far more powerful blast than Mount Saint Helens—happened in 1815 and caused failed harvests around the world. Terry Ann Plank, a magma specialist at Columbia University, warned in 2016 that an explosion of the volcanic formation beneath Yellowstone Park "will disrupt life as we know it on the planet." Some questions do not have answers: nothing can be done to prevent a volcano explosion, little can be done to prepare. But there is one natural existential threat society can prevent: space rocks.

As recently as a generation ago, science assumed that asteroids and other objects had fallen onto Earth only in the far past. Today it's known that a decent-sized space rock struck near the Tunguska River in Siberia in 1908, causing an explosion about a thousand times stronger than the Hiroshima bomb but falling—by good fortune, in a remote region. There's some evidence that a hefty asteroid hit the Gulf of Carpentaria, near Australia, in the year 536, sparing life because it impacted water rather than land; cold summers and poor harvests followed. Astronomers did not develop the means to scan for local space rocks—"near-Earth objects"—until recent decades. In 1980, a total of eighty-six near-Earth objects had been identified. When I wrote about space-rock research for *The Atlantic* in 2008, the total had risen to 5,388 nearby asteroids and similar objects large enough to do global harm. When I wrote this paragraph in mid-2017, the count was up to 16,165 nearby asteroids. By the time you read this paragraph, the count will be higher still. Most of the rocks never will be on a path toward our planet, but only one needs to hit for a calamity equivalent to nuclear war—smoke and debris that mask the sun for years, plus months of rain more corrosive than battery acid.

Protection against asteroids is within the realm of current technology—using, not bombs or lasers, but automated space tugs that alter the path of any big rock likely to impact Earth. Building a space-tug asteroid defense system would require years, so the project must begin before any collision is expected.

Whichever president or prime minister endorsed and funded the work would be mocked by late-night comedians if the system was never used. Space-rock protection would be an insurance policy for humanity—and when purchasing an insurance policy, the best-case result is a total waste of money. Homeowners' insurance, auto insurance, health insurance—ideally you pay the premiums, then never need the coverage. That's the situation with asteroid defense. Great-power nations have spent trillions of dollars, pounds, rubles, francs, and renminbi constructing strategic nuclear missiles they hope never will be used for any purpose: the best-case scenario is that the world's investment in nuclear missiles will be completely wasted. A tiny fraction of what was spent on strategic arms could build space-rock protection that, like the ICBMs, we can hope never will be used. If such a system is needed, stopping an asteroid from causing mass death, and possibly mass extinction, would be the greatest achievement in human history. To our descendants, all else would pale in comparison.

IF POVERTY IN THE DEVELOPING world is to continue to decline, global resource consumption must go up. An oft-heard statistic, that the United States has 5 percent of the world's population and consumes 40 percent of current resources, usually is cited to suggest that American consumption must decline. This is the wrong way to understand the issue: even if the United States stopped consuming resources altogether, those living in privation would not benefit in the slightest. What the statistic means is that global resource consumption—of energy, metals, water, concrete, agricultural chemicals—must rise. Electric grids need to expand from affluent nations to everywhere; the world needs more runways and jets so everyone can access fast, safe travel; hundreds of millions more schools and restaurants need be built. The Earth can sustain a big increase in resource consumption—can society? To use more resources in a cleaner, smarter manner is among the twenty-first century's top challenges. Living standards do not need to keep rising in the West, but they need to rise a great deal in the developing world.

The conventional wisdom is that the whole world cannot live like Americans and western Europeans. To the contrary: for the whole world to live at the Western standard is the only moral course, and given rates of improvement in living standards, coupled to per-capita reductions in pollution and resource waste, is not an impossible dream. An entire world living at the Western standard would bring stress and materialism to the whole world, and not even the rosiest optimist knows where all the cars will park. But society can succeed at a universal Western standard or can fail, and success is a lot more appealing. If the entire world had the living standards, longevity, and education levels of the West, the conditions required for a serene post-scarcity economy might come about.

*   *   *

THE REASON SO MANY PROBLEMS seem unsolvable is that we have not yet attempted to solve them. The past holds innumerable difficulties that seemed as if they could never end. Then they did.

Being sanguine about the human prospect does not justify laissez-faire—"I don't need to worry because things will work out." Things will work out only if society and individuals take action. Greenhouse gas emissions, want amid plenty, refugees risking all for a better life—these and other difficulties may lessen if addressed. Many more people are on the way and should be welcome. Their arrival must be prepared for, even as society deals with the multitude of difficulties that already exist.

The most accomplished reformer of the twentieth century, Franklin Roosevelt, said in 1938, "We observe a world of great opportunities disguised as insoluble problems." Today we observe opportunities disguised as insoluble problems, and we can create the solutions.

Chapter 12

...And It Will Never Be Too Late

ON A WARM MORNING IN a hospital in Peru or Indonesia or South Africa, the most important person of the twenty-first century will be born. She will dodge chaotic traffic to reach an underfunded school to learn her three Rs, later try to fall asleep in a crowded tenement as car horns and gunshots echo on the street. Winning a scholarship to college, she will study molecular biology or cryogenic engineering or poetry. She will have an idea. Then she will go out into the world and save a billion people.

Reading chronicles of history, we encounter countless junctures which instigate the thought, *If only they had done This or That, then The Other Thing would not have happened.* Too often we conclude, *But once they failed to do This or That, it was Too Late.* Such analysis applies not just to the past but the present day—to the recurrent belief that because of some screwup or setback, a good outcome has slipped beyond our grasp.

But it's never too late to make a better world.

Beyond the specific teachings of history are general themes. Some themes of history are deeply negative. Power corrupts and absolute power corrupts absolutely. Weapons tend to be used. Wealth too often fundamentally is theft. Religions preach peace then cause violence.

Some themes of history are neutral. Difficulties exist in an unending chain: problem arises, problem is fixed, new problem arises. Every nation and every person assumes the grass is greener on the other side of the fence. Not long after persons, nations, or societies think *We've finally got it figured out,* the persons, nations, or societies realize they have not got it figured out.

And some themes of history are rich in hope. Most things get better for most people; the human family is ever-larger, yet nature endures; dynamism almost always surpasses catastrophism; optimism almost always bests pessimism.

Uncertainty is inherent in the dynamist view; no one enjoys uncertainty. But the pattern of history is that most challenges get solved, while catastrophes, whether natural or man-made, always are temporary. The pattern of natural or man-made emergencies is that once they end, previous trends resume, and for many centuries the previous trend for the human prospect has been positive. Today many around the world are worried, and with cause, about the wave of despotic cult-of-personality leaders. History suggests this situation will be temporary, and then the positive trends will resume.

Two larger questions than cult-of-personality leaders are the resilience of the Enlightenment and the ability of societies to withstand unceasing change.

Right now every premise of the Enlightenment is being tested as never before in China and India. Should secular democracy, personal liberty, and market economics prevail in those grand tests, the human prospect will increase.

Our habit is to think that all would be well if only change would stop—but change is not the foe. A millennium ago, China was the leading society in mathematics, agriculture, metallurgy, administration (competitive civil service examinations), and shipbuilding, the foremost expression of technology at the time. Then Chinese society turned inward, banning exploration and discouraging trade. The goal was to stop change; the result was a thousand years of decline, plus dozens of generations of suffering by average people. Both the decline and the suffering are ending as China accepts the maddening necessity of modernity. Many other societies wish there were no change, but will be better off for it. Change can be stressful, painful, infuriating. But change is not the foe.

The psychologist Daniel Bar-Tal has proposed that a siege mentality—grounded in past eras of physical sieges of cities—increasingly applies to contemporary life. During a physical siege of a city, beleaguered holdouts resist an onslaught of malevolent intruders. Everything is dichotomized into good (our group) and bad (all other groups) while pessimism rules since the best-case outcome is not a better life, rather, simply avoiding destruction.

Those stricken with the siege mentality want to wall out whatever approaches. During physical sieges in the era of city-states, this was done with stones and revetments. Today the siege mentality manifests as anger—against political opponents, against other identity groups, against the sense of endless uncertainty generated by change. Even anger against optimism. Those who feel fury want others to feel the same, and may actually find the hopeful view offensive.

Yet it not a mere matter of coincidence that optimism is superior to pessimism as a guide. Optimism seeks good outcomes; pessimism tends to spiral downward. Groups that sink into siege mentality usually wind up on the margins, while optimists slowly achieve their goals.

That optimism almost always bests pessimism is why we can be sure the most important person of the twenty-first century is on the way, though of course the specifics of her life can only be imagined. Pessimists want rearguard actions against whatever encroaches: if society is crumbling, then nations really do need walls. Optimists believe any society can be made safer, richer, more fair, and more free, that the world can be a better place in manifold ways.

No one can be certain optimism will continue to best pessimism; all we can know is that this has happened so far. In contrast, it is easy to be certain optimism is the strongest argument for reform. Advances of the past made life better. That is good reason to hope the next round of reforms will succeed too.

If your great-great-grandmother had known that today nearly everyone in the West, and an ever-increasing share of those in developing nations, would live in a society with plentiful food and fuel; with most infectious diseases thwarted; with fast, very-low-risk transportation available to most men and women, including average people traveling aboard jets; with nearly every adult a high school graduate and 470 million people worldwide holding college degrees; with inexpensive, instantaneous global communication available to most of humanity; with more people in desk jobs than sweating in mines or on assembly lines—your great-great-grandmother would say the present represented her era's dreams come true. Many dilemmas of our moment would confound her, and some aspects of the present day would frighten her deeply, as they ought to frighten us. In the main, she would think the human experiment was going well. And she'd want us to get off our duffs and reform what needs to be fixed next.

Today some argue, "We can't reform [insert any word] because that would be too expensive or too disruptive." Looking backward, this is not the lesson drawn from reforms of the past. In most cases, the lesson of past reforms is, "Why didn't we act sooner?" The next round of reforms is likely to be looked back on the same way.

Consider that nearly every important reform of the past century— these are American examples, but most Western nations and some developing nations had similar acts of progress—seems wise and cost-effective in retrospect: environmental conservation; civil rights legislation; safeguarding freedom of speech and of religion; labor laws; legal protection of private property; regulation of business; due process and counsel for the accused; creation of public health care and pension systems; racial and gender equity in marriage, the workplace, and the military; artistic and sexual freedom; disclosure of government secrets; expansion of science and research; expansion of education; maintenance of a strong national defense. "Why didn't we do that sooner!" is the lesson in every instance.

At many junctures in the past, intellectuals, public figures, and religious leaders have pronounced imminent collapse. Extremists of divergent ideologies may make common cause in declarations of crises, to justify the command structures that extremists long to impose—with themselves in charge, of course.

Yet the world keeps refusing to end.

Someday men and women will leave the cradle and live far from Earth. Above us in the galaxy are essentially infinite resources, along with infinite opportunities for kindness or malice. That chapter of the human saga is centuries distant but from the standpoint of geology will appear to have happened in the wink of an eye.

At least 100 billion people have lived on our great spinning globe. Many suffered horribly, their lives rendered sorrowful, short, or both by nature or human heartlessness. Yet most of those 100 billion left society a more welcoming place than they found. That progression is ongoing: a better world is closer than it looks.

History is not deterministic, teleological, or controlled in any manner. But as time passes, in the main the human condition improves—and this can be expected to continue. History has an arrow, and the arrow of history points forever upward.

Acknowledgments

For the realization of this volume, thanks are due to my friends, colleagues, and editors: Ben Adams, Jon Alter, Maya Aubrey, James Bennet, Sandra Beris, Jenny Blake, Lyndsey Blessing, Frank Bowman, David Bradley, David Brooks, Glenn Brooks, Carol Browner, Cindy Buck, Robin Campbell, Michael Carlisle, Stephen Carter, Diane Chandler, Katharine DeShaw, Eric Dezenhall, Martha Drullard, Thomas Dunne, Darcy Eveleigh, James Fallows, Henry Ferris, Franklin Foer, Lindsay Fradkoff, Timothy Fuller, Paul Glastris, Donald Graham, David Gray, Tedd Habberfield, Carla Hall, Laura Hall, Toby Harshaw, Stephen Hayes, Marjorie Hazen, David Hendrickson, Alexis Hurley, Debbie Ida, Walter Isaacson, Bob Jaffe, Martin Janik, Jan Jones, Jonathan Karp, Bob Kerrey, Michael Kinsley, Arkadiy Klebaner, Barbara Klie, Charles Lane, Jaime Leifer, Nicholas Lemann, David Leonhardt, Toby Lester, Jan Lewis, Thomas Lindblade, Ben Loehnen, James Mallon, Jane Mayer, Deborah McGill, Robert Messenger, John Milner, Toni Monkovic, Rosh Moorjani, Michael Mungiello, Cullen Murphy, Timothy Noah, Joe Nocera, Lynn Olson, Steve Olson, Peter Osnos, Sue Parilla, Don Peck, Beth Peters, Charles Peters, Clive Priddle, Melissa Raymond, Diane Rehm, William Reilly, Clay Risen, Janet Robinson, Tina Rosenberg, Claudia Russell, Isabel Sawhill, Aaron Schatz, Greg Shaw, Eric Schmidt, Hannah Schwartz, Charles Sciandra, Greg Shaw, John Skipper, Anne Stadler, Janet St. Goar, Scott Stossel, Claire Swiat, Joseph Tauriello, Nicholas Thompson, John Tierney, Chuck Todd, Peter Wehner, Susan Weinberg, Jenny Witherell, Peter Wolverton, Wendy Woska and Claudia Zahn; to the memories of Benedict Drew 1953–2015, Carolyn See 1934–2016, Pietro Nivola 1944–2017, and Kukula Kapoor Glastris, 1958–2017; to my brothers Frank and

Neil; to my cousins Sharon Benton and David Easterbrook; to my children, Grant, Mara, and Spenser; and to my wife, Nan Kennelly.

I especially thank Jonathan Fanton, Don Randel, Geraldine Richmond, and the fellows of the American Academy of Arts and Sciences, who, by electing me to join their number, metaphorically stuck my finger into an electric socket, jolting me with the energy required to complete this project.

Notes

Chapter 1

3 **Then he went out into the world and saved a billion people:** Gregg Easterbrook, "Forgotten Benefactor of Humanity," *The Atlantic,* January 1997. Other details of Borlaug's life and work are in this article.

3 **In 2015, the United Nations' Food and Agriculture Organization (FAO) reported:** FAO, *Millennium Development Goals Report* (New York: United Nations, 2015).

5 **"Sometime within the next 15 years the end will come":** Clyde Haberman, "The Unrealized Horrors of Population Explosion," *New York Times,* May 31, 2015.

5 **Today there are twice as many people who are overweight as the *total* number who were alive:** Marie Ng et al., "Global Regional and National Prevalence of Overweight and Obesity in Children and Adults," *The Lancet,* August 30, 2014. This study estimates there were about 2.1 billion overweight people in 2013. When Malthus was alive, there were about a billion people in toto.

7–8 **When Borlaug was a boy, US farms produced:** Economic Research Service, *Wheat Data—All Years* (Washington, DC: US Department of Agriculture).

8 **"The global grain harvest has nearly tripled since 1961":** "Vital Signs 2007–2008" (Washington, DC: Worldwatch Institute, 2009).

9 **Farmers likewise have adopted conservation tillage:** "Census of Agriculture 2012" (Washington, DC: US Department of Agriculture, July 2012).

9–10 **breakthroughs such as a means to increase the number of hours in the day that plants metabolize sunlight:** Erik Stokstad, "How Turning Off a Plant's Sunshield Can Grow Bigger Crops," *Science,* November 17, 2016.

10 **Olusegun Obasanjo, a former president of Nigeria, noted in 2016:** Olusegun Obasanjo, "Making African Agriculture Achieve Its Potential," *SciDev .Net,* May 25, 2016.

10 **African coffee plantations sold $2.4 billion worth of green beans:** Calestous Juma, "How the European Union Starves Africa into Submission" (London: Center for Policy Studies, October 2015).

12 **Alexander Hamilton's eighteenth-century policy for the United States:** Hamilton's *Report on the Subject of Manufactures,* presented to Congress in 1791, still is worth reading today. If only someone would set it to music!

12 **The British horticulturalist Noel Kingsbury has noted:** Noel Kingsbury, *Hybrid* (Chicago: University of Chicago Press, 2009). This book also offers a history of crop breeding in previous centuries.

13 **The UN's Food and Agriculture Organization projected:** Nikos Alexandratos and Jelle Bruinsma, *World Agriculture Towards 2030/2050,* ESA Working Paper 12–03 (New York: Food and Agriculture Organization of the United Nations, June 2012).

13 **pesticide application in the United States rose steadily:** "Pesticide Use in US Agriculture: 21 Selected Crops, 1960–2008" (Washington, DC: US Department of Agriculture, 2014).

13 **In 2013, the American Association for the Advancement of Science concluded:** "Statement by the AAAS Board of Directors on Genetically Modified Foods" (Washington, DC: American Association for the Advancement of Science, June 2013).

13 **As Li Jiao has written, the North China Plain water table:** Li Jiao, "Water Shortages Loom as Northern China's Aquifers Are Sucked Dry," *Science,* June 18, 2010.

14 **As the UCLA geographer Laurence Smith has noted:** Laurence Smith, *The World in 2050* (New York: Dutton, 2010).

14 **Today the United States has 21 percent less land under cultivation:** "Census of Agriculture 2012" (Washington, DC: US Department of Agriculture, July 2012).

15 **Currently only about 0.45 percent of the globe:** Zhifeng Liu et al., "How Much of the World's Land Has Been Urbanized?" *Landscape Ecology,* April 2014.

15 **a shocking crisis of "vanishing farms":** Gregg Easterbrook, "Vanishing Land Reappears," *The Atlantic,* February 1986.

15 **Zhifeng Liu, a researcher at Beijing Normal University, found in 2014:** Ibid.

16 **The Dutch scientist Louise Fresco has noted:** Louise Fresco, *Hamburgers in Paradise* (Princeton, NJ: Princeton University Press, 2015).

18 **Just a century ago, 80 percent of humanity:** Max Roser, *Short History of Global Living Conditions* (Oxford: University of Oxford Press). Viewable at Our World in Data, www.ourworldindata.org.

19 **The World Bank reports that the number:** "World Bank Forecasts Global Poverty to Fall Below 10% for First Time" (Washington, DC: World Bank, 2015).

19 **The 3 billion additional men and women who are not impoverished:** One could spend hours comparing—and marveling at the improvements reflected in—the World Bank's *World Development Report 1992* (Oxford:

Oxford University Press, 1992) and *World Development Report 2015* (Washington, DC: World Bank, 2015).

20 **A 2013 survey by Novus:** Mats Elzén and Per Fernström, *The Ignorance Survey* (Stockholm: Novus, 2013).

20 **In 2015, Georgetown University professor Steven Radelet:** Steven Radelet, *The Great Surge* (New York: Simon & Schuster, 2015).

Chapter 2

22 **A top official at the US National Institutes of Health (NIH) declares:** Anthony Fauci, director of the National Institute of Allergy and Infectious Diseases at NIH, said, "It's almost certain that within a reasonable period of time we will experience an influenza pandemic." See "Bird Flu: How Concerned Should We Be?," transcript of meeting of the Council on Foreign Relations, October 8, 2005.

22 **ABC News declares the death toll could reach 150 million:** "How Many People Could Bird Flu Kill?" ABC News, September 30, 2005. Doubling down, in May 2006, ABC aired *Fatal Contact: Bird Flu in America,* a preposterous made-for-TV movie full of fake newscasts and fake White House scenes, depicting much of the US population killed in a few weeks. Donald Trump may cry "fake news" far too often, but it was the networks themselves that conceived the idea of presenting fake news as a form of entertainment.

22 **avian flu has killed about 450 people worldwide:** "Cumulative Number of Confirmed Human Cases for Avian Influenza A(H5N1) Reported to WHO, 2003–2017" (Geneva: World Health Organization, June 2017).

23 **MERS could be the "new Black Death":** Laurie Garrett, "The Middle East Plague Goes Global," *Foreign Policy,* June 28, 2013.

23 **Instead, virologists determined the disease is not especially contagious:** Kai Kupferschmidt, "MERS Surges but Pandemic Jitters Ease," *Science,* March 20, 2015.

23 **warning of "the next AIDS":** "US Health Director Thomas Frieden Says Ebola 'the Next AIDS,'" BBC News, October 9, 2014.

23 **By summer 2015, an Ebola vaccine...was in trials:** Sarah Boseley, "Ebola Vaccine Proves Successful in Guinea," *The Guardian,* July 31, 2015.

23 **Some 11,300 people worldwide died from Ebola in 2014 and 2015:** "Ebola Data and Statistics" (Geneva: World Health Organization, May 2016).

24 **instead, in 2016, about 425,000 did, about 75 percent fewer than would have been expected:** Jane Brody, "Our Parents' Heart Health Mistakes," *New York Times,* April 11, 2017.

24 **"translating to approximately 2.1 million fewer cancer deaths":** Rebecca Siegel et al., "Cancer Statistics 2017," *Cancer Journal for Clinicians,* January 5, 2017.

25 **was positioned on page 5:** Sheri Fink, "Ebola Cases Fall Sharply, WHO Reports," *New York Times,* August 4, 2015.

25 **providing…about $15 billion annually in candy and sweetened soda to food stamp recipients:** "Foods Typically Purchased by Supplemental Nutrition Assistance Program Households" (Washington, DC: US Department of Agriculture, November 2016).

26 **Mexico has the most obesity in the world:** Jean Clemenceau, "Obesity and the State of Cancer Incidence and Mortality in Mexico," paper presented at the 2017 annual meeting of the American Society of Clinical Oncology, Chicago, June 2–6.

26 **sixty-eight people died, but there was no runaway effect:** Gregg Easterbrook, "We're Gonna Die," *Wired,* July 2003.

29 **In 1900, some 80 percent of Americans were employed at manual or semiskilled labor:** Theodore Caplow et al., *The First Measured Century* (Washington, DC: AEI Press, 2000).

29 **Chicago has invested about $4 billion in a deep-tunnel system:** Trevor English, "Chicago Deep Tunnel Project," *Interesting Engineering,* May 21, 2016.

30 **The World Health Organization estimates that indoor air pollution causes 4.3 million deaths:** "Clean Household Energy for Health, Sustainable Development, and Wellbeing of Women and Children" (Geneva: World Health Organization, 2016).

31 **Today the typical man in the Netherlands is five-foot-eleven:** Max Roser, "Human Height," https://ourworldindata.org/human-height/.

32 **The improvement obtains nearly everywhere:** Most statistics in this section can be found in the WHO's Global Health Observatory, http://www.who.int/gho.

32 **in 2017, the CDC reported that older black males live about the same length of time as older white males:** "Health, United States, 2015" (Atlanta: Centers for Disease Control and Prevention).

33 **Already Calico researcher Cynthia Kenyon has shown:** This and Buck Institute work are described in Gregg Easterbrook, "What Happens When We All Live to 100," *The Atlantic,* October 2014.

33 **In 2002, Vaupel published an influential article:** James Vaupel et al., "Broken Limits to Life Expectancy," *Science,* May 10, 2002.

34 **as Claire McCarthy, a pediatrician at Boston Children's Hospital, has written:** Claire McCarthy, "Teen Drug Use Is Down," *Harvard Health Publications,* March 21, 2017.

34 **"Deaths from prescription drugs like oxycodone, hydrocodone and methadone":** "Drug Overdose Deaths in the United States Continue to Increase" (Atlanta: Centers for Disease Control and Prevention, December 2016).

35 **Princeton University researchers Angus Deaton and Anne Case have shown:** Anne Case and Angus Deaton, "Rising Morbidity and Mortality in Midlife Among White Non-Hispanic Americans in the 21st Century," *Proceedings of the National Academy of Sciences,* December 8, 2015.

35 **The Robert Wood Johnson Foundation reports:** "Major Food, Beverage Companies Remove 6.4 Trillion Calories from US Marketplace" (Trenton, NJ: Robert Woods Johnson Foundation, 2014).

36 **"Today's children and young adults may grow up to enjoy":** Margot Sanger-Katz, "Good News Hidden in the Data," *The Upshot,* June 17, 2016.

36 **researchers led by Matthew Pase of Boston University found:** Matthew Pase et al., "Sugar- and Artificially Sweetened Beverages and the Risks of Incident Stroke and Dementia," *Stroke,* April 20, 2017.

37 **Chana Joffe-Walt, a reporter for the public radio show *This American Life:*** Chana Joffe-Walt, "Unfit for Work," NPR, March 22, 2013.

37 **federal disability subsidies are more common in rural areas than in cities:** Brendan Greeley, "Mapping the Growth of Disability Claims in America," *Bloomberg Businessweek,* December 16, 2016.

38 **the best-educated males live fourteen years longer than the least-educated men:** S. Jay Olshansky et al., "Differences in Life Expectancy Due to Race and Educational Differences Are Widening," *Health Affairs,* August 2012.

38 **The Centers for Disease Control have found:** "Current Cigarette Smoking Among Adults, United States, 2005–2014" (Atlanta: Centers for Disease Control and Prevention, 2015).

39 **Samir Bhatt of the University of Oxford has shown:** Samir Bhatt et al., "The Effect of Malaria Control on *Plasmodium falciparum* in Africa Between 2000 and 2015," *Nature,* September 16, 2016.

39 **one promising line of research involves releasing altered mosquitoes:** Annelies Wilder Smith, "Dengue Vaccines at a Crossroad," *Science,* November 6, 2015.

Chapter 3

41 **Los Angeles averaged 125 "stage 1" smog alerts:** "California's Progress Toward Clean Air," report by the California Air Pollution Control Officers Association, 2015.

42 **In 1970, anchorman Walter Cronkite:** Quoted in *Retro Report: The Population Bomb,* produced by Kit Roane and Sarah Weiser, 2015.

42 **International Union for the Conservation of Nature (IUCN), which keeps the books:** "IUCN Red List" (Gland, Switzerland: International Union for the Conservation of Nature, 2017). The bald eagle is listed by its taxonomy designation, *Haliaeetus leucocephalus.*

42 **air that was free of smog, as air almost always is in American cities:** "Our Nation's Air Quality and Trends Through 2015" (Washington, DC: Environmental Protection Agency, 2016).

42 **in general cleanliness was rising:** Suzanne Teller, "The Clean Water Act: 40 Years of Progress in Peril," *Outdoor America* (Izaak Walton League of

America) 4, 2012. "EPA figures show that the number of rivers, lakes, and estuaries safe for fishing and swimming doubled just 25 years after the passage of the Clean Water Act."

43   **exploded with the power of about 1,500 Hiroshima bombs:** The story is well told by Steve Olson in *Eruption* (New York: W. W. Norton, 2016).

43   **"Some 19 million old-growth Douglas firs":** Gregg Easterbrook, *A Moment on the Earth* (New York: Viking, 1995).

44   **the climate activist Bill McKibben would write:** Bill McKibben, "An Explosion of Green," *The Atlantic,* April 1999.

44–45   **according to satellite data compiled by Brazilian researchers:** Jeff Tollefson, "Deforestation Spikes in Brazilian Amazon," *Nature,* November 30, 2016.

45   **The UCLA geographer Jared Diamond has argued:** Jared Diamond, *Collapse* (New York: Viking, 2005).

45   **Researchers led by Thomas Crowther of the Yale School of Forestry:** Thomas Crowther et al., "Mapping Tree Density at a Global Scale," *Nature,* September 9, 2015.

45   **researchers led by Simon Lewis of University College London:** Simon Lewis et al., "Increasing Human Dominance of Tropical Forests," *Science,* August 21, 2015.

45   **sulfur dioxide emissions have declined 81 percent in the United States:** "National Air Quality: Status and Trends of Key Air Pollutants" (Washington, DC: Environmental Protection Agency, 2017).

47   **of the forty bird species Carson named as about to cease existing:** Detailed in Easterbrook, *A Moment on the Earth.*

47   **Audubon's 2016 count tallied 646 avian species:** Geoffrey LeBaron, "The 116th Christmas Bird Count Summary" (New York: Audubon Society, 2016).

48   **The IUCN finds 1.3 percent of species in clear danger:** International Union for the Conservation of Nature, "IUCN Red List."

48   **Katherine MacKinnon, an anthropologist at St. Louis University:** Katherine MacKinnon et al., "Impending Extinction Crisis of the World's Primates," *Science,* January 18, 2017.

48   **Frank Fenner, who was a motivating force behind the eradication of smallpox:** Lin Edwards, "Humans Will Be Extinct in 100 Years Says Eminent Scientist," Physics.org, June 2010.

49   **Stratospheric ozone depletion has now stopped, with the hole shrinking:** Jennifer Chu, "Scientists Observe First Signs of Healing in the Antarctic Ozone Layer," *MIT News,* June 30, 2016.

49   **The world's reaction to artificially triggered climate change:** The unwieldy wording "artificially triggered" sometimes is needed because our civilization, such as it is, came about at the end of an ice age, when natural global warming already was in progress. Glaciers had been receding for thousands of years before fossil fuels were discovered.

50 **In 1991...the US National Academy of Sciences declared "there is no evidence":** National Academy of Sciences, "Policy Implications of Greenhouse Warming" (Washington, DC: National Academy Press, 1991).

50 **"There is now strong evidence that significant global warming is occurring":** "Joint Science Academies' Statement: Global Response to Climate Change" (Washington, DC: National Academy of Sciences, 2005).

50 **China reduced greenhouse emissions by canceling construction of more than one hundred coal-fired power stations:** Michael Forsythe, "China Cancels 103 Coal Plants, Mindful of Smog and Wasted Capacity," *New York Times,* January 18, 2017.

51 **On the day in 1990 when the Germanys were reunified, East Germany's per-capita energy consumption:** Easterbrook, *A Moment on the Earth.*

51 **Today's beer cans...contain about 15 percent as much metal as cans of the past:** David Owen, *The Conundrum* (New York: Riverhead Books, 2011).

52 **A 1972 academic study titled *Limits to Growth:*** Donella Meadows et al., *Limits to Growth* (New York: Universe, 1972).

53 **Now the number is 96 million barrels a day, yet the oil market is glutted:** "Oil Market Report 2016" (Paris: International Energy Agency, 2017).

53–54 **Natural gas was thought in such diminishing supply:** Amory Lovins, "The Road Not Taken," *Foreign Affairs,* October 1976.

54 **John Holdren...predicted natural gas would skyrocket in price:** Noted in Daniel Yergin, *The Prize* (New York: Simon & Schuster, 1991).

55 **In 1943, Secretary of the Interior Harold Ickes Sr. wrote an article:** Ibid.

55 **Navy Secretary James Forrestal told Allied leaders:** Ibid.

55 **Anyone who spent time with oil and gas wildcatters:** Gregg Easterbrook, "Psst—the Energy Crisis Is Over," *Washington Monthly,* October 1980.

56–57 **Stumpf, already paid $19 million for the year in which he made the bank's once-storied name synonymous with fraud:** Stacy Cowley, "Top Leaders Got Big Pay as Crisis Hits Wells Fargo," *New York Times,* March 17, 2017.

57 **today we know that at least 1.7 trillion barrels remain untapped:** "BP Statistical Review of World Energy" (London: BP, 2016).

57 **"Descendants of contemporary oil sheiks":** Gregg Easterbrook, *Sonic Boom* (New York: Random House, 2009).

57–58 **In 2014, the US Geological Survey reported:** Molly Maupin et al., "Estimated Use of Water in the United States" (Washington, DC: US Geological Survey, 2014).

58 **John Steinbeck's masterwork *East of Eden:*** John Steinbeck, *East of Eden* (New York: Viking, 1952).

58 **Smog is so bad in coastal cities of China:** Wei Chen et al., "Air Quality of Beijing and Impacts of the New Ambient Air Quality Standard," *Atmosphere,* August 20, 2015.

58 **Beijing declared a "red alert" for smog, closing schools:** Echo Huang, "Beijing Finally Breathing a Sigh of Relief After Week in Hell," *Quartz,* December 22, 2016.

58   **around three times the World Health Organization standard:** See the WHO Global Urban Ambient Air Pollution Database, updated for 2016 at www.who.int/phe/health_topics/outdoorair/databases/cities/en/.

58   **in China, typical thermal efficiency is about half that amount:** Yinhua Mai et al., "Increasing China's Coal-Fired Power Generation Efficiency" (Melbourne: Centre of Policy Studies, 2015).

59   **the Boston-based Health Effects Institute found a rise in premature deaths:** (many authors), "Global, Regional, and National Comparative Risk Assessment of 79 Behavioural, Environmental and Occupational, and Metabolic Risks or Clusters of Risks," *The Lancet,* October 8, 2016.

60   **Today the City of Angels goes years between stage 1 announcements:** "Annual Emission Reporting" (Diamond Bar, CA: South Coast Air Quality Management District, 2017).

60   **Air quality has improved considerably in Mexico City:** Javier Audry Sánchez, "Recent Trend in Ozone Levels in Mexico City," *Journal of the Mexican Chemical Society,* December 2, 2008.

60   **In the last quarter-century, US air quality shows these trends:** EPA, "National Air Quality."

62   **In 2015, President Barack Obama said he became convinced:** "Obama: Daughter's Asthma Brings Home Climate Change Debate," *Chicago Tribune,* April 8, 2015.

Chapter 4

64   **not to negotiate a treaty, not to denounce Western imperialism, but to order jetliners:** Do a Google search for "Boeing" and "Vietnam celebrates first 787–9 Dreamliner" to behold a photograph that will knock the socks off any Vietnam War veteran, whether American, Vietnamese, or Australian.

66   **"There is no reason for any individual to have a computer in the home":** Quoted in David Boaz, *Beyond the Status Quo* (Washington, DC: Cato Press, 1985).

67   **Hillary Clinton's declaration that she would be:** Avi Zenilman, "Commander-in-Chief of the Economy," *Politico,* March 24, 2008.

68   **the crack-up disproved "the idea of an all-powerful free market that is always right":** Bruce Crumley, "Europe's Conservatives Sour on the Free Market," *Time,* September 26, 2008.

69   **Today, when the Federal Reserve "prints money," no printing may occur:** See Edison Yu, "Did Quantitative Easing Work?" (Philadelphia: Federal Reserve Bank of Philadelphia, 2016).

70   **"Jobless Rate Falls but Many Feel Passed By":** This was the subhead of the page-one story by Patrician Cohen, "Obama's Gift to Successor," *New York Times,* December 3, 2016.

70 **Social scientist Carol Graham of the University of Maryland has shown:** Carol Graham, *The Pursuit of Happiness* (Washington, DC: Brookings Institution Press, 2011).

71 **one of the best books of the twentieth century:** Nicholas Lemann, *The Promised Land* (New York: Alfred A. Knopf, 1991).

71 **American whites on average earn a third more than American blacks:** Patrick Bayer and Kerwin Charles, "Divergent Paths: Structural Change, Economic Rank, and the Evolution of Black-White Earnings Differences, 1940–2014" (Cambridge, MA: National Bureau of Economic Research, November 2016).

72 **the number-one year for US manufacturing output was 2017:** Economic Research Division, "Industrial Production Index" (St. Louis: Federal Reserve Bank of St. Louis). The best source of contemporary US economic data is https://fred.stlouisfed.org. Just Google "FRED."

72 **in 2016 there were 12.3 million US factory jobs:** Economic Research Division, "All Employees: Manufacturing"(St. Louis: Federal Reserve Bank of St. Louis).

72 **Economists Martin Baily and Barry Bosworth...calculate that:** Martin Baily and Barry Bosworth, "US Manufacturing: Understanding Its Past and Its Potential Future," *Journal of Economic Perspectives,* Winter 2014.

72 ***Sonic Boom* described in detail how General Electric:** Easterbrook, *Sonic Boom.*

73 **The sprawling Renton, Washington, facility that assembles Boeing jetliners:** Chris Sloan, "A Historical Look at Boeing's 737 Factory in Renton," *Airline Reporter,* July 2013.

73 **According to the American Iron and Steel Institute:** "ASIS Annual Statistical Report 2016" (Washington, DC: American Iron and Steel Institute).

74 **In the last five years, Canadian Pacific Railway has cut its workforce:** Eric Atkins, "CN and CP Railways on Track for More Layoffs," *Toronto Globe & Mail,* May 17, 2106.

74 **even recently hired employees receive two months of paid family leave annually:** Peter Jamison, "DC Council Votes for Expansive Paid Family," *Washington Post,* December 20, 2016.

75 **Today Steel City's current-dollar per-capita income:** Economic Research Division, "Per Capita Personal Income in Pittsburgh Metropolitan Statistical Area" (St. Louis: Federal Reserve Bank of St. Louis).

75 **extensive media attention, replete with "dying Rust Belt" theatrics:** Gary Younge, "Muncie's Forgotten Factories," *The Guardian,* October 25, 2016.

75–76 **Print newspaper circulation in the United States peaked in 1957:** Michael Barthel, "US Newspapers: Circulation and Revenue Fall" (Washington, DC: Pew Research Center, June 2017).

76 **A 2016 page-one *New York Times* story about unhappiness in middle America:** Roger Cohen, "We Need Somebody Spectacular," *New York Times,* September 9, 2016.

77   **the *Washington Post* ran a harrowing page-one story:** Jessica Contrera, "In Place of Need, an Unhealthy Contradiction," *Washington Post,* March 11, 2017.

77–78   **The New York University professors Pankaj Ghemawat and Steven Altman have shown:** Pankaj Ghemawat and Steven Altman, *DHL Global Connectedness Index 2016* (Deutsche Post DHL Group, 2016).

78   **By 2016, two-thirds of Japanese-marque cars sold in America were built in US factories:** Dan Eaton, "Japan's Big 3 Automakers Built More Cars in US Than Detroit 3 Last Year," *Columbus Business Journal,* June 2, 2016.

78   **Chinese econometric data is unreliable:** Michael Owyang and Hannah Shell, "China's Economic Data: Accurate Reflection or Smoke and Mirrors?" (St. Louis: Federal Reserve Bank of St. Louis, 2017).

78   **Economist Michael Hicks of Ball State University calculates:** Michael J. Hicks, "The Myth and the Reality of Manufacturing in America" (Muncie, IN: Center for Business and Economic Research, 2017).

78   **In 2016, Senator Susan Collins of Maine told Ryan Lizza of *The New Yorker:*** Ryan Lizza, "Occupied Territory," *The New Yorker,* June 20, 2016.

79   **His studies demonstrate that American manufacturing employment:** David Autor et al., "The China Syndrome: Local Labor Market Effects of Import Competition in the United States," *American Economic Review,* October 2013.

79   **that is roughly when Chinese industrial employment, too, started downward:** Michael Schuman, "Is China Stealing Jobs? It May Be Losing Them," *New York Times,* July 22, 2016.

79   **The Wilson Center, a nonpartisan think tank, in 2016 estimated:** Christopher Wilson, "Working Together" (Washington, DC: Wilson Center, 2016).

80   **A magisterial book, *The Sea and Civilization:*** Lincoln Paine, *The Sea and Civilization* (New York: Alfred A. Knopf, 2013).

80   **As the economist Paul Krugman has noted:** Paul Krugman, "Why Don't All Jobs Matter?" *New York Times,* April 17, 2017.

81   **Faster ships and smaller crews have cut the cost of transoceanic shipment to as low as $10 a ton:** Edward Humes, *Door to Door* (New York: HarperCollins, 2016).

82   **Brazil, India, and most of Africa can charge three and a half times what the United States is allowed to:** Compare tariff rules for WTO member nations at http://stat.wto.org/TariffProfile/WSDBTariffPFReporter.aspx?.

82   **Angus Deaton...has studied developing-nation inequality and concluded:** Angus Deaton, *The Great Escape* (Princeton, NJ: Princeton University Press, 2013).

83   **Those who dived into Pew's research:** "The American Middle Class Is Losing Ground" (Washington, DC: Pew Research Center, December 2015).

83 **Stephen Rose, a labor economist at the Urban Institute:** Stephen Rose, "The Growing Size and Incomes of the Upper Middle Class" (Washington, DC: Urban Institute, 2016).

84 **The most-talked-about serious book...bore the subhead:** Christopher Lasch, *The Culture of Narcissism* (New York: W. W. Norton, 1979).

84 **"the simplest and most powerful measure" of inequality:** Thomas Piketty and Emmanuel Saez, "Inequality in the Long Run," *Science,* May 23, 2014.

85 **Piketty's 2013 tome *Capital in the Twenty-First Century* was received:** Thomas Piketty, *Capital in the Twenty-First Century* (Cambridge, MA: Harvard University Press, 2014).

85 **for the typical middle-class family, the value of federal benefits exceeds:** "Distribution of Household Income and Federal Taxes, 2013" (Washington, DC: Congressional Budget Office).

86 **On the first day of the twentieth century, the typical American household:** Caplow et al., *The First Measured Century.*

86 **In 2014 the Brookings Institution economist Gary Burtless asked this question:** Gary Burtless, "Has Rising Inequality Brought Us Back to the 1920s?" (Washington, DC: Brookings Institution, 2014).

86 **Census Bureau statistics show if lower taxes:** Bernadette Proctor et al., "Income and Poverty in the United States" (Washington, DC: US Census Bureau, 2016).

87 **The Labor Department reports that 2016 hourly wages rose at 2.9 percent:** "Average Hourly and Weekly Earnings of Employees on Private Nonfarm Payrolls" (Washington, DC: Bureau of Labor Statistics).

88 **In January 2017, 63 percent of prime-aged, healthy Americans held jobs:** "Labor Force Participation Rate Timeseries" (Washington, DC: Bureau of Labor Statistics).

88–89 **the labor-force participation rate for men has indeed fallen:** Economic Research Division, "Civilian Labor Force Participation Rate" (St. Louis: Federal Reserve Bank of St. Louis).

89 **As the social scientist Charles Murray showed:** Charles Murray, *Coming Apart* (New York: Crown, 2011).

89 **The writer Anne Kim has noted:** Anne Kim, "Why Is Marriage Thriving Only Among the Affluent?" *Washington Monthly,* Spring 2016.

90 **At this writing, unemployment was 4.4 percent:** "Employment Situation Summary, June 2017" (Washington, DC: Bureau of Labor Statistics).

90 **Annualized, from 1950 to 2000 the US economy grew at 3.3 percent:** "Percent Change from Preceding Period in Real Gross Domestic Product" (Washington, DC: Bureau of Economic Analysis).

90 **At the 1950–2000 rate of annualized growth, household income doubles in about twenty-five years:** A handy rule is that any annual percent divided into 72 produces the length of time required for income to double. So, for

example, 2 percent growth, divided into 72, shows that income will double
in thirty-six years.

90 **Phillip Longman has written:** Phillip Longman, "Justice Between Generations," *The Atlantic,* June 1985.

91 **Northwestern University economist Robert Gordon has won praise from
pundits:** Robert Gordon, *The Rise and Fall of American Growth* (Princeton,
NJ: Princeton University Press, 2016).

91 **The Pew Charitable Trusts found in a 2013 study:** "Why Do Some Americans Leave the Bottom of the Economic Ladder But Not Others?" (Philadelphia: Pew Charitable Trusts, 2013).

91 **Economist Martin Feldstein of Harvard University has argued:** Martin
Feldstein, "The US Underestimates Growth," *Wall Street Journal,* May 18,
2015.

91 **By 2013 the fraction was down to 9 percent:** "Aging in the United States"
(Washington, DC: US Census Bureau).

92 **The 2010 census found the average new home was 2,392 square feet:**
"Median and Average Square Feet of Floor Area in New Single-Family
Houses" (Washington, DC: US Census Bureau).

92 **The veteran investment banker William Cohan wrote in 2017:** William
Cohan, "Can Trump Be Wall Street's Savior?" *Vanity Fair,* February 2017.

92 **Studies by the nonpartisan Kauffman Foundation:** Robert Litan et al.,
"How Enduring Is Job Creation by Startups?" (Kansas City, MO: Kauffman
Foundation, 2010).

93 **"Everyone knows how to obey the laws against robbery":** Charles Murray, *By the People* (New York: Crown Forum, 2015).

93 **In 2016, economists at George Mason University estimated:** Bentley Cof-
fey et al., "The Cumulative Cost of Regulations" (Arlington, VA: Mercatus
Center, 2016).

94 **In 2016, the Department of Transportation found that 55,000
bridges:** "National Bridge Inventory" (Washington, DC: Federal Highway
Administration).

94 **Ted Gayer and Alex Gold of the Brookings Institution concluded:** Ted
Gayer and Alex Gold, "Taxpayers Beware: Bidding Wars for NFL Teams Are
Losing Bets" (Washington, DC: Brookings Institution, 2015).

95 **The North Carolina trolley is slated to require *fifteen years* from planning:** Sarah Willets, "The Durham-Orange Light Rail Now Costs More
Than $3 Billion," *Raleigh-Durham IndyWeek,* April 7, 2017.

95 **This short underpass is projected to cost $70 million and take four years
to complete:** "Pedestrian Tunnel Crossing Heading to Planning Board,"
WTOP Newsradio (Washington, DC), December 18, 2013. Starting the
clock at the planning board meetings, a short, simple underpass—at this writing not expected to open until 2019—will take *six years to finish.* A private
business operating under market discipline would take six weeks, if that long.

95 **A federal project to replace the lock has been ongoing for *thirty years*:** See Tyler Kelley, "Choke Point of a Nation: The High Cost of an Aging River Lock," *New York Times,* November 23, 2016.

96 **In a single decade, the United States took on more public debt:** "Historical Debt Outstanding" (Washington, DC: US Department of the Treasury).

97 **"Washington is shifting the burden of bad choices onto the backs of our children and grandchildren":** Glenn Kessler, "Annotating Obama's 2006 Speech Against Boosting the Debt Limit," *Washington Post,* January 15, 2013.

97 **"magic flying puppies":** Jackie Calmes, "Left-Leaning Economists Question Cost of Bernie Sanders's Plans," *New York Times,* February 15, 2016.

97 **The Pew Trusts has found that states have at least $1 trillion in unfunded liabilities:** "The State Pensions Funding Gap" (Philadelphia: Pew Charitable Trusts, 2015).

98 **A 2016 Manhattan Institute study found:** Josh McGee, "Pension Costs Are Crowding Out Education Spending" (New York: Manhattan Institute, 2016).

99 **In 2017, the bond-rating firm Moody's Investors Services downgraded China's sovereign credit:** "Moody's Downgrades China's Rating to A1 from Aa3" (Chicago: Moody's Investors Services, May 24, 2017).

99 **Richard Samans of the World Economic Forum in Switzerland calculated:** Richard Samans, "We'll Live to 100 but Can We Afford It?" (Geneva: World Economic Forum, 2017).

99 **The powerful 2012 book *The Reckoning*:** Michael Moran, *The Reckoning* (New York: St. Martin's Press, 2012).

101 **Polls show Americans think about 25 percent of federal budget is foreign aid:** Andrew Kohut, "Debt and Deficit: A Public Opinion Dilemma" (Washington, DC: Pew Research Center, 2012).

102 **Medicare is on track to be depleted by 2029:** "The 2017 OASDI Trustees Report" (Washington, DC: Social Security Administration).

103 **Michael Mullen, a retired admiral who was chair of the Joint Chiefs of Staff:** Geoff Colvin, "Mike Mullen: Debt Is Biggest Threat to US Security," *Fortune,* May 10, 2012.

Chapter 5

104 **In January 2017, the World Health Organization released a lengthy document:** "The Top 10 Causes of Death" (Geneva: World Health Organization, 2017).

105 **foreign affairs observer Roger Cohen said in 2014:** Roger Cohen, "A Climate of Fear," *New York Times,* October 27, 2014.

105 **"The world is in chaos":** Jeffrey Goldberg, "The Lessons of Henry Kissinger," *The Atlantic,* December 2016.

105 **if writer Elaine Godfrey is right:** Elaine Godfrey, "Trump's TV Obsession Is a First," *The Atlantic,* April 3, 2107.

105 **Speaking to the law students of the University of Chicago in April 2016:** "President Obama Town Hall Meeting on the Supreme Court," University of Chicago Law School, April 7, 2016.

106 **Of top-rated US prime-time TV shows in the 2015–2016 season:** Lisa de Moraes, "Full 2015–16 TV Season Series Rankings," *Deadline Hollywood,* May 2016.

106 **In 1990, some 2,245 people were murdered in New York City:** "Comp-Stat Report" (New York: City of New York Police Department, May 7, 2017).

106 **Data from the FBI show that in the United States:** "Uniform Crime Report 2016" (Washington, DC: Federal Bureau of Investigation).

106 **During Memorial Day weekend of 2017 in Chicago, forty-six people were shot:** Monica Davey, "Drop in Violence Gives a City Hope," *New York Times,* May 31, 2017.

106 **the murder rate in Brazil is seven times that of the United States:** "Global Study on Homicide, 2013" (New York: United Nations, 2014).

107 **not only has homicide dropped out of the top ten causes of death in Centers for Disease Control statistics:** Kenneth Kochanek et al., "Deaths—Final Data for 2014" (Atlanta: Centers for Disease Control and Prevention).

107 **For fifteen consecutive years before the 2016 election, the majority said:** "Crime" (Washington, DC: Gallup, October 2016).

107 **The Pew Research Center found in a 2017 poll that 70 percent:** John Gramlich, "Voters' Perceptions of Crime Continue to Conflict with Reality" (Washington, DC: Pew Research Center, 2017).

107 **Abraham Lincoln and Franklin Roosevelt...utilized war as an excuse to claim for themselves extraordinary powers:** During the Civil War, Lincoln jailed people without charges, suspending the *habeas corpus* clause of the Constitution—which does not allow rights to be suspended. After World War II had begun but before the United States had entered it, Roosevelt gave the military several orders that violated the Neutrality Act, while instructing the FBI to assist British intelligence in planting fabrications in American newspapers. On the latter, see Lynne Olson, *Those Angry Days* (New York: Random House, 2012).

108 **John Adams...employed war or the prospect of war as rationalization for subverting law or Congress or both:** Adams used the XYZ Affair to enter into quasi-war with France, without a declaration of hostilities by Congress. Tyler cited the prospect of war with Mexico as reason to annex Texas in advance of congressional approval. Not asking Congress for approval, McKinley demanded that Spain surrender Cuba, triggering the Spanish-American War. Wilson refused to consult with the Senate on the League of Nations negotiations. Johnson lied to Congress about the Gulf of Tonkin incident to obtain an authorization that would allow him to conduct all-out war without a declaration of war. Nixon had the Air Force attack Cambodia, a neutral, without consulting Congress. Reagan defied clearly stated law by

funding rebels in Nicaragua, then had his senior staff lie to Congress. The younger George Bush had senior staff tell both Congress and the United Nations that Iraq was about to acquire the atomic bomb; this lie justified the 2003 invasion Bush wanted to stage, for reasons that are still unclear. Obama allowed domestic spying in violation of law, prosecuted journalists and service members who revealed illegal actions in Iraq and Yemen, and ordered attacks on Libya and Syria without congressional authorization.

108 **The Conflict Data Program at Uppsala University in Sweden finds:** Uppsala's numbers are updated at www.pcr.uu.se/data.

109 **The 2015 figure of a one-in-70,000 chance of dying because of war:** That year, according to the World Health Organization's "Global Status Report on Road Safety 2015," about 1.25 million people died in traffic crashes; death in a traffic crash was thus about twelve times more likely than death by war.

109 **Maybe the rise was caused by profusion:** See Barry Latzer, *The Rise and Fall of Violent Crime in America* (New York: Encounter Books, 2016).

110 **young males without fathers present in their lives are more likely:** Dewey Cornell et al., "Characteristics of Adolescents Charged with Homicide," *Behavioral Sciences and the Law,* December 1987.

110 **today prosecutors convict, or attain guilty pleas from, more than 90 percent of criminal defendants:** "United States Attorneys Annual Statistical Report 2015" (Washington, DC: US Department of Justice).

110 **the highest incarceration rate in the world:** See "Trends in US Corrections" (Washington, DC: The Sentencing Project, 2017).

110–111 **Raymond Kelly contends that stop-and-frisk:** Ray Kelly, "The NYPD Is Guilty of Saving 7,383 Lives," *Wall Street Journal,* July 22, 2013.

111 **The crime reporter Joseph Goldstein has noted:** Joseph Goldstein, "Changes in Policing Take Hold," *New York Times,* April 2, 2017.

111 **as, beginning in 2013, street stops by the NYPD:** "Monitor's Fifth Report: Analysis of NYPD Stops Reported, 2013–2015" (New York: Arnold & Porter, 2017).

111 **Guatemala, Honduras, Mexico, and a few other nations have seen homicides rise:** UN, "Global Study on Homicide, 2013."

112 **West Baltimore is an exception:** "American Healthy Homes Survey" (Washington, DC: US Department of Housing and Urban Development).

113 **But as the policing analyst Heather MacDonald has noted:** Heather MacDonald, *The War on Cops* (New York: Encounter Books, 2016).

113 **As Paul Butler, a law professor at Georgetown University, has written:** Paul Butler, *Chokehold* (New York: New Press, 2017).

114 **Forty years ago, NYPD officers shot and killed about ninety people per year:** Charles Campisi, *Blue on Blue* (New York: Scribner, 2017).

114 **For 2016, the *Washington Post* assigned reporters to collect information:** Entitled "Fatal Force 2016," the *Washington Post* project is ongoing at https://github.com/washingtonpost/data-police-shootings.

115 **In 2015, the Supreme Court ruled some aspects of mandatory-minimum sentencing:** *Johnson v. United States,* 135 S.Ct. 2551, 2015.

115 **"While legislatures write the laws and cops make the arrests":** Gilad Edelman, "All Criminal Justice Reform Is Local," *Washington Monthly,* January 2017. This article contains many statistics regarding incarceration in the United States, Canada, and other nations.

116 **there are 300,000 laws in the United States:** Data on both federal and state laws are compiled by the Manhattan Institute's Overcriminalizing America project, which is ongoing at www.manhattan-institute.org /overcriminalization.

116 **even the conservative heavyweights Charles and David Koch said they favored shorter sentences:** Molly Ball, "Do the Koch Brothers Really Care About Criminal-Justice Reform?" *The Atlantic,* March 2015.

116 **in recent years a resident of France has been less likely to die in a terror attack than in the 1970s and 1980s:** See the Global Terrorism Database maintained by the University of Maryland at www.start.umd.edu/gtd.

117 **Ninety-eight percent of the victims were in Africa, Afghanistan, the Middle East, or Pakistan:** Lazaro Gamio, "How Terrorism in the West Compares to Everywhere Else," *Washington Post,* July 16, 2016.

117 **As the social-justice advocate Nicholas Kristof has noted:** Nicholas Kristof, "Husbands Are Deadlier Than Terrorists," *New York Times,* February 11, 2017.

117 **Rudy Giuliani, then mayor of New York City, said:** Jane Mayer, *The Dark Side* (New York: Doubleday, 2008).

118 **John Mueller of Ohio State University estimates:** John Mueller and Mark Stewart, *Chasing Ghosts* (New York: Oxford University Press, 2016).

118 **Dana Priest…believes that the post-9/11 enlargement of intelligence agencies and their personnel:** Dana Priest, *Top Secret America* (New York: Little, Brown, 2011).

118–119 *The New Republic* **noted in 2010:** Gregg Easterbrook, "Waste Land," *The New Republic,* November 10, 2010.

119 **Martin Dempsey, a retired Army general who was chair of the Joint Chiefs of Staff:** Quoted by Richard Broadhead in a speech delivered at the Duke University commencement, May 2017.

119 **the Turkish-born social scientist Zeynep Tufekci:** Zeynep Tufekci, *Twitter and Tear Gas* (New Haven, CT: Yale University Press, 2017).

120 **Especially, Goldstein documents the unseen aspects of war—what has not happened:** Joshua Goldstein, *Winning the War on War* (New York: Dutton, 2011). The following also includes information from my interviews with the author, though I did not use any direct quotes.

121 **The Stockholm International Peace Research Institute, which tracks this issue:** See the Stockholm International Peace Research Institute Military Expenditure Database maintained at www.sipri.org/databases/milex.

121 **Not long before her 1989 death, the eminent historian Barbara Tuchman wrote:** Barbara Tuchman, *A Distant Mirror* (New York: Alfred A. Knopf, 1978).

121 **Juan Manuel Santos, president of Colombia, said that year:** Steven Pinker, "Colombia's Milestone in World Peace," *New York Times,* August 26, 2016.

123–124 **The Yale University historian Timothy Snyder has noted:** Timothy Snyder, *Black Earth* (New York: Tim Duggan Books, 2015).

124 **The Polish writer Stanislaw Lem introduced the concept:** Stanislaw Lem, *Fiasco* (New York: Harcourt, 1987).

125 **Fertility per woman remains highest in the warsphere nations:** "Fertility Rate, Total Births per Woman" (Washington DC: World Bank).

125 **The *Bulletin of the Atomic Scientists,* founded by Manhattan Project veterans, calculates:** The *Bulletin of the Atomic Scientists* maintains the Doomsday Dashboard at http://thebulletin.org/doomsday-dashboard.

127 **The former Pentagon official Rosa Brooks has written:** Rosa Brooks, *How Everything Became War and the Military Became Everything* (New York: Simon & Schuster, 2016).

130 **Alfred Thayer Mahan, a member of the society of famous persons:** Kaiser-run Germany followed Mahan's advice in its pre–World War I dreadnaught buildup, and the result was national calamity. Fascist Japan followed Mahan's advice in its attack on Pearl Harbor, and the result was national calamity. Adroitly passing away in 1914, Mahan was spared having to observe his theories proved totally wrong.

131 **naval hegemony cost the United States $155 billion in 2017:** This sum is the Navy's direct share of the 2017 defense budget.

131 **Obama said that the United States does not use its might to acquire territory or seize resources:** Transcript of Obama speech on Afghanistan, CNN, December 2, 2009.

131–132 **Angell was a Labour member of the Parliament who published a 1913 pamphlet:** Norman Angell, *The Great Illusion* (London, 1909, under the title *Europe's Optical Illusion*).

132 **Mueller of Ohio State took up Angell's cudgels in an underappreciated 1989 book:** John Mueller, *Retreat from Doomsday* (New York: Basic Books, 1989).

133 **The…political scientist Graham Allison coined the phrase "Thucydides Trap":** Graham Allison, *Destined for War* (New York: Houghton Mifflin, 2017).

134 **of the arrival of white settlers to California, Steinbeck notes:** Steinbeck, *East of Eden.*

135 **Yale's Snyder has written that Hitler "thought existence meant a struggle for land":** Snyder, *Black Earth.*

137 **Tomasello's 2009 treatise:** Michael Tomasello, *Why We Cooperate* (Cambridge, MA: MIT Press, 2009).

137   **He offers a larger thesis:** Steven Pinker, *The Better Angels of Our Nature* (New York: Viking, 2011).

Chapter 6

140   **Once, Sagan and some colleagues employed a radio telescope:** Gregg Easterbrook, "Are We Alone?" *The Atlantic,* August 1988.

141   **Beck expounded the notion that technology would grow ever more dangerous:** Ulrich Beck, *Risk Society* (New York: Sage Publications, 1992).

142   **Traffic accidents kill twelve times as many people per year, globally, as war:** "Global Status Report on Road Safety 2015" (Geneva: World Health Organization).

142   **Traffic deaths are five times higher, per mile traveled, in Algeria:** See the interactive road safety map maintained by the World Health Organization at http://gamapserver.who.int/gho/interactive_charts/road_safety /road_traffic_deaths2/tablet/atlas.html.

143   **Global production rose from 8 million in 1950 to 25 million in 1971:** See the Production Statistics Database maintained by the Organisation Internationale des Constructeurs d'Automobile (OICA) at http://www.oica.net/category /production-statistics/.

143   **The epidemiologist Devra Davis has documented:** Devra Davis, *When Smoke Ran Like Water* (New York: Basic Books, 2002).

143–144 **originally developed for combat helicopters:** The relationship between military helicopters and contemporary auto safety is detailed in Stefan Duma, "Virginia Tech–Wake Forest University Center for Injury Biomechanics 10 Year History," *Brain Injuries and Biomechanics,* April 2013.

144   **Some studies suggest that pretensioners:** A related paper, "Sample Selection in the Estimation of Airbag and Seat Belt Effectiveness" (*Review of Economics and Statistics,* November 2001), launched the career of Steven Levitt, later to be the popular economist of *Freakonomics.*

144   **Many cars now incorporate:** Available low-cost technology that should be mandated for vehicles in all nations is detailed in WHO's "Global Status Report on Road Safety 2015."

145   **In the United States, traffic deaths...have declined steadily for two generations:** "State Traffic Data" (Washington, DC: National Highway Traffic Safety Administration).

145   **at least 90 percent of crashes involve an impaired driver:** Santokh Singh, "Critical Reasons for Crashes Investigated in the National Motor Vehicle Crash Causation Survey" (Washington, DC: National Highway Traffic Safety Administration, 2015).

146   **A 2016 survey by the State Farm insurance company found 36 percent of drivers:** Nicole Friedman, "Smartphone Use Lifts Car Insurance Rates," *Wall Street Journal,* February 21, 2017.

147 **Researcher Michael Sivak of the University of Michigan found that in 2015:** Michael Sivak, "Sales-Weighted Fuel-Economy Rating of Purchased New Vehicles, 2007 Through June 2017" (Ann Arbor: University of Michigan, Transportation Research Institute, last updated September 5, 2017).

149 **The typical new refrigerator sold in 2010 uses 40 percent as much electricity:** "How Refrigerator Standards Have Saved Consumers Billions" (Washington, DC: US Department of Energy, 2011).

149 **The actual number for 2011 was 98 quads:** "US Energy Consumption Rose Slightly in 2016" (Washington, DC: Energy Information Administration, 2017).

150 **In 2001, Vice President Dick Cheney declared that unless the United States built:** "Dick Cheney, Energy Czar" (editorial), *New York Times,* May 14, 2001.

152 **Studies by researchers at the Massachusetts Institute of Technology suggest:** Matthew Claudel, *How the Driverless Car Could Transform Cities* (New York: McKinsey & Co., 2015).

154 **Labor economists who deride long-haul trucks as "sweatshops on wheels":** Michael Belzer, *Sweatshops on Wheels* (Oxford: Oxford University Press, 2000).

154 **Civilian airliner crashes peaked in 1972 and have declined steadily since:** See the Aviation Safety Database maintained by Aviation Safety Network at http://aviation-safety.net/database/.

154 **The celebrated journalist James Fallows:** See James Fallows, *Free Flight* (New York: PublicAffairs, 2002). The title refers to how future aircraft may operate, not to fares.

155 **The chess grandmaster and Russian dissident Garry Kasparov noted:** Gary Kasparov, *Deep Thinking* (New York: PublicAffairs, 2017).

155 **The death rate has declined almost annually, to one in 29,600 in 2016:** "National Census of Fatal Occupational Injuries" (Washington, DC: Bureau of Labor Statistics, 2016).

155 **Fire, and deaths from fire, are in long-term decline:** Melissa Knight et al., "National Fire Data Survey" (Quincy, MA: National Fire Protection Association, 2017).

156 **In 1996, Ruth Sivard, an economist who worked as a Department of State arms control analyst:** Ruth Sivard, *World Military and Social Expenditures 1996* (Washington, DC: World Priorities, 1996).

157 **an estimated 500,000 civilians were slaughtered:** William Shawcross, *Sideshow* (New York: HarperCollins, 1979).

157 **Barack Obama said in 2016, was "tens of thousands":** "President Obama Town Hall Meeting on the Supreme Court," University of Chicago Law School, April 7, 2016.

157 **As the political scientist John Tirman of the Massachusetts Institute of Technology has written:** John Tirman, *The Deaths of Others* (Oxford: Oxford University Press, 2011).

157 **The Pentagon acknowledged in 2017 that a US airstrike in a crowded section of Mosul, Iraq:** "Executive Summary of the Investigation of the Alleged Civilian Casualty Incident in the al Jadidah District, Mosul" (Washington, DC: US Department of Defense, Operation Inherent Resolve, May 25, 2017). See the Operation Inherent Resolve website maintained by the Pentagon at www.inherentresolve.mil.

158 **5,000 tons of unguided explosives were dropped:** Jan Rüger, *Heligoland* (Oxford: Oxford University Press, 2017).

160 **In 2010, Defense Secretary Robert Gates revealed:** Andrew Quinn, "US Reveals Nuclear Target: Oceans," *Reuters,* April 6, 2010.

160 **individual officers might end up making launch decisions:** Graham Allison (*Destined for War*), director of Harvard's Belfer Center for Science and International Affairs, contends that during the Cold War warship captains could have launched nuclear warheads without approval from Moscow or Washington.

160 **Studies by the Federation of American Scientists:** Hans Kristensen, "Declining Deterrent Patrols Indicate Too Many SSBNs" (Washington, DC: Federation of American Scientists, 2013). SSBNs are submarines that carry strategic missiles with nuclear warheads.

161 **Studies at UCLA have found:** Omar Asensio et al., "Effectiveness of US Energy Efficiency Building Labels," *Nature Energy,* March 27, 2017.

Chapter 7

165 **either democracy won outright or the result was stalemate:** The Korean War ended in deadlock. The Vietnam War is hard to characterize, as the South Vietnam government was not a democracy: the 1975 victory by communism slowly gave way to a reasonably open society. Soviet repression of Czechoslovakia, Hungary, and Poland initially was a win for dictatorship, then a win for freedom. Some imperialist enclaves that achieved post–World War II independence rejected democracy for monarchy (Morocco) or for faux-democracy (Algeria, Egypt). South Africa and Zimbabwe officially embraced free elections, though both show unofficial dictator-lite conditions. Since 2014, the political situation in Ukraine and the annexation of Crimea by Russia are unclear ideologically, but obviously liberty does not prevail. Some post–World War II conflicts have been Communist dictatorship versus military dictatorship, such as the 1977 Ogaden War between Ethiopia and Somalia. These qualifiers stated, in direct military confrontations between dictatorship and democracy, the good guys keep defeating the bad guys.

165 **there has recently been what Larry Diamond, a Stanford University professor, calls:** Larry Diamond, "Facing Up to the Democratic Recession," *Journal of Democracy,* January 2015.

165 **Diamond thought Portugal, not the Soviet Union, was the leading indicator:** Larry Diamond, *The Spirit of Democracy* (New York: Henry Holt, 2007).

166 **Max Roser, of the University of Oxford, calculates:** Max Roser, "The Short History of Global Living Conditions and Why It Matters That We Know It," at Our World in Data, https://ourworldindata.org/a-history-of -global-living-conditions-in-5-charts. Roser shows that if one person in one hundred lived in democracy two centuries ago, today there are fifty-six.

166 **Jonathan Powell of Central Florida University and Clayton Thyne of the University of Kentucky:** Jonathan Powell and Clayton Thyne, "Coup d'État or Coup d'Autocracy? The Impact of Coups on Democratization, 1950–2008," *Foreign Policy Analysis,* February 2016.

167 **Paul Samuelson...predicted the Soviet economy would pass the US economy by the 1980s at the latest:** Samuelson's venerable textbook *Economics* (New York: McGraw Hill), which first went to press in 1948, began including this forecast with the 1961 edition.

167 **The United States outproduces China and Russia combined:** As elsewhere in this book, this is the standard calculation—employed by the World Bank, the CIA, and other authorities—for gauging GDP by exchange rates. If instead the gauge is purchasing power parity, China looks better. Russia remains an economic basket case under all forms of measurement.

167 **As Deirdre McCloskey, an economic historian...has written:** Deirdre McCloskey, *Bourgeois Equality* (Chicago: University of Chicago Press, 2016).

168 **In early 2017, the market capitalization of Apple reached $800 billion:** Anita Balakrishnan, "Apple Market Cap Tops $800 Billion," CNBC, May 8, 2017.

168 **Most of the world's great colleges and universities are in the United States:** Benjamin Wildavsky, *Reinventing Higher Education* (Cambridge, MA: Harvard Education Press, 2011).

170 **"dissent is not permissible," *The Atlantic* said in 2016:** James Fallows, "China's Great Leap Backward," *The Atlantic,* December 2016.

171 **Military historians tend to conclude:** John Keegan, *The Face of Battle* (London: Jonathan Cape, 1976).

171–172 **As the historian Jay Winik has written:** Jay Winik, *1944* (New York: Simon & Schuster, 2014).

172 **the US staging base on Guam was receiving:** Yergin, *The Prize.*

173 **As the analyst Daniel Yergin has noted:** Ibid.

173 **historian Richard Overy called the fact:** Richard Overy, *Why the Allies Won* (New York: W. W. Norton, 1996).

173 **Northwestern University historian Michael Sherry wrote in 1987:** Michael Sherry, *The Rise of American Air Power* (New Haven, CT: Yale University Press, 1987).

174 **Ta-Nehisi Coates has noted:** Ta-Nehisi Coates, "My President Was Black," *The Atlantic,* January 2017.

176 **William Galston...wrote in 2016:** William Galston, "The Populist Revolt Against Failure," *Wall Street Journal,* August 30, 2016.

176 **Lula had been sentenced to prison for stealing public funds:** Ernesto Londoño, "Ex-President of Brazil Sentenced to Nearly 10 Years in Prison for Corruption," *New York Times,* July 12, 2017.

177 **A top official who had just left the Argentinian government was arrested:** "Argentina Ex-Minister Arrested over Cash Bags at Monastery," BBC News, June 15, 2016.

177 **the head of Samsung…was taken to jail in chains:** Hyunjoo Jin, "Samsung Chief Arrested as South Korean Corruption Probe Deepens," *Reuters,* February 16, 2017.

178 **Milan Vaishnav, a researcher at the Carnegie Endowment for International Peace:** Milan Vaishnav, *When Crime Pays* (New Haven, CT: Yale University Press, 2017).

178 **Global Financial Integrity, a nonpartisan think tank, estimates:** Dev Kar and Joseph Spanjers, "Illicit Financial Flows from Developing Countries: 2004–2013" (Washington, DC: Global Financial Integrity, 2015).

179 **The mayor of Detroit was sentenced to twenty-eight years in prison:** Steven Yaccino, "Kwame M. Kilpatrick, Former Detroit Mayor, Sentenced to 28 Years," *New York Times,* October 10, 2013.

179 **The speaker of the New York State Assembly was sentenced to twelve years:** As this book went to press, his conviction was set aside on appeal; a second trial was expected. See Jim Dwyer, "For Sheldon Silver, Three Judges Overturn 12 Jurors," *New York Times,* July 13, 2017.

180 **The result was no jobs other than for prosecutors who filed bribery and bid-rigging charges:** Vivien Yee, "How Cuomo's Signature Economic Growth Project Fell Apart in Utica," *New York Times,* December 27, 2016.

180 **The former head of the Chicago public school system was sentenced to four years in prison:** Derrick Blakley, "Former Head of the Chicago Public School System Sentenced," CBS Chicago, April 28, 2017.

181 **The Associated Press tried without success to establish direct quid pro quo:** Stephen Braun and Eileen Sullivan, "Many Donors to Clinton Foundation Met with Hillary Clinton at State Department," Associated Press, August 23, 2016.

181 **John Mikesell, a professor at Indiana University, estimates:** John Mikesell, "Impact of Public Officials' Corruption on the Size and Allocation of US State Spending," *Public Administration Review,* April 2014.

181 **The Istanbul-born economist Daron Acemoglu of the Massachusetts Institute of Technology:** Daron Acemoglu and James Robinson, *Why Nations Fail* (New York: Crown, 2012).

183 **In 2016, Scott Anderson, for twenty-five years a roving international correspondent:** Scott Anderson, "Fractured Lands," *New York Times Magazine,* August 11, 2016.

185 **Turnout in 2016 was 71 percent for senior citizens:** Thom File, *A Look at the 2016 Presidential Election* (Washington, DC: US Census Bureau, 2017).

187 **In 2016, polls showed a meager 11 percent:** "Congressional Job Approval" (Washington, DC: Gallup, 2016).

188 **In 2017, a federal court in Wisconsin ruled:** *Whitford v. Gill.* Analysis at *Whitford v. Gill, Harvard Law Review,* May 10, 2017.

190 **some studies found Bush the true winner in Florida:** Brooks Jackson, "The Florida Recount of 2000," FactCheck.org, January 22, 2008.

190 **Steve Silberstein, an official of the advocacy group National Popular Vote, has argued:** Steve Silberstein, "How to Make the Electoral College Work for Everyone," *Washington Monthly,* March 2017.

Chapter 8

200 **Former Colorado senator Gary Hart noted of negativism in American annals:** James Fallows, "How America Can Rise Again," *The Atlantic,* January 2010.

200 *The Atlantic's* **1994 cover story:** Robert D. Kaplan, "The Coming Anarchy," *The Atlantic,* February 1994.

200–201 **In 2012, Barack Obama's National Intelligence Council produced a report declaring:** "Global Trends 2030" (Washington, DC: National Intelligence Council, 2012).

201 **David Brooks wrote in 2017:** David Brooks, "The Crisis of Western Civ," *New York Times,* April 21, 2017.

203 **The demographics of the United States and European Union are shifting:** "Structure and Aging" (Brussels: European Commission, 2016).

204 **refusal to admit Jewish refugees until late in World War II:** Recounted in Winik, *1944.*

204 **George Will's memorable phrase:** George Will, "Colleges Become the Victims of Progressivism," *Washington Post,* June 6, 2014.

206 **But Reagan told audiences their liberty was being taken away:** Lou Cannon, *Governor Reagan* (New York: PublicAffairs, 2003).

207 **Gallup polls find it has been a generation or more since:** See the "Confidence in Institutions" page maintained by Gallup at http://news.gallup.com/poll/1597/Confidence-Institutions.aspx.

209 **Reagan said he was surprised to learn that people became angry when rescued:** Cannon, *Governor Reagan.*

209–210 **Figures are higher still in contemporary Europe:** "General Government Spending" (Paris: Organization for Economic Cooperation and Development, 2016).

210 **Gallup has conducted a monthly poll on this question:** See the "Satisfaction with the United States" page maintained by Gallup at http://news.gallup.com/poll/1669/General-Mood-Country.aspx.

211 **Pew Research Center national satisfaction polling has, since 2004:** See the "National Satisfaction" page maintained by Pew Research Center at http://www.pewresearch.org/subjects/national-satisfaction/.

211 **Researchers at the University of Canberra found:** Mark Evans et al., "Who Do You Trust to Run the Country?" (Canberra: Institute for Governance and Policy Analysis, 2016).

211 **or perhaps they had become surrounded by unfounded innuendos:** See Kurt Andersen, *Fantasyland* (New York: Random House, 2017).

211 **The University of Rochester historian Christopher Lasch, who died in 1994:** Lasch, *The Culture of Narcissism*.

212 **As the writer Timothy Noah has noted:** Timothy Noah, "The Death of the Telephone Call," *Slate,* September 18, 2016.

212 **Facebook has about two billion daily users:** Josh Constine, "Facebook Now Has Two Billion Users," *TechCrunch,* June 27, 2017.

213 **Holly Shakya and Nicholas Christakis...found:** Holly Shakya et al., "Association of Facebook Use with Compromised Well-being: A Longitudinal Study," *American Journal of Epidemiology,* February 2017.

213 **Going into the 2016 election, Pew Research reported:** Elisa Shearer, "News Use Across Social Media Platforms 2016" (Washington, DC: Pew Research Center, 2016).

213 **as Robert Thomson has said:** Robert Thomson, "Fake News and the Digital Duopoly," speech to the Asia Society, Hong Kong, 2016.

214 **a political science textbook, *Red and Blue Nation*, said:** Pietro Nivola, ed., *Red and Blue Nation* (Washington, DC: Brookings Press, 2006).

217 **The psychologist Amos Tversky:** Amos Tversky, *Preference, Belief, and Similarity: Selected Writings* (Cambridge, MA: MIT Press, 2003).

218 **Research by Edward Mansfield and Diana Mutz at the University of Pennsylvania:** Edward Mansfield et al., "US vs. Them: Mass Attitudes Toward Offshore Outsourcing" (Philadelphia: University of Pennsylvania, 2014).

218 **As the lawyer and legal analyst Philip Howard noted:** Philip Howard, *The Lost Art of Drawing the Line* (New York: Random House, 2001).

219 **As the Florida State University psychologist Roy Baumeister has shown:** Roy Baumeister et al., "Bad Is Stronger Than Good," *Review of General Psychology,* May 2001.

220 **former attorney general Eric Holder declared:** Speech to the Democratic National Convention, Philadelphia, 2017.

220 **and helped moderate the growth of health care's share of the GDP:** In the five years before ObamaCare was enacted, US health care expenditures rose from 15.3 percent of GDP to 17 percent. In the five years that followed, they rose to 17.2 percent. See "Health Expenditure Total (% of GDP), United States" (Washington, DC: World Bank, 2016).

220 **the civil rights leader Andrew Young asking in 2014:** Speech to the National Prayer Breakfast, Washington, DC, 2014.

221 **as Emily Bazelon wrote in 2017:** Emily Bazelon, "Department of Justification," *New York Times Magazine,* March 3, 2017.

221 **Hitler, Snyder has written, realized that conflating:** Snyder, *The Black Earth.*

222 **The writer Peter Beinart has noted:** Peter Beinart, "Breaking Faith," *The Atlantic,* April 2017.

222 **which social commentator Bill Bishop calls "the Big Sort":** Bill Bishop, *The Big Sort* (New York: Houghton Mifflin, 2008).

224 **A 1992 book titled *The End of Equality:*** Mickey Kaus, *The End of Equality* (New York: Basic Books, 1992).

224 **the investment whiz Warren Buffett said in 2016:** Warren Buffett, Berkshire Hathaway shareholder letter, 2016.

224–225 **As Patrick Sharkey, a professor of sociology at New York University, has written:** Patrick Sharkey, "The Destructive Legacy of Housing Segregation," *The Atlantic,* June 2016.

Chapter 9

226 **northern polar sea ice, which is down about 28 percent since 1980:** "Sea Ice Extent Sinks to Record Lows at Both Poles" (Boulder, CO: National Snow and Ice Data Center, 2017).

226 **as the Russian researcher Sergey Zimov showed:** Sergey Zimov et al., "Permafrost and the Global Carbon Budget," *Science,* June 16, 2006.

227 **The 2005 National Academy of Sciences finding:** "Joint Science Academies' Statement: Global Response to Climate Change" (Washington, DC: National Academy of Sciences, 2005).

227 **In 2014, the National Academy of Sciences concluded:** "Climate Change Evidence and Causes" (Washington, DC: National Academy of Sciences, 2014).

227–228 **from the Climate Change Science Program supervised by President George W. Bush:** "Temperature Trends in the Lower Atmosphere" (Washington, DC: Climate Change Science Program, 2006).

228 **Thomas Kuhn's 1962 book:** Thomas Kuhn, *The Structure of Scientific Revolutions* (Chicago: University of Chicago Press, 1962).

230 **but NOAA does not detect any hiatus in data:** Thomas Karl et al., "Possible Artifacts of Data Biases in Recent Global Surface Warming Hiatus," *Science,* June 26, 2015.

231 **The Geophysical Fluid Dynamics Laboratory, a division of NOAA, said in 2017:** "Global Warming and Hurricanes: An Overview of Current Research" (Princeton, NJ: Geophysical Fluid Dynamics Laboratory, 2017).

231 **Additional mild warming could make Alaska, Canada, Russia, and Scandinavia more valuable:** Gregg Easterbrook, "Hot Prospects," *The Atlantic,* April 2007.

232 **This natural feedback may be a reason carbon emissions from human activity:** "It's Water Vapor, Not the CO_2" (Washington, DC: American Chemical Society). This web page explains the difference between carbon dioxide and water vapor in greenhouse effect terms.

232 **researchers led by Zeke Hausfather of the University of California at Berkeley:** Zeke Hausfather et al., "Assessing Warming Using Instrumentally Homogeneous Sea Surface Temperature Records," *Science,* January 4, 2017.

233   **That same year a Department of Energy study:** "US Energy and Employment Report" (Washington, DC: US Department of Energy, 2016).

234   **Robert DeConto of the University of Massachusetts at Amherst led a team:** Robert DeConto et al., "Contribution of Antarctica to Past and Future Sea Level Rise," *Nature,* April 5, 2016.

234   **James Hansen of NASA, perhaps the world's most proficient climate modeler:** James Hansen et al., "Ice Melt, Sea Level Rise, and Superstorms: Evidence from Paleoclimate Data, Climate Modeling, and Modern Observations That 2°C Global Warming Could Be Dangerous," *Atmospheric Chemistry and Physics,* March 22, 2016.

234   **Hansen first said this in 1988:** Richard Kerr, "Hansen Versus the World on Greenhouse Threat," *Science,* June 2, 1989.

235   **The US Energy Information Administration (EIA) projected:** "International Energy Outlook 2016" (Washington, DC: US Department of Energy, 2016).

236   **At this writing, for three consecutive years the world's emission of greenhouse gases:** Corinne Le Quéré et al., "Global Carbon Budget 2016," *Earth System Science Data,* November 14, 2016.

237   **Oxford University's Institute for Energy Studies has determined:** Malcolm Keay, "Energy: The Long View" (Oxford: Oxford Institute for Energy Studies, 2007).

237   **The nonpartisan World Resources Institute calculated:** Nate Aden, "21 Countries Are Reducing Carbon Emissions While Growing GDP" (Washington, DC: World Resources Institute, April 2016).

237   **The EIA reports that in 2010:** "US Energy Intensity Projected to Continue Its Steady Decline Through 2040" (Washington, DC: Energy Information Administration, 2013).

238   **Researchers led by physicist Nancy Haegel:** Nancy Haegel et al., "Terawatt-Scale Photovoltaics: Trajectories and Challenges," *Science,* April 14, 2017.

240–241   **a coalition of conservative establishment figures:** James Baker et al., "The Conservative Case for Carbon Dividends" (Washington, DC: Climate Leadership Council, 2017).

241   **Jerry Taylor, head of the libertarian Niskanen Center...switched to supporting carbon taxes:** Jerry Taylor, "The Conservative Case for a Carbon Tax" (Washington, DC: Niskanen Center, 2015).

241–242   **as Amy Harder has written:** Amy Harder, "Exxon Touts Carbon Tax to Oil Industry," *Wall Street Journal,* June 30, 2016.

Chapter 10

245   **In 1990, some 67 percent of Chinese citizens lived:** Global Count of the Extreme Poor: Data Issues, Methodology and Initial Results: (Washington, DC: World Bank, 2015).

245 **Benjamin Friedman, an economist at Harvard University, has contended:** Benjamin Friedman, *The Moral Consequences of Economic Growth* (New York: Alfred A. Knopf, 2005).

247 **Some cities had a patronage-controlled "poormaster":** See Holly Metz, *Killing the Poormaster* (Chicago: Chicago Review Press, 2012).

247–248 **As Robert Samuelson has noted:** Robert Samuelson, "How Health Care Controls Us," *Washington Post,* July 24, 2017.

248 **European Union nations spend less per capita on health care than the United States:** See the "Health Expenditures and Financing" page maintained by the Organization for Economic Cooperation and Development at http://stats.oecd.org/Index.aspx?DataSetCode=SHA.

248 **In 2017, the *Wall Street Journal* quoted seventy-nine-year-old Carole Siesser:** Joseph Walker, "Surging Drug Costs," *Wall Street Journal,* May 30, 2107.

249 **By the end of the Obama administration, according to the Congressional Budget Office:** "Distribution of Household Income and Federal Taxes" (Washington, DC: Congressional Budget Office, 2016).

251 **Milanovic's research shows:** Branko Milanovic, *The Haves and the Have-Nots* (New York: Basic Books, 2010).

252 **according to the Economic Policy Institute, think tank of the US labor movement:** Lawrence Mishel and Jessica Schieder, "CEO Pay Remains High Relative to Pay of Typical Workers" (Washington, DC: Economic Policy Institute, 2017).

253 **Nike pays the Indonesian workers who sew the company's sneakers $3 a day:** Bonnie Kavoussi, "Nike Factory in Indonesia Used Military to Intimidate Workers into Giving Up Pay," *Huffington Post,* January 16, 2013.

253 **according to the corporate-board analysis firm Equilar:** "Ranking the Largest CEO Pay Packages" (Redwood City, CA: Equilar, 2017).

254 **according to Congressional Budget Office data:** CBO, "Distribution of Household Income and Federal Taxes."

255 **economists led by William Gale:** William Gale et al., "A Significant Increase in the Top Income Tax Rate Wouldn't Substantially Alter Income Inequality" (Washington, DC: Brookings Institution, 2015).

255 **The Sanders plan would have raised an added $150 billion per year:** Gordon Mermin, "Analysis of Senator Bernie Sanders's Tax and Transfer Proposals" (Washington, DC: Tax Policy Center, 2016).

256 **The proposal came from Milton Friedman:** Milton Friedman, *Capitalism and Freedom* (Chicago: University of Chicago Press, 1962).

257 **In 2015, the United States spent $878 billion on subsidies exclusively for those with low incomes:** "The Federal Budget in 2015" (Washington, DC: Congressional Budget Office, 2015).

258 **Kemp, who died in 2009...said:** See Fred Barnes and Morton Kondrake, *Jack Kemp* (New York: Sentinel, 2015).

259   **the Organization for Economic Cooperation and Development calcu-
      lated:** "Basic Income as a Policy Option" (Paris: OECD, 2017).

260   **The conservative social scientist Charles Murray has proposed:** Charles
      Murray, *In Our Hands* (Washington, DC: AEI Press, 2016).

262   **the typical homeowner had about thirty times the net worth of the typi-
      cal renter:** Matthew Desmond, "How Homeownership Became the Engine
      of American Inequality," *New York Times Magazine,* May 9, 2017.

262   **The Case-Shiller Index of home values shows:** See the "S&P CoreLogic
      Case-Shiller Home Prices Indices" maintained by S&P Dow Jones Indexes at
      http://us.spindices.com/index-family/real-estate/sp-corelogic-case-shiller.

263   **Tyler Cowen, an economist at George Mason University, notes:** Tyler
      Cowen, *The Complacent Class* (New York: St. Martin's Press, 2017).

263   **According to the Census Bureau, fifty years ago, some 20 percent:**
      "Americans Moving at Historically Low Rates" (Washington, DC: United
      States Census Bureau, 2016).

Chapter 11

266–267   **In 2014, the Pew Research Center found:** Kim Parker et al., "Record Share
          of Americans Have Never Married" (Washington, DC: Pew Research Cen-
          ter, 2014).

267   **In a 2010 study, the Pew Research Center found:** Paul Taylor et al.,
          "Women, Men, and the New Economics of Marriage" (Washington, DC:
          Pew Research Center, 2010).

267–268   **Ron Haskins and Isabel Sawhill...have found:** Ron Haskins, "Three
          8Simple Rules Poor Teens Should Follow to Join the Middle Class" (Wash-
          ington, DC: Brookings Institution, 2013).

269   **Research by economist James Heckman of the University of Chicago:**
          Jorge Luis García, James Heckman, Duncan Ermini Leaf, and María José
          Prados, "The Life-Cycle Benefits of an Influential Early Childhood Program"
          (Chicago: University of Chicago, 2016).

269   **Data from New York City suggest that a broad pre-K program:** Kate
          Taylor, "New York City Will Offer Free Preschool for All 3-Year-Olds," *New
          York Times,* April 24, 2017.

269–270   **Studies of the 2016 graduating class from the Los Angeles Unified School
          District:** Sarah Favot, "New Student Data Show That Half of Graduating
          Seniors in LA Not Eligible for California's Public Universities," The 74, April
          2017.

270   **David Freedman has written:** David Freedman, "The War on Stupid Peo-
          ple," *The Atlantic,* July 2016.

270   **as Don Peck has written:** Don Peck, *Pinched* (New York: Crown, 2011).

271   **The sixty-eight-year-old private equity billionaire David Rubenstein:**
          Commencement address, Duke University, May 2017.

273 **James Vaupel...has warned that society's reluctance to face the policy choices:** Vaupel et al., "Broken Limits to Life Expectancy."

275 **Japan, the nation with the longest life spans:** See the "Life Expectancy" page maintained by the World Health Organization, detailing life expectancy around the globe, at http://www.who.int/gho/mortality_burden _disease/life_tables/situation_trends/en/.

276 **The Yale University computer scientist David Gelernter forecast:** David Gelernter, *The Tides of Mind* (New York: Liveright, 2016).

277 **Elon Musk, Martin Rees, Francesca Rossi, Steve Wozniak, and other luminaries:** See "Research Priorities for Robust and Beneficial Artificial Intelligence," an open letter with over 8,000 signatories to date, available at Future of Life Institute, https://futureoflife.org/ai-open-letter/.

278 **Alan Robock of Rutgers University and Owen Toon of the University of Colorado calculate:** Alan Robock and Owen Toon, "The Climate Impacts of Nuclear War," *Bulletin of the Atomic Scientists,* 2012.

278 **Volcanoes pose a natural threat that could manifest at any time:** Some researchers believe a phase of mega-volcanism in Siberia caused the mass extinction that killed at least 75 percent of Earth life about 252 million years ago, via corrosive rain, damage to the ozone layer, and vast amounts of greenhouse gases. See David Bond and Stephen Grasby, "On the Causes of Mass Extinctions," *Palaeogeography Palaeoclimatology Palaeoecology,* July 15, 2017.

278 **Terry Ann Plank, a magma specialist at Columbia University, warned:** Remarks at a meeting of the American Academy of Arts and Sciences, Cambridge, MA, 2016.

279 **When I wrote this paragraph in mid-2017, the count was up to 16,165 nearby asteroids:** Check the Jet Propulsion Laboratory's asteroid-discovery inventory at https://cneos.jpl.nasa.gov/stats/totals.html for the total on the day you encounter this passage. (Google "jpl neo cumulative totals" to avoid having to retype the URL.) In the sixty days between when I wrote the reference to space rocks in the main text and when I wrote this footnote, 282 near-Earth asteroids were discovered.

Index

Gregg Easterbrook is the author of ten books, including the *New York Times* bestseller *The Progress Paradox*. He has been a staff writer, national correspondent, or contributing editor of *The Atlantic* for nearly forty years. Easterbrook has written for *The New Yorker, Science, Wired, Harvard Business Review,* the *Washington Monthly,* the *New York Times,* the *Wall Street Journal,* and the *Los Angeles Times*. He was a fellow in economics, then in government studies, at the Brookings Institution, and a fellow in international affairs at the Fulbright Foundation. In 2017, he was elected to the American Academy of Arts and Sciences.

PublicAffairs is a publishing house founded in 1997. It is a tribute to the standards, values, and flair of three persons who have served as mentors to countless reporters, writers, editors, and book people of all kinds, including me.

I. F. STONE, proprietor of *I. F. Stone's Weekly*, combined a commitment to the First Amendment with entrepreneurial zeal and reporting skill and became one of the great independent journalists in American history. At the age of eighty, Izzy published *The Trial of Socrates*, which was a national bestseller. He wrote the book after he taught himself ancient Greek.

BENJAMIN C. BRADLEE was for nearly thirty years the charismatic editorial leader of *The Washington Post*. It was Ben who gave the *Post* the range and courage to pursue such historic issues as Watergate. He supported his reporters with a tenacity that made them fearless and it is no accident that so many became authors of influential, best-selling books.

ROBERT L. BERNSTEIN, the chief executive of Random House for more than a quarter century, guided one of the nation's premier publishing houses. Bob was personally responsible for many books of political dissent and argument that challenged tyranny around the globe. He is also the founder and longtime chair of Human Rights Watch, one of the most respected human rights organizations in the world.

.   .   .

For fifty years, the banner of Public Affairs Press was carried by its owner Morris B. Schnapper, who published Gandhi, Nasser, Toynbee, Truman, and about 1,500 other authors. In 1983, Schnapper was described by *The Washington Post* as "a redoubtable gadfly." His legacy will endure in the books to come.

Peter Osnos, *Founder*